Praise for *The Global Imagination of 1968*

"A well-informed survey of the global 'New Left' of 1968."
—Eric Hobsbawm, author of *The Age of Extremes: A History of the World, 1914–1991*

"George Katsiaficas's work presents an understanding how we of the New Left used our education as a practice of freedoms: confronting the racist, warmongering status quo with the objective of creative participatory democracy. As we continue to work toward cooperational humanism here at home and the world over, this insightful analysis provides a useful backdrop for social activism and the struggle for future democratic human rights."
—Bobby Seale, former chairman and cofounder of the Black Panther Party

"This is the best book on the New Left, the only truly global history that historicizes the social movements of the 1960s. It is both a cautionary tale and a guide for dark times that require imaginative resistance. This new edition could not have come at a better time."
—Roxanne Dunbar-Ortiz, author of *Outlaw Woman: A Memoir of the War Years, 1960–1975*

"By including feminism prominently in the global insurgency of 1968, this book gives us comprehensive understanding of the broad mobilization that was at the heart of the movement. Everywhere in the world, people simultaneously challenged wars, racism, and archaic politics and also patterns of domination in everyday life."
—Mariarosa Dalla Costa, professor emerita, University of Padua, and theorist of Wages for Housework

"Of all the many studies of the wave of radicalism marking the so-called long sixties, *The Global Imagination of 1968* ranks among the very best. Nothing else rivals the lucidity and succinctness with which Katsiaficas captures not only the liberatory vision but the sheer vibrancy with which the period's global movement was imbued. The book should be considered essential reading by all who seek transformative change."
—Ward Churchill, author and activist

"The year 1968 stands out as a pivotal moment in history, a high point of worldwide revolutionary consciousness, an unbreakable chain of resistance and rebellion. Whether in Asia, Africa, Europe, Latin America, or the belly of the imperialist beast (USA), oppressed people were reclaiming their dignity and humanity. When 1968 is mentioned, I think most profoundly of our party—the original Black Panther Party, which raised to new heights the multiracial slogan of 'All Power to the People!' Read this book and you too will discover the 'eros effect' or revolutionary love that is so necessary in the age of neoliberalism and global capitalist tyranny."
—Shaka Zulu, chairman, New Afrikan Black Panther Party

"It is heartening to see how George Katsiaficas, a radical who has neither dropped out nor burned out, and whose scholarly research grew out of his own activism as a student in the late 1960s and early '70s, has incorporated in his vision an enlarged sense of the necessity for 'genuine revolution [to be] based upon the universal interest of the human species and all life.'"
—Denise Levertov, poet and activist

"Here the New Left is convincingly portrayed for what it was, a profoundly influential world-historical movement."
—Stewart Edward Albert and Judith Clavier Albert, editors of *The Sixties Papers: Documents of a Rebellious Decade*

"This book is a must for those contemplating future struggles for change. It gives a vivid picture of what actually took place as well as an idea of where we fell short so that in the next stage of struggle we can build on strengths and weaknesses and grapple with the even more profound questions that face us."
—James Boggs and Grace Lee Boggs

"I met George Katsiaficas in Berlin in the early 1990s and we took part in the demonstrations of revolutionary May 1 in Kreuzberg. His book on the New Left and 1968 gave me long-lasting connections between the West Berlin Autonomists and the theory and practice of the global revolt at the end of the 1960s. This book has at least a convincing message: 'Beyond your own plate!' This shall be the life-elixir of every autonomous individual in the world. To this the free intellectual George Katsiaficas has made a compelling contribution."
—Geronimo, author of *Fire and Flames: A History of the German Autonomist Movement*

The Global Imagination of 1968

Revolution and Counterrevolution

George Katsiaficas
Preface by Kathleen Cleaver
Forward by Carlos Muñoz

The Global Imagination of 1968: Revolution and Counterrevolution
© 2018 George Katsiaficas
All proceeds received by the author will be donated to the Eros Effect Foundation.

ISBN: 978-1-62963-439-5
Library of Congress Control Number: 2017942912

Cover by John Yates/stealworks.com
cover photo from *Photo*, hors-série no. 128: *Spécial: Les inédits de Mai 68* (May 1978).
Layout by Jonathan Rowland

PM Press
PO Box 23912
Oakland, CA 94623
www.pmpress.org

10 9 8 7 6 5 4 3 2 1

Printed by the Employee Owners of Thomson-Shore in Dexter, Michigan.
www.thomsonshore.com

Contents

For Herbert Marcuse and Jang Doo-sok,
my teachers, friends, and comrades

TABLES AND MAPS

FOREWORD
by Carlos Muñoz

I T IS A PLEASURE TO BE PART OF THE SECOND EDITION OF GEORGE Katsiaficas's book *The Imagination of the New Left: A Global Analysis of 1968*. I consider it to be a classic study of the social movements that became dramatically visible in what is widely considered the key year of the 1960s. During that era I became a leader of one of those movements that came to be known as the broader "Chicano movement." Prior to the publication of the first edition of the book, it was an "invisible" movement because previous books on the New Left had ignored its existence. The Katsiaficas book was the first to acknowledge it.

The book's focus on 1968 is personally very significant to me because I had a life-changing experience that year. I was a Vietnam War–era veteran attending college on the GI Bill and a first-year graduate student activist involved in the anti–Vietnam War movement. I was also president of the United Mexican American Students (UMAS) and became one of the organizers of student walk-outs to protest the racism Chicano students faced in the barrio high schools of East Los Angeles. The protest turned out to be the first major Chicano mass protest action against racism in U.S. history, and it ignited the emergence of the Chicano civil rights movement in the Southwest.

Over ten thousand students walked out of their de facto segregated barrio high schools in East Los Angeles. The walkouts lasted a week and a half and practically shut down the schools. The major students demands were that the school board fire all racist teachers and staff, hire Latino teachers and staff, teach courses about Chicano history and culture, and afford Chicano students the opportunities to enroll in college prep courses. At that time in history, Chicanos had the highest dropout rate in the city. The consequence was that instead of having the option to pursue a college education, many male students were drafted into military service. They suffered the highest casualties of any racial/ethnic group in the trenches of the Vietnam War. I had been one of those drafted a year out of high school but fortunately ended up serving in South Korea instead of Vietnam, where more than likely I would have been part of the casualty list.

My life-changing experience occurred after the student walkouts ended. I was one of the thirteen Chicano civil rights activists who had organized the student walkouts and were arrested after the Los Angeles Grand Jury charged us with "conspiracy to disrupt" the largest school district in the nation. I was thrown into an overcrowded cell with men who had been arrested on felony charges of murder, bank robbery, and rape. The county district attorney Evelle Younger, who had previously been one of FBI Director J. Edgar Hoover's top agents, had redefined organizing protest meetings as a conspiracy to commit misdemeanors and thus a felony crime. Each one of us faced sixty-six years in prison if found guilty. We did not know it at that time, but we were victims of the FBI Counterintelligence Program (COINTELPRO) and were not granted our First Amendment rights. Perhaps J. Edgar Hoover thought Chicanos did not qualify for constitutional rights. In 1970, two years after our arrest, the California State Appellate Court ruled we were innocent by virtue of the First Amendment of the U.S. Constitution.

My imprisonment and the felony crime charges awoke in me the realization that we did not live in an authentic democracy. I therefore made a commitment to devote my life to the struggle for social justice, peace at home and abroad, and to contribute to the remaking of the United States into an authentic multiracial democracy.

Like other activists who considered themselves part of the New Left, I was inspired by revolutions in the Third World, especially the Cuban Revolution. After becoming one of the leaders of the Chicano civil rights movement, I saw the connections between those revolutions and the struggles of Chicanos and other people of color in the United States. George Katsiaficas dramatically captured those connections. In particular, it was the first book that went beyond placing the U.S. social movements of the 1960s and '70s into the limited context of the black-and-white racial paradigm. It was also the first book to include analysis of the Chicano movement, the Asian American movement, and Native American movement. In this second edition, Katsiasficas continues to place the New Left in the context of a theoretical framework that captures both its positive revolutionary contributions and its failures. It is a critical analysis that makes clear why the legacies of our past collective movements should be honored by the youth of the twenty-first century as they engage in the struggle against the oppressive forces of the U.S. Empire at home and abroad.

PREFACE
by Kathleen Cleaver

T HE RISE OF LIBERATION STRUGGLES FROM EUROPEAN DOMINANCE and generations of anticolonial warfare in Africa and Asia set the stage for the cluster of nationalist movements that erupted during the upheavals of 1968. Numerous peoples gained independence from Belgian, French, or British rulers in Asia, Africa, and the Caribbean. Black Americans for the first time saw African diplomats and heads of state on the world stage, such as Ghana's Kwame Nkrumah and the Congo's Patrice Lumumba. Their brilliant inspiration encouraged support and emulation among African Americans. This era saw thousands of American soldiers killed by the ill-fated U.S. Army campaign to retain Vietnamese submission to foreign rule in South Vietnam after North Vietnam under the leadership of Ho Chi Minh won independence from France. The amazing guerrilla war underway in South Vietnam sparked the rise of anti-racist and anti-imperialist movements around the world.

In *The Global Imagination of 1968*, George Katsiaficas points out that "a world-historical movement" from 1968 to 1970 led to forty nations becoming democratized from 1974 to 1991. He demonstrates how the Black Power movement in the United States was moving from a radical organizing project into low-intensity guerrilla warfare. During the mid-1970s, political and ethnic movements demanding empowerment expanded rapidly. This era he describes as invigorated by the "eros effect" also witnessed women's activism explode across the developed world. The Tet offensive the Vietnamese launched during 1968 proved to the world that the United States could never gain a military victory against the guerrilla fighters in Vietnam.

Katsiaficas's analysis includes a gruesome military detail: the United States dropped more bombs on Vietnam than all sides did during the entire duration of World War II. The toll of destruction flaming through the villages and rice paddies of South Vietnam reached genocidal proportions. It is in this global context that Katsiaficas articulates his unifying concept of the "eros effect." This permits him to link worldwide opposition to the Vietnam war with popular support for challenges against colonial rule in Asia and Africa and social protest movements in Europe, South America, the Caribbean islands, and the United States.

xvi   The Global Imagination of 1968

The Global Imagination of 1968 also devotes significant attention to the movement inspired by the call for "Black Power" in the U.S., the Caribbean, and other English-speaking lands. Although antecedents during the Garvey movement of the 1920s and the socialist movement of the 1930s laid a foundation for the concept, the late sixties call for Black Power gained explosive impact given the international context of widespread opposition to the U.S. war in Vietnam. The energies of youth from high schools, colleges, and prisons propelled a tsunami of protests and fueled national liberation struggles on several continents and the dynamism of the Black Power movement both within and beyond the United States. Liberation struggles from Polynesia to Palestine, from Australia to Africa, gained support, and participants demonstrated creative challenges to established authority, including airplane hijackings.

Katsiaficas concludes his book with a distinctive section devoted to a political event called the Revolutionary Peoples' Constitutional Convention. At the time, I happened to be a guest of the government in Pyongyang, North Korea, representing the International Section of the Black Panther Party. Although the radio reception was scratchy, I managed to hear part of the Voice of American report on the event. The Black Panther Party had organized the Revolutionary Peoples' Constitutional Convention taking place in Philadelphia, and Katsiaficas was a participant. His book's final section incorporates the workshop reports generated at the Constitutional Convention that demonstrate how the Constitution of the United States could be revolutionized.

The current release of *The Global Imagination of 1968* is timely. A new generation of readers attuned to the political crises of our day will find it a fertile source of ideas, historical accounts, and analyses to sustain their development. In the confusing world surrounding us, Katsiaficas's book will help readers develop a sense of continuity with those twentieth-century struggles that continue to enlighten us in the process of changing the world.

INTRODUCTION

UNLIKE ANY YEAR OF THE HALF CENTURY PRECEDING IT, 1968 WILL be remembered for the worldwide eruption of social movements, ones that profoundly changed the world without seizing political power. From Paris to Chicago and Prague to Mexico City, unexpectedly popular struggles erupted in a global challenge to the established order. What did these movements want? Where did they go? What were their effects? What about the future? To answer these questions is the purpose of this book.

The literature on the sixties is so vast that it would fill several libraries, yet there have been few attempts to answer the question: What did the insurgents want? In part, its reactive nature—its appearance as the Great Refusal—accounts for this void. Indeed, what the movement aspired to create was scarcely known among many of its participants. Is it even possible to speak of a common vision?

I selected the general strike of May 1968 in France and the crisis of 1970 in the United States as the focus for this book because the actions of millions of people during these situations concretely embodied their vision of a qualitatively different society. More than any individual's speech or written narrative, the character of spontaneously generated forms of dual power and content of enunciated aspirations display the goals of popular movements. In my case studies, I emphasize the form and content of emergent forces during periods of social upheaval. Although there were many leaders, my analysis is focused on the praxis of *social actors*, millions of people who together generate a new dimension to reality by becoming a "class for itself." In word and deed, millions of people not only imagined a new reality but lived one. Their day-to-day lives were based on international solidarity rather than nationalistic pride; on racial solidarity not division; on self-management of the factories, universities, and offices rather than top-down decision making; on cooperation not competition. However briefly these moments existed, they offer a revealing glimpse of a possible future crying out to be realized. By focusing on these two profound crises, I hope to make clear the global imagination of 1968.

To deal with the May 1968 near-revolution in France involved reading dozens of books and articles in French, German, and English, but when I turned to the U.S. crisis of 1970, it was practically invisible. No one analyzed in depth the May 1970 national campus strike, despite it being the largest strike in American history and also one of its most political. The five months from May to September 1970 were the high points of a self-understood revolutionary uprising, when every subaltern constituency reached a climax of activism. The high point of this insurgency came in September at the Black Panthers' Revolutionary Peoples' Constitutional Convention (RPCC) in Philadelphia, when thousands of us, despite threats of police attacks, drafted a visionary new constitution. Like the student strike, the RPCC has been a neglected moment in an otherwise heavily studied social movement, and my chapter on 1970 presents for the first time a comprehensive history that ties them together as the alpha and omega of the greatest U.S. crisis since the Civil War.

Scholars have generally treated civil rights, feminism, and the gay movement as separate phenomena, drawing artificial lines that inhibit comprehension of one of their most important dimensions: synchronous interrelationships with each other. To be sure, each had its own autonomous organizations and beliefs, but my empirical evidence reveals an international movement from 1968 to 1970 that fused these seemingly separate insurgencies into a unified world-historical movement. The imagination and aspirations of this historical force went beyond the needs and beliefs of any of its various component constituencies.

In the period of the fusion of various national, ethnic, and gender movements into a world-historical whole, the vision of a qualitatively different world system (or nonsystem) emerged. The fondest dreams of any individual genius (such as Martin Luther King Jr., today revered as a "Great Man" of history) fell far short of the global imagination of 1968. As eloquent and intelligent as King was, his individual dream concerned racially integrating the existing system. Although near the end of his life he articulated connections between the struggle for civil rights and the war in Vietnam, he did so long after Black Power advocates and radical Latinos like Corky Gonzales had already taken even stronger antiwar stands.

Like millions of others, Martin Luther King was transformed by the global insurgency of the 1960s. In the months before his assassination, he even began to discuss the idea of qualitatively "restructuring the whole of American society." Black Panthers were also transformed by the global movement they helped so much to bring to life. When they convened their constitutional convention in 1970, the revolutionary workshops' proposals were far more visionary than the Panthers' reformist 1966 program. Because the movement's vision of a new society was not publicized nearly as much as King's eloquent dream or the

Panther program, it is often repeated that the New Left was simply a reactive social movement protesting perceived injustices, that it was a rebellious rather than a revolutionary social movement.

For the most part, activists from the pre-1966 period of the U.S. movement have also been its historians, and their versions of events passionately chronicle their own experiences. After 1966, when the movement spread to working-class students and inner-city ghettos, activists adopted "revolutionary" ideas that went far beyond earlier reformism. The resulting situation has left the high point of the movement in 1970 largely unrecorded or, at best, remembered through the prism of personal experiences. "Bourgeois" accounts, memoirs, and biographical portraits focused on individuals thought to be at the center of world events remain essential to the history of 1968. Many such accounts forget to mention that solitary individuals, such as Malcolm X and Martin Luther King (or organizations such as the Black Panther Party) were themselves historical products of the movements in which they participated.

When the first version of this book appeared in 1987, it opened the door to comprehending the movement of 1968 as internationally united. Unlike dozens of previously published memoirs and studies, my analysis was not confined to one country. At a time when "nationalistic" versions of 1968's history were everywhere prominent, my book was the first to comprehend the movement as global. In my understanding, simultaneous and synchronously related global insurgencies were at the heart of 1968's dynamism. I named this phenomenon the "eros effect." In such moments, people's ties to each other become more significant than patriotic allegiances or class and racial identities. New norms and values are acted upon, and it seems the whole world is transformed. By introducing the notion of the "eros effect," I seek to universalize our understanding of the global imagination of 1968 within the framework of objective forces at work in the world system. I expend considerable effort in reconstructing specific events during uprisings because actions by hundreds of thousands of people speak eloquently to their needs and aspirations.

As a researcher, I seek to make apparent the movement's vision, and as a participant, I share it in my heart, a coincidence that is a key reason for my ability to devote myself to the laborious construction of a global analysis. Without the advice of Herbert Marcuse and the confidence with which he showered me, I doubt I would have completed my international research.

It is gratifying that even after the fall of the Soviet Union and integration of China into the realm of Great Power politics, my perspective remains accurate. In his history of the twentieth century, *The Age of Extremes: A History of the World, 1914–1991*, noted author Eric Hobsbawm called this book "a well-informed survey of the global 'New Left' of 1968." In the intervening years, I've lived as a citizen of the world and written two other books dealing with revolutionary movements: *The Subversion of Politics* (concerning European autonomous social movements) and the two-volume *Asia's Unknown Uprisings*.

Despite its apparent failure, the movement of 1968 (or New Left as it was known) continues to define the contours of subsequent insurgencies, structured as they are by the same grammar of direct democracy, autonomous self-organization independent of political parties, and global solidarity. In the 1980s and 1990s, young activists often complained to me that the 1960s movements were a weight on their shoulders overshadowing their daily struggles. In part, this is due to the mainstream media making the 1960s into a spectacle, turning them into something larger than life, while by comparison, subsequent protest movements are made into parodies or ignored entirely. Besides undercutting contemporary activism, the mythology of 1968 has been used to bring former protesters into the very Establishment they once opposed.

Only after years of encouragement from Ramsey at PM Press did I finally agree to produce this new edition. In 1987, my book discussed movements in seventeen countries within a global framework. The present volume expands my analysis to more than fifty countries by adding many places in Africa, Asia, and Latin America. New sections on Latino activism, the women's movement, and artists have been woven into the rich tapestry of the international uprising. In addition, the U.S. crisis in 1970 is now portrayed as lasting from May to September. Although I use 1968 as a shorthand to refer to the global insurgency, movements in the Americas peaked in 1970, an understanding lost by Eurocentric histories. I've deleted portions of my original monograph, especially the last two chapters with theoretical critiques of sociology, systems analysis, and Soviet Marxism, but these parts are available at http://eroseffect.com.

This book changed my life. After Lee Jae-won found it in a library and translated it into Korean, I journeyed there and have never looked back. In preparing this new version, I would like to acknowledge the help of Richard Cambridge, Eddie Yuen, Alda Blanco, Jack Hipp, John Hansen, Dan O'Connell, Beth Vargas, Thomas and Dalal, Park Mi Ok, and Jonathan at PM. I owe an unspoken debt to dozens of 1960s activists who remain incarcerated in the dungeons of the "belly of the beast." Kevin "Rashid" Johnson and Shaka Zulu's fortitude continually inspires me. Cassandra Wildheart's editing and enthusiasm comforted me as I labored at my table, my hands aching from pounding the computer, my shoulders stiffening, my eyesight blurring. Whoever thinks that intellectuals do not work with their hands simply has no clue!

To Kathleen Cleaver and Carlos Muñoz, unquestioned comrades and friends for decades, and I hope for decades yet to come, thank you for your contributions to this project.

We have come a long way from the global optimism of the 1960s. Our vision of a world of peace and harmony, forever memorialized by John Lennon's song "Imagine," hardly seems relevant in a world perpetually at war, where millions of human beings perish needlessly every year, and where the planet is being devastated. Everywhere, we are compelled to work more hours, for more years, for less money. One realistic theme in 1968 France was that working a few hours a day should suffice for all to prosper. Young people today are forced to spend their youth preparing to "make a living" as opposed to living. Many young Americans today graduate from college buried under a mountain of debt. Where we once hoped to uproot the world system and its enslaving mentality, the triumph of capitalism may reward many of us with consumer goods, but the system costs us dearly in terms of the impoverished quality of our society. Fifty years later, the movement's vision of freedom continues to inspire. Loss of hope today is one reason why the imagination of 1968 is so important.

Ocean Beach, California
January 2018

CHAPTER 1

THE NEW LEFT AS A WORLD-HISTORICAL MOVEMENT

> The nature of Spirit may be understood by a glance at its direct oppo-
> site—Matter. As the essence of Matter is Gravity, so, on the other hand,
> we may affirm that the substance, the essence of Spirit is Freedom.
> —G.W.F. Hegel

WORLDWIDE EPISODES OF REVOLT IN 1968 HAVE GENERALLY BEEN analyzed from within their own national contexts, but only in reference to the global constellation of forces and to each other can these movements be understood in theory as they occurred in practice. Particularly since World War II, it is increasingly difficult to analyze social movements from within the confines of a nation-state. The events that catalyze social movements are often international ones. The May 1970 nationwide university strike in the United States is remembered mainly because of the killings at Kent State and Jackson State Universities, but it was enacted in opposition to the U.S. invasion of Cambodia as well as to repression of the Black Panther Party.

The international connections between movements in 1968 were often synchronic, as television, radio, and newspapers relayed news of events as they occurred. In May 1968, when a student revolt led to a general strike of over nine million workers in France, there were significant demonstrations of solidarity in Mexico City, Berlin, Tokyo, Buenos Aires, Berkeley, and Belgrade, and students and workers in both Spain and Uruguay attempted general strikes of their own. Massive student strikes in Italy forced Prime Minister Aldo Moro and his cabinet to resign; Germany experienced its worst political crisis since World War II; and a student strike at the University of Dakar, Senegal, led to a general strike of workers. These are instances of what sociologists have called "contagion effects" (and what I consider "eros effects"); they remain to this day understudied, a moment of neglect which stands in inverse proportion to their significance.

It was not by chance alone that the Tet offensive in Vietnam occurred in the same year as the Prague Spring, the May events in France, the student rebellion in West Germany, the assassination of Martin Luther King Jr., the takeover of Columbia University, riots at the Democratic National Convention in Chicago, and the pre-Olympic massacre in Mexico City. These events were related to one another, and a synchronic analysis of world social movements in 1968 validates Hegel's proposition that history moves from east to west. Global oppositional forces converged in a pattern of mutual amplification: "The whole world was watching," and with each act of the unfolding drama, new strata of social actors entered the arena of history, until finally an internationally synchronized insurgency against war and all forms of oppression emerged. In 1968 and 1970, crises of revolutionary proportions were reached in France and the U.S. These climactic points involved intense struggles between uprisings and reaction, a pivot around which protests ultimately lost momentum as "repressive tolerance" shed its benign appearance.

Looking back half a century later, we can say that 1968 signaled an enormous historical transition. The world today is changing faster than ever before in a dizzying process seemingly without outline. Yet 1968 gave us unusual clarity. As one observer put it:

> History does not usually suit the convenience of people who like to divide it into neat periods, but there are times when it seems to have pity on them. The year 1968 almost looks as though it had been designed to serve as some sort of signpost. There is hardly any region of the world in which it is not marked by spectacular and dramatic events which were to have profound repercussions on the history of the country in which they occurred and, as often as not, globally. This is true of the developed and industrialized capitalist countries, of the socialist world, and of the so-called "third world"; of both the eastern and western, the northern and southern hemispheres.[1]

Prior to 1968, no one knew and few could have guessed what was in store for world history. Without warning, worldwide movements spontaneously erupted. At the beginning of the year, President Charles de Gaulle hailed France as an "infallible beacon for the world," but within months the country teetered on the brink of revolution. If he had known what kind of beacon France would be in 1968, he might never have delivered his New Year's Address. After weathering the revolutionary crisis two years later in the United States, President Richard Nixon (popularly known as Tricky Dick) in his State of the Union address in January 1971 called for a "New American Revolution . . . as profound, as far-reaching, as exciting as that first revolution almost 200 years ago."[2] While some people scratched their hands in bewilderment, many more understood Nixon's Orwellian universe to mean "peace" was war, and "revolution" was counterrevolutionary repression.

Without warning, global turmoil of 1968 erupted against both capitalism and real-world socialism, against authoritarian power and patriarchal authority. The New Left opposed both state "socialism" and American "democracy." In its best moments, the movement challenged the entire universe of capitalist patriarchy—and in doing so, gave future generations an enduring vision of freedom. Although 1968 is often used as shorthand for the New Left, insurgencies were not confined to one year. The 1955 bus boycott in Montgomery, which catapulted Martin Luther King to national attention, did not consider itself a "New Left" movement, but in essential aspects, it certainly was. The 1980 Gwangju People's Uprising (which ultimately brought parliamentary rule to South Korea) took place long after the New Left was supposed to have died, but it too carried New Left features. There was a self-described "New Left" in France as early as 1957, and a "New Left" insurrection in Sri Lanka in 1971.

Despite its brief appearance in history, the New Left regenerated dormant traditions of self-government and international solidarity. In Europe and the United States, after decades of cultural conformity, the possibility of revolution once again was widely discussed—and acted upon. At the same time, the meaning of revolution was enlarged to include questions of power in everyday life as well as the quality of power won by past revolutions. If the idea of revolution in an industrialized society was inconceivable for three decades prior to 1968, the kind of revolution prefigured in the emergent praxis of the movement was unlike previous ones. The goal of revolution was redefined to be decentralization and self-management of power and resources—destruction, not seizure, of militarized nation-states embedded in an international web of war and corporate machinations.

By enunciating the desire for a new world society based on cooperative sharing of international resources (not national or individual aggregation), on a communalism based upon enlarged social autonomy and greater individual freedom (not their suppression), and a way of life based on a new harmony with nature (not its accelerating exploitation), the New Left defined a unique stage in the aspirations of revolutionary movements. A new set of values was born in the movement's international and interracial solidarity, in its rejection of middle-class values like the accumulation of wealth and power, in its fight against stupefying routines and ingrained patterns of patriarchal domination, and in its attempt to reconstruct everyday life, not according to tradition or scientific rationality but through a liberated sensibility. In crises generated by insurgencies in 1968 in France and 1970 in the United States, these values were momentarily realized in spontaneously produced forms of dual power.

The tempo of modern history has been so rapid that what was new in 1968 seems to be as far away from us today as all the rest of history. Although no obvious trace of the movement seems to survive, once we review key events of 1968, it should become clear that, far from ending in failure, the New Left's very success contributed to its disappearance. To give just one example: in the 1960s, only a few people supported the right of South African blacks to rule their country. Today apartheid is a distant memory.

World-Historical Movements

Periods of crisis and turmoil on a global scale are relatively rare in history. Since the French and American Revolutions, it is possible to identify less than a handful of such periods of global eruptions: 1848–49, 1905–7, 1917–19, and 1968–70. In each of these periods, global upheavals were spontaneously generated. In a chain reaction of insurrections and revolts, new forms of power emerged in opposition to the established order, and new visions of the meaning of freedom were formulated in the actions of millions of people. Even when these movements were unsuccessful in seizing power, immense adjustments were necessitated both within and between nation-states, and the defeated movements offered revealing glimpses of the newly developed character of society and types of class struggles that would follow.

Throughout history, fresh outbreaks of revolution have been known to "conjure up the spirits of the past to their service and borrow from them names, battle cries, and costumes in order to present the new scene of world history in this time-honored disguise and this borrowed language."[3] The movements of 1968 were no exception: activists self-consciously acted in the tradition of past revolutions. Public statements issued by French insurgents during the May events invoked the memory of 1789, 1848, the 1871 Paris Commune, and the Russian soviets of 1905 and 1917. Outsiders confirmed what seemed like the collapse of time:

> In the Paris of May 1968, innumerable commentators, writing to celebrate or to deplore, proffered a vast range of mutually exclusive explanations and predictions. But for all of them, the sensibility of May triggered off a remembrance of things past. By way of Raymond Aron, himself in touch with Tocqueville, readers of Le Figaro remembered February 1848; by way of Henri Lefebvre, French students remembered the Proclamation of the Commune in March 1871, as did those who read Edgar Morin in Le Monde; French workers listened to elder militants who spoke of the occupation of factories in June 1936; and most adults, whether or not they had been in the Resistance, relived August 1944, the liberation of Paris.[4]

Such periods of the eros effect witness the basic assumptions and values of a social order (nationalism, hierarchy, and specialization) being challenged in theory and practice by new human standards. The capacity of millions of people to see beyond the social reality of their day—to imagine a better world and to fight for it—demonstrates a human characteristic that may be said to transcend time and space. During moments of the eros effect, universal interests become generalized at the same time as dominant values of society (national chauvinism, hierarchy, and domination) are negated. As Herbert Marcuse so clearly formulated it, humans have an instinctual need for freedom—something we grasp intuitively—and it is this vital need that is sublimated into a collective phenomenon during moments of the eros effect.[5]

Dimensions of the eros effect include the sudden and synchronous emergence of hundreds of thousands of people occupying public space; the simultaneous appearance of revolts in many places; the intuitive identification of hundreds of thousands of people with each other; their common belief in new values; and suspension of normal daily routines like competitive business practices, criminal behavior, and acquisitiveness. Though secular, such moments metaphorically resemble the religious transformation of the individual soul through the sacred baptism in the ocean of universal life and love. The integration of the sacred and the secular in such moments of "political Eros" (a term used by Herbert Marcuse) is an indication of the true potentiality of the human species, the "real history" which remains repressed and distorted within the confines of "prehistoric" powers and taboos.[6]

The reality of Paris at the end of May 1968 conformed less to the categories of existence preceding May (whether the former political legitimacy of the government, management's control of the workplaces, or the students' isolation from the "real world") than to the activated imaginations of millions of people who moved beyond a mere negation of the previous system by enacting new forms of social organization and new standards for the goal-determination of the whole system. Modes of thought, abolished in theory by empiricists and structuralists, emerged in a practical human effort to break out of antiquated categories of existence and establish nonfragmented modes of Being. Debate ceased as to whether human beings were capable of such universal notions as justice, liberty, and freedom. Rather, these abstractions, concretized in the actions of millions of people, became the popularly redefined reality.

The May events, like the Paris Commune, Gwangju Uprising, and other moments of revolutionary upheaval, established a new reality where living human energy and not things was predominant. From this perspective, they can be viewed as a taste of the joy of human life, which will be permanently unleashed with the advent of a new world system qualitatively different than anything that has ever existed. With the end of "prehistory" and the beginning of "human history," human imagination will be freed to take giant steps in constructing a better world. "All Power to the Imagination," written everywhere in May 1968, will become inscribed in the lives and institutions of future generations.[7]

Two years later, the United States underwent its most significant crisis since the Civil War. While a majority of workers did not join, a rupture even more acrimonious and violent than in France took place. U.S. geographical size and the racial fragmentation of its citizens contributed to obscuring the magnitude of five months of climactic confrontations. Beginning in May with a university strike of more than four million people, a simultaneous battlefield revolt incapacitated the U.S. military, the first Gay Pride marches openly dared to take public space, women organized a general strike, Latinos mobilized in the streets as never before, and a rainbow alliance of about ten thousand people responded to the call by Black Panthers and assembled in Philadelphia, despite police terror, to write a new constitution. Insurgents' visions of freedom are contained in their actions, yet the Black Panthers' Revolutionary Peoples' Constitutional Convention (RPCC) also gave explicit details of the conscious outline of a free society.

With hindsight, we may debate today whether May '68 and May–September '70 were revolutionary crises, prerevolutionary situations, or simply "moments of madness," but in both cases self-understood revolutionary movements involving hundreds of thousands of people mobilized millions of supporters who decisively fought to overthrow the Establishment. In the U.S., unlike France, the forces of order used murderous force to crush the insurgency.

Historically speaking, it has often been the case that a particular nation has experienced social upheavals at the same time as order reigned elsewhere. Coups d'état, putsches, and armed takeovers of power within the confines of a particular nation are to be expected. In 1968 (and 1848 and 1905), there were seldom successful seizures of power despite the movement's global character. Nonetheless, social convulsions in these periods profoundly redirected world cultures and political trajectories. Spontaneous chain reactions of uprisings, strikes, rebellions, and revolutionary movements signaled massive proliferation of movement ideas and aspirations, a crucial aspect of their world-historical character.[8]

Some epochs of class struggle are world-historical and others are not, a distinction noted by Antonio Gramsci, who used the terms "organic" (relatively permanent) and "conjunctural" (occasional, immediate, almost accidental) to describe the difference.[9] The apparent climax and disappearance of the New Left led many observers to conclude it conformed to what Gramsci called conjunctural, arising as a unique product of the post–World War II baby boom, the injustice of Jim Crow segregation, or the prolonged intensity of the war in Vietnam. In the twenty-first century, with international acceptance of feminism's goal of gender equality, a global consensus against racism, and growing insurgencies against capitalist inequality and environmental devastation, the organic character of 1968 is evident.

Even in failure, world-historical movements define new epochs in cultural, political, and economic dimensions of society. They present new ideas and values that become common sense as time passes. They qualitatively reformulate the meaning of freedom for millions of human beings. Massive and unexpected strife and international proliferation of new aspirations signal the beginning of epochal change. During the dramatic outbreak of revolts and reaction to them, new aspirations are passionately articulated and attacked, and progress occurs in weeks and months when previously it took decades and half centuries. History does not unfold in a linear direction or at an even pace. As Marcuse observed, "There is no even progress in the world: The appearance of every new condition involves a leap; the birth of the new is the death of the old."[10] He forgot to add that the birth of the new, after its period of celebration and youth, moves into maturity and then decays. In order to appreciate this, let us review what is meant by world history.

Hegel measured the development of world history through emergence of individualized inward subjectivity.[11] Such a transposition of the individual for the species as agent and outcome of world history thoroughly conformed to the ideology of the ascendant bourgeoisie. Limitations of Hegel's outlook are apparent in his conclusion that history culminates in Germany and in his legitimation of the Prussian state.[12] In contrast to Hegel, it is my view that history is nothing but the development of the human species and is not measured through flowering of the individual in isolation from others (that is bourgeois history) but in the unfolding of human collectivities and of an individuality that surpasses bourgeois individualism. Moreover, what for Hegel was a dialectic of mind is analyzed here as a dialectic of praxis, of the consciousness in action of millions of people.

The history of modernity, from struggles for national independence and parliamentary democracy to liberation of oppressed classes and managed masses, follows a logic similar to that uncovered by Hegel, a dialectical framework within which potentialities of the human species as a species-being unfolds. The logic of world history carries an irony which "turns everything upside down," not only posing the new against the old, but simultaneously transforming what was once new and revolutionary into its opposite. In the past two hundred years, we see this in the history of the United States. From challenging and defeating the forces of "divine right," the world's first secular democratic state has long since degenerated, whether in bloodily invading Korea, Vietnam, Iraq, and Afghanistan or in abetting one of the world's last states founded on a notion of "divine right," a religious state whose technological weapons of genocide are provided by the United States to forestall the realization of its own ideal foundation: a secular, democratic state for people of all religions, but this time in Palestine.

But of course, to see the contradictory character of history, we only have to look at the important role of slave owners within the American Revolution of 1776, at the acceleration of genocide against Native Americans after it, and at U.S. refusal to support the Haitian Revolution.[13] Is it surprising that the new republic annexed Texas in 1844 and northern Mexico four years later? Are we amazed by contemporary U.S. support for the Saudi monarchy and for every variety of dictator "on our side"? So much for what can become of world-historical leaps when left adrift in the world of the "survival of the fittest." Let us return to their moments of joyful infancy, to the attempts made by human beings to leap beyond the dead weight of the past.

In the twentieth century, the essential indication of these leaps, the signal for a whole epoch of class struggles, was recognized to be the general strike. Such strikes are not cleverly orchestrated by a small group of conspirators or "world-historical individuals," but involve the spontaneous and conscious actions of millions of people. As Rosa Luxemburg pointed out:

> Political and economic strikes, mass strikes and partial strikes, demonstrative strikes and fighting strikes, general strikes of individual branches of industry and general strikes in individual towns, peaceful wage struggles and street massacres, barricade fighting—all these run through one another, run side by side, cross one another, flow in and over one another—it is ceaselessly moving, a changing sea of phenomena. . . . In a word, the mass strike . . . is not a crafty method discovered by subtle reasoning for the purpose of making the proletarian struggle more effective, but the method of motion of the proletarian mass, the phenomenal form of the proletarian struggle in the revolution.[14]

General strikes not only sum up new historical epochs of class struggle by revealing in utmost clarity the nature of the antagonists, they also indicate future directions of movements—their aspirations and goals, which, in the heat of historical struggle, emerge as popular wishes and intuitions. General strikes create a new reality, negating previous institutions, rupturing the hegemony of the existing order, and releasing seemingly boundless social energies that normally remain suppressed, repressed, and channeled into more "proper" outlets.

In contrast to what has become a commonplace alienation from politics, these moments are ones of the eroticization of politics, as portrayed by the May 1968 slogan, "The more I make revolution, the more I enjoy love."[15] Drudgery becomes play as imagination replaces practicality, and human competition and callousness are replaced by cooperation and dignity. During the Paris Commune of 1871, the streets were safe for the first time in years, even with no police of any kind. As one Communard said, "We hear no longer of assassination, theft, and personal assault; it seems, indeed, as if the police had dragged along with it to Versailles all its conservative friends."[16] The 1980 Gwangju Commune was an "absolute community of love" based upon "the act of recognizing a value larger than individual life."[17] The liberation of life instincts in these moments creates unique qualities of social life. In 1848, 1905, and 1968, for example, anti-anti-Semitism was a recurrent public theme, and international solidarity momentarily outweighed patriotic sentiments.[18]

Such spontaneous leaps are certainly products of long-term social processes in which organized groups and conscious individuals prepare groundwork, but when political struggles come to involve tens and hundreds of thousands of people, it is possible to glimpse a rare historical occurrence: the emergence of the eros effect, the massive awakening of the instinctual human need for justice and for freedom. When the eros effect occurs, it becomes clear that the fabric of the status quo has been torn, and the forms of social control have been ruptured. This break becomes clear when established patterns of interaction are negated, and new and better ones are created. In essence, general strikes (and revolutions) are the emergence of humans as a species-being, the negation of the age-old "survival of the fittest" through a process by which nature becomes history (*Aufhebung der Naturwüchsigkeit*).[19]

The international impact of revolutionary movements that succeed in seizing state power is widely recognized. Few people would question the profound and long-lasting repercussions of revolutions in 1776 in the United States, 1789 in France, or 1917 in Russia. The ruptures of social order in 1848, 1905, and 1968 may not have toppled the dominant institutions, but they marked the emergence of new values, ideas, and aspirations that became consolidated as time passed. These intense periods of class struggle were important to the self-formation of the human species; they dramatically changed human beings. The new realities created by the eros effect changed the conversations. They were not limited to elite regime change, but transformed entire populations, revealing new needs and higher aspirations of millions of people.

Experiences accumulated from political praxis are a significant historical legacy that imbues future struggles with a higher consciousness. Whether in intuitive terms, directly intergenerational, or obtained from the study of history, human beings are transformed by social movements, and the self-formation of the species remains the innermost meaning of history. If history teaches us anything, it reveals the process through which the human species becomes conscious of its own development, an awareness that takes shape with utmost clarity during moments of the eros effect.

Thomas Jefferson observed this phenomenon in his analysis of the global impact of the American Revolution:

> As yet that light (of liberty) has dawned on the middling classes only of
> the men of Europe. The Kings and the rabble, of equal importance, have
> not yet received its beams, but it continues to spread, and . . . it can no
> more recede than the sun return on his course. A first attempt to recover
> the right of self-government may fail, so may a second, a third, etc. But
> as a younger and more instructed race comes on, the sentiment becomes
> more and more intuitive, and a fourth, a fifth, or some subsequent one of
> the ever-renewed attempts will ultimately succeed.[20]

American revolutionaries of Jefferson's day were hemispheric. Beginning in 1776, the brothers Catari protested uninterruptedly against the abuses of authorities in Chayanta (now part of Bolivia). On November 16, 1780, Tupac Amaru proclaimed liberty of slaves during an uprising joined by Creoles, Spanish, Africans, Mestizos, and Native Americans.[21] Riding his famous white horse, Amaru led an insurrectionary army of as many as twenty thousand fighters in fourteen provinces. He exhorted his compatriots to realize that they were "all born in our lands and from the same natural origin, all of whom have been oppressed by European tyranny."[22] By the time the rebellion reached its zenith, it affected a generalized uprising from Buenos Aires to Chile, Quito, New Granada, and Venezuela.

Far from being the result of any single event, abolition of European colonialism and feudalism was a process that required centuries of struggle. Uprisings and revolutions accelerated the birth of a new social formation as part of a process that occurred on many levels. In retrospect, we can observe today that 1848, 1905, and 1968 marked the first acts of the emergence of new social classes on the stage of world history. Despite defeat in their first experiences in the class struggle, these "failed" movements had their moments of success—even if incomplete—in subsequent epochs. Within the context of the world system's escalating spiral of expansion, fresh social movements take up where previous ones leave off. The "failed" social movements of 1848, 1905, and 1968 connected the emergent subjectivity of millions of people over more than a century. The world-historical movements of the working class of 1848, the landless peasantry of 1905, and the new working class of 1968 provide a glimpse of the essential forces that have produced—and are products of—the movement of history.

Although each of these periods of upheaval revitalized social movements, differing economic conditions precipitated the storms. The revolutions of 1848 were preceded by the prolonged economic slump of 1825–48, and the movements of 1905 were also preceded by severe hardships following the worldwide slump of 1873–96.[23] The two decades prior to 1968, however, were ones of immense global economic expansion before the world economic downturn of the 1970s.

Despite differing precipitating conditions and historical epochs, striking similarities can be found in cultural contestation of rules governing everyday life in 1848, 1905, and 1968. As initially pointed out by Alexis de Tocqueville, the first revolution against boredom was in 1848. He makes it quite clear that in the established political life, "there reigned nothing but languor, impotence, immobility, boredom" and that "the nation was bored listening to them."[24] When he turned to the poet Lamartine, Tocqueville commented, "He is the only man, I believe, who always seemed to be ready to turn the world upside-down to divert himself." If 1848 was, at least partially, a revolution against boredom, the May events in France were even more so. As the Situationists put it: "We do not want to exchange a world in which it is possible to die of starvation for one in which it is possible to die from boredom." Shortly before May 1968, the front page of *Le Monde* ran the headline "*France s'ennuie!*" and Godard's film *Weekend* had expressed a similar message. In the United States, Abbie Hoffman's *Revolution for the Hell of It!* sold out as quickly as it was printed.

Leading up to the cataclysmic events of 1848 in Vienna, Jesuit priests were handed control of nearly all the high schools, and when they forbade the old and joyous custom of nude bathing in the river, the first sparks of student protest began to fly. From these small beginnings emerged the revolutionary student brigade that became the government in Vienna for months.[25] In 1968, at Nanterre University on the outskirts of Paris, a few men who had spent the night in the women's dormitory to protest sexual segregation and parietal hours were chased by police into a crowded lecture hall where scores of students were then mercilessly beaten. So began the escalating spiral of the May events.

Berlin in 1848 had a reputation of being gay in every way. Berliners adored picnics, bonfires, parades, and festivals, but one of the many prohibitions included a ban on workers smoking in the public gardens, the Tiergarten. After the first round of barricade fighting in March, a crowd carried some of the 230 dead civilians to the palace, and someone called out loudly for the king to come and see the flower-covered corpses. His Majesty appeared on the balcony and took his hat off at the sight of the dead while the queen fainted. In this delicate moment, Prince Lichnowsky addressed the crowd, telling them their demands were granted. No one moved. Suddenly someone called out, "Smoking too?" "Yes, smoking too." "Even in the Tiergarten?" "You may smoke in the Tiergarten, gentlemen." With that, the crowd dispersed. The fact that another Prussian, Prinz zu Hohenlohe-Ingelfingen, questioned whether it was tobacco or some other concoction that workers were smoking provides another aspect of cultural affinity between the movements of 1848 and 1968.

Such parallels might be regarded as trivial ones, but their significance should not be disregarded unless one refuses to contemplate the need of the established order to control leisure time and the aspirations of popular movements to transform everyday life. Precisely because these movements were rooted in the popular need to transform power structures in everyday life are they "world-historical." The birth of the women's movement in 1848, its revival after 1905, and its reemergence in 1968 are further indications of the "organic" awakening in these years.

1848, 1905, 1968: Historical Overview

These three world-historical movements emerged at different historical conjunctures, and they were composed of differing social classes. Although many groups participated in the revolutions of 1848, these events marked the entrance of the working class on the stage of world history. On February 22–24, 1848, the workers of Paris rose up and toppled the monarchy, sending the king into exile and sparking a continent-wide movement for democratic rights, the end of the monarchies, and economic justice. The French uprising had an enormous international impact in part because of the country's new telegraph system.[26] In March, a bloody uprising in Vienna defeated the army and led to a new constitution. As the fighting spread to Berlin, Bavaria, Baden, and Saxony, the King of Prussia formed a new government and promised a democratic constitution. In Sicily, the Bourbon dynasty was overthrown, and the revolt spread to Naples, Milan, Venice, and Piedmont. The Poles rose against their Prussian rulers, and two nights of bloody barricade fighting broke out in Prague. Altogether there were some fifty revolutions in Europe in 1848 (counting the small German and Italian States and Austrian provinces), and these movements converged in their demands for republics and in their tactic of building barricades for urban warfare.

In June 1848, a new round of insurrections began when the working class of Paris seized control of the city. In four days of bloody barricade fighting, thousands of people were killed. After the revolt, the army held more than fifteen thousand prisoners, many of whom were later executed. Despite their defeat, the workers of Paris catalyzed a new wave of armed insurrections in Berlin, Vienna, and Frankfurt, and vast movements emerged among the peasantry. A revolutionary army appeared in Hungary, where Lajos Kossuth eloquently exhorted people to rise up for self-government and social revolution. The pope fled Rome as the republican movement won control from the French army. If the Hungarian revolutionary army had been able to reach the insurgents in Vienna, a Europe-wide revolution might have consolidated. Instead, counterrevolution reigned as order was brutally restored. The Holy Alliance (fashioned by Metternich in the wake of Napoleon) may not have been shattered in 1848, but Metternich himself was forced to flee Vienna, and greater liberties were won within the confines of existing states.

Rebellion in 1848 swept the distant island of Sri Lanka (then Ceylon), and British imperialism was also opposed in the Punjab. Sri Lankans were aware of the uprisings in India and around the world. One British observer noted that: "intelligence from Europe arrived of the revolution in France . . . and the disturbances in other European countries . . . and almost simultaneously with that there arrived intelligence of disasters to our Army in India. . . . I am assured by intelligent Kandyans that those two circumstances had a very material affect on the minds of the Kandyans . . . and improper use of those circumstances was made by the local press."[27] For the first time in Sri Lanka, in 1848, rural protesters united with the urban intelligentsia. Although the revolt was mercilessly crushed, the system of compulsory labor was brought to an end, and the colonial governor was recalled to England. The controversial poll tax levied on Buddhist monks was also withdrawn.

From 1845 to 1864, in a fusion of Christianity and Eastern philosophies, the Taiping rebellion led to civil war in China in which some twenty million people were killed. Ruling a vast liberated territory from their capital in Nanjing for eleven years, the Taiping were ultimately defeated by the Manchu Qing Dynasty. Although defeated, Taiping notions of communal property and complete equality of men and women subsequently reappeared.

Only after World War I would the Kaiser, the Czar, and the Hapsburgs be permanently dethroned, but after the storms of 1848, modern political parties, trade unions, and democratic rights emerged as bourgeois society was consolidated. The defeats of the insurrectionary governments of 1848 throughout Europe led to a period of stagnation for revolutionary movements. As Austria and Germany became more autocratic, more than one million Germans emigrated. For Immanuel Wallerstein, 1848's failed revolutions created a Left ideology that broke decisively with feudal conservatism and centrist liberalism, thereby paving the way for a long-term socialist organizing project that culminated in the 1917 Russian Revolution.[28] Although challenged in the streets in 1848, centrist liberalism went on to become the dominant "geoculture of the world-system" founded on formal democracy (based on universal suffrage within nation-states) and material improvements for the vast majority of citizens.

In the twenty-five years after 1848, free enterprise experienced some of its most dynamic years. For the first time, industrialization took root in France, Austria, Hungary, Poland, and Russia. Germany quickly developed into a major industrial country. New economic masters whose program of industrialization necessitated freeing the slaves conquered the United States. During this period, there was another wave of global expansion of European powers: the Syrian expedition (1860); Anglo-French war against China; French conquest of Indochina (1863); Maximilian's dispatch to Mexico; and conquest of Algeria and Senegal. There were also wars between capitalist powers, notably those in the Crimea and the Franco-Prussian War (which precipitated the Paris Commune).

Global expansionism after 1848 accelerated accumulation of vast wealth in industrialized nations, and concomitant harnessing of science to production and new mass production techniques (that is, the Second Industrial Revolution) further intensified the system's tendency toward global expansion. The whole world became divided into oppressor and oppressed nations as "free trade" led to imperialist conquest.

Nearly seventy years after the emergence of the working class as a class for itself, the peasants and natives of the periphery, increasingly denied land and liberty by the expanding imperial system, emerged as a force in their own right. At the beginning of the twentieth century, global networks of communication and transportation were limited compared to today, but nonetheless they helped synchronize world movements even more than in 1848. Beginning with Korea (1894), Cuba (1895), and the Philippines (1897), uprisings and movements for national independence appeared throughout the world. From 1904 to 1907, significant social movements erupted in India, Indochina, Madagascar, Angola, Portuguese Guinea, Egypt, Crete, Albania, Serbia, Poland, Guatemala, and Peru. A protracted guerrilla war against German colonial rule in Namibia cost the lives of one hundred thousand Africans, and the Zulus in Natal rose against their British rulers.

The 1905 defeat of Russia, a great European power, by Japan, then a small Asian sovereignty, helped precipitate this global wave of revolutionary activity. At one end of Asia, Sun Yat-sen declared, "We regarded the Russian defeat by Japan as the defeat of the West by the East." Similarly, Jawaharlal Nehru described how "Japanese victories stirred up my enthusiasm. . . . Nationalistic ideas filled my mind. I mused of Indian freedom."[29] At the other end of Asia, a British diplomat in Constantinople reported to London that the Japanese victory made every fiber in Turkish political life tingle with excitement. Three years later, the Young Turk revolt led to an insurrection in Salonika, and a constitutional government was quickly won for the entire Ottoman Empire. In China, the 1911 nationalist revolution led to the end of the Manchu dynasty and the emergence of modern Chinese political parties. Korean "righteous armies" rose against their Japanese rulers.

Popular movements erupted among miners and railroad workers in Germany, England, France, and the United States, and among farm workers in Italy and Galicia. The praxis of the working-class movement from 1900 to 1905 was a demonstration of the historically new tactic of the general strike. In this period, there were general strikes in Russia, Bohemia, Spain, Sweden, and Italy, strikes modeled on the first general strike of 1877 in St. Louis, Missouri. Between 1900 and 1905, there were massive strikes by miners in Pennsylvania (1900), Colorado (1903–4), Austria (1900), and France (1902); a general strike of all production workers in Barcelona (1902); and strikes for universal voting rights in Sweden (1902), Belgium (1902), Prague (1905), Galicia (1905), and Austria (1905). Although no movement came to power, organizations of farm workers in Italy and Galicia were strengthened; the Wobblies (Industrial Workers of the World) came to life in the United States; and in Belgium, Austria, and Sweden, universal suffrage was enacted.[30]

In Persia, general strikes and the emergence of soviets (organs of dual power or *anjomans*) precipitated a constitutional revolution that ultimately deposed the Qajar dynasty. In the course of these struggles, Persian women played an integral role. Organized into secret societies, masked women carried out armed actions while others published feminist newspapers and organized discussion groups. Although these actions achieved only minimal legal change in the status of women, there was a more significant transformation of the social attitude toward women, a change that established the cornerstone for future feminist movements there.[31]

Further to the north, in Russia, the mighty Czar was nearly overthrown. The massacre of hundreds of peaceful marchers in St. Petersburg on Bloody Sunday (January 22, 1905) precipitated a general strike coordinated by spontaneously formed soviets. Only after thousands of workers were killed during months of strikes did the movement temporarily abate. The revolution of 1905 transformed Russian politics by illuminating the brutality of Czarist rule at the same time as it indicated the popular movement's strength. As previously disenfranchised workers and humble peasants found themselves rallying the country to their cause, women of Russia became activated: "There had been no specifically feminist movement in Russia before this time, but there were obvious feminist implications in the idea of universal suffrage. And they encouraged the faint beginnings of a movement that now began to pick up a following."[32]

Although the movement did not seize power, the Czar was forced to grant limited democratic reforms, the Duma (Russian Parliament) was created, and Russian workers won a shorter working day and the right to organize. The spontaneously generated movement of 1905 permanently changed the common sense of Russia, and over the next twelve years, there was a growing wave of strikes that culminated in the reappearance of soviets and overthrow of the Czar in 1917. Russia's defeat in World War I left a vacuum of power. Eight months later, the Bolsheviks seized the state amid an uprising they orchestrated. The Bolsheviks' success helped to catalyze council movements in Germany, Austria, and Hungary, movements of workers and peasants which led to the end of the Austrian and German empires, even though the insurgents were unable to remain in power. From the March 1, 1919, Korean independence uprising to the May 4 movement in China, from the Egyptian revolt to massive strikes in the United States and Great Britain, international repercussions of the Russian Revolution were enormous.

In the decades following 1917, the working class and its peasant allies were successful in a host of countries as the locus of revolutionary movements shifted away from Europe to the world system's periphery. Within industrialized societies, overproduction led to a worldwide depression beginning in 1929, and working-class movements were temporarily revived in the Popular Front government in France, the Spanish Republic, the San Francisco General Strike, the battle of Minneapolis, and the great sit-in movements and factory occupations. Of course, the Comintern (or Third Communist International) played an overdetermining role in many popular struggles of the 1930s. More often than not, it defused vital energies of insurgent movements. Although the generation of the Abraham Lincoln Brigade demonstrated remarkable proletarian internationalism, it was nearly extinguished in the struggle against the fascism that filled the political void in old Central European empires. In the United States and Western Europe, struggles of the 1930s won trade unions new legitimacy, and the working class emerged from these struggles with a new sense of dignity. As one participant explained, he was "fortunate enough to be caught up in a great movement of millions of people, [which] literally changed not only the course of the workingman . . . but also the nature of the relationship between the workingman and the boss, for all time."[33]

In the first half of the twentieth century, although social movements came to power in Russia and China, global expansion of capitalism accelerated in the other half of the world. The origins of the world economy date well before the twentieth century, but in the latter half of this century, transnational corporations have centralized the world's productive capacity under their supervision. Monopoly production has moved from a national to an international level, and modern technology has revolutionized production through cybernetic control. In 1968, the Third Industrial Revolution announced itself with the publication of the *Double Helix*, (which revolutionized knowledge of DNA), marketing of the first microcomputer, and Apollo 8's rounding the moon. Modern space-age production, made possible by global centralization of resources and modern technology, has engendered an increasingly complex division of labor, and, in 1968, new oppositional forces emerged in the most developed capitalist countries: the new working class (technicians, employed professionals, off-line office workers, service workers, and students). As the First Industrial Revolution produced the working class and the Second a landless peasantry, so the Third created the new working class. The rapid growth of universities necessitated by high technology, internationalized division of labor, and consolidation of consumer society all converged to create the new working class. In 1968, their aspirations for a decentralized and self-managed global society transcended previous calls for liberty, equality, and fraternity in 1789; for jobs, trade unions, and employment security in 1848; and for land, peace, bread, and voting rights from 1905 to 1917.

As we will see, the New Left enriched traditions of revolutionary organization and tactics: from insurrectionary parliaments and barricade fighting in 1848; to soviets and general strikes in 1905; to vanguard parties and insurrections in 1917; and finally to decentralized, self-managed councils and popular contestation of public space in 1968. The New Left merger of culture and politics created situations in which contestation of public space was neither an armed insurrection nor a military assault for control of territory. Aspirations of the New Left in the advanced industrialized countries were decidedly not a dictatorship of the proletariat, but "Power to the People" and "All Power to the Imagination." In 1968, issues raised by the movement, like racism and patriarchy, were species issues, and at the same time, a new "we" was concretely defined in self-management which sprang up at the levels of campus, factory, and neighborhood. The chart below summarizes the New Left's relationship to previous world-historical movements.

The Development of World-Historical Social Movements					
Ascendant	1778–1789	1848	1905	1917	1968
Revolutionary class(es)	Bourgeoisie	Urban proletariat	Rural proletariat	Urban and rural working class	New working class
Emergent organization	Representative assemblies	Insurrectionary parliaments and political parties	Soviets/ councils	Vanguard party	Action committees/ collectives
Vision/ aspirations	Formal democracy; liberty, equality, fraternity	Economic democracy; trade unions; democratic constitutions	Universal suffrage; unions; freedom from empires	Socialism as the "dictatorship of the proletariat"; land, bread and peace	Self-management, all power to the people/ imagination
Tactics	Revolutionary war	Popular insurrections	General strike	Organized seizure of power	Contestation of public space/ everyday use

The New Left: A Global Definition
Unlike the centrally organized Communist International, the New Left's international political unity was not mandated from above but grew out of needs and aspirations of popular movements around the world. That is why the New Left can simultaneously be regarded as one insurgency and many social movements.

Despite attempts to construe the New Left as tied to the Soviet Union, Communist parties globally opposed the movement.[34] For its part, the New Left did not regard Communist parties as friends. As an observer in Italy put it:

> The fight of the New Left in Italy is taking place on two fronts: on one side against conservative forces and on the other against the traditional Left. One often gets the impression that the conflict with the Old Left is the predominant element in the choice of criteria for action by the New Left, since the target they set for themselves is to "unmask" the traditional Left as being "non-Left," as aiming at no more than an infiltration of the capitalist system in order to reform it; this they regard as a non-alternative, in fact as strictly organic and functional to the authoritarian and repressive system.[35]

Italy was not the only place where emergent movements opposed Soviet Communism. In 1953, 1956, 1968, and 1970, uprisings that erupted in Eastern Europe against Soviet regimes displayed remarkable similarities to their counterparts in the West. In some cases, they self-consciously identified themselves as New Left,[36] and in almost all cases, activists in the West spontaneously welcomed them as part of a larger international movement.

Despite their international unity, it would be a mistake to equate all movements of 1968. Freedom from foreign domination and freedom from one's own government's attempts to dominate other nations may become the same struggle in the practicality of world events, but they are different freedoms, carrying within them different meanings. More importantly, movements in economically advanced societies must deal with qualitatively different objective conditions and with different immediate goals than those on the periphery of the world system. Despite obvious differences, participants did not act in isolation from one another. When Yippies brought panic to the New York stock exchange by throwing money on the floor, when Dutch Provos wreaked havoc on rush hour traffic in Amsterdam by releasing chickens into the streets, and when Strasbourg Situationists issued their manifesto denouncing boredom, they were using methods obviously different than those of liberation fighters in Vietnam. Despite their tactical differences, all these groups enunciated similar goals—a decentralized world with genuine human self-determination—and they increasingly acted in unison.

Uneven development in the world system conditioned the diverse composition of the New Left as a world-historical movement. Vietnam was fighting for national liberation two centuries after the American colonies broke away from England. The Vietnamese modeled their struggle, at least in part, on that of the United States, even adopting word-for-word part of the U.S. Declaration of Independence. Similarly, their organization was modeled on the Bolshevik Party. The global movement of 1968 was composed of many components: newly emergent social actors, as well as ones continuing unfinished struggles of previous epochs. The complete success of all these struggles would be a global revolution—the first truly world-historical revolution. Such a revolution would necessarily involve the radical transformation of the world system from within its core countries.[37] Successful twentieth-century revolutions, however, have been confined to the periphery of the world system, a situation that resulted in the disappearance of the idea of a world-historical revolution, at least until 1968. My analysis of social movements focuses on the core of the world system to illuminate the possibility of such a world-historical revolution.

Taken as a whole, the New Left was a global movement that sought to decentralize and redistribute world resources and power at a time when their centralization had never been greater. Of course, the movement developed within nation-states, not by people's own choosing but because of national organization of political power. Around 1968, however, the growing feeling among activists in Vietnam, Cuba, Latin America, Africa, and even in the United States and Europe was that they were all engaged in the same struggle. As Marcuse pointed out in that year: "The theoretical framework of revolution and subversive action has become a world framework. . . . Just as Vietnam is an integral part of the corporative capitalist system, so the national movements of liberation are an integral part of the potential socialist revolution. And the liberation movements in the Third World depend for their subversive power on the weakening of the capitalist metropolis."[38]

In the 1970s, international solidarity and coordination between radical movements in the core and periphery became even more intense than in 1968. Thousands of young Americans went to Cuba as part of Venceremos Brigades, helping cut sugarcane during the harvests, building schools and houses, and planting trees. In February 1972, the Indochinese liberation movements hosted a world conference in Paris, and representatives of solidarity groups from eighty-four countries attended. A carefully prepared global action calendar was formulated, and on March 31, the same day that worldwide demonstrations were to begin, a major offensive was launched in Vietnam that included the surprising appearance of tanks among the guerrillas. International coordination of the world movement had never been as conscious or well synchronized.

Since 1972, five other internationally synchronized mobilizations have taken place—all of them emanating from the grassroots:

1. Disarmament movements of the late 1970s and early 1980s, which helped to end the Cold War

2. Asian uprisings from 1986 to 1992, which overthrew eight entrenched dictatorships in six years
3. Turmoil in Eastern Europe that ended seven established Soviet governments
4. Alterglobalization mobilizations from Seattle 1999 to February 15, 2003
5. The Arab Spring, Spanish Indignados, Greek anarchists, and Occupy Wall Street in 2011

The New Left's world-historical character is revealed by insurgencies' recurrent patterns of independence from political parties, autonomous self-organization, direct democracy, and global solidarity. The global movement is increasingly self-conscious of its international synchronicity. In 1972, the Vietnamese revolution provided a centralized organizing group for the world antiwar offensive. Subsequent waves of protests emerged spontaneously from the grassroots without any central organization.

Rather than interpreting the New Left nationalistically, organizationally, or ideologically, I locate it in the praxis of millions of people. A universal definition of the New Left cannot merely be based on organizational ideology, that is, that it developed outside or in opposition to the "Old Left," nor can we clarify what it was in terms of specific organizations or theorists. The Student Nonviolent Coordinating Committee (SNCC), the Black Panther Party (BPP), the March 22 Movement in France, the Sozialistischer Deutscher Studentenbund (SDS) in Germany, and the Students for a Democratic Society (SDS) in the United States were all New Left organizations. Martin Luther King, Malcolm X, and Herbert Marcuse were New Left theorists, but the movement extended beyond these organizations and theorists. They were all part of but not equivalent to the movement.

The primary defining characteristics of the global New Left include:

(1) *Opposition to racial, political, and patriarchal domination, as well as to economic exploitation.*
The movement sought to overthrow the economic exploitation that the Old Left had opposed, but activists' antiauthoritarianism also opposed cultural and bureaucratic domination. Movements for national liberation and civil rights, the primary basis of global turmoil in 1968, insured that racism (including within radical movements) would be a central concern. Women's liberation challenged patriarchal domination, and gay movements questioned established gender identities.

There may be an analogy between the development of Christianity and that of secular liberation. From this perspective, the New Left began a reinterpretation of the scope of freedom in much the same way that the Protestant Reformation redefined the individual's relationship to God by making the church an unnecessary vehicle for salvation and affirming the sanctity of individual subjectivity. The universe of freedom spontaneously envisioned and practiced in 1968 included individual liberty within a framework of social justice and equality.

New Left activists were concerned not only with economic and political issues, but also with domination in everyday life. Called into question were bureaucracy, economic exploitation, oppression of women, repression of children, homophobia, and racism—all aspects of capitalist patriarchy. Attempts to transform everyday life and to politicize taken-for-granted models of interaction, particularly in the practice of women's liberation, rest on a belief that economic and political structures are reproduced through the daily acceptance of predetermined patterns of life, a belief that stands in sharp contrast to the Old Left's economic determinism. Inner reworking of the psyche and human needs—the cultural revolution—lays the groundwork for a new type of revolution, one that does not culminate in the political sphere but that would move the realm of politics from the state to everyday life and transform politics from elite administration to self-management. Through its universal realization, politics would cease to exist as we know it today.

Nationalization of the economy and decision making do not define a free society as envisioned by the New Left. Forms of freedom in 1968 included decentralization of decision making, international sharing of resources, socialization of ecologically sustainable industry, worker and community self-management, and extension of democracy to all aspects of life. In slogan form, the New Left's "All Power to the People"—not the "Dictatorship of the Proletariat"—stood as a political guide to freedom.

All this should not be interpreted to mean that the New Left never reproduced racist, patriarchal, bureaucratic, or exploitative characteristics of the system from which it originated. As offspring of the society they opposed, the movement was stamped with birthmarks of the old order. Despite many shortcomings, when taken as a whole, the movement was profoundly universalistic in its consciousness of oppression, and its theory and practice attempted to transform all its forms.

(2) *A concept of freedom as not only freedom from material deprivation but also freedom to create new human beings.*
Compared with previous social movements, the New Left did not arise primarily in response to conditions of economic hardship but to political and cultural/psychological oppression. The need to change daily life was evident in Che Guevara's "new socialist person," and it applies equally well to Martin Luther King's "new Negro," the subsequent self-definition of Americans of African descent, the emergence of "Latino" and "Chicano" as ethnic markers rather than Hispanic or Spanish, and the new self-definitions of women, gay people,

transgender people, and students. Asian Americans insisted they no longer wished to be called "Orientals."

The movement opposed "cultural imperialism" and "consumerism" at the same time as it sought to build people's culture: black culture, women's culture, Chicano culture, gay culture, and youth culture (as emergent countercultures became known). Insurgent cultures were based on new norms and values developed from a critique of generally accepted patterns of interaction. In retrospect, cultural precursors of the movement stand out—aesthetic and philosophical qualities that found popular embodiment in the 1960s. Existentialism and Godard films in France, the Kafka revival in Czechoslovakia, jazz, blues, rock, pop art, and the theory of the Frankfurt School all contributed to the creation of a social soul which became manifest in political form with the New Left.[39] The massive fusion of culture and politics defined the New Left's uniqueness. As a social movement the New Left represented the political emergence of many of the same human values and aspirations that gave rise to modern art and philosophy. Spontaneity, individual autonomy amid community, and the subversion of bureaucratic as well as economic domination were all values and ideals shared by artists and the movement.

By 1968, the art world's happenings, process art, action painting, kinetic art, pop art, op art, new realism, minimal art, environmental art, and Tachism had long challenged limits of what was considered possible. If sixties movements experimented with new forms of street protests and created communal spaces at be-ins and love fests, these innovative happenings were anticipated by artists already in the 1950s. Contemporary art's lack of coherence and frequent formless tendencies anticipated the New Left's rejection of organizational structure in favor of spontaneity and self-organization. While destroying boundaries between music and performance, Nam June Paik's humanization of technology paved the way for movement attempts to reconstitute social order beyond established borders. Conceptualism similarly questioned the boundaries of art. By prioritizing language over visual relevancy, it helped to create new vehicles for protest.[40]

Anticipating the subsequent merger of disparate political movements into a coherent whole, aesthetic streams of imaginative appropriation of technologies congealed under the name of Fluxus, which even before its 1962 Festum Fluxorum galvanized openness and cross-pollination of traditionally separate domains. Visual artist Joseph Beuys was attracted to Fluxus because he wanted "to create a theory that would go beyond the idea of actions and happenings." Musician Wolf Vostell was lured by "its way of looking at things that went from action music, to life music, thought music, de-collage music, and behavior music, and finally right down to invisible music."[41] Action poet Robert Filliou refused "to be colonized culturally by a self-styled race of specialists in painting, sculpture, poetry, music, etc. . . . This is what *La Révolte des*

Médiocres is all about. With wonderful results in modern art, so far. Tomorrow could everybody revolt?" Long anathema to artists' creativity, nationalism was explicitly negated by international identities such as COBRA (an acronym for Copenhagen, Brussels, and Amsterdam). COBRA attempted to include Czechoslovakia but was prevented from doing so by Cold War politics.[42]

In contrast to rigid aesthetic formalism, postwar artists emphasized play, fun, imagination, and politics, creating new forms of expression that ran parallel to New Left innovations. Spontaneity, festivities, and play were deemed more important to human nature than work, thought, and vacation (a consumerist, individualized version of the festival). "European culture . . . is sick . . . [and] going to die," screamed the Situationists in 1961. They felt it would not be sufficient to have "a social and political revolution if this reorganization does not go hand-in-hand with a similar qualitative reshaping of culture."[43]

Autodestructive art completed the visual task of negating the dominant industrial system at the same time as it undermined the commodity form, which reified art as consumer objects. Dematerialization of the art object followed as another way to negate capitalist intrusions. In conjunction with the Spur Group, the Situationist International clashed with consumerism. They demanded utopia as a dialectical combination of art and life, with "professional amateurs" helping to make everyone an artist of their own life. They believed that "coffee cups can be more beautiful than fancy sculptures. A kiss in the morning can be more dramatic than a drama by Mr. Fancypants. The sloshing of my foot in my wet boot sounds more beautiful than fancy organ music."[44]

At the same time as the United States was the bête noire of world events—overthrowing governments, assassinating political leaders, and conducting genocidal wars—American culture had an undeniable magnetism and attraction. The contradiction between embracing the culture that gave the world nuclear bombs and protesting it did not prevent young British artists from created graphic designs and effective poster art for the antinuclear weapons movement, especially the Committee for Nuclear Disarmament, while emulating U.S.-based artists' use of industrial materials, American pop culture, and abstract expressionism.[45] Collage artist Richard Hamilton attended an Easter protest march carrying a life-sized image of Marilyn Monroe.[46] When sculptor Anthony Caro was asked how his trip to America had affected his art, he replied, "I realized I had nothing to lose by throwing out History—here we are also steeped in it anyway. There's a fine-art quality about European art even when it's made from junk. America made me see that there are no barriers and no regulations—they simply aren't bound to traditional or conventional solutions in their art or anything else."[47] Through such actions, artists embodied the creation of a new planetary culture and liberated human beings.

As anticipated by Herbert Marcuse's *Eros and Civilization*, the body's liberation became a recurrent theme in visual arts and ultimately in radical politics as well. Marcuse called on us to "make the human body an instrument of pleasure rather than labor."[48] The body as art object was central to Yoko Ono's 1964 performance titled *Cut Piece*, in which she invited members of the audience to snip off her clothes. Ono's piece has been hailed as a forerunner to feminism, as was Shigeko Kubota's *Vagina Painting* a year later.[49] Attempts to bring the erotic to consciousness and to thematize the unconscious include Paik's performance pieces, especially his then-notorious 1967 *Opera Sextronique* (during which Charlotte Moorman was arrested as she played the cello in New York).

Marcuse's rethinking of humans' place in the cosmos found similar resonance. Beuys's performance of *How to Explain Pictures to a Dead Hare* came three years before the Yippies ran a pig for president in 1968. The Living Theatre included members of the audience in their performances, thereby helping to break down the distance between audience and actor, a transformation highly valued by both aesthetic and political movements. An early example of how to shatter viewers' distance from art (as insisted upon in the white cubes we call museums) can be found in Beuys's picking up an ax at Paik's *Exposition of Music—Electronic Television* and destroying one of Paik's pianos in 1963. The Situationist critique of the "Society of the Spectacle" followed in 1967.

As artists became politically active, the first demonstration at the Museum of Modern Art in New York took place on January 3, 1969, when sculptor Takis removed his own work. Later he broadcast the message: "Our group has become much bigger and taken the name of the Art Workers Coalition. Art workers! The time came to demystify the elite of the art rulers, directors of museums, and trustees."[50] With Takis's action, artists moved from constituting avant-gardes in the "autonomous" domain of culture to themselves joining protests. Little more than a year later, the New York Art Strike in 1970 seemed to affect the whole art world.

The counterculture that avant-garde artists helped to nurture and develop would, in turn, profoundly influence culture (and the art world) in the 1970s. Rock music and the rise of gay and feminist political cultures are sometimes seen as opposed to each other, but they all arose in the same period of time.[51]

(3) *Extension of democracy and expansion of individual rights, not their constraint.*
Strict principles of democracy were the norm, and bottom-up participatory democracy defined the process of interaction from the largest general assemblies to the smallest action committees. Although the media often focused

on specific individuals, the movement generally avoided selecting leaders, and anyone with major responsibilities was often subject to immediate recall. Important positions of responsibility were rotated. Even among some armed movements in the Third World, extension of the democratic process occurred. In Vietnam, guerrilla units would, when possible, meet before their attacks to discuss tactics and options. In some cases, full-scale models of targets were constructed, and simulated attacks rehearsed with members rotated from one specific task to another until each could function best. Commanding officers for the actual attack were then democratically elected. Once the real attack was launched, of course, orders had to be followed without hesitation.[52] Among Tupamaro fighters in Uruguay, strict democratic decision making was also practiced.

Democratic process was manifest in self-management as represented in consensual decision making at general assemblies involving hundreds of people; in autonomy of black and women's liberation; in aspirations for self-determination for oppressed nations; in calls for community control of police and neighborhood development; and in self-management of factories, schools, and cities during New Left strikes. In contrast to monolithic Old Left organizations, many tendencies coexisted within New Left organizations, from Maoism to feminism, anarchism, democratic socialism, and common sense.

(4) *Enlarged base of revolution.*
At the same time as the movement sought to enlarge the scope of freedom, its praxis involved an enlarged constituency. Its historical experiences transcended a static model of class struggle developed from previous revolutions. The legacy of the New Left is enrichment of that tradition, a practical wealth often obscured by the Old Left's labor metaphysic and "base-superstructure" orthodoxy. In 1968, oppositional forces emerged whose existence could not be contained within the existing typology of class struggle modeled upon previous occurrences. In 1968, it was not predominantly the working class and their parties which rose to challenge the existing social order, but groups normally considered marginal: students, young people, national minorities, women, and the lumpenproletariat. By occupational categories, large numbers of factory workers helped lead workers' insurgencies as part of the overall movement (particularly in France, Poland, Czechoslovakia, and Italy), but the main oppositional constituencies originated in the urban underclass and the new working class. Particularly in France, the participation of the new working class in the radical movement was an important defining contour of the New Left, perhaps as important as the hostilities of the Old Left Communist Party. As the quantitative growth of the new working class has proceeded through intensification of world industrialization, so the practice

of the New Left has demonstrated the "proletarian" aspect of these middle strata.

Part of the reason for the inability of the Left (including the "new Old Left"—the myriad assortment of "Marxist-Leninist" and anarchist groups that emerged in the 1970s) to comprehend the meaning of 1968 lies in the differing roles played by the middle strata, students, and the lumpenproletariat in other times and places. In 1848, the lumpenproletariat of Paris was wined and dined by Louis Napoleon Bonaparte so that it would fight for him against the proletariat. Indeed it was Napoleon III's ability to use these gangsters, thugs, and hoodlums to maintain order that eventually won him the mandate needed to rule France. More recently, in places like Guinea-Bissau, Algeria, Angola, and Greece, the lumpenproletariat has played reactionary roles as well.[53] In the 1960s, in the United States, when the civil rights movement entered its second phase by moving north, the black lumpenproletariat became the catalyst and leadership of the radical movement. Inspired by the example of Malcolm X, former criminals and drug addicts changed their lives and rebelled *en masse* against the conditions of their existence. During the 1980 Gwangju Uprising, lumpen were among the most dedicated freedom fighters.

The middle strata formed the social basis for the Nazi regime and played a distinctly reactionary role in Allende's Chile, but in the core of the world system in the 1960s, middle-class people—particularly women and young adults—were progressive forces. To be sure, there are economic reasons for the changing political role of the middle strata and for the enlarged base of revolution. In our rapidly changing world, farmers increasingly are made landless, proletarianized, and urbanized. Millions of office workers not directly involved in material production are increasingly seen (and see themselves) as part of the working class. Colonization of everyday life means the realm of the cash nexus has been enlarged to include production and consumption, work *and* leisure. Women's liberation arose concomitantly with massive entry of females onto the labor market. Universities have taken on an enlarged and more central role.

When Clark Kerr compared the economic importance of the nation's universities in the last half of the twentieth century to that of automobiles in the early 1900s and railroads in the late 1800s, he made, if anything, an understatement. In the 1960s, there were more students than farmers in the United States, more students than miners, and more people enrolled in formal studies than working in construction, transportation, or public utilities.[54] The new structural position of the universities within the modern world system gave rise to a student movement unlike ones of the past, a movement tied neither to "adult" nor "parent" organizations nor to the nation-state. Similarly, urbanization of African Americans and their central position in the inner cities, the military, and industry were conditions for the emergence of the black liberation movement.

(5) *An emphasis on direct action.*
Whether observed in the formation of the March 22 Movement at Nanterre or as early as the July 26 Movement in Cuba, the New Left was characterized by the belief that action in itself was a solution. Through direct action, activists believed that the movement would become quantitatively larger and qualitatively stronger. The actionism of the New Left was not merely a reversion to pure and simple spontaneity but a new method for the integration of theory and practice, a form of "conscious spontaneity." Sit-ins and building occupations, even teach-ins can be seen as a form of the "actionization" of theory. The New Left's reliance on direct experience and the empirical evaluation of immediate events represented a negation of the Old Left's overemphasis on centralized organization and the primacy of the role of the "conscious element."

Although resulting in increased repression and premature armed struggle tendencies within the movement, the New Left's actionism did not culminate in attempted coups d'état from above. The New Left continually maintained that society could be genuinely revolutionized only from the bottom up by the vast majority of people. Guerrillas in Guinea-Bissau actually delayed the seizure of state power in order to continue building popular power from below.[55] In the industrialized societies, New Left forms of action from sit-ins to university takeovers and freeway blockades were spontaneously developed in accordance with the military and political possibilities of 1968–1970.

In the epoch after 1968, popular movements have reproduced the New Left tactic of massive occupations of public space as a means of social transformation. This tactic's international diffusion can be seen in Oaxaca's Commune, Cairo's Tahrir Square, Istanbul's Taksim Square, Athens's Syntagma, and among Spanish Indignados. As cultural and economic integration of the world accelerates, the significance of the eros effect and the importance of synchronized insurgencies will only grow in importance. In 1848 and 1905, limited communication and economic ties existed, and movements were relatively undeveloped in their spatial and historical integration. Movements in 1968 exhibited remarkable international consciousness and interconnectedness, and their meteoric appearance and disintegration is a reflection of the rapid pace of change in the modern world. As a world-historical movement, the insurgency of 1968 forms the contours of subsequent insurgencies, which similarly will develop in unexpected, globally synchronized explosions.

Notes

1.   Eric Hobsbawm, "1968—A Retrospect," *Marxism Today*, May 1978, 130.
2.   Richard Nixon, "26—Annual Message to the Congress on the State of the Union," *The American President Project*, January 22, 1971, http://www.presidency.ucsb.edu/ws/?pid=3110.
3.   Karl Marx, *The 18th Brumaire of Louis Napoleon* (New York: International Publishers, 1972), 15.
4.   Aristide R. Zolberg, "Moments of Madness," *Politics and Society* 2 (Winter 1972): 184.
5.   For Marcuse's inspired understanding of instinct and revolution, see *Essay on Liberation* (Boston: Beacon Press, 1969).
6.   A new anthology develops our understanding of erotic dimensions of social movements: Jason Del Gandio and A.K. Thompson, eds., *Spontaneous Combustion: The Eros Effect and Global Revolution* (Albany: SUNY Press, 2017).
7.   What the student movement expressed in the slogan *"L'imagination au pouvoir"* came to France from Vietnam. See Jean-Paul Sartre, *Between Existentialism and Marxism* (New York: Morrow Quill Paperbacks, 1979), 125.
8.   See Karl Marx, *The German Ideology* (New York: International Publishers, 1973), 56.
9.   Antonio Gramsci, *The Modern Prince* (New York: International Publishers, 1972), 165–66.
10.   Herbert Marcuse, *Reason and Revolution* (Boston: Beacon Press, 1960), 141.
11.   G.W.F. Hegel, *Philosophy of History* (New York: Colonial Press, 1899), 56.
12.   Hegel, *Philosophy of History*, 108, 343.
13.   See Gerald Horne's informative book *The Counter-Revolution of 1776: Slave Resistance and the Origins of the United States of America* (New York: New York University Press, 2016). His argument that the revolution of 1776 was an attempt to forestall British abolition of slavery in the colonies does not take into account Thomas Jefferson's rough draft of the Declaration of Independence, which blamed the king of England for slavery. Among the "injuries and usurpations" that the king was charged with perpetrating on the colonies, Jefferson included a "cruel war against human nature itself, violating its most sacred rights of life & liberty in the persons of a distant people who never offended him, captivating & carrying them into slavery in another hemisphere, or to incur miserable death in their transportation thither. . . . He is now exciting those very people to rise in arms among us, and to purchase that liberty of which he has deprived them, by murdering the people on whom he also obtruded them: thus paying off former crimes committed against the *liberties* of one people, with crimes which he urges them to commit against the *lives* of another."
14.   Rosa Luxemburg, *The Mass Strike* (New York: Harper and Row, 1971), 44–45. Georges Sorel described the general strike as "the myth in which Socialism is wholly comprised. . . . We thus obtain that intuition of Socialism which language cannot give us with perfect clearness—and we obtain it as a whole, perceived instantaneously." Georges Sorel, *Reflections on Violence* (New York: Collier Books, 1950), 127–28.
15.   Alfred Willener, *The Action-Image of Society: On Cultural Politicization* (New York: Pantheon Books, 1970), 93.
16.   *The Commune of 1871* (New York: New York Labor News, 1978), 7.

17. Choi Jungwoon, *The Gwangju Uprising: The Pivotal Democratic Movement That Changed the History of Modern Korea* (Paramus: Homa and Sekey Books, 2006), 85, 131.

18. Priscilla Robertson, *Revolutions of 1848: A Social History* (Princeton: Princeton University Press, 1952), 221, 269, 274, 289, 291, 300, 304, 391; Karl Marx, *The Revolutions of 1848–9* (New York: International Publishers, 1972), 108–9, 262; Sidney Harcave, *The Russian Revolution of 1905* (New York: Macmillan, 1964), 203.

19. Periods of revolutionary crisis bear little resemblance to crises produced by economic breakdowns. The latter have their roots in the irrational organization of the economy and the state (*Naturwuchs*), while general strikes and revolutions are essentially attempts to provide rational alternatives. A dialectical view of crisis includes both of these types, particularly since they commonly have a close relationship to each other. Traditional usage of the concept of crisis, however, generally denotes only economic dislocations like the Great Depression or the many financial meltdowns that characterize global capitalism. Economic crises are one type of social crisis and differ from crises produced by the eros effect. See the chapter in the 1987 edition titled "The Rationality of the New Left."

20. Thomas Jefferson, Letter, to John Adams, September 4, 1823.

21. Daniel Valcarcel, *La Rebelión de Túpac Amaru* (Mexico: Fondo de Cultura Económica, 1965).

22. Valcarcel, *La Rebelión de Túpac Amaru*, 117–18.

23. André Gunder Frank, *Crisis: In the Third World* (New York: Holmes and Meier, 1981).

24. Alexis de Tocqueville, *Souvenirs d'Alexis de Tocqueville* (Paris: Gallimard, 1942), 30.

25. Robertson, *Revolutions of 1848*, 81.

26. The momentum of that period originated in Greece, followed by Italy. On September 3, 1843, a popular uprising in Athens confronted the European kingdom imposed upon them little more than a decade after the overthrow of nearly four hundred years of Turkish domination. Greek soldiers marched on the palace with virtually the entire population of the city to demand constitutional rights. Eventually the popular movement's continuing insistence compelled King Otho to grant a constitution in March 1844.

27. Emerson Tennent as quoted in Kumari Jayawardena, *Perpetual Ferment* (Colombo: Social Scientists' Association, 2010), 144.

28. Immanuel Wallerstein, *Utopistics; or, Historical Choices of the 21st Century* (New York: The New Press, 1998), 17.

29. L.S. Stavrianos, *Global Rift: The Third World Comes of Age* (New York: William Morrow and Company, 1981), 389.

30. See Rosa Luxemburg, *Theory and Practice* (Detroit: News and Letters, 1980), 45; Richard Boyer and Herbert Morais, *Labor's Untold Story* (New York: United Electrical Press, 1974), 142–64.

31. Azar Tabari and Nabid Yaganeh, *In the Shadow of Islam* (London: Zed Press, 1962), 30.

32. Harcave, *The Russian Revolution of 1905*, 133.

33. Max Gordon, "The Communist Party and the New Left," *Socialist Revolution* 6 (January 1976): 19.

34. Klaus Mehnert, *Moscow and the New Left* (Berkeley: University of California Press, 1975), 41–42.

35. Valdo Spini, "The New Left in Italy," *Journal of Contemporary History* 7, no. 2 (January–April 1972): 51–71.
36. Mihailo Marković, "The New Left and the Cultural Revolution," in Mihailo Marković, *The Contemporary Marx: Essays in Humanist Communism* (Nottingham: Spokesman Books, 1974), 175.
37. Herbert Marcuse, *Counterrevolution and Revolt* (Boston: Beacon Press, 1972).
38. Herbert Marcuse, "Reexamination of the Concept of Revolution," *Diogenes*, no. 64 (Winter 1968): 17–27.
39. For a book-length study of this insight, see Willener, *The Action-Image of Society*.
40. *Global Conceptualism: Points of Origin 1950s—1980s* (New York: Queens Museum of Art, 1999).
41. Klaus Schrenk, ed., *Upheavals: Manifestoes, Manifestations* (Cologne: Dumont Verlag, 1984), 29.
42. Institute of Contemporary Art, Boston, *On the Passage of a Few People through a Rather Brief Moment in Time: The Situation Is International 1957—1972* (Cambridge, MA: MIT Press, 1989), 63.
43. Quoted in Schrenk, *Upheavals: Manifestoes, Manifestations*, 142.
44. See Janet Jenkins, ed., *In the Spirit of Fluxus* (Minneapolis: Walker Art Center, 1993).
45. David Mellor, *The Sixties Art Scene in London* (London: Phaidon, 1993), 14–17.
46. Mellor, *The Sixties Art Scene in London*, 34.
47. *The Gazette* 1 (1961): 1.
48. Herbert Marcuse, "Political Preface" to *Eros and Civilization*, 19.
49. See John Hanhardt, ed., *The Worlds of Nam June Paik* (New York: Guggenheim Museum, 2003), 23.
50. Jeanne Siegel, ed., *Artworlds: Discourse on the 60s and 70s* (New York: Da Capo Press, 1992), 121.
51. See Robert Hewison, *Too Much: Art and Society in the Sixties 1960–75* (New York: Oxford University Press, 1987).
52. Wilfred Burchett, *Vietnam Will Win!* (New York: International Publishers, 1968).
53. Frantz Fanon, *The Wretched of the Earth* (New York: Grove Press, 1968), 136.
54. United States Office of Education, *Projections of Educational Statistics to 1977–1978* (Washington, DC: Government Printing Office, 1968).
55. James Boggs and Grace Lee Boggs, *Revolution and Evolution in the Twentieth Century* (New York: Monthly Review Press, 1976).

CHAPTER 2

A GLOBAL ANALYSIS OF 1968

The past is never dead. It's not even past.
—*William Faulkner*

WORLD-HISTORICAL SOCIAL MOVEMENTS ERUPTED IN NEARLY every country in 1968, but the focus of world attention was on Vietnam. If anyone embodied the Zeitgeist of 1968, it was the Vietnamese people, whose resistance to foreign domination catalyzed the entire global movement. Having defeated France at Dien Bien Phu in 1954, they faced a new threat to their independence: the world's most powerful empire. The prolonged intensity of their struggle against genocidal U.S. violence shattered the illusion of the democratic content of *pax Americana*, giving rise to movements in the industrialized societies aimed at transforming the system that killed millions of human beings in unnecessary wars. At the same time, Vietnamese battlefield victories inspired anti-imperialist movements throughout the Third World.

Before the first month of 1968 had come to an end, the Tet offensive made it clear that the National Liberation Front (NLF) held the upper hand. Half a million U.S. soldiers and billions of dollars' worth of the world's most technologically advanced weapons were unable to defeat a tiny peasant nation's aspirations for independence. Like so many people, Jean-Paul Sartre was amazed: "Who would have thought that 14 million peasants would be able to resist the greatest military and economic power on earth? And yet, this is what happened." Tracing the origin of the most famous slogan of the May 1968 French uprising, "Imagination in Power!" Sartre said it "came to us from Vietnam."[1] Because of the worldwide importance of the Tet offensive, it is there that any analysis of 1968 must begin.

The Tet Offensive

In the early morning hours of January 31, 1968, the third day of Tet (Vietnamese New Year), guerrillas launched synchronized attacks throughout southern

Vietnam. Five of six major cities, thirty-nine of forty-four provincial capitals, seventy-one district capitals, and nearly every U.S. base in Vietnam simultaneously became scenes of vicious fighting.[2] Over five hundred Americans, and many more Vietnamese, lost their lives *each day* of the uprising. In two months of fighting from January 29 to March 31, 1968, at least 3,895 U.S. soldiers and tens of thousands of guerrillas were killed.[3]

As the offensive began, a squad of guerrillas penetrated the grounds of the newly constructed U.S. embassy in Saigon. At the same time, eleven NLF battalions suddenly surfaced in Saigon. They captured the government radio station and surrounded the presidential palace. The fight for the capital city lasted fully a week. The battle of Hue, the old imperial capital in central Vietnam and epicenter of Buddhist and student revolts in 1963 and 1966, was even more intense. A unified revolutionary power was established, and revolutionary Hue held out for over three weeks. Only after bloody house-to-house fighting and massive bombing (which destroyed eighteen thousand of the city's twenty thousand houses) was the NLF flag no longer flying.[4] As a result of the offensive, six hundred rural villages enacted self-government (about one-quarter of the entire country).

After Hue was retaken, Western media abounded with stories of the "bloodbath" supposedly perpetrated by the NLF against its people. A year and a half later, secretly posing as an ordinary professor, CIA-paid Douglas Pike was

Attacking the enemy in Khe Sanh. Photographer unknown.

quoted in the *Los Angeles Times* of December 6, 1969, as having conducted an "intensive investigation" of events in Hue in which he concluded "Communists had slaughtered almost 6,000 civilians for political purposes." This figure was double all previous ones quoted in the mass media. I mention this because the "Hue massacre" was such a prominently used attack on the NLF, when, in fact, the vast majority of the civilian deaths were caused by U.S. aerial bombardments.[5] The mass graves found later had been dug by the NLF and were necessary because of the casualties caused by U.S. bombs.

The lies surrounding events in Hue were part of a campaign of deliberately perpetrated misinformation designed to intensify the war against Vietnam at a time when antiwar sentiment was growing by leaps and bounds. From fabrication of the 1964 Gulf of Tonkin incident to continual promises of quick victory, President Lyndon Johnson systematically misled public opinion in order to expand his military adventure. In a move designed to coincide with the beginning of the election-year primaries in the United States, the offensive's timing was so precise that the attack on the U.S. embassy came early enough in the day for U.S. network news to carry same day coverage. The fortress-like embassy had huge symbolic meaning. It was a place that the American public could understand, unlike Khe Sanh or Hue. With the embassy grounds in the hands of guerrillas, the public could summon a mind's eye picture of the place and understand that the war was being lost. Vietnamese were well aware that theirs was the world's first televised war (a hundred million television sets were in use in the United States in 1968, compared with ten million during the Korean War and only ten thousand at the time of Pearl Harbor). Their massive offensive purposely did not attack power stations, telephones, or telegraphs so the press would be able to wire out reports more or less normally.

Although elaborate planning for the offensive had taken years, the U.S. had no clue that it was coming—at least not in the form it took. When intelligence reported that something big was going to happen, they concluded it would be at Khe Sanh, a remote outpost where thousands of U.S. troops were cut off and surrounded. Worried that another Dien Bien Phu was in the offing, a defeat so large it could not be hidden, the Pentagon dropped the equivalent tonnage of five Hiroshima bombs (103,000 tons) in and around Khe Sanh. The use of tactical nuclear weapons came under consideration as well.[6] We know today that the Khe Sanh battle was waged by the Vietnamese as a huge diversionary attack to provide cover for the offensive in the cities.

For Vietnamese, the Lunar New Year is the most important holiday, so nearly all Vietnamese troops fighting for the U.S. were given leave to go home. The guerrillas were thereby able to fight American troops directly. Tet also marked the anniversary of Quang Trung's 1789 surprise attack on Hanoi to defeat Chinese invaders, an epic event in Vietnamese history. Five days before the 1968 Tet holiday began, the General Association of Students in Saigon University celebrated Quang Trung's 1789 victory by recreating it on stage. At an assembly attended by thousands of people, many of the songs and speeches carried anti-American overtones.

When the offensive seemed over, General William Westmoreland, the commander of U.S. forces in Vietnam, claimed a "major victory," asserting that the enemy had failed to achieve its goals. Westmoreland's pronouncement was as wrong as his now infamous "light at the end of the tunnel" speech. The U.S. had clearly suffered a major defeat on the ground in Vietnam, so much so that its war plans were turned around, and it began to take measures to withdraw.[7] On March 9, as guerrilla attacks continued, Westmoreland publicly asked the president for 206,000 additional soldiers to protect the more than half a million already in Vietnam, a request that was turned down. As Noam Chomsky's reading of Pentagon documents revealed, one of the factors that concerned the Joint Chiefs of Staff was that if they sent more troops into Vietnam, they might not have enough for domestic control. They knew that sending more troops to Vietnam or invading northern Vietnam would cause even greater disruption at home.[8]

All at once, the bottom had fallen out of the U.S. attempt to control Vietnam. For nearly a year before the Tet offensive, Ambassador Ellsworth Bunker and General Westmoreland had insisted that the NLF was exhausted, played out, and all but finished off, but the intensity of the Tet attacks had quickly made it clear that the official reports were far from true. As Frank McGee put it on the NBC Sunday news of March 10: "It is a new war in Vietnam. The enemy now has the initiative; he has dramatically enlarged the area of combat; he has newer, more sophisticated weapons; he has improved communications; he has changed his tactics. . . . In short, the war as the Administration has defined it is being lost."[9]

Two days later, on March 12, Eugene McCarthy, standing on an antiwar platform and aided by thousands of student volunteers who went "clean for Gene," polled 42 percent of the votes in the New Hampshire primary, only 7 percent behind Lyndon Johnson. In the same month, a Gallup Poll showed that for the first time, more Americans were against the war (40 percent) than were for it (26 percent). Finally, on March 31, Lyndon Johnson delivered his most famous speech, the one in which he announced a limitation on the bombing of northern Vietnam, eventual withdrawal of troops, and a promise not to run for reelection.

President Johnson's withdrawal from the elections was immediately hailed as a major political victory by the Vietnamese as well as by antiwar activists in the United States. The dramatic turnaround in U.S. public opinion concerning

Photographer unknown.

Vietnam after Tet was due both to the battlefield success of the Vietnamese and the firm articulation of antiwar sentiments at home. In the midst of the Tet offensive, the National Council of Churches opposed the assertion that peace could be won by military might, and Pax (an association of Catholics and non-Catholics founded in 1962) took a similar stand by adopting two resolutions addressed to the Catholic hierarchy.[10]

    Calls for "Peace Now" quickly caught on with the American public, but those who directed the war machine had little intention of leaving gracefully. Instead, they clung to the twisted logic exemplified in the words of an American officer who told an Associated Press reporter as they surveyed the ruins of the town of Ben Tre, "We had to destroy it in order to save it." The whole of Indochina came under intensified attacks. On March 16, 1968, hundreds of defenseless women and children at My Lai were brutally murdered by U.S. troops under the command of William Calley. A twenty-month cover-up temporarily concealed this massacre from the American public, but an even bigger massacre—an automated air war—was already well underway. By the end of 1968, the United States had dropped more tonnage of bombs on Vietnam than it had used in all of World War II. Hundreds of thousands of innocent people were killed and wounded, and millions more were made refugees. The killing became increasingly indiscriminate and genocidal. During the Tet offensive, the Vietnamese may have freed large parts of their country, but these liberated zones were then targeted for Agent Orange and cluster bombs, for the CIA's Phoenix Program, which murdered more than twenty-five thousand local leaders. When the war finally ended, the total firepower used by the United States and its allies in Indochina had exceeded the total firepower used in all other wars in history combined.[11] The Pentagon would count 57,661 American dead and at least 300,000 wounded. At least two million Vietnamese were killed, and five million more were wounded or made into refugees.[12]

At the Pentagon protest in 1967, protesters put flowers into gun barrels, an action still in use. Paul S. Conklin.

Despite heavy losses, the Vietnamese resistance moved from the strategic defensive to the strategic offensive after Tet. By the end of the year, 14,500 of the 550,000 U.S. troops in Vietnam were dead, nearly as many as had died in all the previous years combined, and the total number of American aircraft shot down was in the thousands. With each day that the war continued, polarization within the United States became more bitter and antagonistic.

At the same time as the circles of the antiwar movement widened, the African American movement became more militant. Martin Luther King Jr. was one of those who became radicalized by the brutality of the Vietnam War—a radicalization evident in his call for the civil rights and the peace movement to unite and in his denunciation of "white colonialism."[13] Vietnam provided a clear dividing line between those who were "part of the problem" and those who were "part of the solution." The war dramatized the gap between the deeply ingrained notion that the United States is a free country and the all-too-evident reality that the government was committing genocide. This moral contradiction broke apart families and churches, led to the disruption of higher education, and eventually found its way into the highest ranks of the rich and powerful.

In the aftermath of the Tet offensive, tens of thousands of demonstrators regularly appeared in cities throughout the world, and U.S. embassies and information offices came under attack. The high visibility afforded radicals in the industrialized West encouraged their counterparts in the socialist East and vice versa. The rising of Vietnam helped catalyze oppositional forces in the industrialized North, forces that in turn sparked new strata of rebellion in the South, like the student movement in Mexico.

As the eros effect operated on a global level, so it did within each nation. In the United States, opposition to the war against Vietnam quickly became part of an emergent youth culture. The war crystallized a political dimension to the "generation gap," and the movement's cultural politics intensified both opposition to the war and disgust with the politics and lifestyle of what became known as "Amerikkka." The growing African American liberation movement had long opposed the war. In 1966, Julian Bond was denied his elected position in the Georgia legislature for his public opposition to the draft, and in 1967, Muhammad Ali was stripped of his world heavyweight boxing title for the same reason. By 1968, the combination of the Tet offensive and the Black Power movement had radicalized tens of thousands of black youth at the same time as campus protests mounted. The women's liberation movement reemerged in 1968, as women articulated their need for autonomy from male militarism and sought to define their own lives and identities, thereby deepening the movement's scope and widening its public and private impact.

Altogether then, the energies of 1968 galvanized millions of Americans into a movement that posed a revolutionary challenge to the Establishment in 1970. The world-historical convergence of radical oppositional movements was not entirely spontaneous and unconscious. A careful reading of the internal documents of the National Liberation Front of Vietnam reveals a high level of consciousness in relation to the potential worldwide effects of its planned offensive, particularly during an election year in the United States.[14] On the other side, many activists in the United States fully understood that their country was wrong and that they could not, in Camus's words, "love their country and freedom too." Theirs was not a passive understanding of freedom, but an active opposition to their country's government. As the gap widened between the official U.S. version of the war and its reality, hundreds of thousands of Americans even went over to the side of Ho Chi Minh and the NLF. The fact that so many Americans embraced their government's official "enemies" as friends and viewed their own government as their enemy is one of the clearest examples of the internationalism of the New Left and its break with established politics and culture.

The victorious resistance of the Vietnamese gave the international movement a basis for its unity. The militant demonstrators who marched in the streets of Paris, Prague, Chicago, and hundreds of other cities in 1968 were all carrying the same flags: not only the red flag of revolution and black flag of anarchism, but the red, yellow, and blue flag of the NLF. In London (which had been relatively quiet in the 1960s), one observer described the situation this way:

> The reports of the Tet offensive had a powerful effect on British campuses where meetings called by local groups of the Vietnam Solidarity Campaign with national speakers could assemble 1,000 students within hours. The intense debate inevitably spilt onto the streets where, aside from dozens of local demonstrations, there were two significant mass demonstrations. On March 17, some 30,000 confronted police horses and drawn batons in Grosvenor Square in front of the fortress United States embassy. That night, 246 demonstrators were in police cells and 117 policemen in London hospitals.[15]

In Rome, some three thousand people attacked the U.S. embassy, and ten thousand people peacefully marched in West Berlin. Throughout the world, protesters went into the streets with the chants: "Ho, Ho, Ho Chi Minh, NLF is going to win!" and "Two, Three, Many Vietnams!"

The latter slogan was derived from a speech Che Guevara gave to the Organization of Latin American Solidarity shortly before he left for Bolivia to open another front. In his view, that was the best way to act in solidarity with the Vietnamese.[16] Che was captured and murdered in 1967, but guerrilla movements in Venezuela, Colombia, Guatemala, Nicaragua, Bolivia, and Peru took up his call to arms. Mistakenly or not, they modeled their armed struggle on his "foco theory."[17] Armed liberation movements in Eritrea, Angola, Mozambique, Guinea-Bissau, the Philippines, Thailand, and many other nations intensified their actions in this period, so many that Fidel Castro named 1968 "year of the heroic guerrilla." Anti-imperialist military coups made their appearance. In Peru, a 1968 coup led to one of the most far-reaching agrarian reform programs ever directed from above, mandating the end of feudalism. In Ireland, massive marches and the founding of the People's Democracy Party in October 1968 marked the renewal of the struggle for independence.

In the Middle East, the defeat of the Arab regimes and the occupation of the West Bank and Gaza by Israel in 1967 led to the reorganization of the Palestine Liberation Organization (PLO) and a new chairperson, Yasser Arafat. There was an upsurge of PLO guerrilla attacks, the first airplane hijacking, the defeat of Israeli troops at Karameh, and massive demonstrations—some led by women—against the Zionist occupation of Jerusalem. The eros effect swept the Arab world, galvanizing an Arab New Left that identified with the Cuban and Vietnamese Revolutions at the same time as it saw through the bankruptcy of the "progressive" Arab regimes and criticized the Soviet Union and Arab Communist parties for their "rigid and fossilized" leadership. In more than ten Arab countries, a New Left developed, stressing popular struggle and, in some cases, "cultural revolution," the need for autonomy from world superpowers, and the significance of the upsurges in Poland, France, and Italy, as well as the black revolt and student antiwar movement in the United States.[18] The year 1968 was also when Khomeini published a collection of essays on Islamic government, a republican government was won in South Yemen, and a July coup brought the Arab Socialist Baath Party to power in Iraq.

In short, the balance of world power shifted in 1968, a change obvious as early as January of that year, when the USS *Pueblo* and its crew were captured by North Korea after the intelligence-gathering ship "wandered" into its waters. In the 1950s, the United States had been able to impose the division of Korea and install friendly governments in Iran and Guatemala, but in 1968, the Tet offensive signaled the end of the epoch in which the United States would be unchallenged in its capability to impose its will unilaterally.

As Vietnam inspired the global movement, the theories of Che Guevara helped direct its energies. His strategic outlook differed from that of the Communist parties in several respects. These differences merit close attention since they provided a strategy quite different from Moscow's.

Che's Foco Theory

The call for armed struggle to be undertaken in the countryside by the "foco," a small and dedicated group of guerrillas, as a way of setting a popular movement in motion, constituted a strategic alternative to the Communist strategy of building an urban vanguard of the working class. If the Communists sought to build their base within the most advanced sectors of production, the guerrillas located themselves among the peasants as far as possible from the military-political-economic concentrations of the Establishment. If Communist parties sought to work whenever possible within the established political process and believed in the possibility of peaceful change, the guerrillas wanted only to overthrow governments. In broad terms, the Communist parties argued for a gradual transition to socialism by continually emphasizing that conditions favorable to revolution were not present, and guerrillas sought to create these conditions by setting in motion "the big motor of the mass movement through the small motor of the foco."

Although the implementation of Che's foco theory was notably unsuccessful in Bolivia, Colombia, and Venezuela, it proved of value to the Nicaraguan revolution. Attempts to duplicate the success of the Cuban Revolution by adopting its strategy were not confined to Latin America or to the Third World. Many organizations—such as the Weather Underground and Black Liberation Army (BLA) in the United States, the Irish Republican Army (IRA), the Red Army Faction (RAF) in West Germany, the Red Brigades in Italy, the Front de libération du Québec (FLQ) in Canada, Euzkadi Ta Askatasuna (ETA, "Basque Land and Liberty") in Spain, and Gauche Proletarian in France—carefully studied Che and Debray (as well as Marighellia, Mao, and Giáp) and—successfully or not—put the strategy that had led to victory in Cuba into practice in their own countries.

Creation of a Guevarist wing within radical movements sparked major splits between the radical Left and Soviet Communists. As early as 1961, Brazilian Communists divided into pro–armed struggle and parliamentary factions. Around the same time, similar divisions occurred within movements in Bolivia, Venezuela, Peru, Chile, and Colombia. Years later, the same split tore apart the Black Panther Party.

Besides differences over strategy and tactics, there was another dimension to the gap between Soviet Communism and the new radicalism, a difference summed up in Che's call for transformation of human beings—for the "creation of a new socialist human." Soviet Marxism has long regarded transformation of basic structures of society as inevitably and automatically leading to cultural and social transformation. The new radicalism demanded a simultaneous transformation of politics, economy, and culture, of social structure and individual subject. Abstractly, refusal to passively accept nonrevolutionary objective conditions as unmodifiable is analogous to the new radicalism's refusal to accept delaying transformation of everyday life until "after the revolution." In calls for direct action and cultural-political revolution (including liberation of women), guerrillas in the Third World and radical movements in the core

Che Guevara meets Egyptian Premier Nasser in Cairo on June 19, 1958. Picture Alliance.

were intimately tied together in theory, and in practice, they forged a unity against a common enemy (U.S. "imperialism") and a common rival (Soviet-style "radicalism").

Although Cuba subsequently developed enormous economic ties to the Soviet Union, its revolutionary movement was neither Communist-led nor tied to the Soviet Union until after the U.S. invasion and economic blockade, and Cuba provided a powerful impetus for the New Left. When Fidel Castro's speeches were published in the United States, their North American editor explained, "The example of Cuba gives the New Left inspiration; it is living proof that a determined people and strong leadership can defeat the most powerful military forces in the world. Fidel's speeches, with their emphasis on struggle and their vision of a new society and a 'new man,' speak not only to the Cuban people but also to the youth of America today."[19] The same book's dedication was unabashedly optimistic in its understanding of the historical possibilities: "This book is dedicated to the Cuban and the Vietnamese people who have given North Americans the possibility of making a revolution and to the young North Americans who have taken advantage of that possibility."

Student Movements of 1968

If 1968 was anyone's year, it was the year of the students. From Peking to Prague and Paris to Berkeley, students sparked the movements of 1968. More than any other group, it was their international practice that made protests in 1968 a global movement. In conjunction with movements for national liberation, particularly in Vietnam, the student movement became a force in international relations, compelling world policymakers to modify—and in some cases to cancel altogether—their grandiose plans. Soon after Richard Nixon was elected to his first term as president, he threatened Vietnam with use of nuclear weapons on Hanoi if they did not immediately surrender. Hundreds of thousands of predominantly student demonstrators marched in cities across the United States in October and November 1969, causing Nixon to modify his choice of weapons.[20] Six months later, the 1970 nationwide campus strike compelled him to limit the U.S. invasion of Cambodia and helped provide the Black Panther Party with some protection from police and FBI attacks.

Within movements for national liberation, students have long played a significant role both in sparking popular mobilizations and in forming revolutionary organizations. In Cuba, the student movement and army overthrew the Machado regime in 1933. When Batista and the army deposed the constitutional government in 1952, it was again students who initiated armed struggle against him. After his regime brutally suppressed the national university strike of 1955–56, students massively dissented.[21] In Vietnam, students played an important role in sparking oppositional movements in cities. As early as 1949, they began to demonstrate against U.S. involvement in their country,[22] and in the early 1960s, their actions helped isolate the Diem regime. In January 1965, together with organized Buddhists, the student movement appealed for a general strike in Hue, and once the strike broke out there, it quickly spread to Danang among workers at the U.S. air base. As the situation grew more desperate, police fired on demonstrators in Hue and Dalat, wounding four students.[23] Police and paratroopers in Saigon wounded thirty more people a few days later. As disturbances continued, the military staged a coup d'état, and ten days later the United States began its bombing of northern Vietnam. Students in Vietnam continued their opposition to foreign domination through general strikes from March to May 1966, and again in the spring of 1970, when more than sixty thousand students participated.

In 1960, C. Wright Mills noted the new role of students.[24] The signs were clear enough: students in South Korea caused the downfall of Syngman Rhee; in Turkey, student riots led to a military coup d'état; massive Japanese student riots against the Treaty of Mutual Cooperation and Security between the United States and Japan compelled President Eisenhower to cancel his visit; in Taiwan and Okinawa, Great Britain and the United States, students were showing signs of becoming, as Mills put it, "real live agencies of historic change."

International connections among student movements were forged as they heard of one another's existence. In describing the origins of the awakening of black students in the United States, for example, Clayborn Carson noted the influence of African movements: "The African independence movement, led by college-trained activists, also affected black youths. . . . Students who later took part in the sit-in movements heard reports of the African independence struggle . . . a few weeks before the initial Greensboro sit-in. . . . Even the most unintellectual black students were envious of the African independence movement and vaguely moved by it."[25]

In 1960, signs of awakening were present, but few people expected that by the end of the decade, the actions of students would precipitate a near-revolution in France or help bring about the greatest crisis since the Civil War in the United States.

Inspired by Vietnam and activated by the global eros effect, anti-imperialist student movements erupted throughout the world in 1968. In Ethiopia, Ecuador, India, Thailand, Peru, Puerto Rico, Uruguay, Venezuela, Brazil, Argentina, Indonesia, Pakistan, Greece, Turkey, Panama, Mexico, Italy, Spain, Japan, Belgium, France, West Germany, and the United States (to make only a partial list), these movements spontaneously acted in solidarity with one another. Even the most conservative observers were compelled to acknowledge the international character of the movement: "With no formal international federation of student radicals, in 1968, campus movements seemed to be synchronized among different countries and uniform in content and technique."[26] Seymour Martin Lipset, a specialist in the study of student movements, observed in 1968:

> Anyone who attempts to interpret the revival of student activism in recent years must face the fact that he is dealing with a worldwide phenomenon. Wherever one looks—at stagnant underdeveloped countries like Indonesia, at rapidly expanding, economically successful ones like Japan, at right-wing dictatorships like Spain, at Communist systems such as Czechoslovakia and Poland, and at such Western democracies as Germany, France, Italy, and the United States—one finds aggressive student movements that challenge their governments for not living up to different sets of social ideals.[27]

The international character of the student movement has long been one of its defining contours, providing a reference point within which its theory and practice were articulated. In 1968, however, television, radio, and traveling spokespersons spread the movement around the world as never before, synchronizing its actions and making the political generation of 1968 truly international. Eric Hobsbawm understood the material basis of the global revolt: "The same books appeared, almost simultaneously, in the student bookshops in Buenos Aires, Rome and Hamburg. . . . The first generation of humanity to take rapid and cheap global air travel and telecommunications for granted,

Major Student Disruptions, 1968–69

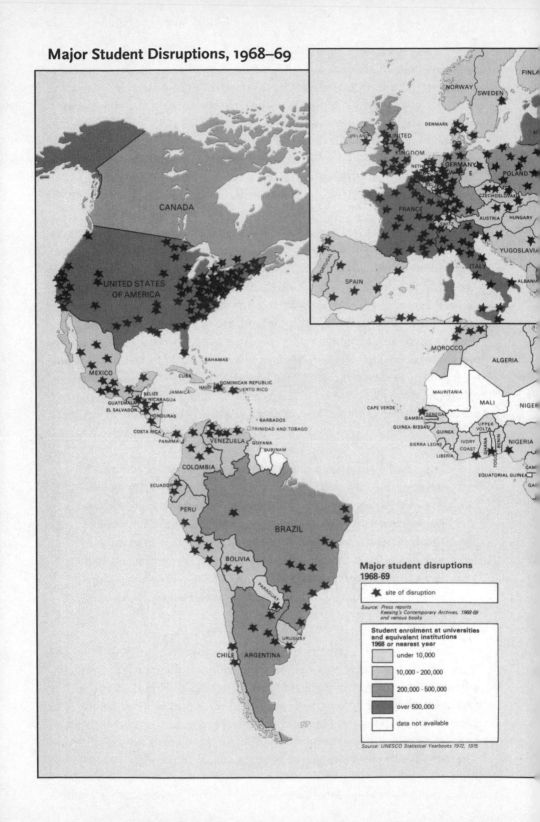

Major student disruptions
1968-69

★ site of disruption

Source: Press reports
Keesing's Contemporary Archives, 1968-69
and various books

Student enrolment at universities
and equivalent institutions
1968 or nearest year

under 10,000

10,000 - 200,000

200,000 - 500,000

over 500,000

data not available

Source: UNESCO Statistical Yearbooks 1972, 1975

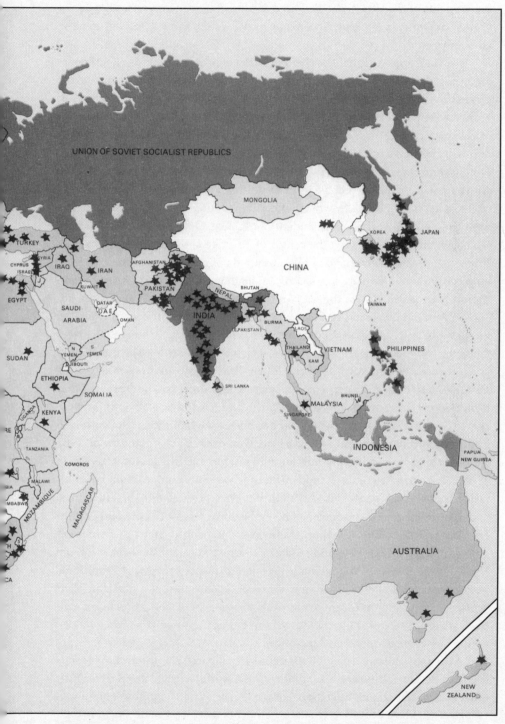

the students of the late 1960s, had no difficulty in recognizing what happened at the Sorbonne, in Berkeley, in Prague, as part of the same event in the same global village."[28]

It is quite apparent that the chain reaction of protests (or eros effect) operated on a global level because so many of the significant outbursts of student protest were related to one another. In February 1968, for example, students in France were heard chanting "Solidarity with SDS," the New Left organization in Germany that was under attack. The next month, four hundred German SDS members formed a prominent contingent at a demonstration in London. After French students erupted in May, police battled five thousand students in Rome who gathered to burn de Gaulle in effigy. In June and July, there were four days of street fighting in Berkeley when police attacked demonstrations in solidarity with the striking workers and students of France. On June 15, ten thousand Japanese students blockaded the center of Tokyo to show their solidarity with French students. In Santiago, Chile, hundreds of students attacked the U.S. embassy on October 4 in support of students in Mexico and Uruguay, who themselves identified with the May 1968 student-led revolt in France.

Seldom in history has such an international general will been formulated in spontaneously generated confrontational movements. In neighborhoods, factories, and offices, day-to-day stories of class struggle seem to be much more concerned with immediate material issues. The transformation of economic struggles into political ones—of self-interest into universal interest (another dimension of eros effect)—occurred globally in 1968 and was obvious for all to see. In Scandinavia, for example, what had been student politics "characterized by an extraordinary tranquility and a virtual absence of mass activism" in 1967 suddenly became remarkably militant and internationally focused activism in 1968.[29] In Turkey, there were suddenly sit-ins, boycotts, and militant confrontations in 1968, although between 1961 and 1968, press statements, meetings, and occasional demonstrations had been the norm.[30] In both core and periphery, East and West, the student movement spontaneously generated coherent global aspirations, which stood in sharp contrast to established reality. From France to Tunisia and Yugoslavia to Mexico, students broke with traditional political parties and developed new forms of organization and practice. Their unified actions and emergent aspirations were a product of centuries of centralization of the world economic system, but at the same time, they helped define new dimensions to global culture.

At their best moments, students defined their particular interests as exactly those of the most oppressed members of the world system, thereby negating entrenched values such as nationalism, elite rule, and the global boundaries of privilege. More than two thousand students sacrificed their lives for their beliefs, as tabulated below.

Numbers of Protesting Students Killed by State Violence, 1967–73

COUNTRY	MONTH/YEAR	MINIMUM KILLED
Spain	January/October 1967	2
Germany	October 1967	1
Japan	October 1967	1
Dominican Republic	February 1968	1
USA	February 1968	3
Brazil	March–August 1968	7
Egypt	May 1968	16
Senegal	May–June 1968	2
France	June 1968	1
Turkey	July 1968	1
Mexico	July 1968	11
Uruguay	August–September 1968	2
Jamaica	October 1968	3
Mexico	October 1968	400*
Lebanon	November 1968	1
Portugal	November 1968	1
Pakistan	November 1968	4
Egypt	November 1968	16
Italy	December 1968	1
USA	May 1969	1
Argentina	May 1969	3
Congo-Zaire	June 1969	10–100*
Philippines	January 1970	6
USA	May 1970	6
Venezuela	May 1970	2
Nigeria	February 1971	2
Bangladesh	March 1971	500+
Sri Lanka	April 1971	1,200+
Thailand	October 1973	77
Greece	November 1973	34

*Corpses were seized by police/soldiers and secretly buried or otherwise disappeared
Note: The table above is a partial list of minimal numbers of deaths. The data indicate that as protests continued, governments became ever more violent.

Counting articles in *Le Monde* dealing with student protests statistically demonstrates the incredible extent to which students became mobilized in 1968, particularly in the period from May 3 to June 18 (when the general strike paralyzed France). It should be remembered that these numbers refer only to student protests that were reported in the pages of *Le Monde*. Actual numbers were much higher.

Incidents of Student Protest as Reported in *Le Monde*

	1967 4th Qtr.	1st Qtr.	1968 Total	2nd Quarter 4/1–5/2	5/3–6/18	6/18–30
France	30	79	1205	41	971	193
Austria	—	—	6	—	6	—
Belgium	—	2	19	1	14	4
Czechoslovakia	4	16	12	7	4	1
Denmark	—	—	1	—	1	—
East Germany	—	1	1	—	—	1
Great Britain	1	3	26	3	20	3
Greece	2	4	4	1	3	—
Ireland	—	—	1	—	1	—
Italy	2	24	34	6	22	6
Luxemburg	—	—	3	—	3	—
Netherlands	1	1	7	—	5	2
Poland	—	33	17	12	4	1
Portugal	1	1	1	—	1	—
Spain	18	49	34	13	19	2
Sweden	1	1	4	—	4	—
Switzerland	—	—	11	—	9	2
Turkey	1	—	10	1	5	4
USSR	1	6	4	2	1	1
Vatican	1	—	1	—	—	1
West Germany	6	13	63	33	25	5
(West Berlin)	—	—	23	6	14	3
Yugoslavia	—	—	14	—	12	2
EUROPE—Total	39	154	296	85	173	38
Algeria	2	21	5	1	4	—
Comores	—	3	—	—	—	—
Congo	—	1	—	—	—	—
Dahomey	1	—	—	—	—	—
Egypt	1	4	2	—	2	—
Ethiopia	—	—	2	2	—	—
Morocco	—	2	2	—	1	1
Mauritania	—	—	2	—	2	—.
Rep. Central Africa	—	—	1	1	—	—
Senegal	—	—	16	—	16	—
Tunisia	—	8	12	6	3	3
AFRICA—Total	4	39	42	10	28	4
Argentina	—	2	21	2	10	9
Bolivia	—	—	2	1	—	1
Brazil	5	2	24	8	7	9
Canada	—	1	1	—	1	—

	1967 4th Qtr.	1st Qtr.	Total	1968 2nd Quarter 4/1–5/2	5/3–6/18	6/18–30
Chile	—	—	6	—	6	—
Colombia	—	1	3	1	1	1
Cuba	1	—	—	—	—	—
Ecuador	2	2	—	—	—	—
Guadeloupe	1	—	1	—	1	—
Guyana	—	—	1	—	1	—
Haiti	—	1	2	—	2	—
Mexico	—		1	1	—	—
Nicaragua	—	—	2	1	—	1
Peru	—	2	4	—	3	1
Santo Domingo	—	3	2	—	—	2
United States	11	12	21	7	12	2
Uruguay	—	—	11		4	7
Venezuela	—	2	2	1	1	—
AMERICAS—Total	20	28	104	22	49	33
Afghanistan			1	—	1	—
China	2	2	12	1	8	3
India	6		1	—	1	—
Indonesia		2	2	—	2	—
Israel		3	3	1	2	—
Japan	3	6	9	3	3	3
Lebanon	—	1	2	2	—	—
Palestine	2	—	2	1	1	—
South Korea	—	1	—	—	—	—
South Vietnam	1	1	—	—	—	—
Syria	—	—	1	1	—	—
Thailand	—	—	1	—	—	1
ASIA—Total	14	16	34	9	18	7
Australia	2		—	—	—	—
Philippines	—	1	—	—	—	—
PACIFIC—Total	2	1	—	—	—	—
Africa	4	39	42	10	28	4
Americas	20	39	104	22	49	32
Asia	14	16	34	7	18	7
Europe	39	154	296	85	173	38
France	30	79	1205	41	971	193
Pacific	2	1	—	—	—	—
General Total	109	328	1681	165	1239	274

Source: Jean Joussellin, *Les Révoltes des Jeunes* (Paris: Les Éditions Ouvrières, 1968), 13–15.

If the actions of students in 1968 were directly political, the impact of their actions was felt on other levels as well. They stimulated a worldwide cultural awakening that accompanied and outlasted the global political revolt. In many countries, the student movement built cultural bases outside universities and established semiliberated territories in places like San Francisco's Haight-Ashbury, in Berkeley, Madison, and Cambridge, in Amsterdam in the period of the Provos, Kabouters, and the Orange Free State, in Berlin's Kreuzberg, in Nanterre and other parts of Paris, and in London's Notting Hill. Free schools, food co-ops, radical bookstores, communes, and collective coffeehouses were established as focal points of this emergent counterculture. New values within these communities could not be extinguished after the political turmoil subsided. In Zurich, ten thousand people demonstrated for an autonomous youth center at the end of June 1968, and the police mercilessly attacked marchers (hospitalizing 200 people and severely beating and arresting 2,500 more). Twelve years later, in 1980, a new generation successfully used tactics like nude marches and roller skate demonstrations and temporarily won an autonomous youth center.

As a general pattern in the twentieth century, students and youth have been in the forefront of those who would end wars and establish a new system of international cooperation. From the May 4 Movement in China to the May events in France, students have been a blasting cap capable of detonating upheavals throughout society. Although there have been important exceptions—notably fascist students of Hitler, Tojo, and Mussolini—students have generally been pro-liberty and antiwar. They have marched peacefully, demonstrated militantly, and formed their own international associations. In terms of massive upheavals, however, the student generation of 1968 was the first since 1848 to erupt globally with such numbers and enthusiasm.[31]

How do we account for the new role played by students around the world in 1968? There are many factors underlying their activism: their youthfulness (which leaves them free from many of the responsibilities that immobilize their elders); their segregation on campuses (which creates a "critical mass"); the relatively free nature of universities in terms of both exchange of ideas and leisure time (both of which contrast sharply to "adult" institutions); and, last but not least, students are *supposed* to study social issues (a demand which brings them face-to-face with obvious problems of the existing world system).

While the above factors may account for student activism, they do not explain why international events catalyzed eruptions on campuses in 1968 or why the vision and demands of the students were international ones. After World War II, the quantitative expansion of universities and increasing interpenetration of national economies in a world economy occurred at a dizzying rate. Far from remaining marginal institutions reserved for training new elites, universities moved to the center of the global system of production. Tens of millions of college students in 1968 represented the ascendant new working class upon whom the functioning of the global system increasingly depends. Not only were (and are) students in a central position in a global system undergoing rapid technological changes, they were also one of the "weakest links" in such a system. As Ernest Mandel put it in 1968:

> A new social group has emerged from the very vitals of capitalism, from all that it considered its essential "achievement": the higher standard of living, the advances in technology and the mass media, and the requirements of automation. There are six million university students in the United States, two and a half million in Western Europe, and over a million in Japan. And it proved impossible to integrate these groupings into the capitalist system as it functions in any of these territories. . . . What the student revolt represents on a much broader social and historic scale is the colossal transformation of the productive forces . . . the reintegration of intellectual labor into productive labor.[32]

Following Clark Kerr's observation that universities stand in relation to the latter half of the twentieth century as railroads did to the nineteenth, then the student movement of 1968 stands historically in line with militant railroad workers of 1905, whose strikes and struggles met with apparent defeat, but whose goals of an eight-hour working day, universal suffrage, and trade unions were realized decades later.

Not only were students in the forefront of others, their numbers were so swelled that they were themselves a force. While many student protests began from campus issues like tuition, poor food, and unsatisfactory instructors, what is striking about 1968 student movements is the degree to which their actions escalated to focus on national and international political issues. In Belgium, Flemish students at the Roman Catholic University in Louvain rioted for three weeks in January after the French-speaking faculty announced that they planned to remain at the university. Even with a purely educational focus, the student movement had *political* repercussions. Tensions over the Louvain University disturbance contributed to the collapse of the government of Premier Paul Vanden Boeynants in February.

Students' international significance was understood by the CIA and the KGB, both of whom organized their own international student associations in attempts to gain control of the movement.[33] In Santo Domingo in 1967, the CIA went as far as organizing an entire "Counter-University."[34]

Coupled as it was with a diffuse cultural revolt, the student movement was controlled neither by outsiders nor by its own hastily organized groupings. The international similarities of student movements in 1968 are evident in the following global review of events.

Asia

From one end of Asia to the other, students profoundly challenged the existing social order. In South Korea and Thailand, they overthrew governments at the cost of dozens killed. In Sri Lanka, a Guevarist uprising in 1971 left more than 1,200 students dead.

South Korea

In South Korea in 1960, fraudulent elections sparked a massive popular uprising against U.S.-backed dictator Syngman Rhee. As soon as voting results were announced, Rhee claimed 90 percent. Immediately, people mobilized peacefully, but murderous violence greeted them in Masan on March 15, where protests and police attacks continued for a month. On April 19, thousands of students took to the streets of Seoul. By the time they approached the presidential palace, their ranks had swelled to as many as one hundred thousand people.[35] For the first time, students found massive support among the general public. During the march, some students chanted, "Let us destroy communism by getting our democracy right!"[36] Here was an early indication of what would become the global New Left's opposition to dictatorships of both communist and capitalist varieties, of a gut-oriented intuition of freedom that cared little for the ideology of governments that unnecessarily limited it.

At the presidential palace, the massive crowd demanded to see Rhee. They were answered when palace guards opened fire, killing at least twenty people in the first volley. Remarkably, students fought back, refusing to be intimidated by clubs and guns. They regrouped and spontaneously formed small action teams that destroyed the headquarters building of Rhee's Liberal Party as well as that of the Anticommunist Youth League, the editorial offices of the government newspaper, and five police substations.[37] Protesters burned houses belonging to Rhee's high-ranking subordinates, wrecked City Hall, and attacked dozens of other buildings linked to Rhee and his party. Throughout the country, thousands of high school students mobilized, especially in Incheon, Jeonju, Mokpo, and Daegu. In Gwangju, high school students demanding new elections surged downtown. Organizers sent runners to visit every school in the city, and thousands of high school students surged into the streets.[38] Police and firefighters fired water laced with red dye but failed to disperse demonstrators. Unpaved roads provided plenty of rocks for ammunition to fight back. Throughout the night, the battle continued and protesters controlled the streets. In Busan, protesters set fire to many government buildings.

Before violence ended, gunfire on "Bloody Tuesday" had claimed dozens of lives.[39] In Seoul alone, more than one hundred people were killed and over one thousand wounded. Ultimately, martial law was declared, the army called out, and a curfew strictly enforced. Remarkably, the army did not open fire. General Song Yo-chan ordered his troops not to shoot, and soldiers and students reportedly shouted to each other, "We are brothers!"

The army refused to fight the 1960 uprising in South Korea. Photographer unknown.

The next day college students massively mobilized. For seven consecutive days, there were major demonstrations in Seoul. On April 24, as the entire country appeared to reject election results, Vice president–elect Lee Ki-bung publicly declared he would not accept office. He and his family subsequently committed suicide. On April 25, some 258 university professors gathered at Seoul National University and issued a message proclaiming that "Student Demonstrations are the Expression of Justice!" They marched through the city to demand Rhee's resignation, as well as those of the nation's chief justice and the speaker of the National Assembly. By the time they arrived at the capitol, more than one hundred thousand people were with them, and people listened intently as professors announced a fifteen-point declaration. This event was significant for many reasons, not least because it marked the first time in Korean history that professors as a group had entered the struggle against tyranny. The spontaneous gathering of so many people was unprecedented in a society where dictatorships had ruled for so long.

After the rally at the National Assembly, some fifty thousand protesters attacked Vice President Lee Ki-bung's empty house. Placing his elaborate furnishings on the street to be photographed so all could see the wealth he had accumulated, people proceeded to burn them before demolishing the house.[40] Their message was clear: not only must Rhee go, so must his entire administration. Evidently, the massive outpouring of antigovernment sentiment and the capacity of people to act despite deadly police violence convinced the U.S. to support Rhee's departure. Without American backing, he would never have been able to become president or to remain in power. On Friday, April 26, the U.S. ambassador offered him the same means of transportation back to the U.S. that had been provided in 1945 to bring him to Korea: a U.S. military aircraft. Rhee announced his resignation and boarded a plane bound for Hawaii.

Joyful gatherings suddenly cropped up everywhere. Thousands of arrested students were released, and police withdrew from public view. Students directed traffic on city streets and took over many police stations. All over the country, as they swept the cities clean of the debris left behind from their hard-won victory, young people proudly stepped into positions of authority amid public acclaim. With the army in the streets, raucous celebrations transpired—spontaneous and joyful expressions of hope for the future of democracy. The success of the uprising in winning power surprised everyone—most of all those who had been at the center of organizing it.

Decades of pent-up grievances were suddenly possible to discuss in public. As one observer described it:

> The April revolution was a giant social revolt. . . . The students . . . touched off a general revolt in society. The people revolted against the government. The young revolted against the old. In many schools, students revolted against their teachers. In some government ministries, junior civil servants revolted against senior civil servants. In a more serious vein, some eight lieutenant colonels revolted against some generals, requesting that the army be cleared of corrupt elements.[41]

People paid a high price for their victory. When the dead were identified and totaled, they numbered 186.[42] At least forty-six were high school students (seventh to twelfth grades), and the majority were teenagers. An additional six thousand people had been injured.

The success of Korean students inspired others around the world. Newspapers reported that protesting students in Turkey bowed their heads to show respect to their counterparts in Korea. U.S. activist Tom Hayden, main author of the Port Huron Statement, the founding document of Students for a Democratic Society (SDS), remembered his feelings when he first heard the news from Seoul:

> I was exhilarated when I saw young people our age overthrow the dicta-
> tor Syngman Rhee. Through that movement, I learned the history of the
> Cold War for the first time. Those events challenged our naive belief that
> our parents were fighting for a free world. I can tell you that movement
> helped inspire SNCC and the Black movement in the South. Two days
> after Syngman Rhee's forced resignation, SDS held its first meeting.[43]

Korea's newly founded popular democracy would last little more than a year, until a U.S.-backed coup on May 16, 1961. Students' euphoric belief in their autonomous power after they had overthrown Rhee led them to intensify their initiative to reunify the country. Four days before a scheduled North-South student conference in Panmunjom, a small coterie of former Japanese officers, led by Park Chung-hee, seized control of the government.[44] Koreans would be forced to persevere through eighteen years of Park's dictatorship. During his rule, protests continued, especially from 1964 to 1965, when 3.5 million people demonstrated against the U.S.-brokered Korea-Japan Treaty. On June 3, 1964, martial law was declared in Seoul, during which the treaty with Japan was signed, followed by dispatch of twenty thousand Korean troops to fight for the United States in Vietnam.

Korean students would continue to be among the world's most advanced activists. Numbers alone fail to account for the central role of universities and high school students.[45] Afforded great respect in the world's most Confucian society, Korean intellectuals and students remain capable of detonating widespread social explosions. In 1980, students sparked the historic Gwangju Uprising. Soon after Park was assassinated in 1979, students in Gwangju refused to accept continuing dictatorship. The military pulled thousands of paratroopers off front lines with North Korea and dispatched them to suppress protesting students. Remarkably, Gwangju citizens fought back with clubs and bamboo spears against machine guns and flamethrowers. At a critical moment, transportation workers took the lead and helped to defeat the army and win control of the city. A general assembly spontaneously organized itself downtown, and citizens converged daily in direct democratic discussions to make decisions. All the while, their Citizens Army continued to fight the army on the city's outskirts. Like the 1871 Paris Commune, there was no looting, and citizens united with each other. Learning about the Gwangju Uprising's direct democracy, "community of love," and self-formation of fighting units are mind-expanding experiences.[46]

China

Beginning in 1966, the Cultural Revolution strove to accomplish some of the same goals articulated by the New Left: abolition of the superiority of mental over manual work, consideration of the political implications of purely "technical" questions, overthrow of bureaucratic domination, and greater democracy.

Public debate on these political issues in China began innocently enough. Students initiated a poster campaign denouncing teachers and admissions policies that favored the children of the Communist Party and the well-to-do. Grassroots calls to revitalize China's revolutionary power were endorsed by Mao's famous big character poster, which he personally attached to the door of the Central Committee to which he belonged: "Open Fire on Headquarters." Beginning on August 18, eight mammoth rallies in Tiananmen Square involving eleven million Red Guards marked the entry of youth into the revolution. Mao called for students to radically change society "by a path that had never been explored" and to give those who had made mistakes "a way out that will allow them to reform and to become entirely new men." He predicted that the Cultural Revolution in China would have a "significance that will exceed that of the Paris Commune itself."

Within four months, the Cultural Revolution's objectives changed into seizure of power largely because of intransigent opposition to revolutionary reforms. On February 5, 1967, the Shanghai Commune was proclaimed with members "elected by the revolutionary masses according to the principles of the Paris Commune." In April, Revolutionary Committees were created throughout the country with executive committees that included many revolutionary

Chairman Mao Zedong autographs a book of his quotations for American activist Robert F. Williams in Beijing, 1967. Photographer unknown.

activists. Chinese official media gave abundant praise to world revolutionary movements in Vietnam, Burma, Thailand, Malaysia, the Congo, Colombia, and India, and to student movements in Western Europe and the United States. Revolutionary leaders from around the world were regularly invited to Beijing and received by high party officials. For example, Mao greeted African American civil rights leader Robert F. Williams personally. When the Soviet Union invaded Czechoslovakia in 1968, Premier Chou En-lai sternly opposed the Russians.

The enthusiasm of Chinese youth ran to excesses. Although Mao had initially encouraged the Red Guards, soon no one controlled them. Violent confrontations on campuses could not be quieted, even after the army halted battles between factions in the fall of 1967. On February 8, 1968, Western news reports gave Maoists control of half of all twenty-six Chinese provinces. In pitched battles in Guangzhou on February 21, more than one hundred students were killed.[47] In March, rival groups of thousands of armed Red Guards continued to fight each other. One faction disrupted the railroad line carrying arms to Vietnam and used the weapons to seize much of southern China.

At the center of the revolt at Beijing's Tsinghua University, students battled each other for control of the campus using homemade cannons, tanks, hand grenades, spears, and Molotov cocktails. Even when thousands of well-organized workers marched from their factories to the campus gates and demanded that all violence cease, students would not relent. They attacked the disciplined throngs of workers, killing 5, wounding 731, and capturing 143.[48] For days, thirty thousand workers stood their ground surrounding the campus as they attempted to convince the students to lay down their arms. (Some estimates placed the number of workers who surrounded the campus at over one hundred thousand.) It was only after Mao's personal intervention that the barricaded students finally relented.

In July, thousands of soldiers took control of China's high schools, colleges, and universities. By the fall, thousands of students had been sent into the countryside to empty cities of warring factions. Despite dispersal of the Red Guards, experiences gleaned during years of struggle helped in the formation of subsequent opposition movements, notably in 1989, when tens of thousands of students took over Tiananmen Square, sparking a national uprising that was bloodily suppressed.

Japan

In Japan, a militant but controlled use of violence, a great deal of it appearing as play, was initially coupled with a rejection of ideologies from Europe and Asia. The Japanese student movement was the first massive student movement to reject both capitalism and communism, and as they denounced both the

United States and the Soviet Union, they were in turn vehemently criticized by pro-American, pro-Soviet, and even pro-Chinese observers.

Like its counterparts elsewhere, the Japanese student movement was conditioned by the rapid expansion of higher education. In 1940 there were only 47 universities in Japan, but by 1960 there were 236 four-year universities and an additional 274 colleges. In 1948, representatives of over 300,000 students from 145 universities created the All Japan Federation of Student Self-Government Associations, or *Zengakuren*, as it became known. One of the first spokespersons of the Zengakuren declared that both capitalist and communist governments were "enemies of peace, democracy, and student freedom" and asserted that if not for the world superpowers, "the innate good sense of ordinary people would make it possible to have minimum control by the government."[49] Despite their hostility to Moscow, the Zengakuren cooperated with Japanese Communists in 1960, and massive demonstrations forced President Eisenhower to abandon his plans to visit Japan.

Although the Zengakuren began as a member of the Comintern-dominated International Union of Students, a split in 1958 created two autonomous groups that claimed the support of almost three hundred thousand members. Hardcore cadres were believed by the CIA to number about two thousand. In 1960, Tokyo had a student population of three hundred thousand—one-third of whom were Zengakuren members, and student demonstrations could draw anywhere from ten to twenty-five thousand on any given day.[50] Thousands of people continually protested against American nuclear submarines in Japanese ports. When the government attempted to give police increased powers, militant protests killed the bill.

As the movement deepened both in experiences of activists and their impact on Japanese society, the theory and practice of the worldwide movement was embraced. A few months after the Free Speech Movement in Berkeley, twelve thousand students at the University of Keio in Tokyo unanimously voted to strike for "democratization of the campus." The Commune of Keio, as the movement became known, won student power, temporarily quieting the nation's campuses. By the fall of 1966, the Chinese Cultural Revolution had electrified the Japanese Left, and with the escalation of the U.S. war against Vietnam in 1967, students again mobilized. They attacked U.S. bases in Japan and confronted Prime Minister Sato when he attempted to board a plane to Saigon, and again when he went to the United States.[51] Trade unions quickly joined the antimilitary movement, although workers and students were unable to unite at critical moments.

On March 10, 1968, thousands of people attacked police formations using six-foot-long wooden poles. Hundreds were arrested and about twice that number injured. On March 15, high school students protested the U.S.

Clashes between protesters and Japanese riot police. Bruno Barbey/Magnum Photos.

war. Ten days later, more than one thousand students demonstrated against a new American military hospital for soldiers wounded in Vietnam. More than a dozen students were injured by police and 179 were arrested. On June 7, there were anti-American protests in more than fifty cities. After railroad workers alerted students to the path of a train carrying ammunition bound for Vietnam, nine hours of street fights were needed to clear the train's path.

By June 1968, a giant poster of Mao complete with his words, "It is right to rebel," adorned the entrance to Todai University. The medical school there is the most prestigious in Japan, but it was also one of the most authoritarian and feudalistic. According to one observer, Herbert Marcuse's books were then more popular in Japan than in Europe.[52] When a strike at the medical school finally broke out in August, it was to "dislocate the imperialist university of Tokyo." Students called on their peers to become "proletarian intellectuals" not "slaves of the technocratic-industrial complex." All through the fall, occupations and protests continued. On October 8, fights broke out in eighteen cities as students commemorated the death of a student at Tokyo airport a year earlier. Campus struggles ignited activism among artists.

The Japanese movement had long been militant and well organized, but the months-long occupation of the medical school proved to be one of its most violent and tenacious struggles. It ended seven months later in January 1969 after a massive and bloody three-day battle involving thousands of police.[53] Although the movement quickly became depoliticized (either through withdrawal of some or armed attacks by a few), the struggle for Narita airport, which began in 1968, lasted over ten years, one of the longest struggles of the global movement.

From 1969 to 1970, campus riots and fights with police continued, resulting in arrests and injuries widely covered on front pages of national newspapers. On "Anti-War Day," street fights with students throwing Molotov cocktails ended after 1,221 arrests. On June 23, 1970, the largest street demonstrations of the postwar period in Japan involved more than one million people in 1,345 cities and towns.[54]

As the popular movement declined, its radical fringe became increasingly militant in such groups as the Red Army, which self-destructed in violence among its own members.

The Philippines

As in nearly every country in the world, student protests rocked the government in the Philippines, where sixties' unrest became known as the First Quarter Storm. On January 30, 1970, named "Black Friday" by Senator Benigno Aquino, six people were killed in cold blood as they rushed to escape a police onslaught on a demonstration at the Mendiola Bridge approaching Malacañang Palace.[55] From torture and disappearances to long prison terms, dictator Ferdinand Marcos gave dissidents little choice but to go underground. Scion of one of the country's leading families, firebrand orator, and teenage Korean War photographer for the *Manila Times*, Senator Aquino soon became President Marcos's chief nemesis. Instead of running for president as he hoped, Aquino found himself serving hard prison time. When his health deteriorated, he was released to the United States, where he and South Korean dissident Kim Dae Jung became colleagues at Harvard University. (Both men would go on to lead democratization movements in their homelands.) Aquino returned but as soon as his plane landed at Manila airport, he was gunned down, setting off a series of massive protests that ousted Marcos in 1986.

The Reform the Armed Forces Movement (RAM)—the spark that ignited the 1986 uprising—was also a product of the First Quarter Storm. During years spent preparing to overthrow Marcos, they studied Egyptian officers who overthrew King Farouk in 1952 and reviewed the history of social movements in many countries, "in particular Gandhi's work and people's experiences in Czechoslovakia and Hungary." Before RAM took over bases in central Manila in 1986, they contacted civil activists to organize "flower brigades" designed to block roads into Manila and prevent troops loyal to Marcos from coming to his rescue.[56] They modeled these flower brigades on "those the American youth movement of 1968 had used to disarm troops breaking up demonstrations against the Vietnam War."[57]

In her 1986 presidential campaign against Marcos (which he fraudulently won), Mrs. Cory Aquino ran under the banner of LABAN (Lakas ng Bayan) or "Power of the People"—a phrase amazingly similar to the Black Panther Party's "All Power to the People." While the phrase's exact origin lies in the flux of popular creativity that congeals in social movements, its common usage speaks volumes about these movements' intuitive ties to each other.

Thailand

Although it blossomed later than most of the world's student movements, Thailand's was among the most successful, almost singlehandedly overthrowing a military dictatorship in 1973—albeit at a high cost. The global wave of youth protests in 1968 had greatly affected the country. As a rear base for the American soldiers fighting in Vietnam, the country was inundated with countercultural music, art, philosophy, and books. Students returning from studies abroad, especially in Berkeley, became active in protests. Translations of Herbert Marcuse's writings and articles about the Black Panther Party helped inform the new generation's sensibility. The May 1968 near-revolution in France also infused people's consciousness with the power of activism, as did an earlier generation of Thai intellectuals. By 1968, illegal student-led demonstrations in Bangkok had succeeded in getting martial law lifted in the capital, and in 1969 students won a brief struggle against a hike in bus fares. From these humble beginnings, a movement for a democratic constitution swept the country.

On October 5, 1973, eleven students were arrested as they handed out anti-dictatorship leaflets. Concerned about the safety of the arrestees, Thammasat University's student union called an emergency meeting that afternoon, and an open mike around the Bo tree in a back courtyard began a public conversation by a few dozen people. The participatory assembly in which people could openly respond to each other spawned many ideas and actions, including an initiative by sixty faculty representatives to visit the detained students. When professors arrived at the jail, however, authorities turned them away. Before leaving, they signed the visitors' log, adding, "We Shall Overcome!"

For days, people remained peacefully in conversation around the Bo tree. Like similar gatherings around the world, the site became a place where deliberative democracy encouraged popular actions—and helped activate the eros effect. By October 9, as many as two thousand students were involved in discussions. On October 10, the meeting grew so large that it moved to the nearby football field. Buddhist monks arrived as part of a continuing stream of thousands of people to support the students. From everywhere, food and flowers were delivered. Within days, the assembly mushroomed in size to more than one hundred thousand people. The coordinating group publicly empowered the general assembly as the final decision-making body. By autonomously organizing themselves, students revealed their own capacity to manage society far better than the generals who had usurped power. That was one reason why so many different segments of society joined them.

Exactly at noon on October 13, a procession of about one million people left the university to demand constitutional government. Praying, singing the National and Royal Anthems, and swearing allegiance to the nation, religion, king, and constitution, the huge crowd was immaculately organized. Scouts were sent ahead to clear the route. At the front were "commando units" with grappling hooks followed by an all-female contingent carrying flowers, Thai flags, and a dharma chakra banner—all organized in rows of five. The procession included groups clustered by school as well as by function—first aid, food, coordination, and commando. Thousands of smiling young students, many carrying portraits of King Bhumibol, made this remarkable display of unity the "Day of Joy," as people referred to it. At 8:00 p.m., even though government radio announced acceptance of students' demands, few people left. Rumors spread that nothing had changed, that their representatives had been killed—or fooled. After a peaceful night in the streets, people tried to disperse, but police blocked exits. In the ensuing scuffles, police opened fire with tear gas and bullets. People responded with Molotovs. Machine-gun fire scattered the crowd, but many people stayed in the streets and fought back. At about 8:00 a.m., a fire engine near Thammasat University was commandeered, and Metropolitan Police Headquarters was attacked. As citizens joined the students, the government brought in army tank units to assist the police.

For thirty-six hours, fighting raged in the streets. Some people used pistols, while others took over buses and used them to charge police positions. Small groups of demonstrators carefully selected symbolically important targets, like the Public Relations building (believed to have propagated false media reports about the protests). People swarmed into the building, took firearms, and set it on fire. The Revenue Department building and National Lottery were burned down. The army attacked with tanks and helicopters.

Only too happy to be seen as the nation's savior, King Bhumibol went on the airwaves to announce the government's resignation. He promised a new constitution. Military leader General Thanom also took to the airwaves, but he attempted to remain in power. Elements of the military and the Royal Thai Navy openly supported the students, as did some army and air force officers.[58] Student teams formed to assault police headquarters. A new battle ensued, and fighting lasted into the following afternoon. Led by a group of engineering students with Molotovs and wearing yellow headbands—the "Yellow Tigers"— repeated assaults were launched on police headquarters. At 1:00 a.m., about four hundred engineering students fought their way to Pan Fah Bridge, but they were driven back by machine-gun fire. The bloodiest fighting took place in front of Chalerm Thai Theatre. All the while, some thirty thousand people huddled around Democracy Monument. The next morning, banks and government offices remained closed. As students in outlying areas mobilized, localized uprisings broke out. In Bangkok, police stations continued to be attacked. Soldiers rounded up and brutalized anyone they could find. Elsewhere in the capital, students and boy scouts directed traffic.

As fighting raged, Bhumibol demanded Thanom and his two top aides leave Thailand, at which point the three ruling generals complied. Government forces withdrew from Bangkok's streets. A palpable sense of victory was felt everywhere, and mourning began for the dead. At least 77 citizens had been killed and 857 wounded. Dozens more were missing and would never be found.

A turning point in Thailand's political development, the democratic breakthrough gave birth to one of the nation's freest periods of time. During the postuprising surge, as hundreds of thousands of workers and farmers mobilized, many student activists remained intensely involved in democratic struggles. A new constitution was drafted by a wide array of citizens' groups, including the women's movement, which emerged from within the democratization impetus as well as from Maoist influences.[59] Approved in 1974, the new constitution addressed gender issues and contained an equal rights protection clause for the first time in Thai history. Sweeping changes were promised in women's opportunities to become judges and prosecutors, and equal wages were promised for equal work.

The victory won by Thai students electrified insurgent movements all over the world. A month after the uprising, Greek students rose against the Papadopoulos dictatorship at Athens Polytechnic. As in Thailand, the military mobilized tanks against students and killed thirty-four on November 15. Before the tanks crashed through the Polytechnic's gate, Greek students had chanted praise of their Thai counterparts' successful overthrow of the dictatorship. The U.S. antiwar movement drew inspiration, while the CIA worried that Burmese students might become activated. In neighboring Indochina, Saigon was liberated on April 30, 1975, and the Cambodian and Laotian royal families were soon overthrown. As economic problems began to mount with the withdrawal of U.S. troops from Thailand, the king permitted dictator Thanom to return. In 1976, Thammasat University was invaded by a mob that brutalized helpless students, killing forty-one. A new military dictatorship not only bloodily curtailed democratic rights, it imposed the harsh economic discipline of neoliberalism.

India

The Naxalite movement, the most significant Indian social movement since independence, erupted in 1967. Assassinating landlords and organizing popular power on a local level, they created vast liberated areas, some of which continue to survive today. In 1968, at least fifty thousand peasants were members of revolutionary organizations that coordinated self-defense committees to defend newly liberated villages.[60] The tea workers of Darjeeling observed three general strikes in support of Naxalites, and an urban student movement acted in solidarity. Amid brutal repression, the Naxalite movement split internally, but the popular revolt in northeast India continued. Looking back at the movement years later, one observer noted the Naxalites' relation to the global movement of 1968, particularly its rejection of Soviet Marxism: "The Naxalbari movement was a part of this contemporary, worldwide impulse among radicals to return to the roots of revolutionary idealism. . . . Its stress on the peasants' spontaneous self-assertion, its plan of decentralization through 'area-wide seizure of power' and the setting up of village Soviets, its rejection of the safe path of parliamentary opposition . . . posed a challenge to the ideological sclerosis of the parliamentary Left in India."[61]

As in many countries, the student movement in India was front-page news. In 1966 and 1967, some one thousand strikes occurred in which at least ten students were killed in clashes with police. Many universities closed down, sometimes for weeks. According to the CIA, the wave of protests in 1966 began at Jodhpur University in Rajasthan when students went on strike to protest an attempt to raise the threshold for passing grades.[62] Protests quickly spread to other universities. In 1968, there were at least fifty-nine student protests that seriously affected the normal functioning of institutions of higher learning, a smaller number than two thousand in 1966, nearly five hundred of which were described as "violent." In 1970 campus struggles became increasingly organized and directed by Naxalites. By November 1970, in West Bengal, between ten and twenty thousand revolutionaries roamed the countryside in an armed struggle that killed thirty-six policemen and wounded four hundred.[63]

International influences permeated India, and Dalit Panthers emerged in Mumbai in 1972.

Pakistan

The isolated actions of students led to general strikes by workers in Pakistan. In October 1968, a student revolt broke out to protest government restrictions on political activity. For two months, students fought for university reforms even though Left parties did not support them. On November 6, riots broke out in all of West Pakistan's major cities. On November 7, the army opened fire on enthusiastic students who had defied a public ban and gathered to greet the former foreign minister and opposition leader, Zulfikar Ali Bhutto. His party's slogan resonated well with global insurgencies: "All Power Belongs to the Masses!" After one student was shot and killed, protests emerged all over the country.

In some cities where curfews were declared, factory workers joined the movement. In response, the government ordered all schools closed and arrested Bhutto on charges of inciting students. Five days of demonstrations were held to protest government repression, and in December, students called for a general strike. When they received the immediate support of many workers, the upsurge continued to spread. In East Pakistan (now Bangladesh), two people were killed by police gunfire on December 7. Mass arrests were used against a general strike a week later. Workers and students successfully fought the police and army for control of many factories. For a week, civil authority broke down in Dacca, the largest city of East Pakistan, which became the center of the revolt.

Faced with spontaneously generated unrest, on the one hand, and the offer by opposition parties for negotiation on the other, President Ayub Khan agreed to meet several student demands and was able to remain in power a few more months.

Bangladesh

Bangladesh's campus movement was noteworthy for its widespread devotion to social justice. Historically low rates of matriculation and the country's high poverty rate meant most students were especially privileged and destined to become part of the political elite, yet they responded with heroic leadership based upon the nation's universal interests.[64] With political parties incapacitated by factional strife, students in Bangladesh led the way forward for decades during which students became known internationally for unparalleled political engagement. In the estimation of Talukder Maniruzzaman, "In no country in the world was student activism in the 1950s and 1960s of greater intensity, continuity and concern than in Bangladesh."[65] When the region was known as East Pakistan, students played leading roles in antidictatorship struggles in 1968. In late 1969, they formulated an eleven-point program and initiated an antigovernment movement that sustained wide support—including large-scale worker actions. In March 1971, they mobilized Bengalis for independence and coordinated a huge noncooperation movement at which "even Gandhi would have marveled."[66] When East Pakistan broke away to form Bangladesh, the Pakistani army invaded. Hundreds of thousands of people were murdered by the invading troops, including at least five hundred students at the University of Dacca on the first night of the fighting. After a midnight raid by a tank battalion, the *London Times* reported, "Outside the university buildings, there was a fresh mass grave. Inside blood streamed from every room."[67]

Sri Lanka

Sri Lanka, formerly Ceylon, is rightfully considered an island paradise, but its tranquility was shattered by centuries of Portuguese, Dutch, and British colonialism. After independence in 1948, postcolonial governments devoted disproportionate resources to expanding the educational system, with the unintended side effect of producing hundreds of thousands of well-educated young people whose career possibilities were practically nonexistent. Frustration with the lack of genuine opportunities and angered by state repression, a massive youth-led uprising in 1971 resulted in the deaths of hundreds if not thousands of youth.[68]

Along with the Cuban Revolution, movements in Vietnam, China, and Russia were admired by the Maoist JVP (Janatha Vimukthi Peramuna or People's Liberation Front), whose leader Rohana Wijeweera believed Sri Lanka could follow in their footsteps. Dubbed Che Kallinya or Che Guaras—the "Che group"—the JVP's 1971 insurrection became internationally known as the Che Guevara Uprising. Che's foco theory, popularized through the writing of Regis Debray, was the downfall of many world movements, but in Sri Lanka, it was particularly disastrous.

At midnight on April 5, 1971, armed JVP militants simultaneously attacked seventy-four police stations across the country.[69] They took over five stations, but more importantly, captured large swaths of the countryside. For two weeks, the army and police failed to curtail insurgents' power. By April 11, at least ninety-two police stations had been attacked. Besides the five that were captured, fifty-six others were damaged, and forty-three more abandoned by the government "for strategic reasons." In nine areas of the countryside, insurgents controlled hundreds of square miles. In addition to many wounded on both sides, some thirty-seven police officers and sixteen members of the armed services were killed.

Declaring a state of emergency, the United Left Front government met the insurrection with ferocious violence. Old Left Trotskyists and Communists were the most vociferous parties in the government calling for its ruthless suppression. These "Golden Brains," as they were known to their admirers, never tired of condemning the "gutter people"—rural youth who joined the JVP. They denounced the JVP as "mad adventurists . . . that must be totally exterminated." Nowhere in the world was the Old Left–New Left schism more violent and hateful than in Sri Lanka.

We will never know the real extent of the murderous spree. More than a thousand rebels and suspected rebels were slaughtered—some say tens of thousands. While imprisoned in 1972, Wijeweera claimed that fifteen thousand revolutionaries had sacrificed their lives, along with as many as thirty thousand civilians who had been killed. Altogether fourteen thousand people where taken into custody. As the prisons overflowed, two universities were converted into large holding cells. Inside the prisons, dissident factions subjected each other to beatings and discrimination. Pro-Wijeweera inquisitors established people's courts, and capital punishment was occasionally meted out along with beatings and various forms of humiliation.[70] So great were the internal schisms that rival JVP politburo members had to be held apart by authorities.

Wijeweera, the insurrection's driving force, took the opportunity of his trial to explain why a New Left had developed: "It was because the old Left Movement had no capacity to take the path to socialism, had gone bankrupt and deteriorated to the position of propping up the capitalist class and had no capacity to protect the rights and needs of the proletariat any longer, that we realized the necessity of a New Left movement."[71] Following his words with bated breath, Western radicals glorified the insurrection and exaggerated its dimensions. Believing that the clash in Ceylon was an indication of future uprisings, Robin Blackburn named Wijeweera "a leading representative" of the "new generation of revolutionaries emerging on the subcontinent." Fred Halliday claimed "despite their defeat, the JVP has shown that armed insurrection is a real and possible form of revolutionary struggle in colonial and ex-colonial countries today."[72] The uprising did have positive effects on the government, compelling land reform as well as changes in housing, education, foreign exchange, income, and fiscal policies.[73] But it ushered in decades of violence that included tens of thousands of political murders and disappearances. For the remainder of the twentieth century, Sri Lankans endured a veritable hell of death squads and bloodshed.

Iran

Iranian students were particularly active against a brutal regime imposed by the U.S. in 1953, when the CIA and a suitcase full of hundred-dollar bills overthrew a democratically elected government.[74] Between the early 1950s and 1963, there were few years without riots and bloody demonstrations.[75] In 1967 and 1968, major protests in Tabriz, Pahlavi, and Tehran resulted in many arrests, and students demonstrated in solidarity with their compatriots in other cities.

The Arab World

The influence of the French May events was felt throughout the Arab world, especially in Lebanon and Egypt.[76] In Jordan, protests began on November 4, 1968, against the king's capitulationism, and before they ended, no fewer than twenty-nine people lay dead (twenty-four civilians, four soldiers, and one policeman.) Lebanon had been relatively peaceful, the "Switzerland of the Arab world," but on November 12, after clashes between students and police turned violent, the government resigned. Prime Minister El-Yafi called for tranquility after one student was killed in Tripoli on November 14.

In Syria, a new critical theatre, revitalized poetry, and "committed art" all accompanied stirrings for democracy.[77] Returning from Germany where he had lived in a commune in Frankfurt, Abu Ali Yassin published *The Taboo Triad: Religion, Sexuality and the Class Struggle*, a pathbreaking book.

On April 28, 1968, more than six thousand Palestinian women marched in Amman against Israeli annexation of Jerusalem. In the occupied territories, girls and boys peacefully protested on many occasions. In October, the mayor of Ramallah, deputy mayor of Jenin, and more than a dozen other prominent political leaders were expelled by Israel on charges they organized youth protests.

Algerian protests were most acute in February 1968, when twenty-eight thousand students went on strike to protest against government control of the national student union. The strike spread from Algiers to universities in Tizi-Ouzou and Oran. Campuses erupted again in January 1971, after six students were arrested at the University of Algiers. The government dissolved the National Union of Algerian Students after militant protests in Constantine and Oran.

Tunisia

In 1968, like today, Tunisian activists were in the forefront of liberty in the Arab world. From 1963 to 1970, the New Left journal *Perspectives Tunisiennes* courageously published ideas and thinking of a new generation that refused to accept dictatorship. A campus movement emerged on February 15, 1965, when college students protested bad food in their cafeterias. The regime responded to such innocent protests with "barbarous repression" by police and National Guard. From 1965 to 1968, high school rebellions against bureaucratic power and arbitrary authority continually occurred. In June 1967, students militantly protested at the embassies of Great Britain and the United States, accusing both countries of being "assassins of Palestinians." Dozens of students, including Mohammed Ben Jennet, were arrested, and Jennet was sentenced to twenty years of hard labor.[78] Student prisoners became a national focal point. On March 15, 1968, Free Assemblies appeared on campuses, demanding freedom for Jennet and other arrestees. A student strike was declared, and on May 1, miners struck in solidarity. While France convulsed in near-revolution that month, Michel Foucault happened to be in Tunisia, where he was astonished to see students go into the streets at the risk of lifelong imprisonment or death.[79] The regime stepped up its repression, condemning as subversives more than two hundred people associated with *Perspectives Tunisiennes*. A few were fined large sums of money, but others were sentenced to anywhere from three months to fourteen years in prison.[80] Inside prison, activists continued their struggle.

Egypt

Beginning on February 21, 1968, student protesters demanded punishment of those responsible for the country's 1967 defeat by Israel. From February

24, after several hundred students barricaded themselves inside Cairo University and were surrounded by police and soldiers, they also called for greater freedom of expression and a truly representative parliament. In ensuing confrontations, workers joined the protests, and at least two workers were killed, 146 policemen injured, and over 600 people arrested.[81] On February 26, President Nasser closed five universities indefinitely but allowed a delegation of two hundred students into the National Assembly for negotiations.

A second round of violent confrontations broke out on May 21 in Al-Mansoura after student strikes demanded greater democracy in the universities. Demonstrations spread to Alexandria and Cairo, where unrest became more political in character. On November 24, all Egyptian universities were closed. Students continued to demonstrate, and sixteen people were killed in Alexandria on November 25 when police with clubs, tear gas, and guns attacked five thousand students. One account told of omnipresent images of Che. President Nasser eventually co-opted student protests.

Iraq

In 1968, in Iraq, the Baath party seized power in what became known as the "July Revolution." The new regime soon was dominated by Saddam Hussein, but at least in its own self-understanding, this revolution was thought to be "laying the foundations of a national, socialist and democratic revolutionary experiment which may serve as a model for Arab countries and for the Third World and will play now, and increasingly in the future, a leading part in the Arab and international revolutionary movement."[82] In the first months after it occurred, the revolution was known as the "White Revolution" because its leadership prohibited bloodshed and sought broad popular support.

Turkey

In the first half of 1968, a "boycott and occupation" movement engulfed Ankara, Istanbul, and every major city, incapacitating the country's system of higher education. On June 10, more than twenty thousand students went on a nationwide strike to demand university reforms. The next day, ten thousand more joined the strike at the University of Ankara. A boycott of examinations by some eighty thousand students convinced university administrators of the need for reforms, including for students to have more voice in key decisions. On July 16, police invaded Istanbul Technical University because of suspicions that it was being used as a staging ground for attacks by antiwar activists on U.S. sailors. One student was killed and twenty-nine others arrested. A week later, renewed confrontations against the American Sixth Fleet took place in Istanbul, and dozens of people were injured.

In December 1968, in Ankara University, right-wing student commandos affiliated with a nationalist party attacked left-wing students who were demanding Turkish withdrawal from NATO. In February 1969, when the United States Sixth Fleet was again visiting Istanbul, thousands of workers and students protested, but right-wing students attacked them. Several people were killed and about two hundred wounded. In the following months, progressive students occupied universities, closing down campuses and using them as organizing bases. Drawing from years of massive campus movements, radical students organized the Federation of the Revolutionary Youth of Turkey in 1969. The next year, many students left the Turkish Labor Party to organize their own militant organizations. Workers and farmers' organizations increased in numbers and in militancy, and government personnel became increasingly restive. In March 1971, a military coup d'état utilized student protests as a pretext to strike down the progressive 1961 constitution. They prohibited worker strikes, banned left-wing organizations, and imprisoned about four thousand intellectuals and students.[83] Among the victims of the 1971 coup were Denis Gezmis, Yusuf Aslan, and Huseyin Inan, three leaders of the 1968 student movement who were executed on May 6, 1972 at Ulucanlar prison in Ankara.

Radical student action combined with militant workers throughout the 1970s, and in 1980 the military staged a third coup d'état—this time to impose a neoliberal regime as they had in Chile in 1973, Thailand and Argentina in 1976, and South Korea following the 1980 Gwangju Uprising.

Pacific

Australia

Despite the best efforts of the government to wall off Australia, international currents of revolution reached its shores.[84] A New Left network of bookstores developed in major cities in the mid-1960s, and a counterculture sprang to life. In 1967, a labor club at Monash University raised money for the NLF in Vietnam at the same time as Australian troops were fighting on the side of the United States, prompting the Australian government to ban such fundraising efforts.[85] Youth culture came to Brisbane in March 1968, when "Foco" opened as a culture club. Within three months, more than 2,500 members inundated it. The French May events had a powerful impact. On July 4, 1968, hundreds of Monash students broke away from an antiwar march and attacked the American consulate in Melbourne, smashing windows and seeking to raise the NLF flag inside the building. With the parallel development of feminism, the first pamphlet was distributed at an antiwar demonstration in December 1969. "Only the Chains Have Changed" called upon women to fight for their freedom "just as Vietnamese are fighting for the right to govern their own country." By

May 1970, feminist Kate Jennings publicly denounced movement men who refused to help stop "backyard abortions" and "personalized slave kitchens."

In 1965, a loose grouping of young indigenous activists blossomed in Redfern, Fitzroy, and South Brisbane.[86] Identifying with Black Power, whose arrival in Australia had been accelerated by books left behind by U.S. troops, they read Fanon and Malcolm X and were especially inspired by the Black Panthers. In Brisbane, they established an Australian Black Panther Party modeled on the U.S.[87] Following in the footsteps of Native Americans' seizure of Alcatraz, indigenous activists began an occupation in front of Parliament House on January 27, 1972, calling themselves the "Aboriginal Embassy." On July 8, police cleared the occupation and arrested eight people. Three days later, hundreds of protesters tried to reoccupy the site but were forced to fight a pitched battle with hundreds of police. Many people were injured and eighteen arrested. On July 30, more than two thousand indigenous activists faced off with thousands of police in the biggest land rights demonstration in Australian history. Confrontation was avoided that day, and soon thereafter the government convened high-level meetings with indigenous representatives to discuss grievances. Activists established the National Black Theatre Company, which staged months of successful shows. The Black Power movement helped to swing public opinion against conservatives, who lost the next election, ending twenty-two years of their rule.

New Zealand

On June 16, 1971, the Polynesian Panther Party arose among Pacific Islanders in New Zealand. Police harassment of indigenous people, including early morning raids on family homes, had become commonplace. In response to police attacks, Panthers staged their own "dawn raids" on homes of the country's leaders. Using floodlights to bang on doors, they roused politicians from sleep and then departed as soon as anyone responded. Evidently, the tactic worked, for morning police raids were soon suspended. Nonetheless, police harassment intensified from 1974 into the early 1980s, and Polynesian Panthers stood firmly against them.

Africa

In Africa, there were major student demonstrations in at least seventeen countries in 1968. Partly as a result of the French May, students and workers in Senegal challenged the government in a general strike. The Black Consciousness Movement emerged in South Africa. In March 1971, students at the University of Abidjan in the Ivory Coast went on strike to protest the Portuguese invasion of Guinea the previous November. In Gabon, the government dissolved all student associations. In Dahomey as well, 1971 was a year of campus turmoil, including among secondary students. In the Sudan, in March 1971, Khartoum University was closed indefinitely after students protested campus conditions.

On December 31, 1968, the National Revolutionary Council led by Marian Ngoubi assumed power in the Congo Republic, renamed it People's Republic of the Congo, and attempted to construct a society freed from neocolonialism.[88] During the 1960s, guerrilla liberation movements in the Portuguese colonies of Guinea-Bissau, Angola, and Mozambique gathered forces and enlarged their bases. In the 1970s, all won liberation.

Nigeria

In Nigeria, a student movement in May 1968 demanded the right of free assembly. The University of Lagos was closed for three weeks. Only when high school students joined the revolt did the government relent.[89] In February 1971, a demonstration of some three thousand students clashed with police, and two students were killed. The university was immediately closed, and police guards were posted. Police used tear gas to repel students who tried to march to the center of the capital. In the fighting that ensued, at least two police posts were burned down, two policemen seriously injured, and at least fifteen students arrested. Students constructed barricades and attacked police buses. Later that year, more than seven hundred students at a grammar school were sent home after they went on a rampage to protest school meals.

Senegal

Senegalese student protests initially centered on dissatisfaction with overall economic and social conditions in the country. Formerly a French colony, the May events in France had a pronounced influence on existing student organizations, many of which were already involved in struggles for recognition of autonomous student unions. When news arrived of the French uprising, the movement was emboldened. As the CIA noted, "events in France and other countries certainly influenced the timing of the demonstrations. Correspondence between FEANF (the Communist front Federation of Black African Students in France) and Senegalese students urging student uprising reportedly was found at Dakar."[90] In 1968, a struggle developed against a new government scholarship policy during which a radical Maoist campus group came to the attention of the CIA. On May 27, when the minister of education announced that the government would not meet students' demands, the Association of Senegalese Students called for a boycott of examinations and a strike. Overwhelming support led to sympathy strikes in high schools in Dakar and other cities. On May 28, the country's president threatened to use force to end the strike. The next day, police invaded Dakar University, and in the ensuing struggle, one student was killed and over nine hundred arrested (including union leaders). On May 31, the National Union of Senegalese Workers called for a general strike and accused the government of mismanaging the economy. Workers went on strike to support the students as well as for higher wages and price controls. The president closed the university and imposed a nationwide state of emergency.[91]

Four days later, labor unions enacted a general strike, and some eight hundred workers were arrested after protesting the occupation of Dakar University by paratroopers.[92] A high school student was killed when force was used to end a high school student boycott. Unable to control the situation, the president requested troops from France. Arriving French soldiers were greeted with more demonstrations and Molotov cocktails. More than two thousand students were arrested. On June 11, Senegal's uprising ended with small pay increases negotiated by "sellout" organizations.

Although the government embarked on an ambitious program of university reforms, student protests continued to confront incompetent teaching and nepotistic appointments. In January 1971, arsonists attacked the center of French cultural exchanges. The next month, when students were arrested for that action, turmoil on campus was heightened by the decision of teachers to launch a strike. Militant student unions called for a boycott of campus examinations. Almost unanimously, students turned in blank examination booklets, and soon thereafter fighting erupted between police and students. The government banned the two most militant student unions and excluded forty-nine students from the university before campuses were quieted.

South Africa

Although 1968 may not have been a high point in South Africa's protracted struggle to abolish apartheid, quite a bit occurred. The assassinations of Martin Luther King and Robert Kennedy profoundly affected South Africans, as did movements in the United States and France. The country suffered under a harsh racist regime, so much so that in 1968, a group of Christians publicly accused Prime Minister Vorster of an "attitude analogous to that of Hitler toward German Christians."[93]

As campuses became centers for organizing, the president of the National Union of South African Students (NUSAS) reported that his colleagues considered Daniel Cohn-Bendit, Rudi Dutschke, and Mark Rudd "heroes" and attempted to import their protest tactics.[94] On August 14, 1968, some one thousand mainly white students condemned the University Council in Cape Town for withdrawing a teaching offer to a black lecturer. More than three hundred students converged at the administration building, pushed through the front doors and conducted a ten-day sit-in—the first in South Africa. On August

19, police attacked about three thousand students outside Witwatersrand University in Johannesburg who were taking part in an illegal march to show solidarity with their striking colleagues in Cape Town. On September 7 in Natal, some three hundred students were suspended for protesting apartheid. When their colleagues protested the expulsions police used dogs to disperse them and arrested seven. Months of protests ensued.

Significantly, Steve Biko emerged as a national leader when he guided black students to leave white-dominated NUSAS and create their own South African Student Organization. Biko's Black Consciousness Movement led to the Soweto uprising in 1976, when the defiant heroism of schoolchildren was answered with the shooting deaths of more than seven hundred unarmed young people and the wounding of at least four thousand more. Soweto sparked a national rebellion among young South Africans.

After his return to South Africa from studying in France, Rick Turner led a sit-in at the University of Cape Town in 1968. An inspiring leader, Turner helped form the white New Left in South Africa. Opposed to both global capitalism and Soviet communism, these young university-based activists subsequently assisted in the formation of progressive trade unions. Police killed Biko on August 18, 1977. Turner fell to an assassin's bullet in January 1978.[95]

The movement of 1968 affected exiled activists as well. On March 17, 1968, future South African president Thabo Mbeki was brutally arrested during the massive anti–Vietnam War demonstration outside the American embassy in London's Grosvenor Square. As the global impetus of 1968 transformed global consciousness, the end of apartheid was only a matter of time. Finally, on February 11, 1990, Nelson Mandela was released from prison after twenty-seven years of captivity.

Congo-Kinshasa (Zaire)

While alienated from the mainstream of Congolese society, Lovanium University, founded in the mid-1950s by Belgian Catholics, became a focal point for transmission of European radical ideas and actions. In 1964, only four years after independence, students won removal of army units then on campus, a precondition they had set for negotiations to end their strike for better instruction and improved living conditions.[96]

On January 4, 1968, the Mobutu government held a public commemoration of the life of the country's first prime minister, Patrice Lumumba, assassinated in 1961 by a Belgian firing squad assisted by the CIA. One of the invited guests was U.S. Vice President Hubert Humphrey. Student activists protested Humphrey's presence, both because they vehemently opposed the Vietnam War and because of the U.S. role in killing Lumumba.[97] Key student leaders were imprisoned or expelled from the university. For the remainder of the year, there were strikes and demonstrations at all three universities in the country. Lovanium was occupied for two weeks by the army. In June, high school students protested the procedures regarding their final exams.

News of the French May events slowly reached the country and helped to inspire a small circle of radical activists. On June 3, 1969, the night before they planned to demonstrate, the secretive group announced the protest at Red Square, the center of the campus. The next day, nearly all of Lovanium's three thousand students turned out for the march. What began as a peaceful walk to protest the Mobutu dictatorship turned into a bloodbath. The army appeared out of nowhere and opened fire, killing dozens of people. No one will know how many were murdered since the bodies of the dead students were taken away and buried anonymously in a mass grave.[98] Mobutu continued to rule the country for another three decades after the massacre, but the bloodshed in 1969 forever stained his reputation and standing.

Two years after the June 4 massacre, a planned commemoration at Lovanium University again resulted in the army shutting down the campus. A Belgian priest was arrested for his organizing. Students mounted solidarity demonstrations in the People's Republic of the Congo and in Zambia. After closing the university, Mobutu ordered all three thousand of its students— the entire student body—drafted into the army. In addition, sixteen activists were sentenced to ten years in prison. Mobutu ordered the university's name changed to the University of Kinshasa, which for years was in a state of ruins left by the regime's designed neglect.

Ghana

Africa's insurgencies were constantly undermined by Western imperialism. Although the murder of Patrice Lumumba is well known, less remembered is the coup d'état in Ghana on February 24, 1966, which overthrew revolutionary leader President Kwame Nkrumah while he was on his way to Hanoi to visit Ho Chi Minh. Ghanaian students militantly fought against the new government. In 1971, the National Union of Ghana Students spurred great protests at graduation. On March 13, students called for the government to oppose apartheid in South Africa and to grant amnesty to all Ghanaians in exile, including former president Nkrumah.

Zimbabwe (formerly Rhodesia)

In 1970, students went on strike when the University of Rhodesia became independent of its counterparts in London and Birmingham. On June 23, 1970, secondary school pupils at Plumtree protested the Smith regime's ties to Britain. Protesters carried posters claiming: "Rhodesia is a police state"; "Stop working for these White Pigs"; and "No Second South Africa." All over the country hundreds of students were arrested in protests against "white imperialism." Years earlier, the Catholic Church had integrated its colleges in Salisbury, a move which brought the settler state to cut off these colleges from all government subsidies for education.[99]

Zambia

On April 16, 1971, more than eight hundred students protested against an incompetent registrar at the University of Zambia, setting in motion a militant student movement that came to protest French support for the apartheid system in South Africa. In July, some sixty-five members of the academic staff publicly supported a student march on the French embassy, where police had attacked them. President Kenneth Kaunda banned all further demonstrations related to South Africa. As confrontations continued, students took control of the university on July 13 and prepared Molotov cocktails and other weapons to defend themselves. That night, as the army and police arrived in force, students left without a fight. The campus was closed, seventy-five students were excluded when it reopened, and two foreign lecturers in the Department of English were expelled from the country.

Ethiopia

For years, aspirations of Ethiopian students were either ignored or heavily repressed. In 1964, the Crocodile Society began to propagate Marxist-Leninist ideology on campus, and by 1967, Maoism had become ascendant. To protest neocolonial penetration of their society, campus radicals attacked a fashion show on March 30 at foreigner-dominated University College of Addis Ababa. Police arrested thirty-eight students; the university was closed and remained so for weeks. The CIA noted that these April protests exhibited the first open expression of anti-U.S. sentiments.[100] By attacking a fashion show, radicals hoped to facilitate a cultural revolution that could reverse the ravages of American neocolonialist culture.[101]

In response to government repression, about one hundred thousand students mobilized. All student publications were banned. Outside the U.S. information office, three days of strident anti-American protests began in April. Students went on strike after the university reopened. As protests continued through November, the prime minister agreed to some of their demands, and students returned to classes.

In March 1971, university students demonstrated in support of a strike by teachers in Addis Ababa, but students' main concerns were campus issues. High school students criticized their university counterparts and mobilized around far more visionary demands such as land reform, high bus fares, and the rounding up of beggars in "poor houses." Most schools in the capital were closed by student protests. Militant actions targeted Mercedes-Benz cars and showrooms. Later, city buses were attacked to dramatize high fares being charged by a so-called charitable organization (His Imperial Majesty's Trust Foundation). Students' most popular actions involved going into the city's markets and compelling merchants to lower their prices to affordable levels. Police refused to intervene, and even after the army was called in, soldiers were arrested for collaborating with students.[102]

Angola, Mozambique, Guinea-Bissau (then Portuguese colonies)

Shortly after World War II, Great Britain and France had been compelled to relinquish political control of their colonial possessions in Africa, but Portugal remained particularly vehement in its desire to hold on to its African colonies in Angola, Mozambique, and Guinea-Bissau. Portuguese army officers, many of whom had been captured and persuaded to act by African guerrillas, would finally overthrow the military dictatorship in 1974. Despite enormous hardships, the capacity of these liberation movements to fight racism and to conduct humanitarian revolutions was remarkable. From the jungles facing aerial bombardment, Amilcar Cabral (leader of the movement in Guinea-Bissau) praised the solidarity of the capitalist metropoles, which he named as sources of inspiration for fighters in their jungle hideouts.

Priests who sided with the liberation movements in the Portuguese colonies of Angola and Mozambique (or those who refused to explicitly support the regimes there) suffered long imprisonments and exile. As the brutality of repression mounted, the expulsion of missionaries and state intervention in the church became more frequent. In 1968, the major seminary in Mozambique was taken out of the hands of its staff and entrusted to conservative Portuguese Jesuits. Two-thirds of the seminarians refused to continue teaching, and a number joined revolutionary groups.[103] Pressure on the pope was brought to bear by the priests, and on July 1, 1970, Pope Paul granted a Vatican audience to leaders of national liberation movements in Portuguese colonies.

Burkina Faso

Within eight years of liberation from its status as a French colony in 1958, Burkina Faso (which means "land of incorruptible people") was impacted heavily by the global sixties. In 1966, trade unions and progressive forces in the military overthrew the postcolonial regime in a coup d'état celebrated today as the "January 3 Revolution." Although a national holiday, the January 3rd coup failed to produce real democracy. It was not until 1983 that Thomas Sankara, the "African Che," was thrust into the office of president. In four years, Sankara implemented one of the most far-reaching reform programs ever attempted in Africa. While many African countries suffered famine, Burkina Faso became self-sufficient in food production.[104] Sankara's government promoted women, built the economy, sponsored world-renowned cultural festivals, and built youth groups through universal education and literacy. To dramatize the country's new independence, he changed its name from Upper Volta to Burkina Faso. Although Sankara was killed by his lieutenant Blaise Compaore in a coup supported by France and the Ivory Coast, many of the young people educated in Sankara's schools led a revolution in 2014 that overthrew Compaore and established the country's current democracy.

Europe

Of all the events of 1968, the near-revolution in France is most important, and all of Chapter 3 is devoted to it. In West Germany, the student movement and extraparliamentary opposition created the country's biggest crisis since World War II. In Italy, militant student protests helped detonate the Hot Autumn of 1969, when five million workers went on strike. A small general strike of workers and students erupted in Spain in 1967, and twenty thousand students were expelled from universities. Creative protests in Holland, Denmark, and Switzerland helped subvert the seriousness of their cultures. Suffering under a military dictatorship, Greek students occupied the Polytechnic in 1973.

West Germany

The German New Left was among the most theoretically inclined and internationally conscious members of the global movement. Students demonstrated against the president of Senegal when he arrived at the Frankfurt Book Fair because he had suppressed the student movement at home; they protested the arrival of Moise Tshombe for his role in the murder of Patrice Lumumba; and they mobilized against the Korean secret service for its treatment of dissidents. The internationalism of the German Sozialistischer Deutscher Studentenbund (SDS) defined that organization's identity from its inception, leading it to break away from its parent organization, the German Social Democratic Party. As the Social Democrats formed a Grand Coalition with the Christian Democratic Union to govern Germany, SDS became increasingly extraparliamentary, using "sit-ins," "go-ins," and demonstrations as a means of precipitating parliamentary action.[105]

Although SDS in Germany and the United States shared the same initials and grew out of similar social democratic labor groups, the two organizations were not formally connected. German SDS was explicitly "socialist," while SDS in the United States (Students for a Democratic Society) contained a more diverse and theoretically underdeveloped membership. Nonetheless, the two groups were intuitively tied together. Although their actions were quite similar

(German SDS adopted the "sit-in"—both the word and the practice—from the United States), the German organization was never able to synthesize a cultural politics like the U.S. counterculture. The German New Left was the first massive opposition to the Cold War consensus that took up the long-abandoned revolutionary tradition of the German working class, a heritage betrayed by the opportunism of Social Democracy and nearly destroyed by the Nazi slaughter and Stalinist purges.

More than any other New Left organization, the roots of German SDS were in the dynamics of European political discourse. Its first president was Helmut Schmidt (later a chancellor of West Germany), and some of SDS's initial campaigns protested the presence of former Nazis in administrations of universities and the government. As the organization grew, its membership became a unique combination of exiles from East Germany, radical Christians, and libertarian socialists. Divided Germany was a focal point for many of international problems of the Cold War era, and the German New Left became increasingly oriented to global issues.

When the Shah of Iran hoped to attend the opera in West Berlin on June 2, 1967, he was greeted by several thousand demonstrators, whose presence made them the targets of vicious attacks by both the Berlin police and the Shah's secret police (SAVAK). One student, Benno Ohnesorg, was shot in the head and killed, an incident that had profound repercussions for the German movement. A few days later, twenty thousand people formed a miles-long funeral procession that was allowed to pass uninterrupted through East Germany without usual time-consuming border checks. After Ohnesorg's funeral, the German New Left convened in Hannover.

Although the Hannover Congress should have been a time for unity, it marked the beginning of the end for the German New Left. It was there that Jürgen Habermas first raised the problem of "Left fascism" for discussion, and the acrimony that ensued eventually led to sit-ins at the Frankfurt Institute for Social Research (where Habermas, Adorno, and Horkheimer taught). Decades after the Hannover Congress, the Frankfurt School continues to be poorly regarded by German activists, while the Bewegung der 2. Juni (or June 2 Movement, a guerrilla group which took its name from the day of Ohnesorg's death) are regarded as folk heroes. In Tehran, there now exists a Benno Ohnesorg street.

By the fall of 1967, much of German society opposed SDS, but the movement had entrenched itself on the campuses, particularly in West Berlin where thousands of people voted to reconstitute the Free University as a "Critical University": a self-managed institution oriented toward changing society and governed by university-wide plebiscites. Of course, university administrators refused to accept the results of the vote reconstituting the university, but there was little they could do to stop the growing involvement of thousands of

Rudi Dutschke.

students in an extraparliamentary opposition (APO).

At the beginning of 1968, German SDS hosted an international gathering of five thousand antiwar activists in Berlin to discuss solidarity actions with Vietnam. Significantly, many participants in the subsequent student revolt in France participated in the Berlin conference. Before the delegates took to the streets for one of the largest peace demonstrations in German history, they issued a call to the world movement: "We call on the anti-imperialist resistance movement . . . to continue to build unified mass demonstrations against U.S. imperialism and its helpers in Western Europe. In the course of this unified struggle, political and organizational working unity between the revolutionary movements in Western Europe must be intensified and a United Front must be built."[106]

Of the many diverse groups that constituted the APO, the largest umbrella organization sponsored an annual Easter March for disarmament. Unlike the Campaign for Nuclear Disarmament in Great Britain (whose membership and base of support began to erode in the early 1960s), the German antinuclear impetus saw its numbers swell: from 100,000 marchers in 1966 to 150,000 in 1967.[107] By Easter of 1968, more than 300,000 Germans marched for peace in the midst of a violent upheaval caused by the attempted assassination of Rudi Dutschke, one of the principal spokespersons of SDS.[108] On March 11, the Thursday before Easter, a Munich house painter carrying a pistol and a newspaper clipping of Martin Luther King's assassination a week earlier, fired three shots at "Red Rudi." One shot hit him in the head, but Dutschke survived, at least until December 1979, when he died from epilepsy caused by the bullet that hit him. The fact that Dutschke's attacker carried a clipping of King's assassination confirmed many people's suspicions that the German media's campaign against SDS had helped cause the attack, and throughout Germany, the APO attacked publications of the Springer Press, a newspaper monopoly that controlled over 80 percent of German daily newspapers. Axel Springer had long used his power over German public opinion to incite readers against the student movement. Not only did the APO blame Springer for Dutschke's fate, they also saw his monopoly of the media as a symbol of the problem of private ownership of social resources.

The anti-Springer campaign was not confined to Germany. Marchers took to the streets in Vienna, Amsterdam, Oslo, Rome, New York, and more than a dozen cities. In London, the demonstration of March 17 on the U.S. embassy prominently included anti-Springer posters carried by at least sixty members of Berlin and Frankfurt SDS. In Paris, two days after Dutschke was shot, more than one thousand people demonstrated in front of the German embassy. Significantly, that demonstration was the first time that a coalition of all New Left groups in France worked together. On March 19, several thousand people again converged on the German embassy, but this time, issues relating to France were also raised.[109] Three days later, the administration building at Nanterre University was occupied to protest the U.S. war against Vietnam, an action which led to the formation of the March 22 Movement, the group often credited with sparking the May events.

After Dutschke was shot and Springer Press was under attack throughout Germany, the stage was set for the German Bundestag (or Parliament) to impose the Notstandsgesetze, emergency laws aimed at social control that had long been desired by the German Right, but which had not been politically possible until the APO's eruption and near-revolution across the Rhine. In a concerted campaign to stop the new laws from being passed, the APO mobilized tens of thousands of Germans. Violent clashes broke out in Munich on May 15 and police killed two students.[110] Students in high schools and colleges boycotted lectures. In Berlin, a "permanent" teach-in of several thousand students was convened. Demonstrations in thirty-one cities protested the new law. On May 20, hundreds of students occupied the Free University. In Bochum, a coordinating center was set up and a call was sent out for a general strike on May 29 (a strike which some believed would match the one of nine million workers which had brought France to a standstill that same month). The strike was endorsed by representatives of 50,000 IG Metall workers in Munich and 120,000 unionists in Cologne, while in Frankfurt, 10,000 workers downed tools in a brief warning strike. Hundreds of steel workers in Bochum went on a wildcat strike, as did two hundred chemical workers and hundreds of Ford workers in Cologne.

On May 27, the APO staged go-ins during theater performances in Berlin, Munich, Bremen, Bonn, and Stuttgart, and the entrances to universities were barricaded in Bochum, Frankfurt, Hamburg, Göttingen, and Aachen. Actors on the stage of the Frankfurt Theater stopped their production and called on the audience to oppose the emergency laws. The cabaret group Floh de Cologne called on all cabaret workers and artists to work against the legislation. Massive demonstrations continued as the Bundestag debated the bill. Finally, on May 30, the date the legislation was to be voted on, the APO blocked traffic in downtown Berlin, Cologne, Hamburg, and Hannover. In Munich, the tracks in the central train station were blockaded by thousands of people. In Bonn, one hundred thousand people marched, while twenty thousand trade unionists mobilized in Dortmund.[111]

The conservative political climate in Germany, however, was such that the German Bundestag overwhelmingly approved the emergency legislation, enabling the government to curtail individual rights during declared "national emergencies." At the same time, the intensity of the movement and attacks on it led to the formation of adventurist guerrilla groups and dogmatic Maoist tendencies within SDS. Soon sexism and internal splits helped destroy the organization. In the late 1960s, the German New Left discovered rock 'n' roll at the same time as the Kreuzberg Hash Rebels came into existence. As guerrilla groups like the Red Army Faction and the June 2 Movement began their armed attacks and bombings, their marginalization as "terrorists" helped depoliticize the mass movement and signaled the end of the APO. Despite its quick demise, the New Left permanently altered the political landscape of West Germany, setting the stage for the emergence of the Autonomen and the Green Party ten years later.[112]

On July 4, 1971, in the Berlin neighborhood of Kreuzberg, a vacant house was occupied and turned into a center for young people. From this inauspicious beginning emerged a movement that built a network of dozens of squatted houses. European squatters successfully won control of group homes, where they lived forms of collective life that negated the atomization to which consumerism had condemned them. They governed themselves through horizontal relationships and organized autonomous campaigns against nuclear power, militarism, and the international system of finance capital. In Berlin alone, dozens of occupied group houses contained hundreds of activists, causing the government enormous problems.

The feminist movement was an important link between 1968 and subsequent autonomous movements. On September 13, 1968, a critical date in the history of the German New Left and of German feminism, Helke Sander, a member of the Berlin Action Council for Women's Liberation, gave an impassioned speech at the national meeting of SDS in Frankfurt calling on her male comrades in SDS to remove "the blinders you have over your eyes" and take note of their own sexism.[113] As expected by some, the meeting returned to business as usual as soon as she finished speaking. But when SDS theoretician Hans-Jürgen Krahl was in the middle of his speech (having nothing to do with the feminist appeal for support), another female delegate from Berlin screamed at him: "Comrade Krahl, you are objectively a counterrevolutionary and an agent of the class enemy!" She then hurled several tomatoes in the direction of the podium. One hit Krahl squarely in the face.

Many SDS women were embarrassed by the action, but the deeds of the Berlin Action Council for Women's Liberation electrified feminists and are considered to be the beginning of the autonomous women's movement. Initially, nothing was more important to the new movement than the campaign to liberalize the abortion laws. Statutes criminalizing abortion had been on the books since 1871,[114] and intermittent struggles at the turn of the twentieth century had failed to win significant reform.

In 1973, Alice Schwarzer published her book *Women's Work—Women's Liberation*, and a few months later a German translation appeared of the classic text by Mariarosa Dalla Costa and Selma James.[115] If the personal is political, as these theorists maintain, then unpaid domestic labor performed by women (estimated to be in the billions of hours) should be considered part of the economy—counted in the calculation of gross domestic product and compensated in cash. They insisted that if women were paid for what is now unpaid work, the division between the world of paid work and that of unpaid labor would be rendered meaningless. This could lead to a complete revaluation of women's roles and an end to their relegation to the home and the private sphere, where they serve as unnoticed appendages to men.

Italy

Beginning in the fall of 1967, Italy witnessed the eruption of a protest movement that built up on campuses until the spring of 1968, when the revolt spilled over to the whole society. In 1968, nearly all Italian universities were taken over by popular movements that governed them through democratic general assemblies. Traditional hierarchies within academia were overthrown, as was the segregation of students from society. Protests began over academic issues like inadequate classroom facilities and archaic standards of excellence, but by November of 1967, students opposing the university's authoritarian power occupied Turin University. In huge assemblies, students debated the meaning of their revolt, and it was there that self-management was first proposed and massively embraced.

As opposed to comanagement, which called for professors and administrators to appoint a few students to serve on joint committees, students in Turin demanded nothing less than full control over the curriculum, classrooms, and life of the university.[116] The University of Urbino had established comanagement in the Faculty of Economics in 1966, but student protesters soon objected to these joint student-faculty groups on the grounds that they were a form of co-optation. When students occupied the University of Turin on November 27, 1967, they refused to negotiate because they felt they couldn't express their demands until an open general assembly of students could freely discuss their needs. After a month of democratic discussions, the students united around the demand that all university decisions be made at open general assemblies

Democratic and leftist students clash with neo-fascists at Rome University. *Black Dwarf.*

of students. After the administration called in police, disruption of classes became the norm for months.

Although there were numerous student protests in Italy in the early 1960s, in the year ending in 1968, the campus movement spread all over the country. The center of protests was at Rome University, where over four hundred people were arrested and hundreds injured in February and March. The university was twice ordered closed. On March 1, 1968, intense clashes with police took place near the School of Architecture with many arrests. On April 27, thousands of university and high school students protested the continuing detention of architecture students. Militant students were armed with iron bars, chains, and Molotov cocktails. Significant protests also occurred in Turin, Florence, Padua, Venice, Naples, and Bologna. Copying German attacks against the Springer Press, many people blocked distribution of newspapers in Venice. Students in Rome demonstrated for the right of opposite sex visitors in dormitory rooms to be legal. Right-wing students clashed with left-wing students at many universities.

In May, as events in France unfolded, strikes and sit-ins spread to campuses in Florence, Turin, Pisa, Venice, Milan, Naples, Padua, Palermo, Bologna, and Bari,[117] touching off a political crisis that forced Prime Minister Aldo Moro and his cabinet to resign. In Italy, as around the world in 1968, the sheer *quantity* of protests produced a qualitative break. Almost everything that transpired had happened before, but this time it mushroomed to involve tens, perhaps hundreds of thousands of students in the space of less than nine months. It was as if isolated actions of the preceding five years had been compressed into one year and multiplied by the participation of thousands of new people. In 1968, for the first time, neither the issues nor the actions were isolated.[118] The movement spread to high schools in the fall. A general student strike in Palermo targeted the entire system of youth repression and capitalist exploitation. In November, students all over the country demanded campus reforms.

New ties to workers were successfully forged, first indicated by a peaceful twenty-four-hour joint strike on November 14, when twelve million workers struck in defense of the retirement system and for educational reform. After police killed two farmworkers in Sicily, a general strike spread throughout the island and to other parts of the country. On New Year's Eve, students in Pisa peacefully protested against wealthy patrons of La Bussola nightclub. When clashes occurred, police killed one student.

In the next year, the student movement transformed itself and joined workers' struggles, hoping to spark an explosion like the "French May" and to seize leadership of the workers' movement from unions.[119] During the Hot Autumn of 1969, unrest spread explosively, and the type of dissent was qualitatively new: the movement had clear revolutionary intent. Factory workers by the thousands took over their factories, not for the purpose of running them but to turn them into bases for organizing in conjunction with their new allies—ex-students experienced in the struggles of the previous year and office workers. "The factory is our Vietnam" was one popular slogan. Creative strikes—hiccup and checkerboard—were autonomously organized through which workers controlled production. (Hiccup strikes involved whole factories suddenly coming to a standstill. When management composed itself and workers were ordered back to work, the workers complied, only to repeat the scenario every half hour. A checkerboard strike involved one section of a factory downing tools and walking off the job until ordered to return—at which point another sector took its turn in a prearranged sequence designed to stop production. Sometimes workers with last names from A-L took the first shift of the strike. At other times, the formula was reversed.) Dual power emerged (notably in the Montecatini-Edison factories in Venice and the Fiat plants in Turin). Five million workers (more than 25

Street protest in Rome, May 1968. SV-Bilderdienst.

percent of the labor force) struck in 1969, and hundreds of thousands of workers demonstrated, occupied factories, and committed sabotage. The government and corporations struck back, arresting thirteen thousand people and firing or suspending thirty-five thousand workers.[120]

As struggles intensified, fifty thousand engineering workers took part in a national demonstration on September 25.[121] At the beginning of October, the city of Milan was brought to a standstill by roadblocks organized by workers from hundreds of factories and joined by thousands of students. In the province surrounding Milan, one hundred thousand engineering workers struck simultaneously on October 7. Estimates told of more than seventy million hours of work lost in 1969 to unrest in the engineering sector alone.[122] As strikes spread throughout the country, they enjoyed overwhelming public support, and the minister of labor was compelled to sign an agreement with the unions that included all major demands. Hoping to pacify the young hotheads, management agreed to mammoth wage increases: 23.4 percent from 1969 to 1970, and 16.6 percent a year later. Nonetheless workers were not quieted. The frenetic pace of work, long a source of agony that unions had been incapable of changing, was slowed by workers' concerted campaigns to reduce the speed at which they worked. The length of the workweek was similarly reduced through absenteeism or by simply leaving work early. Workers were protected from aggressive bosses by bands of "red handkerchiefs," named for the attire they wore to mask their identities when they were called on to intimidate foremen and management.

Trade unions were able to lead the way out of the Hot Autumn by negotiating a settlement which, at least on paper, granted the workers significant wage increases as well as better working conditions. When all was said and done, mammoth wage increases had been won, but even more significantly, the working class had reconstituted itself as a historical force. Their new demands and aspirations fell outside unions' traditional purview.

With unions firmly in control of the workers' movement, numerous New Left parties and groups (Potere Operaio, Lotta Continua, and the group that published *Il Manifesto*) became increasingly active outside the factories, particularly in working-class communities. "Let us seize the city" was a slogan put forth by Lotta Continua in the hope of persuading workers to occupy vacant housing. Despite their failure to liberate the working class from trade unions, the new generation of radicals deepened the political crisis of Italy and created the preconditions for a vast cultural revolt.[123]

Like never before, Italian women organized an autonomous movement that challenged blatant patriarchal laws and practices. During the student movement and Hot Autumn, women who later formed the nucleus for the women's movement gained valuable experience. From the very beginning, many females were active in student protests, and some began to meet in women-only groups. Within the New Left, however, women were often relegated to roles as secretaries inside the movement, a situation reflected in the ironic slogan "From the angel of the hearth to the angel of the copying machine." In 1970, Rivolta Femminile was created in Rome and Milan and Lotta Feminista (Female Struggle) collectives were formed in Rome and Padua.[124]

In Torino, Lotta Continua organized joint worker-student actions. Photographer unknown.

By 1977, a new generation of youth was once again on the offensive on campuses in Italy, and violent attacks by both right-wing conservatives and Communists occurred. Off the campuses, the "Metropolitan Indians" shot back at police in the midst of mass demonstrations.[125] Under the slogan, "1968 has returned," the movement of the late 1970s in Italy exploded in a merger of culture and politics that the first phase of the Italian New Left had never attained. By then, however, the worldwide cultural revolt had been depoliticized, and the Italian youth revolt of the late 1970s suffered the same fate.[126]

Spain

In Spain as in Italy, the student movement erupted and was able to forge significant links with the working class. Although a general strike of workers and students took place in 1967, it was nowhere near the scale of the May events in France. The escalating spiral of confrontation began on January 27, 1967. After two weeks of student protests and police attacks, over one hundred thousand workers in Madrid answered students' call for a national demonstration for an end to the Franco dictatorship and support of independent student and worker unions. It was business as usual when the joint demonstration was viciously attacked and hundreds were arrested. The next day, as students regrouped, police invaded the cafeteria at the University of Madrid. Throughout the country, hundreds more students were arrested. Rafael Moreno, an activist in Madrid, was murdered by police in his family home. When student delegates from all of Spain arrived in Valencia for a meeting of the illegal *Sindicato Democrático de Estudiantes* (Democratic Student Union), they were systematically arrested and beaten. In response, sixty thousand factory workers and thousands of railroad workers went out on strike on January 30.[127] The next day, the University of Madrid was closed, and a week later, thousands of workers joined in a general strike. Over twenty thousand students were expelled from Spanish universities, but the revolt continued to spread and street fighting broke out in all the major cities. Finally the army mobilized to control the country.

Although movement activists suffered incredibly, their spirits remained strong, and they did not give in. In October 1967, teach-ins on Vietnam led to refrains of "Ho, Ho, Ho Chi Minh." At least twenty thousand people became members of illegal student groups in Madrid alone. On October 27, a general strike called by students received the support of Workers Commissions, but it was averted when four hundred delegates of Workers Commissions were arrested. The next week, Spanish students elected delegates to their illegal student union. Those elected were promptly arrested, but over 100,000 students (out of a total of 147,000 in all of Spain) went on strike. Fires were set in the University of Madrid.[128] This time the police response was even more brutal than it had been in January. Another activist, Enrique Ruano, died while in police custody, and a virtual state of siege was declared to combat the "subversion of the universities."

Although heavily repressed, the Spanish students maintained the integrity of their vision. Their union, which they had fought for since 1956, continued to be organized along absolutely horizontal lines. In January of 1968, activists concluded that the actions of the government precluded reforms, adding "we know that it will be possible to destroy it only through violence."[129] After police used water cannons to prevent students from meeting, one thousand workers protested repression of students as well as the U.S. war in Vietnam. Carrying posters reading "Yankees out of Spain," on May 1, the first May Day protests since the Civil War occurred. More than 250 people were arrested in Madrid and 50 more in Barcelona.

From March 28 to May 6, 1968, Madrid University remained closed. Four days of riots at the University of Madrid involved students using Molotov cocktails and police responding with batons, water cannons, and horses. Not until the government agreed to campus reforms at the end of May did violence subside. In November, the University of Madrid was again closed when students refused to submit to new repressive measures. Strikes spread to universities in Oviedo, Granada, and Valencia.

Intense struggles both on and off the campuses in Spain gave new energy to movements for regional autonomy, particularly in the Basque country. In 1968, ETA (acronym for Basque Land and Liberty) began its armed struggle, joining numerous other guerrilla groups fighting the Franco dictatorship. With the transition to a corporate democracy ten years after the renewed upsurge of 1967, the movements for regional autonomy intensified. In 1982, five decades after their bloody civil war, a socialist government was democratically elected, but its policies failed to achieve substantial changes.

The Netherlands

A creative use of happenings characterized the Dutch movement in the 1960s. Although the Provos numbered no more than a few hundred, they attracted attention by releasing chickens in the streets during rush hour and placing free white bicycles around Amsterdam. In 1966 municipal elections, they were able to attract thirteen thousand votes. Provos gained their name from Amsterdam's chief of police when he tried to describe marginalized youth protests against U.S. policy in Vietnam, air pollution, traffic congestion, and even against the marriage of the crown princess. Following their voluntary dissolution, the Kabouters (Gnomes) emerged as a political party. By the mid-1970s, thousands of squatters lived in hundreds of formerly abandoned buildings, and squatters' councils provided opportunities for democratic participation in planning group actions.

Provos hoist a white bicycle on March 19, 1966. Cor Jaring.

Denmark

Like the Dutch Provos, Danish activists emerged as cultural radicals in the early 1960s. In February 1963, a building slated for demolition was occupied and a group home survived until 1968, when police evicted it. One of the groups that emerged took the initiative to take over Christiania, an abandoned military base in Copenhagen.[130] Residents built homes and businesses, established assembly democracy, and defended their territory. Their Rainbow Army was able to mobilize thousands of people to defend the free space both from police and motorcycle gangs. More recently, the state's legalization campaign and gentrification have changed Christiania, but it remains an important symbol of grassroots initiative and peaceful capacity for coexistence.

On March 21, 1968, the Danish university movement began when students in Copenhagen spray painted campus walls with slogans like "Break the Power of Professors" and "Participation Now!" University students occupied the Faculty of Psychology until their demands were met to have more say in university affairs. After lawmakers abolished free railroad tickets for children, ten thousand pupils threw tomatoes and apple cores at the Parliament building. In early April, thousands of people protested outside the American embassy, but police attacked and beat them. On April 27, more than twenty-five thousand protesters, the largest demonstration in Danish history, gathered outside the U.S. embassy in Copenhagen. Clashes with more than six hundred police left many injured on both sides.

Belgium

On March 2, 1968, about ten thousand antiwar protesters clashed with police outside the U.S. embassy in Brussels. By May, as the society became activated, a student revolt convened daily free assemblies of students and staff. Aspiring to make the university truly democratic as a "step toward democratization of the society," there were fifty days of free assemblies. A huge banner outside the occupied university read, "The university is open for the entire population."

England/UK

The global energies of 1968 galvanized a host of small publications and autonomous action groups such as squatters and anarchists. The most significant demonstration came on March 17, 1968, when thirty thousand protesters confronted police at the U.S. embassy in Grosvenor Square. Besides future South African president Thabo Mbeki, others among the thousands present including Mick Jagger and John Scarlett, subsequently head of MI6—British foreign intelligence.

In England, university students are particularly elite, and the thrust of the movement at schools like the Royal College of Art and Cambridge, Oxford, and

Hull Universities was largely confined to educational reform. In 1968, there were several significant upsurges of political activity. The first manifesto of the British student power movement was published on May 10, a week after several hundred radical students at the University of Leeds confronted conservative parliamentarian Patrick Wall and his wife for their support of racism in Rhodesia. On May 26, a thousand students tried to storm the French embassy in London in solidarity with the French uprising. In the same month, inspired art students at Hornsey School of Art transformed a teach-in on art education into a takeover of campus buildings that lasted from May 28 to July 8. Remarkably, a localized struggle turned into one in which students called for a fundamental transformation of the educational system.[131] On June 8, the administration building at the University of Hull was taken over by students who insisted they be given voting rights in all major decisions as well as control over dormitories. In October the student union at LSE voted to occupy the campus in protest of the Vietnam War. On October 27, over one hundred thousand people peacefully paraded through London. Militant sit-ins occurred at the London School of Economics and at Essex, Hornsey, Hull, and Birmingham.[132]

In 1970, there were direct actions at one-third of Britain's universities following disclosures that secret political files were being assembled on movement teachers and students. At Cambridge University, after a militant demonstration against supporters of the Greek junta, the subsequent trial of fifteen activists resulted in six receiving prison terms ranging from nine to eighteen months.

The movement in Great Britain never reached the proportions of its counterparts in Germany, France, or the United States, in part because many activists went into the Labour Party in the belief it could be radicalized.[133] The working class in Britain became activated with the world economic downturn beginning in 1968, and in the next four years, a record number of strikes prompted Tony Benn to remark that "we can speak of Labour's own New Left as a force to be reckoned with." In August, a thousand nurses marched on Downing Street to protest working conditions. Within factories, the labor movement led by shop stewards massively contested the capitalist order. One estimate tells of two hundred occupations from 1969 to 1970 and over one hundred in the following three years.[134] In 1972, a miners' strike paralyzed the country, and two years later, a second miners' strike led to elections that brought the Labour Party to power (but like the Spanish socialists, progressive politicians failed to satisfy even minimal needs of New Left partisans).

Old Left Trotskyists, notably from the International Socialists, International Marxist Group, Socialist Workers Party, and *New Left Review*, played a disproportionate role in the British movement, but many New Left theoreticians remained distant from the activist milieu. Women began to raise feminist issues within many of these parties, and at the same time the influence of American feminism helped galvanize autonomous women's groups through-out the country.

Beginning in 1968, squatters first appeared in East London when activists took over abandoned government-owned buildings. Artists in Notting Hill took control of Powis Square, and the movement spread to Hackney, Brixton, Battersea, Hammersmith, and Fulham. In the mid-1970s, Brighton alone had 150 squats, and a campaign there successfully stopped a project that would have destroyed hundreds of homes to build a highway.

On December 1, Black Power arrived in Britain with a conference that drew participation of seven hundred immigrants, mostly from South Asia.

Greece

In 1968, the Papadopoulos dictatorship tightly censored news, so the May events in France were simply not reported when they happened. Of course, it is impossible to seal off borders to information flows, and the ideas of the '68 movement slowly arrived. On November 3, the funeral of former Prime Minister George Papandreou, who died under house arrest, turned into an antidictatorship protest. Clashes with police resulted in forty arrests. All except four of the arrestees received prison sentences of one-and-a-half to four years.

The American counterculture had a huge effect on Greek youth, from folk music cafes to rock music. Small groups of radical publishers translated texts from around the world, including Jerry Rubin's *Do It!* The youth movement grew until the police could no longer contain it. In 1973, the first buildings at the Polytechnic in Athens were occupied by anarchists, who were immediately called CIA provocateurs by the Greek Communist Party. Within a few days, young people flooded into the occupied university. At that point, Communist youth were sent into open assemblies. Party youth created a radio station and attempted to claim credit for the occupation, but the free flowing direct democracy had little to

In 1967, a U.S.-supported, right-wing military government took control of Greece. Many groups, both in exile and in Greece, organized to oppose this junta. Relief print, 1969.

do with their Stalinist variety of hierarchical discipline. The first libertarian slogans, such as "Challenge Authority," appeared at the Polytechnic, and students also chanted praise for the courage of their counterparts in Thailand who had overthrown their military dictatorship a month before. At the occupied Polytechnic, a giant banner reading "OXI!" ("NO!") drew inspiration from indigenous refusal to submit to Italy in World War II, as well as from Herbert Marcuse's characterization of the New Left as the "Great Refusal." On November 17, soldiers using a tank, bazooka, and automatic weapons retook the Polytechnic. In the process, they killed thirty-four people. Eight days after the slaughter, Papadopoulos was overthrown from by his own army, but the military's days in power were numbered, and it fell within a year.

Portugal

Portugal had been quiet for decades, ruled harshly by the Salazar dictatorship and, after he went into a coma, by one of his closest aides, Marcelo Caetano. The first protests against the dictatorship occurred on November 11, 1968, when hundreds of students marched in downtown Lisbon to protest the torture death of student Daniel Teixeira. By the end of the year, two thousand students participated in a sit-in for university reform, and five thousand at the University of Coimbra fought police in the name of campus reform.

Beginning with the overthrow of the Portuguese dictatorship on April 25, 1974, the "Carnation Revolution" indicated just how much the floodgates of change had been knocked open by the world-historical movements of 1968. From 1974 to 1991, some forty countries democratized.

Eastern Europe: New Left vs. Old Left

Tension between the Soviet Left and newly emergent popular movements has a long and tragic history. In 1935, the Communist International accused Augusto César Sandino of having gone over to the side of the United States and the counterrevolution.[135] Marxists faithful to the Soviet Union similarly misinterpreted the popular movement in Spain. After World War II, an insurgent movement in Greece liberated the vast majority of the countryside, but Greek Soviet Communists tragically betrayed it.[136] In 1968, the Communist Party of Nicaragua dismissed the Sandino National Liberation Front, an organization that had adopted Che's foco theory, as "petit bourgeois." These examples help clarify historical limitations of Soviet Marxism and explain why the New Left developed autonomously and remained unattached to existent parties.

American Communist leader and noted activist Dorothy Healey clearly understood her party's failure to act properly: "The Party's hostile attitude toward the New Left was probably the greatest political liability we had to contend with in the 1960s."[137]

Communists opposed the French revolutionary movement of May 1968, and did little to advance the Cuban Revolution in its infancy—to say nothing about popular uprisings against Soviet regimes in East Berlin in 1953, Poland and Hungary in 1956, Czechoslovakia in 1968, and Poland in 1970. Whether or not it is appropriate to label movements of 1968 in Czechoslovakia, Yugoslavia, and Poland as New Left, it is clear that the eros effect penetrated Eastern Europe. In Hungary, students of Lukács explicitly began to call themselves New Leftists.[138] In the Soviet Union, amid protests against arrest and trials of dissident writers, words coined by the New Left found their way into the Russian language: *kontrkultura, khippi, kampus, marginalnost, kheppening, ekolog, tick-in, stsientism.*[139] In 1967, a wave of dissent grew out of the trial of protest leader Vladimir Bukovsky, who maintained the right to demonstrate and criticize the government. Protesters throughout the region were emboldened by Czechoslovakia's courage and vision. East Germany in 1968 did not have a flamboyant or well-known movement. Although marginalized protests against the Soviet invasion of Czechoslovakia remained relatively unknown, popular disillusionment with "real existing socialism" spread widely after the Prague Spring.

Yugoslavia

In Yugoslavia, the student movement first acted in solidarity with emergent movements in Poland, West Germany, and France. As one observer described repercussions of the global movement:

> What is completely new and extremely important in the new revolutionary movement of the Paris students—but also of German, Italian, and U.S. students—is that the movement was possible only because it was independent of all existing political organizations. All of these organizations, including the Communist Party, have become part of the system; they have become integrated into the rules of the daily parliamentary game; they have hardly been willing to risk the positions they've already reached to throw themselves into this insanely courageous and at first glance hopeless operation.[140]

While drawing inspiration from the New Left in other countries, Yugoslav activists self-consciously attempted to create a New Left for themselves. In May 1968, there was a discussion organized at the Faculty of Law under the title "Students and Politics." The "theme which set up the discussion" was:

the possibility for human engagement in the "New Left" movement which, in the words of Dr. S. Stojanovic, opposes the mythology of the 'welfare state' with its classical bourgeois democracy, and also the classical left parties—the social democratic parties which have succeeded by all possible means in blunting revolutionary goals in developed Western societies, as well as the communist parties which often discredited the original ideas for which they fought, frequently losing them altogether in remarkably bureaucratic deformations.[141]

On June 2, the student movement exploded when a controversial theater performance that was to be held outdoors was rescheduled for a room too small to fit everyone. Those who could not get in began to protest, and their ranks spontaneously swelled to several thousand outside student dorms in New Belgrade. As they marched toward downtown government buildings, police riot batons and arrests greeted them. After police opened fire, students commandeered a water cannon truck and drove through student neighborhoods to alert people.

The next day, general assemblies convened at the Karl Marx Red University (as the University of Belgrade was renamed). In the streets of New Belgrade, students met outside their classrooms and animated discussions ensued. In large assemblies, students emphasized gross social stratification within Yugoslav society, unemployment, increasing private wealth of a few, and the impoverished condition of a large section of the working class. Talks were interrupted by loud applause and calls like "Students with Workers," "We're Sons of Working People," "Down with the Socialist Bourgeoisie," and "Freedom of the Press and Freedom to Demonstrate!" The June 4 issue of the newspaper *Studen* was banned, but censorship only served to expose the regime's attempts to isolate and muzzle the student movement. By June 5, protests spread to Zagreb and Ljubljana. Representatives of factory workers in Belgrade publicly supported students.

The government attempted to portray students as only interested in their own material well-being or as under the influence of "foreign elements"—as Tito put it in a speech on June 10. For their part, the week before Tito's speech, the Yugoslav Student Federation proclaimed a "Political Action Program" emphasizing larger social issues, and the Belgrade Youth Federation journal declared:

The revolutionary role of Yugoslav students, in our opinion, lies in their engagement to deal with general social problems and contradictions. . . . Special student problems, no matter how drastic, cannot be solved in isolation, separate from general social problems: the material situation of the students cannot be separated from the economic situation of the society: student self-government cannot be separated from the social problem of self-government: the situation of the University from the situation of society.[142]

Soon thereafter, Tito had a change of heart and began to co-opt the movement through publicized consideration of its Political Action Program. One commentator, M. Krieza, put it well within the Situationists' domain when he described the events as "not only a conflict between production and creation, but in a larger sense—and here I have in mind the West as well as the East— between routine and adventure."[143]

Student rally in Belgrade on June 3, 1968, to demand higher education reform and protest the military's brutal treatment of student demonstrators. Picture Alliance.

Czechoslovakia

Rooted as it was in the working class, sectors of the Communist Party, and the government, the movement in Czechoslovakia could hardly be classified as a student movement. Students and intellectuals played a catalyzing role, both in the Kafka revival beginning in 1963[144] and in agitation for an autonomous student union, an issue first raised in the stormy days of May 1956, after Khrushchev had denounced Stalinist purges, and movements had risen up in Poland and Hungary. For nearly a decade, students in Czechoslovakia continued to demand an autonomous union. At a national conference in December 1965, students proclaimed their right to criticize society publicly and even asked to be represented in the parliament. As students organized, they "influenced the growing awareness in other parts of the awakening infrastructure that artificial organizational unity was a restrictive factor and a barrier to assertion of group interests."[145] By November 25, 1966, those favoring an autonomous union were the majority at a national student conference. When one of their key activists was expelled from school and drafted into the army, it was clear that autonomy was not yet in the realm of possibilities. Czech youth have long been spontaneous and nature-loving. They have never responded well to governmental attempts to rule them. It was no surprise that they had nothing but derision and scorn for the authorities who tried to control the student union, banned rock music, and arrested musicians like the Plastic People of the Universe.

The opposition long defined itself within larger domains than that of politics alone. Beginning in 1956, a number of nonconformist cultural journals appeared, and although somewhat censored, these journals prepared the groundwork for the more direct political criticisms of the 1960s. Film, mime, theater, variety shows, and music became increasing sources of antibureaucratic values. One observer noted: "A typical line of thought, quite popular in Czechoslovakia after 1956 in connection with the inimitable and by now legendary atmosphere of the Reduta Jazz Club, attributed a symbolic importance precisely to jazz. . . . Take a jazz band, people used to say, with its freedom of improvisation, spontaneity and joy of free expression. Is it not the exact contrary of what the regime wants us to do?"[146] Jazz clubs and other such associations also provided members with informal meeting spaces where forbidden public topics could be broached.

As student agitation continued for an autonomous union, a cultural gap and political squabble were greatly intensified by events of Halloween 1967. That night, the lights went out in Charles University dormitories in Strahov as they had done many times before, but this time, hundreds of students poured into the streets and began marching toward downtown Prague shouting, "We Want Light!" When they arrived at the bottom of the hill, police greeted them with clubs and were heard to say, "Here's your light!" as they savagely beat them. Meetings were quickly organized to protest the "unhealthy situation in the country." Students forged links with dissidents within the Writers' Congress. Even the National Assembly denounced police and demanded an investigation, the first time that a majority of the Assembly had supported any antiregime activity.[147]

Events moved rapidly. The right wing of the Party charged students with trying to "return capitalism, unemployment, hunger, and poverty to Czechoslovakia," but with Novotny's resignation as Party Chairman and the ascension of reformist leadership under Alexander Dubček in January 1968, the political struggle opened by students spread to the whole society. On March 12, 1968, significant forces within the government, the Party, and the working class moved to liberalize state control of society, and students went ahead and reconstructed their organization on the basis of "socialist humanism" and "self-management."[148]

A notable influence on this movement was the March student revolt in Poland. Prague press and radio carried detailed coverage of these events and publicized the dismissal of students and faculty there. Two Polish professors, Leszek Kolakowski and Bronislaw Baczko, were later invited to speak at Charles University in Prague, and the Czechoslovak Academy of Sciences sent a letter protesting their firings to the Polish embassy.[149]

Although students were co-opted by Dubček's technocratic reform program, openings provided by Party attempts at reform lent credibility to nonconformist thinkers. In May 1968, one journalist had the boldness to recall that the Party Central Committee had not even discussed foreign policy for over twelve years.[150] Even though fresh thinking entered Czechoslovak political discourse, the Action Program of the Party (adopted on April 10, 1968) was moderate, continually calling for expert management and equating material wealth and science with socialism. It was not a revolutionary program, merely a streamlining (a word the program itself used on many occasions) of the existing Russian-dominated system. Although it had the distinction of reformulating Rosa Luxemburg's insistence on the need to expand democracy, neither worker self-management nor a critique of technocratic values was part of the program. Indeed, technocratic values were precisely those that the reform program advocated, since they were considered necessary to lift the country from the outgrown bureaucratic centralization of the epoch of industrialization into the epoch of the "scientific-technological revolution." Although the slogans of "self-government" and "councils" modeled on Yugoslavia were raised and discussed, they were considered too far-reaching.[151]

Even a moderate reform program proved unacceptable to the leadership of the Soviet Union.[152] On the night of August 20, 1968, over half a million Soviet bloc troops invaded. Popular resistance was massive. At least twenty people were killed in Prague alone, and the overwhelming majority of people refused to cooperate with the invaders. In Prague, citizens quickly removed street signs, and it took over a week for the Soviets to find the post office. More than one person told me that Russian soldiers believed they were in Germany to put down an uprising of Nazis.

In a secret post invasion meeting, a thousand Czechoslovak Party delegates were smuggled into a Prague steel factory under the noses of Soviet guards, but the Dubček-led Party decided only to passively resist in order to avoid precipitating bloodshed on the scale of Hungary in 1956. The Soviet invasion did bring

(TOP) Soviet tanks enter Prague on August 21, 1968. Topham Picturepoint. (MIDDLE) Czech students protest in the streets against the Soviet invasion. GAMMA/Frank Spooner Pictures. (BOTTOM) A Soviet tank and truck burn on the streets after a student onslaught with Molotov cocktails. Corbis-Bettmannn/UPI.

Occupation of Wenceslaus Square on August 22, 1968. GAMMA/Frank Spooner Pictures.

calls for armed resistance, notably from novelist Ludvík Vaculík, whose "Two Thousand Words" had already gotten him expelled from the Party. In a remarkable change in style, the gentleness of his remarks at the Writers' Congress in June 1967, that "politics are subordinate to ethics," became a confrontational call for defense "with weapons if necessary."[153] Nonetheless, the main form of resistance was passive and spontaneous. As reported in the *Sunday Telegraph* of August 24: "People are using Hippie methods—sticking flowers into the helmets or into the gun barrels. For the Russians it is absolutely weird. . . . It is very peculiar and sometimes even rather gay." Free speech and assembly, first won in the post-January reforms, intensified under the barrels of tanks as people staged sit-ins, organized vigils, and demonstrated against the occupation. Underground radio broadcasts and newspapers abounded, and graffiti was everywhere. A sign in Russian in Prague's Wenceslas Square read, "Moscow—1800 kilometers." Another said, "Lenin wake up—Brezhnev has gone mad." Two days after the invasion, there was a one-hour general strike. For days, railroad workers stopped trains bringing in equipment from the Soviet Union.

Although Party leadership did not actively oppose the Soviet invasion, workers, students, and intellectuals continued to intensify their resistance. At the beginning of October, workers threatened to strike if there was any attempt "to return to the pre-January (pre-reform) position."[154] What was described as a "typically Schweikian form of resistance to the Russians," that is, passive non-compliance, occurred throughout the country. Finally on October 16, a joint treaty was signed which permitted "temporary" stationing of Soviet troops in Czechoslovakia.

A new wave of student demonstrations greeted the announcement, and students renewed attempts to forge an alliance with workers. There was a total university strike in November, and action committees modeled on those that had been so prominent during the general strike in France in May 1968 were created. In December, a meeting between the Student Commission for Cooperation with Workers and the Congress of Czechoslovak Metal Workers (representing ninety thousand workers) reached a political accord. All industrial unions in Bohemia and Moravia concluded similar agreements with student unions there, and worker-student action committees were established throughout the country. Workers' councils were elected, and people mobilized to defend civil liberties.

It quickly became clear, however, that the Soviet Union was not about to let Czechoslovakia break free of its sphere of influence. In a desperate act, Jan Palach, a philosophy student, burned himself to death in Wenceslas Square on January 16, 1969, calling for a general strike in support of three demands: abolition of censorship, a ban on *Zprávy* (the publication of Soviet troops in Czechoslovakia), and resignation of Czechoslovak collaborators. The oppositional movement intensified, and in his inaugural speech in April 1969, new Party Chairman Husak declared: "Some people go into the factories and stir up anti-Party tendencies, on every occasion there appear slogans such as 'Students and Workers Together,' or 'Students, Intelligentsia, Workers Unite.' We all know that this platform is contradictory to the policy of our Party."[155] He continued: "We received information that a conference of students and workers in Prague is being held without the knowledge of the appropriate organs. What are they up to? Planning strikes perhaps?" On August 23, 1968, Fidel Castro characterized the Czech uprising as "a counterrevolution that embraced capitalism and imperialism."

Popular resistance in Czechoslovakia could in no way match the severe repression suffered by dissidents.[156] As its situation deteriorated year after year, the opposition movement reorganized itself in 1977 as "Charter '77," but activists suffered even worse controls and more arrests after joining it, measures which seemed to mimic the kinds of grotesque bureaucratic domination portrayed by Kafka.[157]

Whether or not the movement in Czechoslovakia should be labeled "New Left," there certainly was much similarity to other movements of 1968, and the global movement intuitively identified with Czechoslovakia. The week after the invasion of 1968, demonstrators brutalized by police in Chicago at the Democratic National Convention carried placards reading "Welcome to Czechago," and in the battle for People's Park in Berkeley, "Welcome to Prague" was spray-painted on the streets. In France and Germany (as throughout Europe), there were massive shows of support. In East Germany, four thousand people gathered in Eisenach on August 24, 1968, at a protest rally, and there were smaller rallies and protests by writers in Moscow and Leningrad.[158]

There were also those within Czechoslovakia who deliberately identified with the New Left. According to Vladimir Kusin: "A certain affinity with the

'New Left' was expressed . . . within the reformist theories of the Party, but was never accepted as a program for action."[159] Although professing adherence to "authentic Marxism," historian Karel Bartosek called for the formation of a Czechoslovak "New Left" in June 1969. He summed up the opportunities available to the defeated reformers as follows:

> In the immediate future the following should be the aims of the forces of the New Left:
>
> a)   To work out a coherent programme of a revolutionary transformation of our society, primarily arising from the theoretical analysis of the specific experience of 1968.
>
> b)   To combat defeatism and despondency which are "normal" features of every period of defeat and which are spreading in our country . . .
>
> c)   To make use of all legal organizations to project a new programme, to unmask the bureaucratic system and to establish the nuclei of new political organizations of the future. If the New Left is to be historically new, it must direct its entire activity at encouraging the formation of several, not just one, political organizations of the working class and the working population, and to pave the way for their public activity. . . . Utopianism has been an impediment only when it has suppressed critical reflection on reality and on itself, and when it has transformed a potential will for a change of reality into an illusion about such will and reality.[160]

Poland

The movements of the 1980s far overshadow the student revolt of March 1968, which the Polish working class largely ignored, yet that step was not insignificant. Two years later, in the midst of the 1970 uprising in Gdańsk, workers marching on local Party headquarters entered the Polytechnic chanting, "We apologize for March 1968." A decade later, *Solidarność*'s exhibition of Polish history had displays focused on workers' revolts of 1956, 1970, and 1976, as well as the 1968 student movement. Just as the student revolt did not find massive support from workers in 1968, neither was the 1970 working-class uprising supported by many Polish students. Embryonic movements of 1968 and 1970 prepared the groundwork for overwhelming popular support and unity of the movement in the 1980s.

Demands of students and intelligentsia for an end to cultural censorship stand in stark contrast to the 1970 worker rebellion for affordable food prices. In both cases, revolts occurred as *reactions* to unpopular measures by authorities: suppression in January 1968 of an Adam Mickiewicz play (written in 1831 after the defeat of the Polish uprising but applauded by audiences for continuing political relevance of its anti-Russian passages) and the 1970 decision of the regime to raise prices of basic groceries. As much as the movement of the 1980s combined both aspirations (cultural and political autonomy as well as a greater degree of economic equality), it was itself a *subject* of changes in vision and policy as prior movements were *objects* of excesses of the regime. In order to comprehend this dramatic change in initiative and momentum, it is helpful to review several episodes of political struggle.

As early as 1962, students had organized informal discussion clubs, each with a distinctive name like "Contradiction Seekers."[161] During 1963 and 1964, the Gomułka regime (which came to power as a result of the revolt of 1956) shut down independent literary magazines and dissolved the main discussion club at the University of Warsaw, beginning an escalating spiral of repression and dissent, a dynamic in which Kuron and Modzelewski's "Open Letter" and subsequent three-year jail sentences were but one example. The tenth anniversary of the 1956 "Polish October" was ignored by the regime but celebrated by the Socialist Youth Organization at the University of Warsaw, and Kolakowski was the main speaker. The next day he was expelled from the Party, and six student organizers were suspended from classes.[162]

The revolt of 1968 was precipitated when the government banned Mickiewicz's play and *Dziady*, an independent magazine. The first demonstrations were allowed to transpire, but as winter relented and public support grew, so did violence of specialists in crowd control. On March 2, in its first special meeting, the Warsaw Writers' Union voted to condemn censorship, and the Actors' Union soon took a similar stand. In defiance of a ban on demonstrations, over 1,500 people assembled at the University of Warsaw on March 8 to protest arrests of students who had led the fight for freedom of expression. Shouts of "Long Live the Writers!" and "Long Live Czechoslovakia!" were heard at the same time as workers passing by were pelted with coins and snowballs for siding with authorities.

Brutal attacks by groups of club-carrying "Party activists" soon incited students, bringing tens of thousands of them into street actions. On March 11, some workers joined students, and together they fought police for eight hours. Protesters tried to reach Party headquarters but were unable to do so. The next day, renewed struggles broke out at the University of Warsaw, where students held an American-inspired "sit-in." Fighting occurred in Poznań, Kraków, and Katowice, and protest meetings were held in Lublin, Gliwice, Gdańsk, Łódź, Szczecin, and Wroclaw. On March 13, a national call went out from Warsaw for a general strike. Thirteen demands were formulated (including freedom of speech, press, and assembly, as well as against both anti-Semitism and Zionism), but even though thousands of students acted, the working class did not. Many working-class women brought bundles of blankets and food to students occupying the universities, but without massive participation of workers, the regime was able to arrest thousands of students and dismiss thousands more from universities, thereby bringing the movement under control by May.

What began in Poland in March of 1968 was a student movement, but aspirations of activists pertained to the whole society. In "Theses of the Program of the Young Generation," they wrote: "The principal objective of our action, that which gives meaning and value to our struggle, is the total and real liberation of humans, the abolition of all forms of human slavery (economic, political, cultural, etc.) from all elements of human life that prevent progress and make being pitiful. We struggle for humanism in practice."[163]

Two years later, the working class in Poland initiated the next phase of class struggle, and this time the response of the regime was bloody. Official reports confirmed forty-six deaths in Gdańsk, and it is rumored that as many as three hundred people were killed.[164] Beginning in November 1970, workers in and around Gdańsk went on strike to protest the regime's new system of "economic incentives" which caused lower wages, higher prices, and a scarcity of food. When radio and TV announced on December 13 that price adjustments would cause a 30 percent increase in food prices, two sections of the striking Gdańsk shipyard workers immediately elected delegates to go to Party headquarters for discussions. All were promptly arrested.[165]

These arrests marked the beginning of an insurrection, since they transformed a strike for wages into a political confrontation. The next day thousands of workers marched from an assembly at a Gdańsk factory toward the Party's regional headquarters. On the way, the procession more than doubled in size as sailors, workers, women, and youth joined in. They unsuccessfully tried to force their way into the northern shipyards and then changed direction for the Polytechnic (where only a few students joined them despite the crowd's apology for their passivity in 1968). Another column of several thousand workers left the shipyards and headed downtown, but, divided from one another and frustrated by lack of support from students, they soon withdrew.

The following afternoon, fighting began in earnest. In Gdańsk, Party headquarters was momentarily set on fire, as were numerous stores, cars, and even a fire engine. Tear gas and gunshots could not stop attackers. Demonstrators took police cars to obtain arms and loudspeakers. At least thirty-five people were wounded and hundreds arrested. The next day, when the prison where arrested demonstrators were being held was attacked, the army bloodily defended it. Local Party headquarters was completely burned, and "shoot on sight" orders were issued from Warsaw. That day alone, local authorities admit that six people were killed and three hundred wounded.[166] According to the most conservative figures, the fight for Gdańsk claimed the lives of forty-five workers and resulted in nineteen buildings and over two hundred shops being set on fire.[167]

Although the army won control of Gdańsk, fighting spread to Gdynia, where workers took managers hostage, and crowds attacked city hall seven times. In Szczecin, workers assembled and drew up a list of demands including independent unions, reduction of food prices, a 30 percent wage increase, release of all those currently arrested, limitation of salaries of Party and state employees, better housing, and a meeting with members of the Parliament. Once again their delegation to the Party was arrested. Renewed fighting broke out. Assembled workers marched to the city singing the "Internationale" and were joined by students, workers, women, and schoolchildren:

> The crowd set fire to the Party building. . . . They first brought out, in a remarkably orderly and calm fashion, the furniture, documents and supplies which were in the building. "All the archives were methodically piled in the street along with the luxury provisions (champagne, sausages, caviar) prepared for the Party's New Year's celebration." The villa of Walaszek, local Party secretary, was also burned. On the walls of the city you could see: "We are workers, not hoodlums."[168]

A Central Strike Committee in Szczecin became the epicenter of the whole revolt. Of its thirty-eight members, seven were Party members, one a shipyard director, and the rest were workers, the majority of whom were under twenty-five. They organized production, food subsidies, and communications: "The city was transformed into a veritable workers' republic where all power was held by the strike committee. A strike committee was set up which took over all authority in the city, all activities of the Party organs and the city government. The general strike did not end until the strike committee had been guaranteed complete immunity for everyone."[169]

In the midst of the crisis, on December 20, Edward Gierek replaced Wladyslaw Gomułka as first secretary of the United Polish Workers' Party. Gierek admitted that the revolts were not against socialist ideals, and he moved to alleviate the "crisis of confidence." Special concessions of 450 *zloty* were allotted to each Szczecin shipyard worker at the same time as others were fired in Gdańsk and Gdynia. In January, after Gierek refused to meet with workers in Gdańsk and went to Moscow instead, strikes again broke out in Gdańsk (although workers maintained gas, electricity, and water services), and the Central Strike Committee in Szczecin sent messengers to factories throughout the country. Scattered strikes broke out among transport workers, and official unions came under heavy attack. From this point on, the state changed its approach and began to encourage workers' councils.

Gierek met with workers' delegations rather than arresting them. He announced he was taking legal steps to restore church property and launched negotiations with the clergy. Numerous high Party and union officials were fired. Nonetheless, workers in both Gdańsk and Sczecin continued to strike. They demanded an accurate list of those who had died, the release of those jailed, democratization of the unions, better economic conditions, and that Gierek come to shipyards for discussions. In their meetings, workers debated such issues as the role of workers' councils and choices between investments for production as opposed to other human needs. Gierek discussed with workers substantive issues. After newspapers contained long denunciations of *"enragés"* (the same word used in France to defame militant students) who sought to lead the majority of honest workers astray, Gierek humbled himself in front of television cameras by meeting with assemblies of workers in both Gdańsk and Sczecin. If this, his final effort to placate workers, had failed, few observers doubt that the bloodshed would have been even greater than in December, since the army was positioned to rescue Gierek if he had been detained.

Polish demonstrators outside Communist Party headquarters on March 8, 1968. Photographer unknown.

His homage to the power of workers, however, helped to end the second phase of struggle: the January phase in factories that had been created by the December actions in the streets. Although he did not suspend price increases, he did concede retroactive pay raises for 40 percent of Poland's ten million workers, better retirement and child allowances, free elections of delegates to workers' councils, dismissal of union officials, and reorganization of the Party in Sczecin. Even when women textile workers in Łódź went on strike in February, the government quickly gave in, canceling price increases and ignoring the fact that authorities (including the prime minister) that had come to Łódź for discussions had been held hostage by striking women. At a Łódź meeting of delegates from factories and workers' councils, a union official stressed "the fundamental importance of restoring the authority of trade unions and of gaining the confidence of large numbers of people."[170] Such reforms were considered necessary for the regime to prove capable of harnessing the benefits of the "scientific-technological revolution" and the energy of the workers. In saving the regime from crisis, the stage was then set for the emergence of Solidarność—the organization that went on to overturn Poland's government in 1989.[171]

Similarities between movements in Poland and France abound. The vocabulary of the rulers—their use of *enragé*—treated the French May events as an historical antecedent to the Polish uprising. As in Paris, Polish students in 1968 helped to detonate explosive struggles of the working class, although the fuse took much longer to burn in Poland than the two weeks it had taken in France. Furthermore, the forms of the uprisings closely resembled one another. In both countries, the contests were social, political, and economic in nature. In both cases, essential services like gas and electricity continued amid general strikes because of workers' own initiative and their concern for the vast majority of citizens. The responsibility of workers is one noteworthy aspect of these movements, although it is a double-edged sword, as evidenced by their return to work and docility in the face of Gierek at shipyards in Sczcecin.

As the "maturity" of working-class movements in France and Poland functioned in some ways to undermine their effectiveness, so the very youthfulness of student movements prevented them from going beyond the first phase of their struggle (the contestation of power) to the second phase (the reconstruction of life according to more humane values).

Latin America

Student movements in Latin America reached their culmination in 1968, but their roots predate the global eruptions of that year. In the 1950s, Colombian students sparked a popular revolution that overthrew the Rojas dictatorship, and in Venezuela a militant student uprising led to the ouster of Pérez Jiménez. When the military threatened a coup against the new government, armed student militias guarded the autonomy of the universities and the capital from the threatened attacks by reactionary sectors of the army.[172] In 1966, thousands of paratroopers invaded the Central University of Venezuela in Caracas, forcibly clearing dormitories and searching the entire campus. Tanks, infantry, and police occupied the university for over three months. In the same year, in Ecuador, the military junta fell as a result of a general strike sparked by university students. In Argentina, Brazil, Colombia, and Mexico, troops were called out against students who were protesting educational policies. In Panama, Nicaragua, and Uruguay, student protests caused severe unrest in 1966.[173]

In 1968, students were shot dead in Brazil and Uruguay, leading to even larger campus confrontations. In Chile student protesters were able to win concessions. The bloodiest repression was in Mexico, where several hundred protesters were killed as the Olympics approached. Students in Panama protested the military regime that took over the country in October, and more than two hundred were arrested. In 1969, an insurrection in Córdoba, Argentina, gained control of the city before being bloodily suppressed. Throughout the continent, clergy became active as liberation theology emanated from continent-wide solidarity with the poor.

Mexico

Students in Mexico have a long tradition of sacrifice and struggle. As in much of Latin America, their activism intensified in the early 1960s. In Puebla in 1964, Morelia in 1966, and Tabasco and Sonora in 1967, campus movements combined with remnants of militant railroad workers and teachers who had gone on strike in 1958. A student strike in Hermosillo was brutally suppressed when police invaded the campus and bloodily dispersed protesters. In violating traditional autonomy of the university, the police action quickly became notorious.

In the summer of 1968, inspired by French students, Mexican students hoped to win social reforms by using the spectacle of the coming Olympics. Few people expected the government to resort to murderous violence against unarmed students. Activists hoped that by threatening to compel postponement or cancellation of the Olympics, they could win freedom for political prisoners (especially Demitrio Vallejo and Valentín Campa, railroad union leaders imprisoned since the big strike of 1958), dismissal of the hated police chief of Mexico City, and the allocation of more public monies on domestic needs. Even though campus demands were moderate, rather than compromise with the movement, the government used secret police, torture, and murder to stifle it.

To complicate matters, students were internally divided. On July 23, rival student groups from secondary schools in Mexico City were both attacked by riot police, causing students to set aside their differences. Three days later, not coincidentally the anniversary of the July 26, 1953, attack on the Moncada army barracks in Cuba, thousands of students took to the streets to protest police brutality. Again, riot police attacked. This time seven people were killed, five hundred wounded, and hundreds arrested. More than 150,000 students took part in a general strike. All schools in Mexico City were ordered closed on July 29. Despite being commanded to leave campuses, students occupied their classrooms and used them for discussions, poster making, and movement building. Without provocation, the next day police invaded a small junior college in Mexico City and used a bazooka to destroy ornate seventeenth-century carved wooden doors. Four more students were killed. The strike spread to high schools. College students held daily demonstrations against continuing army and police invasions of campuses.[174] By the end of the month, antipolice protests and street fighting spread throughout the country.

The government called the movement communist and revolutionary, even though students were asking the government for concessions, not rising up for revolution. But of course, the relationship between reform and revolution is complex, and some activists hoped that their demands would draw new activists into a movement that eventually would challenge the entire system. Public opinion supported the students. For Octavio Paz, students were "real beings in an unreal world" and acted because "they were not the spokesmen of this or that class but of the collective conscience."

On August 1, more than 100,000 students marched from the National Autonomous University (UNAM) on the far outskirts of Mexico City to the Zócalo. Four days later, 150,000 students gathered at the Polytechnic Institute. By mid-August, alongside colleges and universities on strike, the Teachers' Coalition for Democratic Freedom brought 200,000 people into the streets in front of the national palace. Every day the strike spread. Its power lay in the movement's horizontal cultural forms, in its capacity to bring in new activists who felt free to take initiatives.[175]

By the end of August, demonstrations with hundreds of thousands of people marched behind revolutionary banners, chanting Che's slogan, "Create two, three, many Vietnams." A strike council drew up a multipoint petition which had little to do with the problems of students alone: besides freedom for political prisoners, they called for repeal of the laws under which "subversives" could legally be arrested, disbanding of the riot police, aid for victims of police aggression, and a role for the public in determining which officials were responsible for the police attacks on universities.[176] As the country's keepers of a higher rationality, students organized a Silent Demonstration on September 13 that so moved the population that 400,000 people spontaneously joined them, "something never before seen in Mexico."[177] The student movement's maturity was evident for all on September 13. Thousands of young people packed into the Zócalo, and the day ended peacefully.

As the strike continued, UNAM was occupied by the military and police on September 18. When they tried to take over the Polytechnic, days of street fighting produced a stalemate. Continuing violations of university autonomy caused an outpouring of criticism of the military, and the army withdrew. Strikers felt they had achieved a major victory. Secretly the forces of order made plans to escalate their use of violence. Whether because of inept intelligence services or the movement's participatory character, the government was unable to single out leaders, so they plotted to attack the movement as a whole.

On the other side, the National Strike Council representing 128 schools hoped to negotiate a peaceful settlement to the burgeoning national crisis. "Combat Committees" at the local level chose Strike Council delegates, and a National Coordinating Committee of six hundred students was the final decision-making body. When President Gustavo Díaz Ordaz refused to make negotiations with the Strike Council public, a rally was called for October 2—ten days before the Olympics were to begin. As rain fell on the plaza at Tlatelolco housing project in downtown Mexico City, six thousand people listened quietly to speakers standing above them on a high platform. At 6:10 p.m., a helicopter dropped two flares—the signal for an attack. Without warning, hundreds of soldiers and police suddenly opened fire, mercilessly killing as they charged forward. Some of the first to die were those who had addressed the rally, gunned down by undercover police among the crowd. Machine guns strafed the speakers' platform, leaving key members of the Strike Council and a number of journalists mortally wounded. Many of the injured were later killed as they lay in the streets. Police combed nearby hospitals and killed wounded students. The attacks lasted into the next morning. Corpses were piled up and carted away to unknown destinations.

On July 30, 1968, the Mexican army used a bazooka to invade a school in Mexico City. Photographer unknown.

To this day, no one knows how many people were killed at Tlatelolco. At the time, initial government reports claimed four deaths, but common knowledge refers to the "four hundred comrades" who lost their lives in one of the most violent confrontations between a government and students in history.

October 2, 1968, is still remembered as the "Night of Sorrow." In February 1969, the police chief in Mexico City quietly resigned, but no one has ever been punished for the massacre. Indeed, Luis Echeverría, then minister of interior, went on to become president.

The government's terror was effective. Although the National Strike Council had repeatedly insisted that the strike would continue until all political prisoners were released, a month after Tlatelolco, they announced that all students should return to class.

Colombia

The French May events stimulated a vibrant student movement in Colombia. As one Colombian put it: "The student movement of 1968 was the first movement that was able to set off critical self-reflection on the global system. . . . They all had something in common: they rejected the primacy of the economy over life."[178] Three years later, they awoke the entire nation when students in Cali went on strike because the Universidad del Valle refused students' and professors' nominations for the position of rector. All over the country, student councils supported Cali's movement. In Bogotá, student power movements became so powerful that the government closed the departments of sociology and social work.

Peru

Copying the Cuban model, guerrilla movements in Peru emerged in the early 1960s, but they failed to mobilize the super-exploited rural population. While Old Left Communist parties sought inclusion in Peruvian "democracy," a plethora of New Left groups emerged, especially on the campuses. On October 3, 1968, a left-wing military coup d'état seized power announced the end of serfdom. Decades later, intensive repression all but destroyed large guerrilla insurgencies, leading to the quieting of popular movements.

Venezuela

Decades later, intensive repression all but destroyed large guerrilla insurgencies, leading to the quieting of popular movements. As in Colombia, Venezuelan New Left groups were focused mainly around participating in campus decisions. In June 1968, the army was sent to occupy the Universidad Central de Venezuela in order to quell student protests. Through exploitation of its vast oil resources, Venezuela consistently had one of the region's highest standards of living. With the onset of neoliberal austerity measures in 1989, a vast revolt broke out and was put down with hundreds of citizens killed. Ultimately, Hugo Chávez was swept into power. His visionary programs brought U.S. countermeasures that devastated the economy and led to polarization of the society.

Argentina

The French May events empowered Argentine students, but they were met by a harsh regime response. Hundreds of students occupied the University of La Plata in Buenos Aires on June 12 to protest the government's repression. Thousands of students fought with police in Buenos Aires, La Plata, Tucumán, and Rosario. At least sixty students were arrested. In early July, over five hundred students were jailed in La Plata after stones and firebombs were thrown from rooftops. Two months later, a student strike in the capital turned into a bloody clash with police.[179]

A year after the French May, a worker-student uprising in Córdoba (the *Cordobazo*) led to the demise of the regime of army general Juan Carlos Onganía, who had taken power during a 1966 coup. Protests began in mid-May 1969, when sugar mill workers took over their factory and held the manager hostage as they demanded long overdue wages. On May 15, police killed a student in Rosario during protests against a 500 percent rise in cafeteria costs. Within a week, police had killed two more protesting students in other parts of the country.

As state violence continued to escalate, Renault worker Máximo Mena was shot dead in Córdoba on May 29, triggering a massive uprising. One of the initial leaders was Agustín "Gringo" Tosco of the General Confederation of Labor in Argentina, a radical formation established in 1968 in opposition to mainstream, progovernment unions. A skilled organizer, Tosco led a march that wound its way through the city. One participant related that "People's reaction was incredible; they came into the street to hand us things, women, old ladies, gave us matches, and bottles or brooms to protect ourselves with. Everyone was in the street, old men, kids. . . . There was a certain feel to the moment, joyous I would say, until then the worst hadn't happened."[180] When police attacked the procession, the whole population was drawn into the struggle. Citizens erected self-defense barricades and took control of most of the city. Central government offices and headquarters of multinational corporations were put to the torch. Showing great care for each other's well-being, citizens voluntarily helped firefighters to insure the conflagrations did not spread to residences. The liberated city had few if any incidents of looting or civil violence.

Onganía mobilized the army to quell the uprising. As the military entered the Barrio Clinica neighborhood, small groups fired at them with hunting rifles and pistols from rooftops. Others threw Molotov cocktails. Of course, such improvised weapons could not hold off tanks, bazookas, and machine guns. Using overwhelming force, the military subdued the city. The uprising may have been brought to an end, but it led to the fall of the Onganía dictatorship and gave the country a momentary respite from state violence.

A new coup brought an even worse government to power in 1976. As only became known years later, the Argentine student movement was brutally liquidated by the 1970s "Dirty War" that resulted in at least thirteen thousand opponents of the military killed or disappeared. [181]

Uruguay

A month of fighting between students and police led to strikes by public service workers, teachers, and bank employees in early July 1968. To head off a potentially explosive situation, the government imposed martial law on July 14. In September, more than 2,500 workers were dismissed at a government-owned coal storage facility, and trade unions called a twenty-four-hour general strike, during which fifty people were injured in clashes with police.

Student unrest continued through the fall. On September 22, following a week of particularly violent clashes in Montevideo, the government ordered all universities and high schools closed for a month. Students had opposed government plans to raise bus fares, and their protests turned into some "Latin America's longest and most intense."[182] High school students erected roadblocks to collect tolls and conducted other creative actions coordinated by grassroots councils. At one point, sugarcane cutters joined urban protesters.

On June 6, 1969, university demonstrations were attacked. Five people were shot and wounded. During the next days of intense fighting, hundreds of students were arrested. On June 12, at least three hundred were arrested and many more injured. When the School of Medicine was occupied, it was surrounded by police, and hundreds more students were arrested and injured in subsequent battles. Workers struck for economic demands, while protests against repression took place at the School of Architecture. Near the oldest part of the capital, protesters targeted Pan Am and General Electric as representatives of U.S. presence.

In Uruguay, more than almost anywhere else, Old Left and New Left mixed together, producing urban guerrillas known as Tupamaros (named after Tupac Amaru), who practiced a form of participatory democracy even as they waged war on the state and its U.S. advisors. After the Tupamaros kidnapped Ulysses Pereira Reverbel, head of the state power company, police raided the university on August 9 but failed to locate him. Eventually, he was released unharmed. Continual street fights resulted in the shooting death of dentistry student Líber Arce a few days later. Protests continued to build in intensity in September, and a workers' general strike was called on September 19. The next day, student Hugo de los Santos was shot by police. Susana Pintos attempted to rescue him, and she too was shot. Neither survived. To avert any further escalation of the conflict, the government mobilized the military and ordered all schools in Montevideo closed until October 15.

Brazil

Continuing campus-based movements led to major crises in Brazil. Between 1964 and 1965, at least three thousand students were expelled from Brazilian universities to stem the rising tide of protests. No matter what measures the government took, students continually rose up against the dictatorship imposed in 1964, when the CIA funded a coup d'état that overthrew the democratically elected Goulart government.

In 1968, dissent reached a high point. On March 29, police killed a student in Rio de Janeiro, sparking two weeks of heavy riots that did not stop after closing of schools and occupation of the city by the army. Two nights of clashes between police and students in Rio resulted in more than one hundred arrests after the U.S. embassy was stoned. On April 1, when more than one thousand students protested against the regime, three people were shot and killed, one in Rio and two in Goiania. More than two thousand students clashed with police after the memorial mass for the student killed on March 28.

At the Polytechnic in Curitiba on May 13, police used bayonets, tear gas, and water cannons against students, who responded with Molotov cocktails and fireworks. More than one hundred students were arrested. Three days later students at Parana University built barricades and occupied the university to protest undiscussed curriculum changes. They held the rector and ten professors hostage for several hours. Riots continued through June as the student movement demanded an end to President Costa de Silva's government and reforms in the educational system. Over eight hundred students were arrested on June 21, when students at the Federal University protested the government's failure to give enough aid to Brazil's forty-one universities. Three days of riots outside the U.S. embassy in Rio resulted in five students and one policeman being killed and 150 people injured. The government ordered all schools closed one week before vacation. Nonetheless several thousand

Rio de Janeiro students opposed to Brazil's military dictatorship clash with riot police. Corbis-Bettman/UPI.

students in São Paolo took to the streets to protest police brutality in Rio. While police stood by they broke all the windows of the First National City Bank of New York. On June 26, an estimated eighty thousand people demonstrated in Rio against the military regime.

In August, 1,500 soldiers and police were mobilized to prevent a student demonstration in Rio. When the unrest spread to other cities, a ban on demonstrations was enacted, and only the arrest of 1,240 students attending the secret congress of the Brazilian National Students Union near São Paulo on October 13 temporarily quieted the revolt.[183] On October 22, when hundreds of students in Rio protested the arrests, police attacks killed one more student.

Chile

In the early 1960s, Chile was in the midst of parliamentary reforms, including significant land reforms. While much of Latin America suffered from military dictatorships, Chileans enjoyed increasing liberties and economic opportunities. As expectations rose, campesino unions with student support took over four hundred large estates. An autonomous radical organization, the Movement of the Revolutionary Left (MIR) evolved from those struggles (and continues today to lead popular resistance).

After a fifty-day student strike at the Catholic University of Chile won curriculum reform in 1967, similar and even more militant campus movements emerged around the country that caused the resignation of Santiago's bishop and many deans at the universities. In May 1968, students from the Education School occupied the administration building at the University of Chile. In June, farmers on the Fundo San Miguel went on strike for higher wages—the first legal farmers' strike in the country's history. When they failed to win any concessions, they took up arms and seized the farm. When the army was sent in, they arrested the campesinos without bloodshed. On December 3, 1968, police tried to remove barricades erected by five hundred students demanding reforms at Santiago's Technical University. Dozens of people, including about seventy police, were injured and about seventy students were arrested.

On March 9, 1969, police killed ten squatters as they evicted them in Puerto Montt. In 1970, Salvador Allende was elected president of the country—the first democratically elected Marxist president in the Americas. President Richard Nixon and Henry Kissinger conspired with the giant U.S. corporation International Telephone and Telegraph to oust Allende. Chile's democratically elected government was bloodily overthrown on September 11, 1973. To this day, the U.S. has never acknowledged its role in the bloody coup that killed two thousand people and imposed the world's first neoliberal regime on Chile.

As the Zeitgeist of 1968 energized the entire world, it also found its way into the Catholic Church.

Theology of Liberation

As the injustices of poverty were obvious throughout the Third World, the eros effect of 1968 resulted in radicalization of the church in Latin America. Coinciding with the Tet offensive was the first Latin American meeting of Christian revolutionaries in Montevideo, Uruguay. A certain number of priests, the best-known being Camilo Torres, had already joined guerrilla movements in Peru, Venezuela, Colombia, and Guatemala, but 1968 marked a massive shift in the ranks of the church. On March 9, a group of priests in Peru publicly denounced the "economic exploitation of the country's resources" and called on priests and laymen to fulfill their mission as prophets of justice.[184] Another letter, this one signed by the Latin American provincial superiors of the Jesuits at their meeting in Rio de Janeiro in 1968, opened with the acknowledgement that the majority of Latin Americans lived in destitute conditions "which cry to heaven for vengeance."[185]

There were many similar religious appeals in this period, including those of Pope Paul VI during his visit to Bogota in 1968, when he said, "In the vast continent of Latin America, development has been unequal . . . while it has favored those who originally began the process, it has neglected the great masses of the native population."[186] A letter signed by nine hundred Latin American priests was addressed to the Medellín Conference of 1968, an international meeting of the Catholic hierarchy which embraced the theology of liberation: "Because the privileged few use their power of repression to block this process of liberation, many see the use of force as the only solution open to the people. . . . One cannot condemn oppressed people when they feel obliged to use force for their own liberation to do so would be to commit a new injustice."[187]

The concluding statement of the Medellín Conference condemned "the tremendous social injustices that exist in Latin America. These injustices keep the majority of our peoples in woeful poverty, which in most cases goes so far as to be inhuman misery."[188] The Medellín Conference's strong denunciation of injustice motivated priests and bishops in many countries to gather and discuss social problems. In Peru, for example, the 36th Assembly of Bishops took an even stronger stand than that of Medellín: "This situation of injustice . . . is the result of a process that has worldwide dimensions. It is characterized by the concentration and economic power of a few and by the international imperialism of money, which operates in league with the Peruvian oligarchy."[189]

To be sure, the Vatican was not the center of a New Left organization. In addition to many progressives, it contains within it some of the most conservative people on earth. When the global insurgency of 1968 swept into the church, it fractured traditional clerical support for the forces of order. The Vatican momentarily came to recognize the needs of the impoverished millions in the Third World, but it also maintained its opposition to feminism, cracking down on the more than one hundred U.S. theologians who publicly voiced their disapproval of the pope's ban on birth control.

On the whole, however, there was more than a superficial affinity between the new radicalism within the church and New Left ideas,[190] and the gradual elaboration of this new symbolism within Christianity was part of the world-wide eruption of 1968. Like the movements of 1968 as a whole, the clerical liberation movement drew inspiration from a global membership. Beginning in 1968, Dom Hélder Câmara modeled his movement for peace and justice in Latin America on Martin Luther King and the activism of black theologists in the United States.[191] On Easter Sunday 1970, he published a joint appeal with the Reverend Ralph Abernathy, Martin Luther King's successor as head of the Southern Christian Leadership Conference, for a "non-violent protest against the political, economic, and social structures of the world which subject so many to destitution or the constant threat of war."

North America

Canada

Growing out of university-based campaigns for nuclear disarmament, the Canadian New Left followed a pattern similar to its U.S. counterpart. Militant campus protests against Dow Chemical Company (then manufacturing napalm used in Vietnam) led to the crystallization of groups who began organizing in ghettos and insurgent communities. After years of significant actions, the chief movement organization, Student Union for Peace Action, splintered and disappeared by 1967. Nonetheless, Canadian youth linked up with Czech, Mexican, German, and Caribbean activists. As a vibrant multicultural movement of 1968 emerged, ever more militant student protests swept through rural provinces.[192] The Canadian movement's center was in Montreal, where a general strike of fifty thousand students carried on for six weeks. During the same period the Front de libération du Québec carried out dozens of bombings and armed actions in a struggle to achieve independence.

Radical students regarded the "co-opting of Canada into the American 'Great Society' as distorting our country's internal development in the broadest sense." One analyst took the matter even further when he said, "The Canadian student in his university is a colonial, even as the Canadian worker is within his enterprise, whether branchplant or not; and the Canadian economy, within the American empire."[193]

The Caribbean

As the Zeitgeist of 1968 everywhere infused the world with vibrant insurgencies, it appeared simultaneously on more than a dozen islands in the Caribbean.

The winds of world revolution fanned flames of discontent into uprisings in a region where nations had only recently gained formal independence but still suffered under the shackles of predominantly white oligarchies. As a result, the movement especially embraced Black Power. In more than a dozen places, a diverse assortment of revolutionary groups were crystallized, some more radical than others, but all united in the belief that fundamental change was needed. Looking back in 1995, Selwyn Ryan described how:

> The cries of "black power" and "power to the people" found responsive echoes not only among high school and university students, but among substantial elements of the working class and the unemployed as well. The massive strikes and street demonstrations which erupted in Curacao, Bermuda, the Bahamas, Jamaica, Trinidad, Aruba, and Anguilla in 1968, 1969, and 1970, and the army mutiny which almost toppled the Trinidad government in 1970, all in the name of "black power," were evidence enough of the strength of the movement.[194]

The international dimension of Black Power is apparent through its theoretical elaboration on many continents. Its roots can be traced to Africa, particularly to Kwame Nkrumah, founder and first president of independent Ghana until he was overthrown by a military coup d'état in 1966. For Nkrumah, Black Power was "part of the vanguard of world revolution against capitalism, imperialism and neo-colonialism . . . part of the world rebellion of the oppressed against the oppressor, of the exploited against the exploiters."[195] C.L.R. James understood Black Power as a "banner which the 20th century will need in the great efforts to overcome the crisis that imperialist domination has imposed upon the whole world."[196] According to Harold Cruse, the vanguard role of the proletariat as understood by Marxists had passed into the hands of African people, who possess a wealth of historical understanding and had little to lose but their chains. Walter Rodney, its foremost theoretician in the West Indies, articulated three dimensions:

1. A break with white, racist imperialism
2. Assumption of power by the masses—who are predominantly black—on the islands
3. Cultural reconstruction in the image of blacks[197]

Although Black Power had a variety of names and organizations, none of the above formulations meant simply filling existing political positions with African American faces, yet in practice that is sometimes what Black Power came to mean. While warning that "it could prove disastrous to the interests of the region itself, British Intelligence plainly understood that "'black' and 'white' apply less to pigmentation then to ideology. . . . Black moderates are also 'puppets' while Mao, Che and Ho Chi Minh are Black Power heroes."[198]

The main target of the Black Power movement was the "white power structure," which was all too obvious in a region where African and East Indians toiled their whole lives, while a small white elite lived incredibly well without seeming to work one day in their entire lives. Despite its progressive role in much of Latin America, the Catholic Church also came to be included in the ranks of those on the wrong side. Trinidad's National Joint Action Committee (NJAC, a confederation of radical groups) believed, "The Christian churches have done the most to destroy the message of Christ. They have made it a virtue to be oppressed, to content the black man with his suffering, while the church is in control of the affluent white oppressors in the Society. Their role in the machinery of oppression is to pacify Black People. . . . The churches propagate the anti-Christ values of Capitalism."[199] This is but one example of widespread anti-church sentiment in Trinidad.

Once the movement sprang to life, it resonated widely and spread into more than a dozen countries in the region. Some of the principal organizations that were galvanized from grassroots struggles are summarized below.

Black Power Organizations in the Caribbean, 1968–70

Country	Organization
Antigua	Afro-Caribbean Movement
Barbados	People's Progressive Movement
Bermuda	Progressive Labor Party, Black Beret Cadre
Dominica	United Black Socialist Party
Grenada	The Forum
Guyana	African Society for Cultural Relations with Independent Africa
Montserrat	Black Power Party
St. Kitts	Black Power Group
St. Lucia	The Forum
St. Vincent	Educational Forum of the People
Trinidad and Tobago	Black Panther Party, National Joint Action Committee

Sources: *Black Power in Bermuda*, 90; Central Intelligence Agency, Directorate of Intelligence, "Black Radicalism in the Caribbean," Secret Report, August 6, 1969, Number 1839/69, approved for public release August 22, 2012; British Intelligence and H.M. Diplomatic Service file entitled "Black Power in the Caribbean," 1970.

Whether in the English-speaking or Spanish-speaking Caribbean, the movement's generalized character is what is most noteworthy. Even on the normally tranquil Dutch-speaking island of Curaçao, a revolt in May 1969 against Royal Dutch Shell (which accounted for more than 90 percent of the national income) led to a massive workers' movement that could only begin to be controlled by the arrival of six hundred Dutch marines.[200] Rioters set fires in the center of Willemstad, chanting, "We will teach them to respect us." Police gunfire killed two people and wounded several more before the government stepped down on June 5, as a general strike loomed.

While less-informed observers attempted to blame the sudden appearance and rapid proliferation of radical movements (not only in the Caribbean) on an international Communist conspiracy, especially one emanating from Cuba, both the CIA and British Intelligence dispassionately noted that Cuba had little interest in these Black Power groups and had done very little to assist them.[201]

Jamaica

On October 16, 1968, the government forbade Guyanese activist-theoretician Walter Rodney from reentering Jamaica where he was teaching at the University of the West Indies (UWI). While many people on campus were antagonistic to Rodney's Black Power group, everyone opposed the ban. Immediately some nine hundred students assembled to show solidarity. Peacefully carrying petitions to the prime minister, they were met with tear gas at Jamaica House. One of the first canisters landed at the feet of Pat Rodney, Walter's pregnant partner, further enraging the public. The state had moved from attacking freedom of speech to a palpable assault on family life.

Students wearing scarlet robes had initiated the march, but as the crowd quickly grew to over two thousand, its ranks swelled with Rastafarians, workers, and unemployed. In front of a trade union building, police attacked again, and this time, people retaliated and destroyed several cars, lighting the torch for a larger conflagration in Kingston that evening. Police cordoned off the downtown commercial center, but looting and car smashing carried well into the night, even spreading to Spanish Town Road. Big businesses were especially targeted: Canadian Imperial Bank of Commerce, Bank of London and Montreal, Pan American Air, and Woolworth were all attacked. To protest recent fare hikes, fifty-three buses were burned or damaged—a direct response to the economic deprivation forced upon the majority of people. Sadly, three students were killed that night, tragically marking the events of October 16 for years to come.

When students regrouped on campus, UWI was surrounded by the military. Although students were permitted to enter, they were not allowed to leave campus. In ensuing clashes, police killed another person. The minister of home affairs banned all marches and meetings downtown. With repression increasing, the movement appeared to die down. Within a few years, however, more than a dozen radical newspapers had been published, and Black Power developed an organic relation to the public, affecting millions of people through Rastafarianism, reggae music, and Garveyism, as well as poetry and art and publications like *Abeng* (with a circulation of twenty thousand after only fifteen weeks),[202] *Miko*, and *Blackman Speaks*. Political Black Power was "merely the visible crest of a much larger wave," as Richard Drayton penned. In 1972, progressive Michael Manley was elected prime minister.

Barbados

One example of the worldwide proliferation of movements during this prolonged period of confrontation and solidarity was the effect of Caribbean activists on Canada as well as on the islands. In November 1968, the Hemisphere Conference to End the War in Vietnam took place in Montreal. This meeting in turn helped to galvanize opposition to university racism, which led two hundred people to occupy and damage the computer center at Sir George Williams University on January 29, 1969. Weeks later, ninety-seven of the protesters, mainly Caribbean students, were arrested. Ten Trinidadian students were among those charged with arson, a crime that carried a possible life sentence. Those arrested included Rosie Douglas, who would go on to become prime minister of Dominica.

The Canadian arrests also had a huge impact in Barbados, particularly since local resident Anne Cools was another of those facing charges. As a

On February 26, 1970, protesters confront the Royal Bank of Canada in Trinidad. Photographer unknown.

militant opposition congealed, both of the island's main department stores burned to the ground in December 1969 and January 1970. In March 1970, students at Cave Hill blockaded the administration building to show solidarity with students in Jamaica. Theology students called for a "Black God for Black Priests," and union leaders called for structural economic change, including nationalization of the Anglican Church, the telephone company, and Barbados Light and Power as part of the "first revolutionary law."

As the region changed, in 1971, the British high commissioner wrote: "More and more of the old Barbadian commercial families are coming to accept—however reluctantly—that their economic future depends on their ability to accept the realities of the present and to forget the unpleasant past in which the black man accepted his subordinate status."[203]

Trinidad and Tobago

In Trinidad, the movement jumpstarted by Canadian events was most notable. During the February–April 1970 "Black Power" Revolution, thousands rose up to challenge the People's National Movement, a political party that had captured much of the state's administrative power but left the economy in the hands of colonial and neocolonial strata. The National Joint Action Committee (NJAC), first created at the Saint Augustine campus of UWI, organized many of the most significant mobilizations. From the very start, East Indian students and lecturers also participated alongside Black Power students. NJAC spread immediately into town—to the streets of San Fernando and the hills of Laventville and Morvant. So resonant was the cry for unity that the calypsonian Valentino, regarded widely as a voice of the people, offered this refrain:

> But we must all try to bridge the gap
> My Indian and Afro brother
> Remember one hand could never clap
> So let us unite at once and come together

On February 26, 1970, the same night that students in Montreal had been arrested, NJAC organized a support demonstration, which began and ended peacefully at the Cathedral of the Immaculate Conception at the top of Independence Square. While the theatrical character of the demonstration may have seemed like a meager threat to power, after the incursion into the Port of Spain cathedral on February 26, the movement unleashed a dynamic life that ultimately led to a near-revolution. "As if by magical transformation" a second demonstration on March 4 grew within minutes from three hundred to ten thousand.[204] Upper-middle-class, lower-class, and working-class people converged for common cause. Overnight, new organizations formed and mushroomed. Dubbed the "People's Parliament," Woodford Square in the heart of Port of Spain became the movement's nerve center. In the words of Lloyd Best: "What you will notice here, right under our noses, is being created a new and exciting form of democracy. Five, ten, fifteen, twenty thousand citizens have been marching to the bugle call: power, power to the people. Young men rush to sell newspapers, old women rush to buy them. As militants demand the power, even the little children take up the chant: power to the people!"[205]

Mobilizations spread throughout the entire country. On March 6, some twenty thousand people marched. When police violently attacked spontaneous protests, people responded with stones and Molotovs. Nocturnal arson became commonplace. Foreign banks, party offices, police stations, and racist social clubs were all targeted. On March 12, a thirty-three-mile march to Caroni to show Black Power's embrace of East Indian sugar workers drew at least ten thousand participants.

Two days later, the government agreed to pay the fines levied against the arrested students in Canada, and on March 22, several flew home to heroes' welcomes. During the victory party on March 23 that NJAC organized in Woodford Square, Prime Minister Williams (often called "The Father of the Country") took to the airwaves to bolster his image. He promised the government would soon own more of the economy than "Cuba's Castro." After a storeowner threatened marchers with a gun, the situation rapidly deteriorated. Police gunfire and riot squad batons were met with counterviolence. An NJAC leaflet described how "We replied with bottles, stones, anything that could be thrown."[206] By March 24, "open warfare" took place in the streets around Woodford Square. The next two weeks were one continuous march. On April 9, at the funeral march for Basil Davis, a twenty-four-year-old killed by police, some twenty to thirty thousand people accompanied his casket from Woodford Square to San Juan cemetery.

On April 15, the government announced it would not allow Stokely Carmichael to return home to Trinidad from neighboring Guyana. (In the late 1960s, Carmichael changed his name to Kwame Ture.) Ture was one of Black Power's most famous advocates, and the fact that he was born in Trinidad endeared him to locals. During Carnival in the spring of 1970, giant posters of Malcolm X, Eldridge Cleaver, and Ture were prominently part of the celebration as it wound its way through Port of Spain. By banning him, the government unmasked itself and empowered the opposition.

On April 17, the organized working class decisively joined the struggle even though conservative trade unions were estranged from the movement. Employees at the Water and Sewage Authority stopped work, followed by a similar action on April 19 by Brechin Castle sugar estate workers. In the period between March 15 and April 21, "almost every single manufacturing and industrial enterprise

(TOP) Black Power march through the streets of Trinidad. (MIDDLE) On March 12, 1970, holding a chain as a symbol of past servitude, young demonstrators set off for the cane fields of Caroni marching with a unity banner. (BOTTOM) Mutineers from the Trinidad Regiment.

(including government services) was hit by a strike at least once."[207] On April 21, the Transport and Industrial Workers Union called for a general strike, and a broad alliance of groups—including Afro-Trinidadian oil workers, Indo-Trinidadian sugar workers, and NJAC—all called for a massive march on Port of Spain. Most impressively, East Indian sugar workers went on strike in four factories and three estates. This new grassroots unity seemed to spell the end of Williams's reign.

The same day that the call for a general strike went out, the government declared a state of emergency. Police rounded up as many leaders of Black Power organizations as they could find and isolated them in the notorious prison on Nelson Island. Seeing the avenue of democratic change foreclosed, about three dozen young activists went into the hills to begin an armed struggle, but their camps were quickly raided. At least eighteen fighters and three police were killed.

Urban militants defied the dusk-to-dawn curfew and battled police for control of downtown. When the 750-man Trinidad Regiment (the island's sole army unit) was ordered to take up arms and suppress protesters, three young lieutenants led a mutiny. Refusing to enforce the emergency decree, rebels captured Teteron Bay army base on the northwestern tip of the island. In a panic, the government ordered the Coast Guard to recapture the base. At the critical moment, when the rebel army had approaching Coast Guard ships in their gun sights, they declined to fire, deciding not to take the lives of innocent sailors guilty of nothing more than following orders. The rebels had at their disposal sufficient firepower to destroy the vessels, but they could not rain death upon their "black brothers." Minutes later, when a shell from one of the Coast Guard ships killed a young rebel, Clyde Bailey, many of the mutineers dropped their rifles and headed home over the hills.[208]

With love in their hearts, the mutineers' noble choice led to defeat of the movement. Four years later, Raffique Shah reflected on his experience: "if we had been politically conscious to the point to understand revolution, to understand what it's all about, that it means life or death, it means making tremendous sacrifices, we would've blown those two boats out of the water, but we did not do this. We felt that there were innocent people on those boats. In a revolution you do not have innocent people."[209]

Immediately after the April near-revolution, however, repression was the order of the day. As Bill Riviere put it:

> The ruling clique, in the absence of moral authority to decide for the people, has intensified repression. Public gatherings have been banned. Radical newspapers have been terrorized into silence. The Regiment is gradually being phased out. The Police have been granted powers of arbitrary search and arrest. Spies are everywhere. Victimization has become part of the national ethic. Dictatorship is complete. But the Black Man

has found his inner being. Organizations are growing. Trinidad and Tobago will never be the same.[210]

Although not a revolution, the movement changed Trinidad and Tobago's political landscape, ushering in a number of long-needed reforms and dramatically improving decades of hostile relations between East Indians and Africans. Throughout the Caribbean, the main long-term effects were cultural, visible in the blossoming of calypso, the widespread popularity of reggae, innovative visual arts and literature, and people changing their names and clothing to African ones.

For Ivar Oxaal, "The central point about the 1970 Trinidad movement was that it represented another local battle in the contemporary international struggle against Western neo-imperialism, being waged, frequently by the young in virtually every country where private enterprise, particularly when foreign-owned, is seen to be incompatible with the general welfare, that is to say, everywhere in the capitalist world."[211]

Bermuda

Bermuda's anticolonial Black Power movement threatened not only to end British colonialism but also to disenfranchise the "Forty Thieves," as locals derisively referred to the island's small white oligarchy. On April 25, 1968, a spontaneous riot broke out when youths from a "back-a-town" neighborhood of the capital were denied entry to a fair. Problems of egregious segregation, racism, and police brutality were to blame, and once an outlet for decades of frustration was found, violence and counterviolence escalated dramatically. The riot turned into a weeklong uprising. Police and the Bermuda Regiment failed to bring quiet even after a state of emergency was declared, and order was finally restored only after the British sent a company of 150 Royal Inniskilling Fusiliers from Northern Ireland to suppress the movement. The *Royal Gazette* described the events as the "worst civil disturbances in the colony's history." During the next four years, the movement grew by leaps and bounds, and British troops had to be sent ashore at least four more times. Each time, their brutality produced an ever more militant response. Both the British police commissioner and governor were assassinated in 1972 and 1973.

U.S. movements had a profound effect on Bermuda, where activists adopted previously formulated manifestos and uniforms. Following their participation in Black Power conferences in New Jersey in 1967 and Philadelphia in 1968, activists in Bermuda were called upon to plan the next gathering in 1969. Leading up to the conference, a variety of liberation movements endorsed it—including North Vietnam, the PLO, and North Korea. Kwame Nkrumah called it a part of "world rebellion of the oppressed against the oppressor." In his opening speech at a packed football stadium, C.L.R. James exhorted thousands keenly listening to his every word to "join the mighty struggle against the forces of American imperialism," not to "play with revolution," and to "mobilize massively."

From across the Caribbean, Black Power groups actively participated. More than one thousand people attended a range of workshops on themes such as Revolutionary Education, Economics, Politics, Religion, and History. (The CIA estimated attendance at 1,100, while the British claimed a higher number of 1,600.) Conference attendees were clear they did not want to produce "Black copies of existing White institutions." A memorandum entitled "Black Power 1969" encouraged people to redouble their activism for "world humanism" that would "eliminate hunger, disease, poverty, ignorance" and bring "dignity to all people."[212] The conference was enormously successful in accelerating the growth of organizations in the region: the Black Beret Cadre and the Vanguard Party of the Bahamas emerged after it. A year later, the Congress of African People was formed in Atlanta.[213] In October 1970, British Intelligence estimated that Black Power movements "at least doubled in number" since the conference in July 1969—although they also noted, "An alliance between elements from the extreme left and Black Power factions in the Caribbean now seems less probable."[214] So threatened were world powers by such transnational gatherings that the governments of the U.S., the UK, France, and Holland threatened to stop all tourism to Barbados if the next Black Power conference in 1970 was allowed there.[215]

John Bassett, friend of Black Panther leaders Fred Hampton and Mark Clark, became Chief of Staff of the Black Beret Cadre. Their "10–10 Program" was modeled on the Black Panthers' ten points. Their 1971 manifesto called for black revolution to end exploitation by British imperialism and to dispossess the local white oligarchy. The Cadre advocated an egalitarian society, including an end to male chauvinism. In April 1970, the British sent a frigate to defend City Hall from a planned Black Beret demonstration in protest of SNCC leader Rap Brown's trial in the U.S. (While in prison in the early 1970s, Brown adopted the name Jamil Al-Amin.) In August 1970, undeterred by the military power arrayed against them, Black Berets burned a British flag outside City Hall to commemorate the 1960 Sharpeville massacre in South Africa. As they came under increasing attacks, a low-scale urban guerrilla war ensued. Arson and sniper attacks across the island were a favored response to arrests of leaders. Fearful of the military's radicalization, at least sixty soldiers from the Bermuda Regiment were discharged or disciplined for having Beret aims.

The British government's harsh repression in colonial Bermuda persisted. On December 2, 1977, the British-controlled government executed Larry Tacklyn and Erskine Burrows—movement leaders who had been convicted of five murders, including that of the British governor. For three days after the executions, riots convulsed the island. More than $100 million in property was destroyed before the Royal Fusiliers again arrived to reinforce the Bermuda Regiment and restore order. Regional insurgencies continued to move ahead. On March 13, 1979, the New JEWEL Movement, a vanguard party first organized in 1973, seized power in Grenada and held it until 1983—when six thousand U.S. troops invaded the island to stop its revolution.

While most European movements reached their climaxes in 1968, in the Caribbean and the United States, the high points of the movements came two years later. Everywhere, 1968 is celebrated without concrete exploration of the period's history. What are we to make of the fact that hundreds of histories have failed even to mention Caribbean incarnations? Racially exclusive and nationalist histories continue to play too great a role in our own collective comprehension of our past. What are we to make of the fact that Daniel Cohn-Bendit and Rudi Dutschke are known to tens of millions of people while practically no one has heard of Larry Tacklyn and Erskine Burrows? Why have we not embraced Rex LaSalle, Raffique Shah, and Michael Bazie, the three mutinous lieutenants whose kindness prevented them from taking lives for the revolution? Millions travel to the Caribbean for memorable vacations, yet how many people can utter one intelligent phrase about its recent history? We are all apparently caught in an overwhelming system of indoctrination and domination—at work and at play—even when we wish to oppose it.

The United States

Onset of Counterrevolution

With the global awakening of 1968, no country or institution could defend its borders from the infiltration of the Eros effect. Even the center of the modern world system, "the belly of the beast," soon found itself embroiled in bitter domestic conflicts. At first, the highest circles of power could do little but watch in horror as the war against Vietnam came home. In 1968, the system moved to repress movements, and counterrevolutionary violence emerged with a vengeance. The "generation gap" was widely discussed before the Tet offensive in Vietnam, but after Tet, the U.S. government abandoned policies of appeasement and embarked on a program of systematic domestic repression.

Barely a week after Tet began, on February 8, 1968, three black students were shot dead and thirty-four wounded at a peaceful demonstration in Orangeburg, South Carolina. All those killed had been shot in the back. The Orangeburg murders led to renewed questioning of the legitimacy of nonviolence and integration as the means and ends of the civil rights movement—means and ends which already had been heavily eroded by riots in 1967 and emergence of Black Power. In late March 1968, advocates of Black Power in

Memphis, taking their cue from Adam Clayton Powell Jr.'s words that "the day of Martin Luther King has come to an end," broke away from a march led by "de lawd" (as they called King) and began breaking windows. The rioting spread, and when the police response was over, one demonstrator had been killed and sixty wounded. The National Guard was needed to control the city. Tensions continued to mount between King and more militant blacks right up to April 4, when he was assassinated in Memphis.

The public outrage at the assassination of this man of peace has few precedents in U.S. history. In over 168 cities, ghettos exploded. Flames reached to within six blocks of the White House. For the first time since the Civil War, federal troops were called in to protect government buildings, and machine guns were mounted on the Capitol balcony and the White House lawn. The combined forces of the police, army, and National Guard occupied ghettos and ruthlessly enforced a curfew. By the time a ceasefire was established, at least forty-six people lay dead, over 21,000 had been injured, and another 20,000 were in jail. In Washington, DC, alone, more than 7,600 people were arrested, over 13,500 federal troops were needed to restore order, and more damage was done to the city than had been inflicted by the British during the War of 1812. All told, over 50,000 federal troops (more than were used in any single battle in Vietnam) were necessary to restore order, and property damage was estimated at over $130 million.[216] As late as April 9, snipers in Washington and Baltimore continued to attack police.

White backlash quickly set in. In one day, President Johnson established a riot control center in the Pentagon and an Urban Institute to monitor the inner cities. On the same day that 150,000 people attended King's funeral in Atlanta, Congress was busy cutting antipoverty funds, and the *New York Times* editorialized against "black criminals." A little over a week later, the FBI publicly claimed that King "was closely associated with Communists and sex deviates. His program for America was an unadulterated Communist program."

The national and international repercussions of events in this period are easy to underestimate. On April 6, police in Oakland, California, killed Bobby Hutton. The Black Panthers' first martyr was cold-bloodedly murdered as he surrendered with his hands raised. He was the first of more than two dozen Panthers who would be killed in the next few years under the aegis of the FBI's COINTELPRO (counterintelligence program), which went into full operation on a national basis on May 10, 1968. In the same period, the CIA's illegal domestic spying program, Operation CHAOS, intensified activities inside the United States. The offices of the Black Panther Party, the organization thrust into the leadership of the burgeoning movement, were attacked across the country. On December 4, 1969, Fred Hampton, leader of the Black Panther Party in Chicago and founder of the original Rainbow Coalition, was murdered by police while asleep in his bed after having been drugged the night before by an FBI informant.[217]

Campus activists intensified their protests. The day that King was assassinated, black students at Cornell University held the chairperson of the Department of Economics hostage for six hours to struggle with his racism.[218] At Tuskegee, 250 students held twelve trustees captive for twelve hours on April 7 to demand an end to ROTC and changes in campus curfews.[219] Nineteen days after King's murder, students at Columbia University began their now famous occupation of five university buildings. They temporarily took a dean prisoner and lived in the offices of Grayson Kirk, president of Columbia. Their reasons included opposition to the war against Vietnam and racism, the latter symbolized by plans for a new gymnasium for Columbia students but not for residents of the neighboring ghetto, many of whose houses would be demolished to make room for the gym. The police waited a week, and then they "simply ran wild. Those who tried to say they were innocent bystanders or faculty were given the same flailing treatment as the students. For most of the students it was their first encounter with brutality and blood, and they responded in fear and anger. The next day almost the entire campus responded to a call for a student strike. In a few hours, thanks to the New York City Police Department, a large part of the Columbia campus had become radicalized."[220] The police rampage lasted only a few hours, but over 150 people were seriously injured and 700 arrested before it ended.

The occupation at Columbia was one of the most famous spectacles of the U.S. student movement, and it was afforded wide coverage by the mass media as the subject of numerous retrospective books, television shows, and even a full-length Hollywood production, *The Strawberry Statement*. Columbia quickly became a model for similar university takeovers in the months after it, not only in the United States (as at Ohio State University, where students held two vice presidents and four staff members hostage), but throughout the world.[221] Tom Hayden, himself one of the participants at Columbia, called for "raids on the offices of professors doing weapons research," noting that, "Columbia opened a new tactical stage in the resistance movement which began last fall; from the overnight occupation of buildings to permanent occupation; from mill-ins to the creation of revolutionary committees; from symbolic civil disobedience to barricaded resistance. Not only are these tactics already being duplicated on other campuses, but they are sure to be surpassed by even more militant tactics."[222]

Beneath the radar of photo spreads in *Life* magazine devoted to elite students at Columbia and Tinseltown remakes of occupations at Ivy League colleges, tens of thousands of student activists mobilized. On April 26, more than two hundred thousand students in high schools and universities in New York participated in a strike against the Vietnam War. The next day, in seventeen cities, sizeable antiwar demonstrations occurred. The largest was in New York with more than eighty thousand people. Despite media inattention, such partial strikes and local mobilizations prepare the ground for future actions, creating infrastructure and possibilities that are subsequently realized in national actions and dramatic outbreaks of protest (as occurred in May 1970).

By June 1968, the newly elected leaders of Students for a Democratic Society were "revolutionary communists" committed to violent revolution. According to SDS National Secretary Mark Rudd, the organization had over three hundred autonomous chapters and an active membership of around one hundred thousand.[223] As radical beliefs spread among white students, the number of campus confrontations continued to escalate. By conservative estimates there were 136 in the academic year 1967–68; at least 272 in 1968–69; more than 388 from September 1969 to April 1970; and finally when the student movement reached its peak during the nationwide strike of May 1970, there were at least 508 violent confrontations in one month.[224] During the entire school year of 1969–70, the FBI listed 1,785 student demonstrations, including the occupation of 313 buildings.

Violence and male aggressiveness of leaders at Columbia, however, made it all too clear that the old values of the movement had been surpassed. As Sara Evans remembered, "The new left had begun by raising the 'feminine' values of cooperation, equality, community and love, but as the war escalated, FBI harassment increased, and ghettos exploded, the new left turned more and more to a kind of macho stridency and militarist fantasy."[225]

In 1968, the escalating spiral of violent confrontations drew millions of people into it. Although the war was supposed to be in Vietnam, there was also one going on at home. In the three years leading up to the 1970 national campus strike, the National Guard was called to domestic duty over two hundred times to deal with protests.[226] Between 1964 and 1969, there were more than 239 major violent confrontations between African Americans in inner cities and the forces of law and order in which at least 191 people died and over 8,000 were injured. In the same period, there were over two hundred nonpolice attacks on members of the civil rights movement which caused at least 23 deaths and 112 injuries.[227] These federal statistics are quite low, and they do not include twenty-eight Black Panthers killed as a result of FBI COINTELPRO operations.

For student radicals, the question of violence may have been the focus of intense debate, but off the campuses, whether in the ghettos or in Indochina, the level of political violence was such that even Resurrection City II, a peaceful encampment near the White House of three thousand followers of Martin Luther King's Poor People's Campaign, was cleared out by the government, further intensifying the atmosphere of confrontation. When Robert Kennedy was killed because of his support of Israel, it seemed that Malcolm X had correctly predicted the chickens would come home to roost (i.e., that the violence exported by the United States would come home to haunt it).

Whether or not the student New Left in the United States unanimously approved the new militancy, the Establishment had no qualms about murder. On August 8, six blacks were killed during riots that coincided with the Republican National Convention in Miami. Two days of fighting in Liberty City left over one hundred people wounded and hundreds more arrested, and it only ended when thousands of National Guard arrived. At that time, however, the media gave the murders only scant coverage. Censorship across the nation became more overt, even beeping out a line in the 1968 Smothers Brothers show: "Ronald Reagan is a known *heterosexual*." There was a "silent majority" that was said to have nodded their heads in agreement.

On August 28 came the spectacle of the Chicago Democratic National Convention. The nationally televised police riot revealed how far the new hard line within the Establishment had reached. Nonviolent sitting protesters were bloodily clubbed in front of television cameras, and even network anchors were not immune from what was later characterized as a "police riot" by the official Walker Commission report.[228] At least sixty-five news people were arrested, maced, or beaten. One was attacked and carried out of the convention while broadcasting live. Chicago's Mayor Richard Daley had carefully waited for demonstrators, assembling more than twenty thousand law enforcement officials, and their sadistic attacks took place in full public view.[229]

Chicago had an immense impact both on the movement and the Establishment, particularly since the police violence was carried *inside* the convention. Eugene McCarthy's bid for the presidential nomination may have been doomed to fail, but when Chicago police mercilessly attacked his supporters, it appeared as an assault on the "democratic" process and "free" press. Before the convention, there were signals of the country's growing division from

Chicago police after confiscating Pigasus the Pig, Yippie presidential candidate, outside the Democratic National Convention in 1968. Fred W. McDarrah.

forty-three black GIs of the First Armored Division, all decorated Vietnam veterans who refused to leave Fort Hood, Texas, for riot duty in Chicago.

Although the violence in Chicago was blamed by a federal commission on a "police riot," no officials were ever punished. Instead, new repressive measures were legislated. The new Federal Law Enforcement Assistance Administration was mandated to better arm and train local police departments. The Omnibus Crime Bill had passed both houses of Congress, a measure deemed necessary by "rising crime rates," but clearly a measure aimed at the movement. In the first applications of this new law, the Chicago 8 (including Bobby Seale, chairman of the Black Panther Party) were indicted for conspiring to cause riots in Chicago. Jamil Al-Amin was arrested for violating provisions of the new law and received a sentence of five years in prison, and thirteen Chicano activists in Los Angeles were indicted and jailed. A new spectacle of government violence in Chicago was then publicly orchestrated. When Bobby Seale demanded his constitutionally guaranteed right to choose his own counsel, the judge in the case had him bound and gagged in the courtroom. By making an example of Seale, the state sought to intimidate its opponents, but protests continued to grow in Chicago. Graham Nash's song "Chicago" brought national attention to the case. Finally, to dispose of Seale, the judge sentenced him to years in prison for contempt of court and shuttled him off to face the death penalty on a trumped-up murder charge in Connecticut.

Alongside domestic counterrevolutionary violence, a major international reorganization of Pax Americana began. The U.S. would accept formal political independence in the Third World so that economic penetration could continue. China would be befriended as a wedge against Vietnam and the Soviet Union. After the United States experienced its first major military defeat in two hundred years, Richard Nixon and Henry Kissinger, arrogant power brokers schooled in the cheap tricks of anticommunism and the "elegance" of order, ascended to the highest positions of world power. The sinister adjustments they would manage in the international constellation of power would reverberate in distant corners of the planet for decades to come.

With the assassination of Martin Luther King, the failure of the near-revolution in France, the Soviet invasion of Czechoslovakia, the pre-Olympic massacre of hundreds of students in Mexico City, and the election of Richard Nixon, global reaction gained the upper hand. Although 1968 was a clear turning point, there were earlier signals of the coming counterrevolution. On April 27, 1967, a fascist clique of Israeli-trained and U.S.-armed colonels activated a NATO plan and seized power in Greece.[230] Che Guevara was captured and murdered in Bolivia. In the United States, the 1967 uprisings in Detroit, Newark, Atlanta, and Cincinnati were brutally suppressed by the National Guard, and dozens of people were killed. In Detroit alone, forty-five people lost their lives and over two thousand were wounded before the fighting stopped. The Newark uprising lasted six

Art by Jay Belloli, 1970.

days, during which twenty-three people were killed.[231] Detroit and Newark revealed escalating government violence, but they also marked a new phase in the development of the African American movement. Not without reason, Jamil Al-Amin called Newark and Detroit "dress rehearsals for revolution." Already long beyond Martin Luther King's civil rights focus, the movement's cutting edge went through Black Power and openly embraced international social revolution as the solution to the world's problems.

At that time, the American auto industry was concentrated in Detroit, and hundreds of thousands of African Americans had migrated there to find work on "Motown" assembly lines. The 1967 rebellion was a crucible for the steeling of African American resistance to racist police attacks on segregated neighborhoods. Within a year, Detroit would spawn a spectrum of black revolutionary unions and organizations.

From Civil Rights to Revolutionary Internationalism

Although there were several streams of thought in the revolutionary current, they all advocated overthrowing the U.S. government, not simply integrating it as the civil rights movement had long proposed or creating Black Power bases within it. In 1965, SNCC had abandoned pacifism and embraced Black Power, an ideology that had already made its way from Africa to the Caribbean. SNCC's program for black autonomy meant expelling all white members, and they insisted whites should organize to break down racism in their own communities, rather than paternalistically aid minorities. SNCC had long endorsed strident antidraft and antiwar positions, but new leaders Kwame Ture and Jamil Al-Amin embraced not just radical ideas of liberation movements but also their tactics. By moving to the next level of struggle, SNCC lost much of its student base, and the organization was unable to generate a new popular base. The transition was part of a dynamic series of developments in the African American liberation struggle, as depicted in the table below.

The Black Liberation Movement in the United States

Phase	Civil Rights	Black Power	Revolutionary Internationalism
Type of Social Movement	Reform	Rebellion	Revolution
Organizations	NAACP, SCLC, CORE	SNCC, RNA	BPP, LRBW
Key Events Time Frame	Montgomery, Selma 1955–65	Watts, MLK Assassination 1965–68	Malcolm X Assassination, MLK Assassination 1968–71
Leaders	Martin Luther King Jr., Jesse Jackson	Jamil Al-Amin, (H. Rap Brown), Kwame Ture (Stokely Carmichael), Malcolm X, Amiri Baraka (Leroi Jones)	Bobby Seale, Huey Newton, Eldridge Cleaver, Malcolm X
Key Constituencies	Ascendant Middle Class Clergy, Educators, Businesses	Lower Middle Class: Tenants, Farmers, Students; Farm Workers	Lumpen (Including Prisoners), Working-Class Youth, GIs
Goal	Integration	Black National/ Separatism	Revolution (Intercommunalism)
Tactic	Nonviolence	Self-Defense	Any Means Necessary
Ideology	Pragmatism, Christianity	Increasingly Pan Africanist	Revolutionary (Intercommunalism)
Slogan	We Shall Overcome	Black Is Beautiful	All Power to the People

The radicalization and decline of SNCC coincided with the rise of the Black Panther Party (the heirs of Malcolm X). Founded in Oakland, California, in 1966, the Panthers immediately embarked on a courageous program of armed self-defense. Following police patrols while legally armed under California laws, they did their utmost to ensure an end to routine brutalization of African Americans. In resultant confrontations, dozens of Panthers were arrested. Many were killed. At least seventy-five Panthers languished in jails and prisons by late 1967, when in the early morning hours of October 28, Minister of Defense Huey P. Newton was arrested after being found wounded and unconscious at the scene of a shootout where a policeman lay dead and another wounded. His trial electrified the country's insurgent youth, and Panther recruits and supporters rushed to his defense. Overnight, the Panthers became internationally prominent. In at least a dozen countries, Panther emulators organized. On February 18, 1968, the remnants of SNCC formally merged with the Black Panther Party.

Art by Emory Douglas, 1969.

Less than two years after they formed, the Panthers had grown from dozens of members to hundreds. After King was assassinated, they became thousands strong within weeks. In the month of June 1968 alone, they recruited nearly eight hundred members in New York City. By the end of the year their newspaper, the *Black Panther*, was selling over one hundred thousand copies every week. As part of the Panthers' commitment to build a multicultural insurgency, Minister of Information Eldridge Cleaver became the Peace and Freedom Party's candidate for president, and numerous other Panthers ran for public office as well. By 1969, they had chapters in forty-five cities. At the Party's high point, Chairman Bobby Seale counted at least five thousand Panthers in forty-seven chapters.[232] Members were responsible for daily "survival programs" that included fourteen medical clinics, a robust campaign against sickle cell anemia, buses to help families visit loved ones in prison, clothing programs, liberation schools, and, most famously, the free breakfast for children program that daily fed thousands of youngsters in church basements before they went to school.

Organized as a Marxist-Leninist party, all Panther chapters were under the authority of the central committee in Oakland, and within each chapter a strict hierarchy was observed with field marshals, section leaders, subsection leaders, members, community supporters, and the underground—small cells that carried out secretive actions. With names like Wolverines, these underground groups were unknown to each other in order to prevent police infiltration. In 1969, FBI director J. Edgar Hoover named the Panthers "the greatest threat to the internal security of the country." Shortly thereafter, police stepped up their attacks. By 1970, only one central committee member had not been killed, imprisoned, or forced into exile. Altogether twenty-eight Panthers were killed and more than sixty wounded, while some fourteen police were killed and more than thirty wounded in their war on the Panthers.

Although they did not allow white members, the Panthers worked closely with a broad range of constituencies, not only in forming defense committees but also in visionary quests like Fred Hampton's organizing the original Rainbow Coalition of Chicago street gangs, which included the Young Patriots from Appalachia. To fight racism, Panthers eloquently intoned, solidarity, not hatred, is needed. Their message resonated deeply among countercultural youth—and many others. By 1970, the Panthers emerged as vanguard of a revolutionary multicultural alliance that articulated a vision for a world at peace based upon sharing of global resources and international cooperation. They articulated open support for liberation movements around the world (including the Vietnamese NLF). In addition, they called for the United Nations to sponsor a plebiscite of African Americans to decide whether or not a separate black nation should be formed in the U.S.

In Detroit, radical autoworkers involved in organizing black unions became the Party's local chapter, but they quickly broke away from the BPP.[233] Soon after the 1967 uprising, about thirty activists had founded a black monthly newspaper, *Inner City Voice*. An early editorial indicated the group's revolutionary ambitions: "If the Koreans and Vietnamese can overthrow imperialism in Asia, then Asia will be free. But if the black revolution can overthrow capitalism and imperialism in the U.S., then the whole world will be freed."[234] As the paper's monthly circulation grew to ten thousand copies, staff members discussed how to bring revolutionary action into their workplaces. A month after King was assassinated, the Dodge Revolutionary Union Movement (DRUM) held its first major action, a wildcat strike at Dodge Main in Hamtramck. Both black and white workers protested speedup of the assembly line. Three weeks later, about three hundred workers from the plant marched to the local United Auto Workers (UAW) office with a set of fifteen demands, including investigation of racism in the company, placement of an African American on the Chrysler Board of Directors, and equal pay for black workers and their white counterparts at a South African Chrysler plant.[235] The next day, about three thousand black workers remained outside the back gate when work finished, again staging a wildcat strike against speedups. That fall DRUM union candidates received 40 percent of the vote in union elections.

The movement spread to Eldon Avenue Gear and Axle plant, where the Eldon Avenue Revolutionary Union Movement (ELRUM) formed, eventually leading to formation of the League of Revolutionary Black Workers (LRBW) with a core membership of at least 250 activists at more than a dozen Detroit factories. Unlike the centrally organized Black Panther Party, the LRBW was composed of semiautonomous components with specific work areas. An executive committee of seven tightly controlled its central staff of about eighty people.

Although the LRBW helped to create a Black Student United Front that included junior high school, high school, and college groups, they treated students with disdain and used them as adjuncts for leafleting and picketing at factories. The 1969 masthead of the *South End*, the daily organ of DRUM, proudly proclaimed, "One Class-Conscious Worker is Worth 100 Students." Their relationships to feminism and whites were similarly problematic. When leafleting outside factories, League members would often pass their literature only to African American colleagues—and refuse to give them to white workers. Despite pressure from the Panthers, they resisted working with John Sinclair and the White Panther Party.[236]

A more restrictive nationalism was contained in groups like Ron Karenga's US (United Slaves) Organization and the Republic of New Afrika (RNA), which held its founding convention in Detroit's Shrine of the Black Madonna in March 1968. Nearly two hundred delegates signed a Declaration of Independence making all blacks "forever free and independent of the jurisdiction of the United States." RNA struggled to create a black nation in South Carolina, Georgia, Alabama, Mississippi, and Louisiana. Black Power advocates generally shunned alliances and built autonomous black initiatives. In many large cities, including Philadelphia, Boston, Denver, Los Angeles, and Washington, DC, Black United Fronts formed out of struggles for community control. After inventing Kwanzaa as a celebration of African heritage, US was a particularly emblematic group, whose cultural nationalism proved to be fertile soil for the FBI to plant seeds of mistrust and division with the Panthers. In 1969, FBI COINTELPRO efforts paid dividends when U.S. gunmen killed two leading Los Angeles Panthers, Bunchy Carter and John Huggins, on the UCLA campus. While Panthers' politics pointed toward global revolution, Black Power was often a vehicle for African American politicians to use when they ran for office in gerrymandered districts. Business owners also found much of value in advocating "blackness" in their communities, as well as in front of government agencies seeking to fund programs for minorities.

Although much of the country was unaware of it, there was a material basis for rejection of integration. The isolation of urban blacks in ghettos following World War II was hastened by racist federal laws granting whites (and

not blacks) access to low-cost federal loans to buy homes in white suburbs. Formal integration of the armed forces aside, African Americans faced continuing racism and segregation in the military. On the job market as well, blacks were relegated to the end of the hiring line. The blue-ribbon Kerner Commission (the National Advisory Commission on Civil Disorders formed to study the rebellions of 1967) made America's racism all too apparent when it released its report to President Johnson on February 29, 1968: "Our Nation

Students activists are arrested after being clubbed by police at San Francisco State College. *Black Dwarf*.

(TOP, left) Black Power leaders Stokely Carmichael and H. Rap Brown face reporters during the Columbia University occupation. Corbis-Bettmann/UPI. (TOP, right) Fred Hampton. Alan Copeland. (BOTTOM) Little Bobby Hutton and Bobby Seale storming the California State Capitol at Sacramento, May 2, 1967. Ward Sharrer/Sacramento Bee.

is moving toward two societies—one black and one white—separate and unequal." The Commission's report regarded the growing radicalism among blacks as unique.[237] If they had taken the time to conduct their polls among a broader cross-section of Americans, however, they would have found that injustices and insurgencies were far from confined to African Americans.

Emergence of Latino Opposition

As the eros effect made its appearance among Chicanos, a militant student movement emerged in high schools and colleges, and a self-conscious Chicano culture was born, transforming the identities and aspirations of Mexican Americans.[238] For the first time, Americans of Mexican descent took the "national stage as self determined agents rather than subservient and racialized others."[239] Over a span of years, movement activism produced new identities: "Chicanos" or "Latinos," which millions of people chose to replace Eurocentric labels such as "Hispanic" or "Spanish."[240]

Founded in 1965 by "Corky" Gonzales, the Crusade won strong support in the barrios with its work for La Raza. Denver Public Library.

In 1965, Corky Gonzales founded the Crusade for Justice in Denver. An ex-boxer, poet, and playwright, he was quite radical, having been raised by a father who fought alongside Pancho Villa during the 1910 Mexican Revolution in Chihuahua. In August 1966, months before Martin Luther King came to oppose the Vietnam War and when white radicals were only beginning to call for peace, Gonzales spoke truth to power: "The ruthless financial lords of Wall Street are the only real recipients of the tremendous profits to be made by the conduct of a wanton, ruthless war. The great and powerful corporations who control our industries, who control the purse strings of the nation, calmly play a chess game trading the lives of innocent American boys, confused and bewildered Vietnamese men, women, and children for green dollars that do not show the red stain of blood."[241] Gonzales worked with a spectrum of activists, but his principal aim was to build unity among Mexican Americans.

The Latino movement was heavily working class, a reflection of Latinos being denied opportunities, suffering inadequate education, and facing severe discrimination. They were compelled to accept jobs that many Americans refused to take. The United Farm Workers were symbolically important to the Latino movement. Hardworking and scandalously underpaid Filipino and Mexican agricultural workers formed the organization in 1966. Under the visionary leadership of Cesar Chavez, people of many races and ideologies came together in unprecedented harmony and found ways to fight the system using weapons of love and solidarity. Although the farmworkers' Plan de Delano explicitly called for "a revolution of the poor seeking bread and justice," they insisted that "Our revolution will not be armed, but we want the existing social order to dissolve, we want a new social order." Chavez sought to create "new men and women" whose "natural dignity" would elevate them above the rule treatment they suffered at the hands of profit-hungry corporate executives.

One of the most spectacular indications of the awakening of Mexican Americans came on June 5, 1967, when Reies Tijerina and the Alianza Federal de Pueblos Libres seized the county courthouse in Tierra Amarilla, New Mexico. Holding the staff hostage, they freed eleven prisoners. The group vowed to implement the 1848 Treaty of Guadalupe Hidalgo (which had ended the war between Mexico and the U.S.) and to legally reclaim lands stolen from their ancestors despite guarantees to the contrary in the treaty. Explaining the courthouse raid, Corky Gonzales summarized, "The United States government itself is part of a criminal conspiracy in taking these people's lands, making out fraudulent titles, and selling the land to others." He insisted that "Hispanos" should "die in Tierra Amarilla. . . . Instead of dying in Vietnam."[242]

Not since Pancho Villa's 1916 attack on Columbus, New Mexico, did the indigenous population of the Southwestern United States have such a hero to celebrate. Even as police searched for Tijerina, *corridos* (folk ballads) celebrated his courage. In response to this first militant armed action by Mexican Americans in the Southwest in more than a century, the government mobilized the National Guard with tanks and created a regional state of siege. In the end, Tijerina was acquitted of all charges stemming from the courthouse raid, although he was later sentenced to two years' imprisonment for burning a U.S. National Forest sign. The movement he helped create came to exert a significant cultural hegemony among the native peoples of the Southwest.[243]

Inspired by the Black Panther Party, Mexican-American urban youth formed the Brown Berets. The Young Lords, a Puerto Rican street gang in Chicago, also aligned with the Panthers. Both groups diligently sought to defend their communities from police attacks and racist intrusions. They also established survival programs modeled on those of the Panthers. Emulating Panther attire, both the Brown Berets and Young Lords wore similar uniforms and adopted parallel programs. In Los Angeles, in September 1967, Brown Berets founded a coffeehouse named La Piranya, a moniker adopted from the LAPD's shorthand for beret-wearing youth.[244] Within two years there were as many as ninety chapters stretching from Los Angeles to Chicago and San Antonio.[245] While some Brown Berets were internationalist revolutionaries, others were exclusively nationalistic. David Sanchez, a key leader, was reported to be a "strident anticommunist."[246]

On March 3, 1968, over one thousand students walked out of Abraham Lincoln High School in East Los Angeles to protest racist teachers, the absence of Mexican and Mexican-American culture and history from the curriculum, and repression of their free speech. By the end of the day, more than ten thousand young people from four other nearby high schools joined the "walkouts" or "blowouts," as they became known. Despite—or should I say, because of—police violence that day against unarmed youth guilty of nothing more than leaving school, the movement gained wide community support, and walkouts continued for a week and a half. Three months later, thirteen of the organizers (including four Brown Berets) were imprisoned on charges of conspiracy under the new federal Omnibus Crime Bill just enacted by Congress. Walkouts spread throughout Texas and the Southwest. College students also took action. In October 1968, the Mexican-American Student Confederation occupied the office of the president of the University of California system to protest his refusal to respect the United Farm Workers boycott of grapes.[247]

Latino internationalism and working-class consciousness infused the movement at the same time as cultural nationalism mingled with accomodationist reformism. The emergence of so many tendencies revealed the release of long-suppressed energies. Aztlán was extolled as the mythical homeland of the Aztecs in the Southwestern United States. Radical nationalists compared even the best white radicals to "Catholic Spaniards" and decried "European Puritanism."[248] Others built alliances and called for global revolution. In 1968, both Tijerina and Gonzales joined SCLC's Poor People's Campaign in Washington. Gonzales brought with him a contingent of "Native Americans from Colorado, New Mexico, Arizona, Nevada, and Oklahoma; young California Black Berets and Brown Berets; elderly New Mexico land-grant heirs and Asians from California's Bay Area; Black Panthers, hippies, and white radicals; pacifists and advocates of revolution."[249]

Chicano organizations such as the Brown Berets initiated community programs and protected neighborhoods. Photographer unknown.

The Los Angeles "blowouts," March 1968: students demonstrate in front of the Board of Education. Raul Ruiz.

The Latino movement found its center in Denver largely because of the charismatic presence of Corky Gonzales. In its first ten years, the Crusade grew from a "small, male-dominated group" to a "multifaceted, multi-issue organization with hundreds of members" before it declined in the mid-1970s.[250] The Crusade was among the most visionary and militant revolutionary organizations in the U.S.—a fact not lost on the FBI, whose COINTELPRO targeted it as early as August 25, 1967. The Crusade purchased an old church on Denver's Downing Street in the summer of 1968, and it became a focal point for dances and cultural events—to say nothing of its importance as an organizing center. Continually harassed by police and FBI agents, Gonzales hoped to defuse their concerns and agreed to be interviewed on October 8, 1968.[251] Speaking to law enforcement officials, he patiently explained how Mexican Americans are victims of discrimination, how corporations benefit from the Vietnam War, and how use of the term "wetback" is pejorative (like "kike" and "wop").

The apartment on Downing Street in Denver. The greater part of the damage stemmed from demolition ordered by city officials on March 17, 1973. The slogan on the wall originated from the uprising at New York's Attica Prison. Pablo Castro.

From March 27 to 31, 1969, the Crusade hosted the first Chicano Youth Liberation Conference in their church. They expected only a few hundred people to attend, but there were almost that many organizations. At least 1,500 people came, including more than two busloads of Puerto Ricans organized by the Chicago Young Lords. The conference adopted El Plan Espiritual de Aztlán. Noted poet Alurista's preamble decried the "brutal 'Gringo' invasion of our territories" and promised to reclaim "our lands" in the struggle against "foreign 'Gabachos' who exploit our riches and destroy our culture." The Plan was firmly nationalistic: "With our hearts in our hands and our hands in the soil, we declare the independence of our mestizo nation. We are a bronze people with a bronze culture. Before the world, before all of North America, before all our brothers in the bronze continent, we are a nation, we are a nation of pueblos, we are Aztlán. Nationalism is the key to organization that transcends all religious, political, class and economic actions or boundaries. Nationalism is the common denominator that all members of La Raza can agree upon." The conference was not without criticism, especially from women involved in planning it

El Teatro Campesino in La Carpa de los Rasquachis (The Tent of the Underdogs). Artist unknown, 1973.

who felt they had been cast in traditional family roles.[252] Their insights became the basis for subsequent discussions. In framing both future conversations and actions, the conference was an enormous success.[253]

A month after the Denver gathering, student leaders in California met at the University of California Santa Barbara, producing a detailed and lengthy Chicano Plan for Higher Education. In addition, they formed MEChA—El Movimiento Estudiantil Chicano de Aztlán—which soon became an activist presence on dozens of campuses. Militant movements called for Third World studies programs in San Francisco, Los Angeles, and San Diego.[254] Lively street performances of El Teatro Campesino inspired protesters; local bands serenaded demonstrators.

The Puerto Rican independence movement, active since the end of the nineteenth century, was rejuvenated by a new generation of activists. The Puerto Rican Socialist Party, an organization formed in the 1960s, led massive antiwar demonstrations in Puerto Rico and New York. The Young Lords were an integral part of the Rainbow Coalition brought together by Panther leader Fred Hampton. Under the leadership of José (Cha-Cha) Jiménez, they established a significant presence in a city where police brutality was (and remains) a daily fact of life. In 1969, they took over a public meeting inside a police station and compelled discussion of police harassment. They mobilized more than ten thousand people to march in honor of heroes of Puerto Rican independence, organized survival programs, and did their utmost to end police violence. Several members of the Lords were callously murdered by police.

Hearing about the Chicago Young Lords, New York activists radicalized by the Columbia University strike traveled to meet Jiménez in June 1969.[255] Together they agreed to form a unified group, the Young Lords Organization. Wearing purple berets, the New York branch developed survival programs, such as breakfast programs and day-care centers, at the same time as they built prisoner support groups and veterans' organizations. They famously blocked some of the city's main thoroughfares with weeks of uncollected trash, thereby winning regular garbage collection in the neighborhood. The Lords transformed a vacant church into a childcare facility with breakfast programs and a community artists' center. They helped form a Health Workers Revolutionary Union Movement modeled on Detroit's LRBW and took over Lincoln Hospital in the South Bronx to demand it meet community needs. A Lesbian and Gay Caucus, as well as a Women's Caucus, existed within their ranks. By the end of 1970, they had grown to more than eight thousand members with offices in three places as well as branches in five cities, a weekly newspaper and a sizable number of supporters on the island.[256]

There was a rebirth of active resistance among Native Americans as well, an opposition which has been continuous for hundreds of years, but one that was intensified by the global upheavals of 1968. That year both the American Indian Movement (AIM) and a national newspaper, *Akwesasne Notes*, were founded. In 1969, the occupation of Alcatraz Island symbolized the intensification of revolutionary consciousness among Native Americans. In late 1972, the Trail of Broken Treaties caravan went to Washington, DC, where it was allowed to arrive peacefully. The same was not true for the occupation of Wounded Knee beginning on February 28, 1973. The FBI surrounded the encampment, killed key activists, and framed others, notably Leonard Peltier, for murder.

Asian Americans, Filipinos, and other minorities whose cultural roots are in the Third World also became radicalized and mobilized in this period.[257] A veritable rainbow of ethnic power movements erupted in 1968, including even small groups such as Arab Americans, Filipinos, and Japanese Americans. As Laura Pulido tells us: "While the civil rights movement raised the consciousness of potential activists, Black Power pushed them into action, eventually resulting in the Red, Yellow, and Brown Power movements."[258] Activist Warren Furutani noted that "Whether it was LA, the Bay Area, Seattle, New York or the Midwest, people we ran into all over the country had the same epiphany at the same time."[259] Yellow Power activists rejected the "colonialist" label "Oriental" and instead embraced a more inclusive moniker of Asian American. In the Bay Area, ex-prisoners and community activists broke away from mainstream self-help group to form the Red Guard, modeled on the Black Panther Party.

Their platform included, "We Red Guard want an end to the exploitation of the people in our community by the avaricious businessmen and politicians who are one and the same."[260]

Radicalization of the African American movement not only led to the galvanization of other minorities, but new demands appeared on the nation's campuses. Black students at Howard University were the first to raise the issue of self-management when they staged a four-day sit-in on March 19, 1968. At San Francisco State College, after years of trying to convince the administration to recruit more minority students, a Third World Liberation Front formulated a visionary program for ethnic studies that would include Native Americans, Latinos, African Americans, and Asian Americans. In alliance with white students, especially SDS members, a strike began on November 6. An intense struggle lasted for five months, ultimately winning an ethnic studies program. Similar efforts were launched at UC Berkeley and UCLA, as well as in Southern California.[261] In Berkeley, then-governor Ronald Reagan declared a "state of extreme emergency" and ordered National Guard, Highway Patrol, and Alameda County sheriffs to the campus, where teargas and mace caused dozens of injuries. Over 150 students were arrested.[262] At the University of California San Diego, faculty and students created a Lumumba-Zapata College, which they hoped would be a base for revolution.

The Working Class

Historical accounts of the 1960s have largely ignored the U.S. working class for a variety of reasons. Workers existed in the shadows of great insurgencies, but not as sometimes thought because they were uneducated. In 1966, *Business Week* described a typical union member as "militant, confident, and loaded for bear. He intends to press for substantial wage increases—as a matter of justice, to match booming profits, and as a matter of need, to compensate for rising living costs. He is remarkably well-informed about both these phenomena."[263] When workers rebelled, they did so after uprisings in the ghettos and campus protests, and the issues which motivated strikes were not universalistic. A 1968 longshoremen strike initiated from the membership lasted 116 days, the longest strike in their history. But it involved a complicated relationship to progressives, since it was led by the same man who had bragged about beating up antiwar protesters a year earlier and threatened to boycott Swedish ships because of the country's liberal asylum laws for American deserters.[264] Illegal, militant school strikes in the mid to late 1960s involved tens of thousands of teachers, but their strikes in both New York City and Newark, New Jersey, collided with black cultural nationalism.

Beginning in 1967, as real wages began to decline because of inflation fueled by the Vietnam War,[265] there were more strikes, contract rejections, and wildcats by workers than at any time since the Great Depression. New York was called a "city of strikes" in 1968, as hundreds of thousands of workers walked off their jobs. On January 19, 1968, some seven hundred women working for AT&T long-distance in New York walked off their jobs and formed a picket line "manned by the girls around the clock," as the union local announced. The next day, thousands of other AT&T and electrical workers refused to cross the picket lines.[266] Across the country, as unions failed to represent properly the needs of workers, dozens of wildcat strikes won very specific demands. The emergence of autonomous rank-and-file strikes and associations gave some life to an otherwise near-moribund union movement dominated by a business model.

Workers mobilized around their needs, but antiwar protests were far less frequent, in part because union bureaucracies were so conservative. Yet there were notable exceptions. On November 11, 1967, less than a month after 175,000 antiwar demonstrators marched in Washington, DC, a two-day conference of unions with over five hundred representatives from thirty-eight states unanimously called for an immediate end to the bombings of Northern Vietnam and U.S. recognition of the NLF in Southern Vietnam.[267] In 1968, the United Auto Workers quit the AFL-CIO because of George Meany's support for the war, but the UAW was accused by black workers of racism and vote fraud.

Global Women's Liberation

Atlantic City, 1968: First mass action by Women's Liberation. Beverly Grant/Newsreel

Nineteen sixty-eight was also a year in which the women's liberation movement globally blossomed. The media made events like the anti–Miss America demonstration in Atlantic City and the wounding of Andy Warhol seem all important to the women's movement, but more significantly, an unreported grassroots network of women's consciousness-raising and action groups sprang up in every major U.S. city, as well as in many smaller towns.

Modern feminism was crystallized as silently endured personal pain of women became public topics in small, intimate group discussions. As Redstockings explained, "If all women share the same problem, how can it be personal? Women's pain is not personal, it's political."[268] Although women strongly articulated the need for inclusion of feminism within both SDS and SNCC, their efforts were initially greeted with silence or heckling at these groups' conventions. Betty Friedan had published *The Feminine Mystique* in 1963, but within the movement, women's attempts to raise the problem of sexism were ridiculed and dismissed. In 1964, Black Power prophet Kwame Ture was heard to say: "The only position for women in the movement is prone." In 1966, the same year NOW was founded, women demanded that SDS include women's liberation in a resolution. Some men threw tomatoes at them and kicked them out of the convention.[269] The LRBW was publicly disdainful of "the white women's liberation movement" and considered women's liberation divisive. In the U.S., Italy, and Germany, movement men often met the emergent women's movement with hostility and even violence. Ruth Rosen precisely places her felt need for an autonomous feminist movement in January 1969 during an incident in Washington, DC, the day before Richard Nixon's inauguration. At a mammoth antiwar "counterinauguration" rally, soon after they began to give their speeches, two female speakers were shocked when men in the front yelled, "Take her off the stage!" and "Fuck her. . . . Rape her in a back alley!"[270] Gathering later in private, female activists resolved to break away from SDS and the "male Left" and to "become an autonomous movement."

Thereafter, women formed their own autonomous organizations. Many marched in separate contingents during antiwar demonstrations and convened women-only national meetings. Radical feminism developed in this female-only environment, and a younger generation of women developed programs directed at building women's culture and alternative institutions (like women's health clinics and rape crisis centers) as part of a militant and confrontational movement aimed at the revolutionary transformation of society.

The autonomous women's movement proliferated far beyond anyone's expectations. In the largest U.S. cities, hundreds of groups formed from the grassroots. Step by step the feminists developed their self-understanding. In March 1968, Jo Freeman helped publish the first issue of *The Voice of Women's Liberation*, in which she wrote, "It is time Movement men realize they cannot speak the language of freedom while treating women in the same dehumanizing manner as their establishment peers."[271] Within a year, the journal had eight hundred subscribers.[272] In 1968, numerous feminist journals were being published. By 1970, New York City alone had over two hundred consciousness-raising groups.[273]

In late November 1968, the first National Women's Liberation Conference convened outside Chicago with over one hundred women from thirty-seven states and Canada. Naomi Weisstein presented her powerful critique of academic understanding of females' inner being: "Psychology has nothing to say about what women are really like, what they need and what they want, essentially, because psychology does not know."[274] In 1969, Marge Piercy wrote a powerful and still-relevant critique of informal power within the movement in which she discussed how men become charismatic spokespersons while women do the actual work of the organizations.[275] Within their ranks, women concerned themselves with dampening celebrities as they sought to deny the authoritarianism and hierarchy of the male Left.

Examining conditions of their existence, women determined that patriarchy and capitalism are twin dimensions of their oppression.[276] Participatory democracy, they said, begins at home.[277] Unpaid domestic work was revalued, and men were encouraged to do their share. At the same time, they

Chicago W.I.T.C.H. coven "hexing" the Transit Authority after a fare hike in 1970. Louise Brotsky.

began vigorous campaigns against institutional sexism. In February 1969, Redstockings women disrupted a legislative panel on abortion, thereby making a public issue of thousands of secretive, illegal abortions. In little more than a year, they proudly watched as New York law was changed to make abortion legal. As the feminist movement grew, women's liberation became central to the idea of a qualitatively new social order, and the entire culture—including the movement—was ultimately changed from within.

The women's movement rapidly became an international phenomenon. Women in the U.S., Holland, Germany, Italy, Denmark, and many other countries engaged in similar feminist campaigns, an indication of international diffusion of feminist theory and practice. Forging connections with women's movements in other countries, feminism in Germany helped negate national chauvinistic tendencies. At a time when anti-Americanism was a growing force among Germans, women translated and studied numerous texts from the United States. They also rediscovered the existence of a first wave of German feminism, a vibrant movement dating to the mid-nineteenth century whose history had largely been hidden.

Influenced by U.S. feminism, Italian women formed consciousness-raising groups and initiated collective projects such as bookstores, journals, and women's centers. In their discussions, they began distinguishing liberation from emancipation, the former dealing with the radical transformation of everyday life, whereas the latter was seen as having a more limited focus on public life, including the workplace.[278] Taking up significant issues of everyday life ignored by established political parties (including the Left), they gathered wide-ranging support. Their alternative health centers became popular sites for women to find information on mothering, questions of female health, and birth control. (Contraceptives were illegal in Italy until 1971.) Of special importance was the issue of abortion. Fascist laws still on the books dictated that only in cases of rape or incest would abortions be allowed, an obsolete ruling that meant that well over a million illegal abortions were performed in Italy every year, and an estimated twenty thousand women died annually as a result of improper procedures.[279]

In the UK, Juliet Mitchell had published a Marxist critique of women's exploitation in 1966, but only in 1968 did autonomous women's groups begin to meet. In May 1969, a feminist newsletter, *Shrew*, appeared. After men disrupted discussions by feminists at a "Festival of Revolution" at Essex University, the first national conference of women's liberation convened at Ruskin College in Oxford in February 1970. Without advance intentions to do so, the conference reached consensus on four demands: equal pay, equal education and opportunity, twenty-four-hour nurseries, and free contraception and abortion on demand.[280] According to Sheila Rowbotham, it was only from that meeting that "a movement could be said to exist."[281] Out of the Oxford meeting, the Women's Street Theatre Group formed and critically engaged spectators by performing a "flashing nipples show" outside the November 1970 Miss World contest, as well as helping to prepare the first Women's Day march in London in March 1971. Quickly, a host of feminist and gay theatre groups appeared in the UK. That year, however, sectarian tendencies doomed the Women's National Coordinating Committee. Similar internal problems also enervated Britain's emergent gay liberation movement. Both feminism and gay liberation had long-lasting international impacts on nearly every country in the world. Although they may have been marginalized in their starting points, their lasting effects continue to transform cultures.

At the same time as the global counterrevolution resorted to violent repression, the feminist movement was caricatured and made into televised spectacles by the mass media. Coverage of demonstrations at the 1968 Miss America pageant gave wide circulation to the notion that the women's liberation movement burned bras. In fact, no bras were burned there.[282] Society greeted displays of nudity, love-ins, be-ins, and rock 'n' roll by turning them into profitable commodities. At first glance, many people were happy when the antiwar play *Hair* opened on Broadway in 1968. Yves St. Laurent designed an evening see-through blouse and a similarly styled full-length dress, great sellers in the fashion world. Prominently featuring interviews with radicals, sales of *Playboy* magazine skyrocketed. That the emergent counterculture proved useful was evident by the Chicago Democratic Convention, when *Esquire* sent both Jean Genet and William S. Burroughs to report on it. The Doors were offered $5 million by Universal Studios to appear in a motion picture, and the Jefferson Airplane and the Grateful Dead became millionaires. What the counterrevolution's murderous violence could not suppress, it blunted through "gentle" assimilation into consumerism. If not the carrot, then the stick. In the same year that *The Money Game* rose to number one on bestseller lists, is it any wonder that LSD gave way to heroin in Haight-Ashbury and to speed in the East Village?

From the unknown periphery of ghettos and barrios, the movement suddenly appeared everywhere. American athletes at the 1968 Olympics in Mexico City raised their fists when they received their medals. Muhammad Ali, heavyweight champion of the world, steadfastly opposed the war even after his title was taken away and he faced imprisonment. Ho Chi Minh became more popular on American college campuses than Richard Nixon, and Che Guevara remains an enduring cultural icon.

Looking back at those heady days, 1968 marked the first act of an unfolding *species-consciousness*—the emergence of a global "we" that negated capitalist consumerism, patriarchy, white racial identity, and patriotism. In the short run, when it didn't destroy what was new and revolutionary, the system turned currents of liberation into avenues of profitability and domination. On a more profound level, however, in the hearts and minds of human beings, 1968 was a year when national heroes and cultures were transcended, when *global* consciousness and action emerged as historical forces. In the rebirth of new forms of freedom, the movement helped to create a global political culture that improved the everyday lives of millions of people and continues to inspire actions.

Women's strike, Reykjavík, Iceland, October 1975. Photographer unknown.

Notes

1. Jean-Paul Sartre, "France: Masses, Spontaneity, Party," in *Between Existentialism and Marxism* (New York: Pantheon Books, 1974), 125.
2. Liz Hodgkin, "People's War Comes to the Towns: Tet 1968," *Marxism Today* 22, no. 5 (May 1978): 147–52.
3. Don Oberdorfer, *Tet* (New York: Avon Books, 1972).
4. Hodgkin, "People's War Comes to the Towns," 147.
5. See Paul M. Sweezy and Harry Magdoff, "Historic Victory in Indochina," *Monthly Review* 27, no. 1 (May 1975): 1–13; Noam Chomsky and Edward Herman, *The Washington Connection and Third World Fascism* (Boston: South End Press, 1979), 345–54.
6. See Daniel Ellsberg's "Introduction" to E.P. Thompson and Dan Smith, ed., *Protest and Survive: Stop Nuclear War* (New York: Monthly Review Press, 1981); Michio Kaku and Daniel Axelrod, *To Win a Nuclear War* (Boston: South End Press, 1987).
7. Ho Khang, *The Tet Mau Than 1968 Event in South Vietnam* (Hanoi: The Gioi Publishers, 2001), 108.
8. Interview with Noam Chomsky, *Indochina Newsletter*, November–December 1982, 4. The Vietnamese began a second phase of their offensive on May 5,

launching simultaneous offensive on thirty-one cities and towns and fifty-eight district capitals. Wave after wave of attacks was launched. In August, artillery was the main weapon. In May 1990, in Ho Chi Minh City, I met General Tran Van Tra, commander of the NLF during the offensive, and he revealed to me that a plan for another phase to coincide with the U.S. November elections had been canceled.

9.   Oberdorfer, *Tet*, 289–90.
10. François Houtart and André Rousseau, *The Church and Revolution* (New York: Orbis Books, 1971), 148, 154.
11. Interview with Noam Chomsky, *Indochina Newsletter*, 12.
12. "Vietnam War Casualties," Wikipedia, https://en.wikipedia.org/wiki/Vietnam_War_casualties; Nick Terse, *Kill Anything That Moves: The Real American War in Vietnam* (New York: Picador, 2013).
13. Houtart and Rousseau, *The Church and Revolution*, 167.
14. See Troung Chinh, *To Mobilize and Unite All Anti-U.S. Forces in the Country and the World* (Berkeley: Asia Information Group, 1971). Also see *Vietnamese Studies* (Hanoi), particularly numbers 26 and 31, *Glimpses of U.S. Neo-Colonialism* (Parts I and II). For a specific analysis of Tet, see *South Vietnam: A Month of Unprecedented Offensive and Uprising* (South Vietnam: Giai Phong Publishing House, 1968).
15. David Triesman, "Cultural Conflict and Political Advance in Britain," *Marxism Today* 22, no. 5 (May 1978): 166.
16. This speech is fully reprinted in John Gerassi, ed., *Venceremos: The Speeches and Writings of Che Guevara* (New York: Simon and Schuster, 1969), 413–24. For an explanation of Che's "foco theory," see Régis Debray, *Revolution in the Revolution* (London: Penguin Books, 1968).
17. "Unsuccessful" is a mild word for the bloody repression suffered by these movements. Repeated calls for armed insurrection from the Tri-Continental Conference in Havana (January 1966) and the OLAS conference in 1967 brought swift reactions from Latin American governments and the U.S., which as sole coordinator and source of military supplies (at that time) had established a Southern Command in Panama. By 1968, Special Forces who had received anti-guerrilla training in Panama had carried out fifty-two operations. In 1966–1967, they intervened in Guatemala, Venezuela, Nicaragua, and, of course, in Bolivia. See Houtart and Rousseau, *The Church and Revolution*, 206–7.
18. Tareq Ismael, *The Arab Left* (Syracuse: Syracuse University Press, 1976), 92–125, 183.
19. Martin Kenner, "Introduction" to Martin Kenner and James Petras, ed., *Fidel Castro Speaks* (New York: Grove Press, 1969), xvi.
20. Daniel Ellsberg, "Introduction"; *Los Angeles Times*, June 2, 1983, 12.
21. Jaime Suchlicki, *University Students and Revolution in Cuba, 1920–1968* (Miami: University of Miami Press, 1966). Fidel Castro's first political involvement was at the University of Havana in the late 1940s, when he was active in the *Union Insurreccional Revolucionaria*.
22. *Vietnam Courier*, October 1982, 24.
23. Franz Schurmann, Peter Dale Scott, and Reginald Zelnik, *The Politics of Escalation in Vietnam* (Robinsdale, MN: Fawcett Publications, 1966), 45.
24. C. Wright Mills, "The New Left," in *Power, Politics and People*, ed. Irving Louis Horowitz (New York: Oxford University Press, 1963), 257–58.

25.   Clayborn Carson, *In Struggle* (Cambridge, MA: Harvard University Press, 1981), 16.
26.   Edward Shils, "Dreams of Plenitude, Nightmare of Scarcity," in *Students in Revolt*, ed. Seymour Lipset and Philip G. Altbach (Boston: Beacon Press, 1970), 5.
27.   Seymour Lipset, "The Possible Effects of Student Activism on International Politics," in Lipset and Altbach, *Students in Revolt*, 495.
28.   Eric Hobsbawm, *The Age of Extremes: The Short Twentieth Century* (London: Abacus, 1994), 446.
29.   R.F. Tomasson and E. Allardt, "Scandinavian Students and the Politics of Organized Radicalism," in Lipset and Altbach, *Students in Revolt*, 96–126.
30.   Claude Durand, ed., *Combats étudiants dans le Monde* (Paris: Editions du Seuil, 1968).
31.   Anthony Eisler, *Bombs, Beards and Barricades: 150 Years of Youth in Revolt* (New York: Stein and Day, 1971); Edith H. Altbach, "Vanguard of Revolt: Students and Politics in Central Europe, 1815–1848," in Lipset and Altbach, *Students in Revolt*; Jürgen Habermas, *Toward a Rational Society* (Boston: Beacon Press, 1972), 40.
32.   Ernest Mandel as quoted in Tariq Ali, *1968 and After: Inside the Revolution* (Essex: Blond & Briggs, 1978), 47–49.
33.   Alexander Cockburn and Robin Blackburn, ed, *Student Power: Problems, Diagnosis, Action* (Harmondsworth: Penguin Books, 1969), 141–62.
34.   Fidel Castro, "Rede über die Zuknft der Universität vom 8," *Kursbuch* 18 (October 1969): 155.
35.   Ingeborg Göthel, *Geschichte Südkoreas* (Berlin: Deutscher Verlag der Wissenschaften, 1988), 73; Mi Park, *Democracy and Social Change: A History of South Korean Student Movements, 1980–2000* (Bern: Peter Lang, 2008), 65.
36.   Namhee Lee, *The Making of Minjung: Democracy and the Politics of Representation in South Korea* (Ithaca: Cornell University Press, 2007), 106.
37.   Göthel, *Geschichte Südkoreas*, 73.
38.   Interview with Kim Ye-Hyan, 4.19 Institute, Seoul, December 13, 2001.
39.   Sungjoo Han, "Student Activism: A Comparison Between the 1960 Uprising and the 1971 Protest Movement," in *Political Participation in Korea: Democracy, Mobilization, and Stability*, ed. Chong Lim Kim (Santa Barbara: Clio Books, 1980), 145.
40.   Mi Park, *Democracy and Social Change*, 65.
41.   H.B. Lee, *Korea: Time, Change, and Administration* (Honolulu: East-West Center, 1968), 119, as quoted in Alice H. Amsden, *Asia's Next Giant: South Korea and Later Industrialization* (New York: Oxford University Press, 1989), 42.
42.   See Sungjoo Han, "Student Activism," 159; Interview with Kim Ye-Hyan, 419 Institute, Seoul, December 13, 2001; Göthel, *Geschichte Südkoreas*, 76.
43.   Tom Hayden made these remarks in Gwangju during a speech at the International Conference Commemorating the Thirtieth Anniversary of the Gwangju Uprising in May 2010.
44.   Bruce Cumings, *Origins of the Korean War*, Vol. 1 (Princeton: Princeton University Press, 1981), 175.
45.   Kang Man-gil, *A History of Contemporary Korea* (Kent: Global Oriental, 2005), 318.
46.   See my article "The Commune: Evolving Form of Freedom," *ROAR*, no. 1, Spring 2016, https://roarmag.org/magazine/katsiaficas-paris-commune-gwangju-uprising/. Like after so many other revolutionary upsurges, conservative forces have taken over part of Gwangju's movement. They propagate accounts of

pro-American journalists and CIA agents about Korean responsibility for the bloodshed in 1980 and a U.S. "mistake." One formerly progressive organization even invited notorious ex-CIA bureaucrat Donald Gregg, key operative in the Phoenix Program in Vietnam, originator of Iran-Contra arms smuggling, and supervisor to Félix Rodríguez (who was instrumental in the assassination of Che Guevara), to speak at the United Nations.

47. Rolf Werenskjold, *Report No. 13: A Chronology of the Global 1968 Protest* (Volda: Volda University College, 2010). This well documented chronology is my source for many specific actions mentioned in this chapter.

48. William Hinton, *Hundred Day War: The Cultural Revolution at Tsinghua University* (New York: Monthly Review Press, 1972), 187.

49. Nobua Aruga as quoted in George Paloczi-Horvath, *Youth Up In Arms* (New York: David McKay Co., 1971), 197.

50. "Restless Youth," CIA Secret Report, number 0613/68 (September 1968): 103. My thanks to Martin Klimke for providing me a copy of what he received from the Lyndon Baines Johnson Library.

51. Michiya Shimbori, "Student Radicals in Japan," *Annals of the American Academy of Political and Social Science* 395, no. 1 (May 1971): 153.

52. Yoshihiko Hanawa, "Le radicalisme de la violence chez les étudiants japonais," *Esprit* 5 (May 1969): 754–63.

53. Jeanne Habel, "Les luttes étudiants et ouvrieres au Japon," *Partisans* 44 (October–November 1968): 79–92.

54. Peter Gerald Kelman, "Protesting the National Identity: The Cultures of Protest in 1960s Japan" (PhD diss., University of Sydney, 2001), https://ses.library.usyd.edu.au/bitstream/2123/2443/4/04chapter2.pdf, chap. 2: "Discovering Autonomy in Protest: Ampo 1960 and 1970."

55. See Benigno Aquino Jr., *A Garrison State in the Making* (Manila: Benigno S. Aquino Jr. Foundation, 1985), 243.

56. Almonte quoted in Angela Stuart Santiago, *1986: Chronicle of a Revolution* (Manila: Raintree Publishing, 1996), 49; see also Jose T. Almonte, *My Part in the People Power Revolution* (Manila: n.p., 2006), 14.

57. In 2009, I interviewed Philippine Senator Gregorio Honasan, a key leader of the mutiny in 1986. He described RAM as "children of First Quarter Storm," the Philippine movement of 1970.

58. Ross Prizzia and Narong Sinsawasdi, "Evolution of the Thai Student Movement: 1940–1974," *Asia Quarterly* 1 (1975): 44.

59. See Virada Somswasdi, "The Women's Movement and Legal Reform in Thailand," *Cornell Law School*, April 1, 2003, http://lsr.nellco.org/cgi/viewcontent.cgi?article=1001&context=cornell/biss.

60. Samar Sen, ed., *Naxalbari and After* (Calcutta: Kathashilpa, 1978).

61. Sumanta Banerjee, *India's Simmering Revolution: The Naxalite Uprising* (London: Zed Press, 1984).

62. "Restless Youth," 65.

63. Arif Dirlik, "The Third World," in *1968: The World Transformed*, eds. Carole Fink, Philipp Gassert, and Detlef Junker (Cambridge: Cambridge University Press, 1998), 303.

64. Bazlul M. Chowdhury, *Class and Social Structure of Bangladesh* (Dhaka: Ankur Prakashani, 2008), 66.

65. Talukder Maniruzzaman, *The Bangladesh Revolution and Its Aftermath* (Dhaka: University Press, 1988), 53.

66. Talukder Maniruzzaman, "The Fall of the Military Dictator: 1991 Elections and the Prospect of Civilian Rule in Bangladesh," *Pacific Affairs* 65, no. 2 (Summer 1992): 203–24.

67. *London Times,* April 2, 1969.

68. Hundreds of people were killed—some say tens of thousands. In 1971, government figures of the total killed range from twelve to fifty thousand, although Prime Minister Sirima subsequently calculated the number killed at twelve hundred.

69. Godahewa Indradasa, *Failed Revolts in Sri Lanka (1971 and 1987–1989): Indepth Analysis of an Intelligence Officer* (Moratuwa: Opro Publishing, 2012).

70. C.A. Chandraprema, *Sri Lanka: The Years of Terror—The JVP Insurrection 1987–1989* (Colombo: Lake House Bookshop, 1991), 41–42.

71. Quoted in Robert N. Kearney, "Youth Protest in the Politics of Sri Lanka," *Sociological Focus* 13 (August 1980): 304.

72. Fred Halliday in Robin Blackburn, *Explosion in a Subcontinent: India, Pakistan, Bangladesh, and Ceylon* (Harmondsworth: Penguin Books, 1975), 218.

73. K.M. de Silva, *A History of Sri Lanka* (Colombo: Vijitha Yapa, 2005), 664.

74. So said CIA operative Kermit Roosevelt in his *Counter-Coup: The Struggle for Control of Iran* (New York: McGraw-Hill, 1981).

75. "Restless Youth," 85.

76. Ibrahim Farghali, "Egypt: From Romanticism to Realism," in *1968: Memories and Legacies of a Global Revolt,* ed. Philipp Gassert and Martin Klimke (Washington, DC: German Historical Institute, 2009), 106; Rachid al-Daif, "Lebanon: Of Things That Remain Unsaid," in *1968,* 119.

77. Mouffaq Nyrabia, "Syria: The Children of the Six-Day War," in *1968,* 150–52.

78. *Perspectives Tunisiennes,* June 1968.

79. Jeremy Varon, *Bringing the War Home: The Weather Underground, the Red Army Faction, and Revolutionary Violence in the 60s and 70s* (Berkeley: University of California Press, 2004), 102.

80. *Perspectives Tunisiennes,* October 1968, 7.

81. Ahmed Abdalla, *The Student Movement and National Politics in Egypt* (London: Al Saqi Books, 1985), 149.

82. *The 1968 Revolution in Iraq: Experience and Prospects,* The Political Report of the Eighth Congress of the Arab B'ath Socialist Party in Iraq, January 1974 (London: Ithaca Press, 1979), 12.

83. Choe Sug-Man, "Students and Their Role in Developing Countries: A Historical Study of Brazil and Turkey" (PhD diss., Pennsylvania State University, 1985), 196.

84. Jon Piccini, "A Whole New World: Global Revolution and Australian Social Movements in the Long Sixties" (PhD diss., University of Queensland, 2013); Jon Piccini, *Global Radicals: Transnational Protest, Australia and the 1960s* (London: Palgrave Macmillan, 2016).

85. Jon Piccini provided much-needed assistance. Chris Kerr graciously sent me a copy of his book. See Piccini's "'We Are on the Side of the Vietnamese'—Imagining and Practicing Transnational Connection in 1960s Australia," https://www. academia.edu/19016163/_We_are_on_the_side_of_the_Vietnamese_Imagining_ and_practicing_transnational_connection_in_1960s_Australia.

86. Gary Foley, "Black Power in Redfern, 1968–1972," Koori History Website, October 5, 2001, http://www.kooriweb.org/foley/essays/essay_1.html.

87. Kathy Lothian, "Seize the Time: Australian Aborigines and the Influence of the Black Panther Party, 1969–1972," *Journal of Black Studies* 35, no. 4 (March 2005): 179–200.

88.   For the significance of this "toehold of freedom in black Africa," see *Target Zero: Eldridge Cleaver, a Life in Writing*, ed. Kathleen Cleaver (New York: Palgrave Macmillan, 2006), 236–39.

89.   Otto Klineberg, Marisa Zavalloni, and Christiane Louis-Guérin, eds., *Students, Values, and Politics: A Crosscultural Comparison* (New York: Free Press, 1979), 293.

90.   "Restless Youth," 4.

91.   William J. Hanna, "Student Protest in Independent Black Africa," *Annals of the American Academy of Political and Social Science* 395, no. 1 (May 1971): 172.

92.   Andy Stafford, "Senegal: May 68, Africa's Revolt," in *1968*, 129–35.

93.   *Informations Catholiques Internationales*, October 15, 1968, 17.

94.   John Daniel and Peter Vale, "South Africa: Where Were We Looking in 1968?," in *1968*, 139.

95.   Ian Macqueen, "How the Failed Ideals of 1970s Activists Haunt Post-apartheid SA," *Mail & Guardian*, October 12, 2015, https://mg.co.za/article/2015-10-12-how-the-failed-ideals-of-1970s-activists-haunt-post-apartheid-sa. Thanks to John Hansen for sending me the article.

96.   "Restless Youth," 33.

97.   On May 15, Irish students protested the Belgian king's visit and carried posters reading, "Lumumba and black people were murdered by Belgian imperialists."

98.   Pedro Monaville, "The Destruction of the University: Violence, Political Imagination, and the Student Movement in Congo-Zaire, 1969–1971," in *The Third World in the Global 1960s*, eds. Samantha Christiansen and Zachary A. Scarlett (New York: Berghahn Books, 2013), 159.

99.   Houtart and Rousseau, *The Church and Revolution*, 243.

100. "Restless Youth," 37.

101. Fentahun Tiruneh, *The Ethiopian Students: Their Struggle to Articulate the Ethiopian Revolution* (Chicago: Nyala Publishing, 1990), 65.

102. Colin Legum, "The Year of the Students: A Survey of the African University Scene," *Current Affairs*, June 1972, A19.

103. Legum, "The Year of the Students," 253.

104. Stephie Melina Kabre, "Burkina Faso Revolution," unpublished Chonnam National University graduate seminar paper, June 2017.

105. Tilman Fichter and Siegward Lonnendonker, *Kleine Geschichte des SDS* (Berlin: Rotbuch Verlag, 1977).

106. SDS, *Der Kampf des vietnamesischen Volkes und die Globalstrategie des Imperialism* (Berlin, February 17–18, 1968).

107. F.C. Hunnius, *Student Revolts: The New Left in West Germany* (London: War Resistors' International, 1968).

108. According to figures from the West German Minister of Interior and reported by the CIA, membership in SDS was 1,600 in early 1968. At the Free University of Berlin, SDS members were estimated at between 400 and 500; enrollment was over 15,000. The West German student Left was never as big as that in the United States partly as a result of right-wing culture that survived Nazism. The ratio of SDS members to total population was one in 7,000 in the United States, while in West Germany it was one in 30,000. These numbers do not include movements among African Americans, Latinos, and other groups outside the universities.

109. Heinz Grossman and Oskar Negt, eds., *Die Auferstehung der Gewalt* (Hamburg: Europäische Verlagsanstalt, 1968).

110. Werenskjold, *Report No. 13*, 159.
111. H.J. Giessler, *APO-Rebellion Mai 1968* (München: Pamphlet Verlag G. Rosenberger, 1968).
112. The emergence of post–New Left cultural politics in Central Europe at the beginning of the 1980s is empirical evidence of the world-historical nature of 1968, and an entire chapter of this book's version as my doctoral dissertation was originally written to document the emergence of the Punk Left in Central Europe. That chapter was deleted in order to focus this book on the events of 1968–1970. It appeared in 1997 in an expanded form as *The Subversion of Politics: European Autonomous Social Movements and the Decolonization of Everyday Life* (Oakland: AK Press, 2006).
113. This speech is translated and excerpted in *German Feminism: Readings in Politics and Literature*, eds. Edith Hoshino Altbach, Jeanette Clausen, Dagmar Schultz, and Naomi Stephan (Albany: State University of New York Press, 1984), 307–10.
114. Alice Schwarzer, "Ewig zittere das Weib," in *Emma Sonderband*, 137. It should be noted that German law was a hodgepodge of various statures. After World War II, the United States essentially rewrote Germany's basic laws according to the U.S. Constitution. In January 1949, the Bundestag approved an equal rights statute, but it had little enforceability. Another equal rights statute in 1957 modified rigidly patriarchal marriage and family laws.
115. Mariarosa Dalla Costa and Selma James, *The Power of Women and the Subversion of Society* (Bristol: Falling Wall Press, 1975).
116. Bernhard Schütze, "Widerstand an Spaniens Universitäten," *Kursbuch* 13 (June 1968): 55.
117. *Facts on File Yearbook 1968* (New York: Facts on File, 1969), 205–6.
118. Barbara and John Ehrenreich, *Long March, Short Spring* (New York: Monthly Review Press, 1969), 60.
119. Valdo Spini, "The New Left in Italy," *Journal of Contemporary History* 7, no. 1 (January–April 1972): 65–66.
120. Frank Brodhead, "Strategy, Compromise and Revolt: Viewing the Italian Workers' Movement," *Radical America* 18, no. 5 (1984): 54.
121. Robert Lumley, *States of Emergency: Cultures of Revolt in Italy 1968–1977* (London: Verso, 1991), 211.
122. Lumley, *States of Emergency*, 226.
123. Arrigo Levi, "Italy: The Crisis of Governing," *Foreign Affairs* 49, no. 1 (October 1970): 147–60.
124. The collectives of Lotta Feminista developed from the groups associated with Female Revolt in the same period when Lotta Continua was formed.
125. Donald Katz, "Tribes: Italy's Metropolitan Indians," *Rolling Stone*, no. 252 (November 17, 1977): 60–65; "Indies Metropolitanos," *El Viejo Topo*, July 1977.
126. For a more complete analysis of Italian feminist and youth movements, see George Katsiaficas, *The Subversion of Politics*.
127. Schütze, "Widerstand an Spaniens Universitäten."
128. Manuel Tunon de Lara, "Le problème universitaire espagnol," *Esprit* 5 (May 1969): 848.
129. *Democracia Popular*, January 1968.
130. See Bart van der Steen, Ask Katzeff, and Leendert van Hoogenhuigze, eds. *The City Is Ours: Squatting and Autonomous Movements in Europe from the 1970s to the Present* (Oakland: PM Press, 2014), 181–82.

131. See Robert Hewison, *Too Much: Art and Society in the Sixties, 1960–75* (New York: Oxford University Press, 1987), 161.

132. Lin Chun, *The British New Left* (Edinburgh: Edinburgh University Press, 1993), 93.

133. David Widgery, *The Left in Britain, 1956–1968* (London: Penguin Publishers, 1972).

134. Chun, *The British New Left*, 173n3.

135. Luis Aguilar, ed., *Marxism in Latin America* (Philadelphia: Temple University Press, 1978), 152–57.

136. See Dominique Eudes, *The Kapetanios: Partisans and Civil War in Greece, 1943–1949* (New York: Monthly Review Press, 1972). Further analysis of the Comintern's sabotage of popular social movements in the 1930s and 1940s can be found in Fernando Claudin, *The Communist Movement* (New York: Monthly Review Press, 1974).

137. Laura Pulido, *Black, Brown, Yellow & Left: Radical Activism in Los Angeles* (Berkeley: University of California Press, 2006), 94.

138. *Telos* 25 (Fall 1975).

139. Klaus Mehnert, *Moscow and the New Left* (Berkeley: University of California Press, 1975), 117–18.

140. M. Markovic, *Student*, May 21, 1968; "The Topic Is Action," *Student*, May 14, 1968, 4, as quoted in Fredy Perlman, *Revolt in Socialist Yugoslavia: June 1968* (Detroit: Black and Red, 1973), 7.

141. "The Topic Is Action," 7.

142. *Susret*, May 15, 1968, 7–8.

143. *Politika*, December 29, 1968.

144. Vladimir Kusin, *The Intellectual Origins of the Prague Spring* (Cambridge: Cambridge University Press, 1971), 63.

145. Kusin, *The Intellectual Origins of the Prague Spring*, 139.

146. Kusin, 60.

147. Robin A. Remington, ed., *Winter in Prague: Documents on Czechoslovak Communism in Crisis* (Cambridge, MA: MIT Press, 1969), 17.

148. "Studenren in Prag," *Kursbuch* 13 (June 1968): 69–70.

149. Remington, *Winter in Prague*, 162.

150. Kusin, *The Intellectual Origins of the Prague Spring*, 128.

151. Kusin, 114–15.

152. Serge Mallet, *Bureaucracy and Technocracy in the Socialist Countries* (Bristol: Spokesman Books, 1974); Remington, *Winter in Prague*, 5–7, 195–212.

153. Michael Randle and April Carter, *Support Czechoslovakia* (London: Housemans Press, 1968), 10.

154. Remington, *Winter in Prague*, 455; Tamara Deutscher, ed., *Voices of Czechoslovak Socialists* (London: Merlin Press, 1977), 6–7.

155. Deutscher, *Voices of Czechoslovak Socialists*.

156. Jirí Pelikan, *Sozialistische Opposition in der CSSR* (Berlin: Europaische Verlagsanstalt, 1973).

157. Hans-Peter Riese, ed., *Since the Prague Spring* (New York: Vintage Books, 1979).

158. Randle and Carter, *Support Czechoslovakia*, 14–17; *Facts on File Yearbook 1968* (New York: Facts on File, 1969), 387, 489.

159. Kusin, *The Intellectual Origins of the Prague Spring*, 127.

160. Kusin, 127, 147–48.

161. "Warschauer Bilanz," *Kursbuch* 13 (June 1968): 91–107.

162. Jacek Kuron, Karol Modzelewski, Antoni Zambrowski, and Isaac Deutscher, *Revolutionary Marxist Students from Poland Speak Out, 1964–1968* (New York: Merit Publishers, 1970).

163. Zugmunt Bauman, "Le combat des etudiants polonais," *Espirit* 5 (May 1969): 865.

164. *Boston Globe*, May 9, 1981; *Le Monde*, January 28, 1971.

165. Informations Correspondence Ouvrieres, *Poland, 1970–71: Capitalism and Class Struggle* (Detroit: Black & Red, 1977), 11–12.

166. Informations Correspondence Ouvrieres, 23.

167. Michael Dobbs, K.S. Karol, and Dessa Trevisan, *Poland, Solidarity, Walesa* (New York: McGraw-Hill, 1981).

168. Informations Correspondence Ouvrieres, 43.

169. Risto Bajalski in *Le Monde*, January 2, 1971.

170. *Contemporary Poland* 5, no. 3 (March 1971): 48.

171. For continuity with even earlier development of the Polish movement, see Jane Leftwich Curry on "Poland's permanent revolution," in Jane L. Curry and Luba Fajfer, *Poland's Permanent Revolution: People vs. Elites 1956 to the Present* (Washington, DC: American University Press, 1996).

172. Heinz Rudolf Sonntag, "Versuch liber die lateinamerikanischen Universitäten," *Kursbuch* 13 (June 1968); Jean Meyer, "Le mouvement etudiant en Amerique latine," *Esprit* 5 (May 1969): 740–53.

173. Robert Scott, "Student Political Activism in Latin America," in Lipset and Altbach, 404.

174. Judith A. Hellman, *Mexico in Crisis* (New York: Holmes and Meier Publishers, 1979).

175. Carlos Monsiváis, *El 68: La Tradición de la resistencia* (Mexico City: Ediciones Era, 2008).

176. Arthur Liebman, "Student Activism in Mexico," *Annals of the American Academy of Political and Social Science* 395 (May 1971): 165; Elena Poniatowska, *Fuerte es el Silencio* (Mexico City: Ediciones Era, 1980).

177. Octavio Paz, *The Other Mexico: Critique of the Pyramid* (New York: Grove Press, 1972), 13–14.

178. Santiago Castro-Gomez, in Gassert and Klimke, *1968*, 47.

179. Luisa A. Brignardello, *El Movimiento Estudiantil Argentino. Corrientes ideológicos y opiniones de sus dirigentes* (Buenos Aires: Ediciones Macchi, 1972).

180. See James P. Brennan's excellent analysis: "Working Class Protest, Popular Revolt and Urban Insurrection in Argentina: The 1969 Cordobazo," https://libcom.org/library/working-class-protest-popular-revolt-urban-insurrection-argentina-1969-cordobazo#footnote34_gha57dq.

181. Gassert and Klimke, *1968*, 27.

182. Vania Markarian, *Student Activism from Global Counterculture to Molotov Cocktails* (Oakland: University of California Press, 2016).

183. M. Pheline, "Crise universitaire et mouvement etudiant au Bresil," *Partisans* 44 (October–November 1968): 93–113.

184. Houtart and Rousseau, *The Church and Revolution*, 214.

185. *Between Honesty and Hope: Documents from and about the Church in Latin America* (Maryknoll, NY: Maryknoll Publications, 1970), 144.

186. Speech to the Peasants, August 23, 1968, in *La Documentation Catholique* no. 1524 (Bonne Press, 1968), col. 1545, as quoted in Houtart and Rousseau, *The Church and Revolution*, 215.

187. Houtart and Rousseau, *The Church and Revolution*, 214.

188. *Between Honesty and Hope*, 211.

189. Houtart and Rousseau, *The Church and Revolution*, 228.

190. Arthur Gish, *The New Left and Christian Radicalism* (Grand Rapids, MI: Eerdmans, 1970). For a discussion of Black Power and the church, see James Cone, *Black Theology and Black Power* (New York: Seabury Press, 1969).

191. Houtart and Rousseau, *The Church and Revolution*, 214.

192. Dimitri Roussopoulos, "Canada: 1968 and the New Left," in *1968*, 39–40.

193. Dimitrios I. Roussopoulos, ed., *Canada and Radical Social Change* (Montreal: Black Rose Books, 1973), 51, 183. The "branch plant" referred to is a facility in Canada whose headquarters are located in another country.

194. Selwyn Ryan, "The Struggle for Black Power in the Caribbean," in *The Black Power Revolution 1970*, eds. Selwyn Ryan and Taimoon Stewart (St. Augustine, Trinidad: University of the West Indies, 1995).

195. Kwame Nkrumah, *The Specter of Black Power* (London: Panaf Books, 1968), 10–11, as quoted in Bill Riviere's insightful study *Black Power, NJAC and the 1970 Confrontation in the Caribbean: An Historical Interpretation* (St. Augustine, Trinidad: University of the West Indies, 1972), 5.

196. Speech on Black Power delivered in London in August 1967 and reprinted in *New World's* special issue on Black Power, 1971.

197. Kate Quinn, ed., *Black Power in the Caribbean* (Gainesville: University Press of Florida, 2014), 2; James Millette, *The Black Revolution in the Caribbean* (Trinidad: United National Independence Party, 1971), 9

198. Black Power had many tendencies and a variety of conflicts arose among its advocates. When Kwame Ture visited Guyana in May 1970, his view that Indians could not be part of Black Power organizations contradicted years of local organizing which had sought to unite Blacks and Indians into a majority capable of controlling the government. Extract from the Permanent Undersecretary's monthly letter, marked "secret" in April 1970, paragraph 15, located in the packet of information released with "Black Power in the Caribbean."

199. As quoted in Riviere, *Black Power, NJAC and the 1970 Confrontation in the Caribbean*, 23.

200. See C.L.R. James, *A History of Pan-African Revolt* (Oakland: PM Press, 2012), 126–27.

201. Central Intelligence Agency, Directorate of Intelligence, "Black Radicalism in the Caribbean," Secret Report, August 6, 1969, Number 1839/69, approved for public release August 22, 2012, 12–13; H. M. Diplomatic Service, "Black Power in the Caribbean," 1970, National Archives Ref.: FCO 63/380 C692040.

202. British Intelligence, 7.

203. Quinn, *Black Power in the Caribbean*, 130.

204. Riviere, *Black Power*, 32.

205. In Quinn, *Black Power in the Caribbean*, 97, as quoted in Brinsley Samaroo, *The February Revolution (1970) as a Catalyst for Change in Trinidad and Tobago* (Wallerfield: University of Trinidad and Tobago, 2010)

206. Pantin, *Black Power Day: The 1970 February Revolution, a Reporter's Story* (Santa Cruz: Hatuey Productions, 1990), 174.

207. Franklin Harvey as quoted in Ryan and Stewart, *The Black Power Revolution 1970*, 166.

208. Pantin, *Black Power Day*, 187.

209. As interviewed by Brian Meeks in 1974. See Meeks, "The 1970 Revolution: Chronology and Documentation," in Ryan and Stewart, *The Black Power Revolution*

1970, 171. Unbeknownst to the mutineers, as well as to most Trinidadians, the United States and Venezuela had immediately dispatched warships at top speed to intervene in Trinidad. With the approval of the Williams's government, more than two thousand U.S. Marines and helicopters were poised to invade, and additionally, an airlift of small arms and ammunition was already underway, setting the stage for a bloody suppression of the movement. Williams also called on Jamaica and Guyana for troops to support his government, but Forbes Burnham, prime minister of Guyana since its independence from Britain in 1966 and arguably the most progressive political leader in the entire region (including Castro), refused to come to the assistance of the embattled government of Trinidad. In this context it is worth recalling that in 1965 the United States had sent forty-two thousand marines to prevent the democratically elected government of Juan Bosch from governing in the Dominican Republic. Two decades after the near-revolution in Trinidad, the United States intervened ninety miles north on the spice island of Grenada, when a revolutionary movement arose that was at least partially inspired by the 1970 Black Power movement. Besides obvious geopolitical interests in the region, U.S. economic interests, worth well over $2.5 billion, were also at stake according to British intelligence. Confidential discussion paper, "Black Radicalism: A New Caribbean Phenomenon," in the packet of British intelligence documents, 6.

210. Riviere, *Black Power*, 67.
211. As quoted in Pantin, *Black Power Day*, 159.
212. Quito Swan, *Black Power in Bermuda* (New York: Palgrave Macmillan, 2009), 84.
213. John T. McCartney, "The Influences of the Black Panther Party (USA) on the Vanguard Party of the Bahamas," in *Liberation, Imagination, and the Black Panther Party*, eds. Kathleen Cleaver and George Katsiaficas (New York: Routledge, 2001); Swan, *Black Power in Bermuda*, 89.
214. Quinn, *Black Power in the Caribbean*, 2.
215. Swan, *Black Power in Bermuda*, 89.
216. John Hersey, "1968: The Year of the Triphammer," *San Diego Union*, October 22, 1978, C-5; Joe Fagin and Harlan Hahn, *Ghetto Riots* (New York: Macmillan, 1973), 105.
217. National Lawyers Guild, *Counter-intelligence: A Documentary Look at America's Secret Police* (New York: National Lawyers Guild Counterintelligence Documentation Center, 1978).
218. *Facts on File Yearbook 1968*, 212.
219. *Facts on File Yearbook 1968*, 200.
220. Daniel Bell, then professor of sociology at Columbia, as quoted by *U.S. News & World Report* 62 (March 6, 1967).
221. See Immanuel Wallerstein and Paul Starr, *The University Crisis Reader*, vol. 2 (New York: Random House, 1971), 160–62.
222. Tom Hayden, "Two, Three, Many Columbias," *Ramparts*, June 15, 1968.
223. Dimitrios Roussopoulos, *The New Left: Legacy and Continuity* (Montreal: Black Rose, 2007), 81.
224. Garth Buchanan and Joan Brackett, *Survey of Campus Incidents* (Washington, DC: The Urban Institute, 1970), 15.
225. Sara Evans, *Personal Politics* (New York: Vintage Books, 1980), 200.
226. Scranton Commission, *The Report of the President's Commission on Campus Unrest* (Washington, DC: U.S. Government Printing Office, 1970), 12.
227. National Commission on the Causes and Prevention of Violence, *Progress Report* (Washington, DC: U.S. Government Printing Office, 1969), A-11.

228. Daniel Walker, National Commission on the Causes and Prevention of Violence, *Rights in Conflict* (New York: Signet Books, 1968).

229. Hersey, "1968" C-5.

230. Stephen Rousseas, *Death of a Democracy: Greece and the American Conscience* (New York: Grove Press, 1967).

231. Kerner Commission, *Report of the National Advisory Commission on Civil Disorders* (Washington, DC: U.S. Government Printing Office, 1968). Despite many facets of progress since 1968, a comprehensive report by the Economic Policy Institute on the fiftieth anniversary of the Kerner Commission told of worsening conditions. The percentage of U.S. children living in poverty increased from 15.6% in 1968 to 21% in 2017; public schools are resegregating; African American homeownership is declining; and the prison population has mushroomed from about 200,000 in 1968 to over 1.4 million today. See http://www.chicagotribune.com/news/nationworld/ct-no-progress-african-americans-20180226-story.html.

232. Wentworth Institute of Technology student Sylvester Spencer interviewed Seale in Boston in 1994. By 1973, when he ran for mayor, only 1,000 members remained, a number that dropped to 190 by the time he left the Party on July 31, 1974.

233. By 1971, the LRBW was history, and many of those members who wished to remain active joined the Communist League.

234. February 29, 1968, editorial, as quoted in Dan Georgakas and Marvin Surkin, *Detroit: I Do Mind Dying, A Study in Urban Revolution* (New York: St. Martin's Press, 1975), 20.

235. Aaron Brenner, Robert Brenner, and Cal Winslow, *Rebel Rank and File: Labor Militancy and Revolt from Below during the Long 1970s* (London: Verso, 2010), 290.

236. Georgakas and Surkin, *Detroit: I Do Mind Dying*, 63, 84, 171.

237. Kerner Commission, *Report of the National Advisory Commission on Civil Disorders*, 89, 95–112.

238. See Carlos Muñoz Jr., *Youth, Identity, Power: The Chicano Movement* (London: Verso Books, 1989; new edition published in 2007).

239. George Mariscal, *Brown-Eyed Children of the Sun: Lessons from the Chicano Movement, 1965–1975* (Albuquerque: University of New Mexico Press, 2005), 2.

240. "Chicano" refers to U.S.-born citizens of Mexican ancestry. Some say it originated from "Chico Mexicanos" (small Mexicans) while others claim it has no fixed origin, that it was a product of increasing mixtures and fusions of cultures and identities. Mario Garcia heard it used in the barrios of El Paso in the early 1960s; in late August 1970, James Baldwin told Margaret Mead the term was "absolutely new" for him. (Mariscal, *Brown-Eyed Children of the Sun*, 171.) In the twenty-first century, Chicano is heard infrequently as Latino has largely replaced it.

241. Ernesto B. Vigil, *The Crusade for Justice: Chicano Militancy and the Government's War on Dissent* (Madison: University of Wisconsin Press, 1999), 28.

242. Vigil, *The Crusade for Justice*, 207.

243. In 1966, Alianza membership was over twenty thousand people in six states. Richard Gardner, *Grito! Reies Tijerina and The New Mexico Land Grant War* (New York: Harper-Colophon, 1971), 120; Patricia Blarvis, *Tijerina and the Land Grants* (New York: International Publishers, 1971).

244. David Montejano, *Sancho's Journal: Exploring the Political Edge with the Brown Berets* (Austin: University of Texas Press, 2012), 4.

245. Laura Pulido, *Black, Brown, Yellow, Left: Radical Activism in Los Angeles* (Berkeley: University of California Press, 2006), 116.

246. It would not be unfair to say that many Mexican Americans were reluctant to build coalitions with African Americans. One study found that between 1965 in 1972 those agreeing with coalition politics doubled to a meager 32 percent, Pulido, *Black, Brown, Yellow, Left*, 7, 57.

247. Muñoz, *Youth, Identity, Power*, 69.

248. Mariscal, *Brown-Eyed Children of the Sun*, 79.

249. Vigil, *The Crusade for Justice*, 55.

250. Vigil, 18.

251. Vigil, 67.

252. Vigil, 97.

253. Vigil, 97–100.

254. Mariscal, *Brown-Eyed Children of the Sun*, 213.

255. Miguel Melendez, *We Took the Streets: Fighting for Latino Rights with the Young Lords* (New Brunswick, NJ: Rutgers University Press, 2005), 76, 86.

256. Andrés Torres and José E. Velázquez, *The Puerto Rican Movement: Voices from the Diaspora* (Philadelphia: Temple University Press, 1998), 157. After Jiménez gave a speech denouncing U.S. imperialism at the University of Puerto Rico, students torched the ROTC building.

257. Amy Uyematsu, "The Emergence of Yellow Power in America," in *Roots: An Asian-American Reader*, eds. Amy Tachiki, Eddie Wong, Franklin Odo, and Buck Wong (Los Angeles: UCLA Asian American Studies Center Press, 1971), 9–14.

258. Pulido, *Black, Brown, Yellow, and Left*, 91.

259. Karen L. Ishizuka, *Serve the People: Making Asian America in the Long Sixties* (London: Verso, 2016), 75.

260. Ishizuka, *Serve the People*, 82.

261. Pulido, *Black, Brown, Yellow, and Left*, 82.

262. Ishizuka, *Serve the People*, 86.

263. Brenner, Brenner, and Winslow, *Rebel Rank and File*, 130.

264. Peter B. Levy, *The New Left and Labor in the 1960s* (Urbana: University of Illinois Press, 1994), 50–51.

265. Stanley Aronowitz, "Trade Unionism and Workers' Control," in *Workers' Control*, eds. Gerry Hunnius, G. David Garson, and John Case (New York: Vintage Books, 1973).

266. Brenner, Brenner, and Winslow, *Rebel Rank and File*, 258

267. *Veterans Stars and Stripes for Peace* 1, no. 3 (1968): 1.

268. Redstockings, *Feminist Revolution* (New York: Random House, 1975), 21.

269. Robin Morgan, ed., *Sisterhood Is Powerful* (New York: Random House, 1970), xxi.

270. Ruth Rosen, *The World Split Open: How the Modern Women's Movement Changed America* (New York: Penguin Books, 2000), 134–35.

271. As reported in Rosen, *The World Split Open*, 132.

272. Susan Brownmiller, *In Our Time: Memoir of a Revolution* (New York: Dial Press, 1999), 18.

273. Robin Morgan, *Sisterhood Is Powerful*, xxv.

274. Naomi Klein, "'Kinder, Kuche, Kirche' as Scientific Law: Psychology Constructs the Female," in *Sisterhood Is Powerful*, 205–20.

275. Marge Piercy, "The Grand Coolie Damn," in *Sisterhood Is Powerful*, 421–38.

276. Sheila Rowbotham, *Woman's Consciousness, Man's World* (Harmondsworth: Penguin Books, 1973), 117–20.

277. Pat Mainardi, "The Politics of Housework," in *Sisterhood Is Powerful*, 447.

278. See Judith A. Hellman, *Mexico in Crisis* (New York: Holmes and Meier Publishers, 1979), 46–47.

279. This was a minimal number. Rivolta Femminile estimated the number of illegal abortions at one to three million per year. The more conservative World Health Organization gave a figure of eight hundred thousand to three million, and attributed twenty thousand female deaths per year to improperly performed procedures. See Hellman, *Mexico in Crisis*, 42, and Sandra Kemp, *Italian Feminist Thought: A Reader* (Oxford: Basil Blackwell, 1991), 214.

280. Hewison, *Too Much Art*, 217.

281. Hewison, 217.

282. Morgan, *Sisterhood Is Powerful*, 521.

CHAPTER 3
REVOLUTION IN FRANCE? MAY 1968

It is truly with confidence that I envisage, for the next twelve months, the existence of our country . . . in the midst of so many lands shaken by so many jolts, ours will continue to give the example of efficiency in the conduct of its affairs.
—*President Charles de Gaulle*, New Year's Broadcast, January 1, 1968

T HE MAY EXPLOSION CAME AS A SURPRISE NOT JUST TO DE GAULLE. No one planned it. Few expected it. In the apparent tranquility of a modern industrialized society, a student revolt precipitated a general strike in France, momentarily posing the possibility of revolution. Although the May events were but one of the many uprisings which shook the world in 1968, they were a significant one, shattering the myth of "the end of ideology" and inspiring revolutionary struggles in countries on six continents.

The events of May demonstrated a unity between generations of people who came to consciousness along different roads. The main forces of the explosion were workers and students who had not known material scarcity at any time in their lives. There were also those who had lived through the Great Depression and Nazi occupation, and, despite the appearance of affluence in post–World War II France, fought for a new type of social order.

Throughout France in May and June of 1968, millions of people refused to continue their normal day-to-day activities. Students closed their universities and high schools, many demanding a new mode of education. Workers occupied their factories and offices, frequently calling for a new mode of production. Some cities established new forms of government, as in Nantes, where a Central Strike Committee representing autonomous unions of workers, peasants, and students took over the town hall for six days and even issued their own currency.[1]

The dimensions of the 1968 explosion are difficult to comprehend. In less than thirty days, business as usual in France was brought to a halt. As many as ten million workers were on strike, and tens of thousands of people were rioting in Paris, battling with police for control of the city. The uprising threatened to transform not only previous modes of production, education, and government but the entire epoch of civilization. What began as springtime student protests against U.S. involvement in Vietnam and sexual segregation in university dormitories was rapidly transformed into a potentially revolutionary situation.

Tactics of the government contributed to escalation of conflict. In the first eleven days of May, various ministers closed universities and called on police to suppress the student revolt. When police invaded campuses, it was the first time in the twentieth century (with the lone exception of the Nazi occupation) that university autonomy had been violated. As hundreds were arrested and many more injured, thousands of people took to the streets, building barricades against the police onslaught and refusing to submit. People all over Paris witnessed police savagery and were sickened by the system's dependence on brutality to enforce its order. On May 8, after nearly a week of riots, the French public opinion poll IFOP reported that four-fifths of Parisians were sympathetic to rebellious students.[2]

By Saturday, May 11, the day following the "night of the barricades," the government abandoned its strategy to repress students and attempted, instead, to defuse their revolt. Police were withdrawn from universities and the streets of Paris, amnesty was granted to all those who had been arrested, and it was promised that closed universities would be reopened the following Monday. These measures, seen as government capitulation to students' demands, brought legitimacy to those who had fought the police and gave them a renewed feeling of strength.

From the start, the Communist Party of France (PCF) and General Confederation of Labor (CGT) militantly struggled to isolate the student revolt, calling students the "children of the big bourgeoisie" in the Party's paper, describing their leaders as agents of Gaullism, and keeping students out of occupied factories. The student revolt challenged the influence that the PCF and CGT held over the French proletariat, a legacy from past trade union struggles. Feeling its power threatened, the CGT did its utmost to split students and workers. In early May, an official statement very negatively portrayed the student uprising: "Some petty bourgeois with feverish brains slander the workers' movement and pretend to teach the workers a lesson. The working class rejects these stupidities; it has come of age a long time ago; it needs no tutelage."[3] Suddenly, after the victory of May 11, all the country's major trade unions announced their support for a general strike in support of students to begin on May 14.

On May 12, university occupations spread. The University of Strasbourg was occupied and declared its autonomy from the National Ministry of Education. The Censier Annex of the University of Paris Faculty of Letters (Sorbonne) was taken over. These actions catalyzed new motion among workers and students throughout France.[4]

On Monday, May 13, eight
hundred thousand workers and
students took to the streets of
Paris and marched in solidarity
with the student revolt.[5] At the
end of the march, thousands
joined the Sorbonne occupation and a student soviet was
declared. Over the next month,
the occupied Sorbonne served
as a meeting place for students
and workers where questions of
strategy and tactics were openly
discussed and democratically
decided. As factory after factory was occupied, the fighting
in Paris intensified and spread
throughout France.

Defiant Paris protest. Marc Riboud/Magnum Photos.

The massive popularity of
occupations made it impossible
for the army to intervene. Moreover, there were many within the government
who feared that soldiers would fight side by side with workers and students,
not against them. Fearing radicalization of the military, the government called
up all reservists and kept military personnel on bases and out of touch with
the outside world, even with state-run radio and television. For a time, strikers themselves were able to close down the mass media, making it even more
difficult for the centers of power to function and precipitating intensified discussions in streets, cafes, and neighborhoods. So popular was the impetus to
express needs that even several dozen female ballet dancers from the Folies
Bergère cabaret in Paris went on strike for better working conditions and wage
increases. On May 24, an attempt to set fire to the Paris stock exchange failed,
protests demanded the resignation and expulsion of de Gaulle, at least three
police stations were attacked, almost eight hundred people arrested and more
than four hundred injured. On May 25, intense street fights were reported in
Lyon, Strasbourg, Grenoble, Rouen, Nantes, and in Paris.

Prime Minister Pompidou banned all demonstrations, and simultaneously,
in an attempt to buy off workers, he organized negotiations with all major
trade unions at the Rue de Grenelle in Paris on the weekend of May 25–26.
Agreed upon reforms were modeled after the Matignon agreements of 1936,
when the working class was guaranteed a minimum of rights, such as collective bargaining, unionization, and election of shop stewards. The 1968 Grenelle

settlement was even more stupendous: a 35 percent increase in the minimum wage (agricultural workers received a 56 percent raise, and, in some industries, wages were increased by as much as 72 percent); a shorter work week; a lower retirement age; more family and elderly people's allowances; and more union rights. To top it off, the strikers were to be paid at half their normal rate for all days of the occupations.[6]

To everyone's surprise, striking workers rejected the results. When Georges Séguy, secretary-general of the largest trade union in France, the Communist-dominated CGT, and Benoît Frachon, CGT president and a signatory of the Matignon agreement, drove directly from concluded negotiations to the huge Renault plant at Boulogne-Billancourt to address twenty-five thousand workers assembled there, their speeches were met with boos and catcalls. Shop stewards from around the country telephoned and telegraphed CGT headquarters turning down the agreements.

Workers continued to occupy factories and offices, and at this point, revolution seemed to be the order of the day. On May 27, the PCF announced it was against any further student demonstrations. The Party also warned the nine million workers on strike that the police would use all possible force to suppress on new outbreaks of violence. De Gaulle left Paris, and, according to his own admission, he was tempted to resign. There was a vacuum of power in France on Monday, May 29. For over six hours, no one even knew where to find the president. Later, it became known that he spent these mysterious hours in Baden-Baden, Germany, where, in close collaboration with top French Army generals, he was plotting his comeback. On May 30, de Gaulle dismissed Parliament and announced new elections would be held in June. That same day, almost one million people marched in Paris to demand he leave office. The next night, May 31, tanks and paratroopers positioned themselves surrounding Paris, and French troops in Germany were placed on high alert. The release on June 14 of General Raoul Salan, former head of the paramilitary right-wing Secret Army Organization (whose actions included an attempted assassination of de Gaulle in 1961), and ten other imprisoned OAS leaders prompted many to wonder what deals or promises had been made to the paramilitary Right.

Global Connections

French political life during the 1950s and 1960s was intimately connected with successful anticolonial movements in Vietnam and Algeria. Within national liberation support movements in France, many activists gained their first experiences in extraparliamentary political praxis.[7] The refusal of the Parti Communiste Français (PCF) to support the Algerian Front de Libération Nationale (FLN) in the early 1960s caused many people to leave the PCF and its affiliates, leading to creation of independent "groupuscules," small, ideological groups generally credited with sparking the May events.

French students have long acted in solidarity with movements in other countries. Hundreds of activists went to an international conference in Berlin in February 1968, to help organize pan-European actions against U.S. involvement in Vietnam. The next month, various groupuscules in Paris united for the first time to demonstrate against the Springer Press's sensationalist attacks on German SDS. The arrest of three students protesting the U.S. war against Vietnam precipitated occupation of the administration building at Nanterre University on March 22, bringing into existence the March 22 Movement. Prior to the May events, membership in all French New Left groups and organizations was miniscule, numbering at most two thousand, but these activists comprised a political force of great importance, one that detonated an explosion throughout the entire society.[8]

We might wonder whether the May movement could have enjoyed such massive participation before the Comintern's influence over the PCF had waned or before NATO troops had been asked to leave France. For the first time since World War II, the nation's relative military autonomy left its fate in its own hands. In the immediate aftermath of May 1968, André Glucksmann summed up the situation:

> At present, everything at stake in France is decided in a neutralized military space; no foreign power can act physically to alter a relation of forces decided within the national frontiers. For the first time for more than a century, Marx's formula is true again for Western Europe, and the revolutionary struggle may be national in form (not nationalist in content): "The proletariat of each country of course, first of all has to settle matters with its own bourgeoisie."[9]

It is never certain that foreign powers will refrain from intervening during another nation's moments of crisis. There are many methods of intervention in the modern world: covert and overt, economic, political, and military. The power of transnational corporations and their U.S. protectors was demonstrated in 1973 by their subversion of the democratically elected Allende government in Chile. A minimum of outside military strength was necessary to destabilize Allende, and even in 2018, the U.S. government continues to deny its role in the military coup there.

The French movement was the *product* of global forces, but it also acted as a *producer* of the worldwide turmoil of 1968. The May events were internationally significant since the vast majority of the working class in France, unlike their peers in other industrialized countries, joined with the students and nearly made a revolution. As in 1848, the revolutionary movement of 1968 in France revealed a new epoch of class struggles at a more intense and advanced level than in other economically advanced countries. It may be coincidental that the Paris peace talks between the United States and Vietnam began in the first part of May 1968, but this correspondence in time and space illustrates essential social forces of 1968 that affected France. Is it a mere happenstance that revolutionary aspirations and actions reappeared in Europe at the same time that the American Empire, the last Western colonial empire, reached its limit in Vietnam?

That the French explosion came exactly in May was as much an accident as it was a product of the specific sociohistorical developments inside and outside of France. Government mistakes and stupidity played roles in the rapid escalation of the revolt. What is clear after the crisis is that a host of forces converged in 1968, and the totality of French society convulsed in a near-revolution.

Roots of the May Events

The industrial revolution originated in Western Europe, but for many reasons, France was not in the center of it. Not until after World War II did French industry develop parity with neighboring Germany or England. Industrial production in France increased by 75 percent from 1948 to 1957. From 1953 to the first quarter of 1958, the increase was 57 percent (compared to 53 percent in West Germany and 33 percent for Western Europe as a whole).[10]

It was not simply the quantity of industrial production that changed dramatically. There was a vast movement from the countryside to the cities as agriculture was intensely industrialized. From nine million French people working on the land in 1921, to seven and a half million in 1946, there were only three million in 1968.[11] There were a host of business mergers, and the state took on a larger role in the economy.

The French state is one of the most centralized and bureaucratic political instruments ever created. A series of popular uprisings and near-revolutions in the nineteenth century, as Marx said, "perfected this machine instead of smashing it." Bonapartism, characterized by strong and unlimited state authority, urbanization, and preponderance of the army, had already accelerated centralization of power in Paris. As in all industrialized societies, the modern French state has taken on more economic powers.

The role of college training has become increasingly important to industrialized societies. Large-scale industry needs more technicians within its offices to coordinate space-age production, more managers to administer it, more psychologists to find ways of keeping employees working, advertising specialists to market the goods of consumer society, and sociologists to maintain the system's overall direction.[12] As bureaucratic organization of industry and

Demonstration of May 13 at Gare de l'Est. Maurice Grimaud.

politics developed after World War II, the educational sector was expanded in response. In 1946, there were 123,000 college students in France; in 1961, 202,000; and in 1968, 514,000.[13] New universities were hurriedly constructed, including a concrete jungle in Nanterre on the west end of Paris.

French education is almost entirely state-organized and run by the huge Ministry of National Education, which employed more than 700,000 people in 1968, making it the country's biggest employer.[14] The rigidity of French education, its ultracentralization and adaptation to an earlier society, enabled it to resist all attempts at serious reform for over 150 years. Paternalism toward students and neglect of their needs were part of its regular mode of operation, and rapid expansion exacerbated its nascent contradictions.

That there was a structural and human crisis in higher education was common knowledge long before the explosion of 1968. In November 1963, France's universities had been shut down by a national student strike called to protest overcrowded conditions and lack of government foresight in accommodating increased enrollments caused by the postwar baby boom. During the May events, however, many faculty and students questioned the entire organization of the university system, not just its inadequate management. In an interview during May 1968, Alain Geismar, general secretary of the Syndicat National de l'Enseignement Supérieur (National Union of Higher Education) said:

> We have been saying that there is a profound crisis in the universities for several years. It has various kinds of underlying causes, in particular the maladaptation of the university structure to its economic and social functions, in research as well as in education and hence in the training of the cadres. . . . Our proof? Seventy percent of those who attend the French university fail to complete their courses, and even among those that do graduate, there is an absolutely astonishing number of unemployed. As for the internal organization of the university, it is completely inadequate in an advanced country, with its compartmentalization of the various disciplines, a hierarchy of disciplines dating from Auguste Comte and of faculty structures inherited from the Empire.[15]

In another May interview, Jacques Sauvageot, vice president of the Union Nationale des Étudiants de France, reiterated some of the same thoughts: "Students are expected to have a certain critical intelligence, while their studies are such that they are not allowed to exercise it. On the other hand, they realize that in a few years' time they will not be able to find a part to play in society that corresponds to their training. This dual phenomenon is, I believe, the basic cause of their revolution."[16]

Even those who managed French education recognized some of its shortcomings before May. The Fouchet plan of reforms had already proposed a two-year degree, seeking to modernize education and bring it more in harmony with the needs of industrialized France. Student opposition to this plan was widespread since it seemed designed to decrease the numbers of working-class people who would have access to a university education, as well as to fundamentally reduce humanitarian content of university courses to a technocratic version.[17]

It is possible to define a central contradiction within French universities: on the one hand, an archaic orientation to training of elites and an authoritarian structure; on the other hand, an enlarged need for college graduates and increasing diversity among faculty and students. In an attempt to resolve this contradiction while remaining within the bounds of the existing socioeconomic system, several programs were proposed. They included Fouchet's reforms as well as far more visionary notions like departmental reorganization, student and faculty power, and an end to archaic centralization. Students and faculty flocked to the banner of academic reform during May, and in the aftermath of the explosion, they saw many "radical" proposals implemented.

While many faculty and students conceived of universities' problems as solvable through adjustments in the existing system, others were more skeptical because of university dependence on the social system as a whole. They therefore raised questions about the nature of society's structures and universities' role within them. Those involved in the May events who had less at stake in the university, who were less careerist in their life orientation, or who were simply more visionary than their reformist friends, brought the issue of the universities' role within an unfree and unjust society to the forefront of the student revolt.

Following the pattern of general strikes of the past, specific grievances were translated into universalized insurgency. Demands and actions were formulated which focused on the whole society and included such issues as the need to abolish the privileged status of students, the nature of jobs which graduates might find, and the mystification of knowledge in the hands of experts.[18] During May, these visionaries opened the universities to all people ("a university without borders") in the hope of using their resources to overthrow the entire system. By the end of the month, French art students produced posters calling for the end to capitalism while workers held control of factories.

Academic freedom, the traditional autonomy of academia from politics, was originally challenged not by campus activists but by the development of advanced capitalism. In the modern era, science and technology have become one of the system's main productive forces, capable of drastically altering old methods of production (or warfare) in a short time. As scientific research, one of the essential functions of universities, has come to the center of the system's needs, higher education has increasingly become directed by the economic, political, military, and cultural needs of the entire society.[19] In France, this meant the needs as defined by the central government.

The crisis of French universities was part of the total crisis of society. Contradictions within the universities simultaneously reflected and embodied larger social contradictions, chief among which in the era of contemporary capitalism is: incessantly expanding forces of production are contained within ancient social relationships. In less than two centuries since 1789, capital succeeded beyond anyone's expectations for technological development and economic prosperity. For the first time in history, space-age production was capable of providing the vast majority of people in industrialized countries with sufficient food, clothing, and shelter. With their socialization, modern productive forces could bring prosperity to the entire world. The accumulation of generations of labor, embodied in cities, factories, and universities, is controlled by derelict billionaires, mad dog generals, and plastic politicians. This global problem weighed heavily on the thoughts of activists and helped to detonate an explosion in May 1968 which reaffirmed the possibility of a new world, one freed from the scarcity and exploitation of "prehistory."[20]

The general strike that shut down France for nearly a month would never have occurred without workers' massive participation. By itself, the student revolt would have remained utopian, unable to question in practice the entire society. Many workers empathized with the brutality suffered by students at the hands of police, especially since the most brutal treatment came from the Compagnies Républicaines de Sécurité (CRS), first organized after workers' strikes in 1947. But there were also grievances within the working class that students' struggles helped to crystallize.

The Workers

The long tradition of working-class militancy in France, often attributed as the primary reason for the unique juncture of worker and student movements in 1968, does not fully account for workers' actions. Tradition is double-edged, providing a source of revolutionary inspiration in France, but also inertia to maintain old patterns of social interaction. The PCF's Marxism helps to explain why French factory workers were not as dominated by the ideology of capitalism as their counterparts in the United States, West Germany, or England, *as well as* why the French May uprising gave way so easily to restoration of order.

Although the French working class in 1968 was one of the lowest paid and had one of the longest workweeks in Europe, they had seen a dramatic rise in their standard of living since the Nazi occupation. With the postwar economic expansion of 1945–68 and the rise of a consumer society, French workers saw their standard of living improve, a fact that led many sociologists to believe that class struggle in its traditional forms had come to an end. Of course, theories that posited the impossibility of a qualitatively new social order were temporarily swept aside in May. What radical sociologists had not been able to accomplish in years of painstaking debate in the universities occurred almost overnight in the streets.

Growth of higher education in France and open admissions common to continental systems gave an increasing number of working-class children opportunities for individual advancement. As sons and daughters of the working class were seen to be rubbing elbows with children of the rich, it was argued

Striking workers held weeks of discussions in occupied factories. Photographer unknown.

that workers received the same cultural artifacts mass produced by consumer society: television programs, movies, and, it was argued, even theaters were "democratically" available. Although cars and refrigerators were less common among families of factory workers, "postindustrial" society brought to many what previously had been available to only the privileged few. In the decade since de Gaulle seized power on May 13, 1958, the French economy had prospered. The gross national product rose 63 percent, foreign trade tripled despite the shift from colonial to more competitive markets, and the once empty Bank of France was filled with $6 billion worth of gold and foreign currency.[21]

Official French estimates at the beginning of 1968 showed that 40 percent of wage and salary earners received less than $1,800 per year. Only one household in four simultaneously owned a refrigerator, washing machine, and television, while only one in five had all these and a car.[22] These figures may indicate poverty to some, but they serve to outline the level of comfort in a society where there is freedom from hunger and disease for the vast majority (in contrast to much of the world). Not all economic problems had been solved.

Unemployment hovered around the half-million mark, inflation began to eat away at disposable income, and a new world economic crisis was beginning.

In 1968, workers in France did not go on strike simply for a greater share of the capitalist pie. Their overwhelming rejection of the Grenelle agreements, the many proposals for self-management, the effigies of capitalism found hanging outside many factories during the general strike and the widespread discussions of expropriation are ample proof that they had a more radical agenda. The break with the usual short-term, goal-oriented activities of the working class can be explained, at least in part, by the new type of workers engendered by advanced capitalism and by productive relationships common to all industrialized societies.

The New Working Class

With the advent of monopoly capitalism, the unity of ownership and control of the means of production has become more and more fragmented. Large-scale financial organizations and corporate structures involving such people as managers and systems analysts have taken over what had been the individual entrepreneur's functions of ownership and control. Greater numbers of employees have become supervisors and specialists, giving rise to a new division in the working class both in terms of levels of authority and functional fragmentation.[23]

Executives, along with an increasing number of bureaucrats who exercise authority, constitute the administrative apparatus of modern industrial, academic, military, and political organizations. At their command are manual workers as well as a growing number of white-collar workers like researchers, technicians, secretaries, and teachers. Expressed as either the proletarianization of intellectuals or the mass education of the proletariat, contemporary capitalism and large-scale bureaucratic organizations have created an increasing number of workers whose jobs defy traditional distinctions between manual and intellectual work.[24] As the proletariat was the ascendant social class in the period of the First Industrial Revolution, these technicians are growing in the period of the cybernetics revolution, or Third Industrial Revolution. As machinery is the accumulated labor-power of manual workers, computer memory and cybernetically controlled processes are the accumulated labor-power of the new working class.

Rapid expansion of this new section of the working class is a common feature of industrialized countries. In 1968, employment in health and education exceeded one and a half million people in France, or about 7 percent of the total labor force. The number of technicians and scientists, excluding executives, rose from 457,000 in 1954 to 877,000 in 1968.[25] In the same year, the extractive and manufacturing industry employed only 41 percent of the workforce (33 percent in the United States, a more advanced stage of economic development).

The industrial struggles of early capitalism were generally between skilled factory workers and owners. Decades later, these conflicts largely became institutionalized through negotiated settlements between trade unions and management. In modern times, a new level of conflict has developed within what was formerly the small and obedient staff of the supervisor: the conflict between technocrats who give orders and technicians who receive orders. As the general strike spread, the participation of the new workers was impressive. As Alain Touraine put it:

> The fact that most of the workers actively participated in the May–June strikes should not mislead us. Those who were responsible for the social movement character that these strikes often had were neither skilled workers nor the great organized labor groups such as the miners, the longshoremen, and the railroad workers. The leading role in the May movement was not played by the working class, but by those whom we can call professionals, whether they were actually practicing a profession or were still apprentices.[26]

An example of conflict between technocrats and technicians during May was the popular strike by government radio and television workers. Some thirteen thousand producers, journalists, and technicians stayed out longer than any other section of the working class, denying the government the capability to make significant use of mass media during the general strike. Not on strike just for more money, these workers were motivated by a desire to no longer be obedient tools.[27] They launched a creative public campaign with slogans like, "The police on the screen means the police in your home."

We are the power.

Some journalists of large newspapers sought power over the orientation of their papers by demanding changes in the structure of their ownership. In a few cases, printers and journalists published newspapers but changed them, as in the case of *Le Figaro*. When news it was supposed to carry misrepresented the aims of the student movement, workers corrected the article. At one point in the general strike, the technicians responsible for communication between the Ministry of Interior and police headquarters went on strike, disrupting a sensitive and important connection in what was by then the fragmented repressive forces of the French state.

Strikes among technicians marked the emergence of a new social movement for some observers. While the conflict between technocrats and technicians is peculiar to advanced capitalism,[28] the May movement consistently located itself in the socialist tradition of the nineteenth and twentieth centuries. What seems clear is that the rapid pace of change in the French economy in the postwar years helped precipitate the May movement, particularly among the new workers. The blind hand of change that rests solely on internal developments of the economy (*Naturwuchs*) was slapped aside by attempts to rationally reorganize France. Whether we look at new workers engendered by the system's inner logic or at the rapid rate of urbanization in the same period, we can see that the social conditions of existence of the people of France were rapidly transformed in the period leading up to 1968. Is it surprising that such rapid social change was accompanied by the rise of a vast social movement hoping to give reasonability to the quality of change?

Differences between the classical proletariat and modern technicians are real, but both groups experience similar oppression as workers. While some technicians may be elevated to executive status and some proletarians to roles of bureaucratic authority in their unions or companies, the vast majority of people in both categories are employed in positions distant from the decision-making top. They both receive orders from technocrats and hold jobs with narrowing creative outlets and rewards, a common situation in the modern world.

Capitalist Relations of Production

In a capitalist system, producers sell their labor for material rewards like wages and consumer goods. In exchange for human energy, workers receive things. In this way, capitalist society tends to transform qualitative human factors into quantifiable commodities. The terms of the exchange are unequal on both quantitative and qualitative levels.

Quantitatively, despite vigorous and long-term efforts of trade unions, workers' productivity is far greater than their wages. Surplus value continues to be extracted from their energy. No matter how vigorously the science of economics attempts to mask or apologize for this inequality by arguing that capitalists contribute to production and should be reimbursed, the fact remains that workers produce more than they are paid. Otherwise, how could profits be made? The participation of capitalists through the use of "their" machinery is a sham. Long ago, Marx demonstrated that the capital owned by the rich is stored labor-power ("dead labor") extracted from workers of the past.[29] Dead and neutral property comes alive in this context.

Unions have traditionally fought only for a more "equal" and safer quantitative exchange between capitalists and workers. "Unions help workers *have* more, not *be* more. They serve to increase the quantity of goods the worker receives in exchange for his alienated labor; they do not serve to abolish alienated labor."[30] This analysis seems to be especially revealing in terms of trade unions' role in the May events. In entering into the ill-fated Grenelle agreements, in trying to keep the student revolt separated from the working class, and in preventing whenever possible the formation of autonomous strike committees by the workers, the CGT continually attempted to channel the general strike toward reformist objectives.

Qualitatively, the exchange between capitalists and workers differs in kind: energy for things. Workers might get higher wages but that does not alter this qualitative inequality. Industrialization and pressure from unions have resulted in more things being allocated to workers, but qualitative inequality of exchange continues. It is a structural backbone of the capitalist mode of production, and it was this backbone that was challenged and nearly broken in May. Capital's control of the products and process of production excludes 99 percent of us from making decisions vital to all of us. This glaring undemocratic relationship was revealed in utmost clarity in May.

Cultural Poverty of Consumer Societies

Roots of the May explosion can be found in the dynamic conflict between forces and relations of production and in the rapid changes in France in the decades immediately preceding 1968. The May events reveal broader human grievances such as cultural fragmentation and unmet human needs that became glaringly obvious in France and in "affluent" countries generally.

A CGT trade union leader urges striking Citroën employees to return to work. EDIMEDIA.

For most people in the industrialized core of the world system, the drastic rise in standards of living during modern times—the allocation of more things to workers—has come at a high human cost. Energy at the workplace has become more automated and fragmented, and what was formerly "free time" has become increasingly objectified and controlled. Assembly-line production, the basis for consumer society, has routinized jobs, reducing workers to mere appendages of machinery. Vast differentiations in the division of labor, necessary for assembly-line production, have caused workers to specialize in jobs that block the use of nearly all creativity. The increasing separation between decision-makers and executants has reinforced alienation and passivity. As space-age production has given human beings atomic weapons, for example, the decision to pull the trigger is beyond the power of the vast majority.

In university classrooms, military service, and virtually all the institutions of modern society, the role of the individual has been reduced to a passive cog in the social machinery. The transition from public to mass, to use C. Wright Mills's words, has been accompanied by the growth of one-way communication and the demise of dialogue and collective discussion.

In the realm of consumption, mass society reproduces the primacy of things, not people.[31] Instead of a person going to a cobbler, for example, and having a pair of shoes specially made, one now goes to a shoe store where a variety of styles and prices are available. Instead of the commodity being matched to the person, the person must match the commodity. Free time has become leisure, a huge arena for profit making and standardization.

Service industries have risen in importance, providing for cash what used to be available in the family. From acts of intimacy and love to cooking and cleaning, mass society gains what the atomized individual has lost. The exchange of human energy for things and the proliferation of the cash nexus to nearly all aspects of life have combined in their effects on the human psyche. People tend to view themselves, not simply others, as objects—things to be sterilized by deodorants for various parts of the body, much as cleaning aids are available for different parts of the house.

Consumer society's chief strength has been its ability to "deliver the goods" to a majority of people within the industrialized nations. Urbanization and the mass media have centralized consumer markets, and as disposable incomes have risen, new markets have been developed through colonization of everyday life. Using a variety of advertising techniques, new ways of manipulating human consumption are continually devised. Desire for unnecessary products is created through advertising. On a covert level, advertisers and marketing experts design subliminal techniques for stimulating unconscious needs and desires in order to sell products. After establishing its capacity to profitably satisfy the physical needs of humans—food, clothing, and shelter—capitalism has moved on to new markets: manipulation of cultural and psychological needs for profit.

The increasing importance of consumer markets for monopoly capitalism has created a new situation in industrialized countries. Henri Lefebvre taught that "Organizational capitalism now has its colonies in the metropolis, and it concentrates on the internal market in order to utilize it according to a colonial pattern. The double exploitation of producer and consumer carries the colonial experience into the midst of the erstwhile colonizing people."[32]

Coercion needed to maintain these internal colonies is predominantly psychological, in distinction to the Third World where physical force is more common. The human regimentation and standardization which capital imposes on its subjects in the industrialized core are hidden behind the freedom to choose among gadgets, pretty politicians, and other consumer rewards.

Is it surprising that the May explosion erupted in spontaneous actions that challenged the power of manipulation and regimentation? As Raoul Vaneigem put it, "Who wants a world where the guarantee of freedom from starvation means a risk of death of boredom?"[33] The implicit message during May was "DO IT," not watch it. Leaflets called for the formation of autonomous action committees (ACs) in schools, workplaces, and

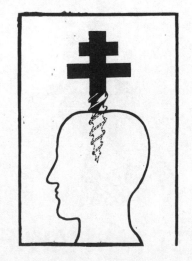

communities—wherever people could organize themselves. In contrast to the ultracentralization of France, self-reliance and self-management were stressed as new means for social organization. As one leaflet said: "If you are a group of comrades, form a committee, draw up your own leaflet, set a place for daily meetings, make dates for demonstrations. Contact the provisional coordination committee of the AC's and name a liaison delegate. If you are alone, contact the coordination committee."[34]

Within two weeks, hundreds of ACs formed throughout France; more than 250 came into existence in Paris alone. A General Assembly of ACs was created, subject to instant recall and with no power beyond coordination. *Action*, the newspaper of the ACs, was an immediate success with a daily circulation of thirty thousand. In contrast to rigid bureaucratic structures of the traditional Left, new forms for liberation and a new content of freedom were developed during May. The Freud–Che Guevara Action Committee called on the movement to unite "all those who are crushed or excluded by an inhumane system: The struggle must have as its final objective the establishment of a socialist system in which, through the destruction of barriers, the creativity of each individual will be set free. This objective implies a revolution not only in the relations of production, but in the mode of life, in ways of thought, in human relations, and in the concept of the sexual life of all."[35]

It is difficult to overestimate the antibureaucratic thrust of the May insurgents. The pomp of officials, Communist or not, was everywhere held up for public ridicule. Rules, an essential ingredient of rational-legal forms of authority, were flaunted according to the slogan: "It is forbidden to forbid." Economic and bureaucratic domination were simultaneously challenged: "Mankind will not be free until the last capitalist has been hanged by the entrails of the last bureaucrat."

In word and deed, May marked the merging of a social movement for economic liberation with a vast cultural revolt. Romanticism of nonfragmented lives of the past was combined with modern awareness of the possibilities opened by space-age production. Science was not rejected, yet material progress was made secondary to human needs.

Beauty is in the street.

Political struggles around culture preceded May. In February 1968, when the government removed Henri Langlois from his position as the head of the Paris Cinémathèque, an internationally prominent archive and theater, organized protests succeeded in restoring Langlois to his position.[36] In a social-psychological study of the May events, Alfred Willener viewed cultural concerns as a prime cause for the May explosion:

> Whatever the situation was in 1968, there was no question of Gaullist France being in ruins; nor did the economy show any major signs of crisis, such as widespread poverty or unemployment, at least for the overwhelming mass of opinion. On the other hand, the extent of the cultural ruin was steadily increasing. . . . A whole civilization, which no one will call "Western" and "Christian," survives only as a skeleton.[37]

Cultural roots of the May events can be found in Dada, Surrealism, free jazz, the Living Theatre, and Godard's films. All share a desire to return to a "natural state" as far as possible from established structures, and they create a space where free play of the imagination and work of the hands and mind can find new unity. Far from being atypical of industrialized societies, the May 1968 explosion was a social manifestation of the same human values and needs contained within modern forms of art. The surrealist ethic of living for one's fantasies was matched by the popular May slogan: "I take my desires for reality, for I believe in the reality of my desires." Another May slogan, "As long as we have not destroyed everything, there will remain ruins," was reminiscent of Dada's attempts to destroy dead art in order to create a living one. The perception of cultural injustices and attempts to overturn them during May demonstrated the nonreducibility of human beings to economic factors.

A strong impulse in May, especially among the more youthful participants, was to consciously reshape themselves to become different kinds of people than those the mass system produced. Everyday life became a topic for politics. The personal values of yesterday were held up for collective reevaluation. One sociologist, who happened to be with members of the March 22 Movement as they were waking up one afternoon, was amazed as they evaluated their previous night in the streets: "The astonishing thing was that what interested them were the little incidents that arose from their own practice, their relations with each other in the gang—and as boys and girls—for sexual problems were not divorced from politics, even during the night of the barricades. . . . Either we're at the antipodes of politics, or it's a new way of seeing politics."[38]

In contrast to the human fragmentation engendered by mass society, the May events' vision called for a new integration of the individual in a different kind of society. The totality of life under the previous mode of existence came into question in theory and practice as new future possibilities were developed. Norman Birnbaum viewed this concern with integration and fragmentation as an essential one:

> The (admittedly precarious) coexistence since the French Revolution of bourgeois routine and bohemian cultural innovation, of bourgeois domination and working-class challenge, of Catholicism and laicism, has proven so fruitful in the sphere of culture precisely because of a common language. The continuation into an industrial epoch of these conceptions, combined with the absurdly backward aspects of much of French social organization, in May of 1968 provoked a convulsion. Typically, French debate about the convulsion has been concerned to a considerable extent with restoring the fragmented unity of the cultural community.[39]

Social fragmentation of French culture was answered by activists' calls for transformation of relationships between human beings and with nature. "The forest precedes man, the desert follows," said one inscription. The notion of the unlimited interrelation of all life was present within the spontaneous and dramatic nature of protests and in the appearance of love at the barricades. If the May insurgents challenged middle-class cultural hegemony, they affirmed new values for life, not ones having to do with domination of nature but on playful and loving interaction with it.[40] From this source flowed such demands as the liberation of the Luxembourg Gardens and freedom for the animals in the zoos.

The May critique of the impoverished culture of contemporary society is an important contribution to the continuing development of revolutionary aspirations. The fusion of cultural and political revolt within a vast social movement gave the May events a new character within the long tradition of insurrections. At one point, de Gaulle said that the situation was *insaisissable*, impossible to grasp or control. The universities and workplaces were not held by armed force but through massive participation of their members, and demands were incomprehensible to those in power. Insurgents were not concerned with traditional political power, and they envisaged their victory through transformation of the general strike into an "active strike":

> the workers would set their factories back into motion on their own account. Then with the economy beginning to turn again, but for the workers and not for their former bosses, the state would succumb in impotence and be ripe for overthrow. A parallel power would arise in each town and village as workers coordinated their efforts with each other and the farmers. Socialism would be initiated from below as self-management and not handed down from above in nationalizations.[41]

May 1968, love at the barricades. *Les inédits de Mai 68* (May 1978).

Such a strike made it difficult for the state to intervene. When occupied buildings were retaken by the government, there was considerable bloodshed but not of the scope that followed the 1871 Commune. In this sense, the fusion of the forces of production and culture in May presented a new method and new goals for the transformation of society. The imagination of May opened possibilities for construction of a qualitatively new future, one where not only material needs but also cultural needs would be of prime concern, where liberation would not be decreed from above but achieved by an activated population.

May 24. Gilles Caron.

The Political Meaning of May 1968: Internationalism and Self-Management

The May insurgents did not act with an already developed model for a new society. Spontaneous escalation of the student struggle necessitated improvisation of strategy and tactics and brought new forms of social organization into existence. A vision where nations, hierarchies of domination, boredom, toil, and human fragmentation no longer would exist came to light during the general strike. A brief investigation of some of the aspects of this vision will be undertaken to demonstrate its qualitative difference from the status quo.

Patriotism and Internationalism

Insurgents in May knew no national boundaries. "To hell with borders," expressed a popular feeling. Through leaflets and posters (*Frontiers =*

Repression), a systematic campaign against petty nationalism was conducted, a campaign that encouraged international students in France to participate in the May events. As the student revolt intensified, foreign students' residence halls in Paris were occupied by their more radical members. Democratic reorganization of residences and support for liberation movements at home and in France were called for. (Of course, there were exceptions, notably the Brazilians who literally closed their doors to the movement in May.) A Tri-Continental Committee was established in Paris that proclaimed that "to contest capitalist structures within a national framework is also to contest the international relations set up by these structures."[42]

Bilingual posters urged such seemingly antagonistic groups as Arabs and Jews to "turn against your common enemy: imperialism and capitalism." One episode of May occurred during a demonstration in support of Daniel Cohn-Bendit, the German-born Jew who was expelled from France after he and the March 22 Movement helped spark the explosion. As the support demonstration unfolded, fifty thousand people, including a prominent contingent of Arabs, chanted: "We are all German Jews."

Daniel Cohn-Bendit symbolized the movement of 1968. Topham Picturepoint.

Foreign workers in France, traditionally considered a threat to jobs of French workers and subject to racist attacks, were received as comrades during May. Immigrants from nearby countries have long been compelled to find work in French industry, even though they are hired for the worst jobs at the lowest pay. For the most part unable to speak French, these workers were often used by management to break strikes, or in periods of relative calm, to disrupt communication and organization among laborers at the point of production. Working at the grueling pace of an assembly line provides little time or space for discussion, especially if there is a Yugoslav on your left and an Algerian on your right. Moreover, foreign workers in France generally lived in company-owned houses where they were purposely assigned roommates who spoke a different language.

The general strike temporarily transformed workers divided by language and nationality. Multilingual worker-student action committees very successfully canvassed the housing projects where foreign workers lived. Not only was management unable to mobilize strikebreakers, but the vast majority of foreign workers joined in the general strike. In early June, the General Assembly of Worker-Student Action Committees passed a resolution "For Abolition of the Status of Foreigner in France." Invoking the example of the Paris Commune, where a Hungarian was minister of labor and a Polish worker the military chief, the resolution went on to call for an end to residence cards, work cards, and deportations:

> These foreigners come under an oppressive special statute which subjects them to almost permanent special police checks and threats, which we Frenchmen avoid simply because of our nationality. This concept of "nationality" is profoundly reactionary. People work, are exploited, dream, and fight for their freedom in a specific geographic and social context; there they have every right.[43]

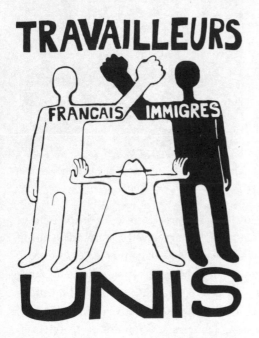

Workers—French and immigrants—united.

In contrast to the internationalism of the insurgents, the government attempted to seal off French borders to the many young people from Germany and Italy who attempted to get to Paris. Deportations were used to rid France of foreign activists. In response, an Action Committee for the Abolition of Borders was formed in Paris and urged Europeans to spread the revolution throughout the continent. Their call to action did not go unheard, particularly in Germany and Italy.[44]

Traditional French ethnocentrism was swept aside by unleashed imaginations. The Gaullist counteroffensive in June, on the other hand, played heavily on the myth of foreigners who had caused the disruptions and riots. What may surprise some was the nationalism of the French Communist Party, an organization originally committed to proletarian internationalism. On June 10, Waldeck Rochet, the Party's secretary-general, proclaimed, "We Communists have always fought and shall continue to fight remorselessly the lack of national feeling that certain anarchist elements vaunt as a sign of their revolutionary ardor. We, for our part, are proud to have restored to the working class what Aragon so nobly called 'the colors of France.'"[45]

FRONTIERES = REPRESSION

Radical activists questioned the nation-state as a rational form for social organization in May, but national sovereignty had already been undermined long before 1968. Modern transnational corporations, which today account for well over one-third of the world's total production, are capitalist forms of global organization that transcend national boundaries. Is it so surprising that the New Left's vision for the future included a world without borders?

Borders = repression.

Authoritarianism and Self-Management

With the rise of large-scale modern industry and fragmentation of production, managers of all varieties have become a necessary part of the productive apparatus. Are they really? The May events indicated not. Many factory occupations exposed managers as essential to a profit-oriented economy, but also as superfluous, if not destructive, to a human-oriented system.

In the first days of the general strike, many managers found themselves prisoners in their offices at the mercy of occupying workers. The first two factories to be taken over by workers who then detained their managers were Sud-Aviation in Nantes and Renault at Cléon. Hostage-taking caused uproar in the government, as well as in the largest trade union in France, the Communist-dominated CGT. Georges Séguy, secretary-general of the CGT, broadcast an appeal to the workers in Nantes to release the management team, and he even sent a delegation by private plane to intervene. Alarmed by workers' drastic actions, the CGT issued a public statement praising the "responsibility" of its membership and guaranteeing safety for management and means of production.[46]

It should be noted that during the same period, some managers expressed sympathy for the aims of the strikers, and a few even contributed money to the movement. At Orly Airport, for example, the Air France staff donated 10,000 francs at the start of the strike, and the vast majority of management helped the strike committee in negotiations and upkeep of the ninety-odd planes grounded during the strike.

In general, however, workers' actions against management revealed a fundamental aspiration of the general strike: *autogestion* (or self-management). The main thrust of the vision of self-management was to abolish hierarchical authority, but this kind of authority was only one of many permeating France. As scientific innovations in production progressed, so did the need for experts with technical qualifications to develop and implement them, and knowledge became even more a means for power over others. The self-managed institutions of 1968 aimed to socialize such specialized knowledge.

Workers take over the massive Renault plant at Boulogne-Billancourt. EDIMEDIA.

Because participation in the general strike included large numbers of professionals, technicians, and off-line office and service personnel (the new workers), the united working class was able to synthesize what had been a fragmented and partial view of production. The compartmentalization of knowledge and concomitant need for privileged experts and managers were refuted not only in desire but often in reality.

In some factories, the workers continued production without the "help" of management. Utility workers, for example, insured regular supplies of gas and electricity for the community. At the electricity plant in Cheviré, workers refused to readmit managers to the plant despite an offered increase in monthly wages averaging 150 francs. As one worker said, "The managing staff has been away for two weeks, and everything is going fine. We can carry on production without them."[47] At the Atomic Energy Center in Saclay, the Central Action Committee, the organ of dual power, organized production to such an extent that when gasoline was running low in the area, thirty thousand liters were delivered with the compliments of the Finac strikers in Nanterre. In Vitry, at the Rhône-Poulenc factories, workers established direct exchange with nearby farmers and made contact with various chemical workers in Western Europe, hoping to develop similar relationships.

These examples indicate a profound aspiration of French workers for control over their jobs and lives, not simply for more things in exchange for obedience to superiors. The absence of specific demands for the first ten days of the workers' occupation at the Atlantic shipyards in St. Nazaire, even though under pressure from their union, is a spectacular demonstration of workers' disdain for management, whether capitalist or "communist." As advances of capitalism in the days of Marx relegated the capitalist to an unnecessary component of the productive process, so it seems that modern capitalism has carried managers to the abyss of irrelevancy. Indeed, in 1976, forty-five thousand professional and managerial personnel were unable to find work in France, compared to only fourteen thousand in 1971.[48]

The concept of self-management did not originate in workplaces during May, but in universities. Nonetheless, it quickly became a general aspiration of the May explosion, a spontaneously created form for dual power. The student soviet at the Sorbonne developed a comprehensive plan for restructuring goals and methods of the university system. The occupied Sorbonne was managed by a general assembly that had final decision-making power. Medical services, food, space allocations, and all other functions within the liberated Sorbonne were taken care of by occupiers. In Nantes, a democratically elected Central Strike Committee conducted food and gasoline distribution, traffic control, and other activities in the life of the city. This committee even developed its own currency.[49]

Occupied high schools, universities, offices, and cities established direct control, concrete realizations of a new vision for society that existed among nearly all sectors of the population. An eloquent articulation of this vision came on May 28 from a student-worker action committee:

> Self-management as an economic and social system has as its goal fully to achieve free participation in production and consumption through individual and collective responsibility. This is therefore a system created above all for human beings, to serve them and not to oppress them. Practically, for working-class comrades, self-management consists in having their factories . . . doing away with the hierarchies of salaries as well as the idea of employees and employers . . . setting up workers' councils elected by themselves to carry out the decisions of everyone together. These councils should be in close relationship with the councils of other companies on regional, national, and international levels. The members of these workers' councils are elected for a determinate period and tasks are to be rotated. We must in fact avoid the recreation of a bureaucracy that

would tend to set up a leadership and thus recreate a repressive power. We must show that worker management in business is the power to do better for everybody what the capitalists were scandalously doing for a few.[50]

As a universal aspiration of the May explosion, self-management affected not only the occupied institutions, but also, as mentioned, unions that controlled large parts of the working class. Many younger workers struggled against the CGT from within, and others left that structure entirely. In the Wonder Batteries factory at Saint-Ouen, workers elected their own strike committee and refused to let CGT officials inside the occupied plant. (The vast majority of takeovers, however, were controlled by the CGT, which encouraged occupations but not dual power.)

In contrast to French ultracentralization and authoritarianism, self-management provided a realistic alternative based on autonomy and direct participation. In contrast to passivity of consumer society, self-management demanded active involvement. In contrast to compartmentalization of knowledge, self-management required collectivity and pooling of individual skills. In short, self-management implied a qualitatively different social reality.

Limits of Spontaneity

During May, the fusion in action of subjective and objective forces of transformation brought France to the edge of revolution. The June reaction necessitated their separation. Without unified alliances of grassroots initiatives, the government was able, despite heavy resistance, to disperse localized protests in early June. On June 3, French radio and television workers went on strike to demand administrative autonomy from government control. Military personnel were brought in to replace them. On June 6, some public sector employees began returning to work as did transport workers. Two thousand well-armed riot police suddenly appeared in Flins and took control of the Renault factory without resistance from workers who had occupied the factory for three weeks. The next day, however, thousands of workers fought back at Flins and Elisabethville, but police used tear gas and batons to maintain control.

On June 10, fighting continued at Flins, while clashes broke out in the Latin Quarter. In the chaos of attacks and counterattacks, a young high school student drowned in the Seine River. Although one million workers remained on strike, scabs showed up at the Citroen factory and fought with striking workers. The next day, as students threw Molotov cocktails from the roofs of buildings, renewed barricade fighting in Paris took place. Hundreds of people were injured, and more than 1,500 people arrested. In Sochaux, a demonstrator was shot and killed by police.[51] On June 12, rioting continued and Paris became a battlefield, with police resorted to ever more force. Using a law from 1936, the government banned eleven small revolutionary groups. Two days later, right-wing OAS leaders were pardoned and quickly released from prison. The next day police surrounded the Sorbonne and evicted several thousand remaining students. The heroism of those who fought in June is impressive, but without a firm alliance, separate contingents could be defeated one by one. Furthermore, activists involved in isolated regional conflicts were often unaware of specific features of the uprising's generalized character as well as the state's systematic application of force (a problem that also existed in the U.S. during the crisis of 1970.)

Gilles Caron.

Elements of the May movement that at first glance appeared as strengths were also weaknesses. Spontaneity, a refusal to accept any form of hierarchy or leadership, and initiative solely from the base cannot be permanently maintained in a new social formation except after destruction of existing political power. The centralized organization of modern capitalism necessitates creating seeds of a new society—revolutionary culture and organizations—prior to overthrowing the system. Since the possibility of revolution was unrecognized for decades prior to 1968, even its partisans were surprised by the rapid development of the crisis.

The May insurrection developed outside Left parties for good reasons. Bureaucratization of the PCF made that organization incapable of comprehending the totalized impulse for liberation, which emerged in May, and the Socialist Party was virtually nonexistent at that time. The inability of May insurgents to advance the political crisis (except to the extent that cultural revolt and social movements precipitated it) had its corollary in a rebellion against traditional Left organizations without a dialectical negation of obsolete organizations. No development of a concrete political platform or plan for revolutionary power was evident.

In the aftermath of 1968, many insurgents (like André Gorz) envisioned construction of a new kind of party. Besides destroying the traditional state, such a revolutionary party would need to be capable of fusing partial concerns of the subjects of social transformation—students, factory workers, new workers, the ecology and women's liberation movements—into a totalized future vision. Without bringing together the movement's autonomous streams into a revolutionary river, the fragmented consciousness engendered by capitalism would in time insidiously reassert itself through regeneration of specialized self-interest issues and concerns.

Analyzed in isolation, each sector of the May movement was incapable of conceptualizing, let alone implementing a new society. The student movement was able to detonate a larger social explosion. Despite the modern-day entrance of academia into the "real world," the limits of the student movement were marked by the confines of its environment. Students embodied a particular expression of the general contradiction between capitalist relations of production and productive forces. Only their momentary integration into a larger movement in 1968—the abolition of a purely student movement—allowed the student revolt to trigger such a vast upheaval.

By themselves, the new workers tend toward the modernization solution. As educated executives, they tend to look for a better way to do this, a less painful way to implement that. The immense birth pains involved in creating a new society make it easier for new workers to adopt technical solutions to human problems. Generally speaking, new workers are relatively better paid than other sectors of the working class. This relative privilege cut the other way in May 1968, however, as new workers, more often than others, stressed qualitative demands and were relatively unconcerned with pay raises. In the midst of the explosion, the majority of these new workers allied themselves with students and factory workers. Together they constituted a united force, which, if it could have been maintained, might have served as a basis to abolish different categories of existence while establishing a new mode of life.

The student revolt would not have become much more than now usual springtime festivities had it not been for the general strike. In their rejection of the Grenelle agreements and examples of dual power they created, French factory workers momentarily demonstrated aspirations to transform the entire society. By themselves, however, factory workers neither initiated nor successfully concluded the general strike. Only after two weeks of student-led street fights in Paris did the working class act. What students had proposed—a new social formation—workers were in a social position to implement. Unfortunately, when all was said and done, the working class by itself proved incapable of carrying through what many regard as its historic task.

Neither absence of a revolutionary party nor reformism of the PCF totally accounts for limitations of the May movement. The questions must be asked: Why did workers ultimately remain obedient to their unions and return to work? Why did students obey commands of CGT officials to leave factories, as on May 16 when over one thousand students marched from the Sorbonne to the huge Renault plant at Boulogne-Billancourt? The next day an even larger march was not admitted inside the factory by CGT officials. Even after some chemical workers went to the Sorbonne and invited students to their factory occupation, few went and many opposed the idea, using the "revolutionary" argument that "we would be substituting ourselves for the workers."[52]

Some of the answers to these questions can be found in the social conditions of modern capitalism, a system that has consolidated its hold on over half the earth while fragmenting people's needs, desires, and relationships to the whole. As Marcuse understood:

> In the domain of corporate capitalism, the two historical factors of transformation, the subjective and objective, do not coincide: they are prevalent in different and even antagonistic groups. The objective factor, i.e., the human base of the process of production which reproduces the established society, exists in the industrial working class, the human source and reservoir of exploitation; the subjective factor, i.e., the political consciousness, exists among the nonconformist young intelligentsia. . . . The two historical factors do coincide in large areas of the Third World.

"Workerism" was common during May, accepting as it did a fundamental social category of capitalism. Marcuse's notion of a "psychic Thermidor," an internally conditioned impetus to return to the *status quo ante*, applies to the workers as well. At Saclay and elsewhere in May 1968, some workers showed how they viewed the long-term prospects of their strike by punching their time clocks in the usual fashion. Even at Saclay, the well-organized workers did not question the propriety of nuclear power.

To overcome workerism and self-defeating behavior, a vision for a new society transcending fragmented realities of modern capitalism would have been needed. In such a society, property would be socialized, and the vast majority, not simply a fraction of the population, would view the modern productive forces as their responsibility. In advance of such a transformation, it would be necessary to recognize and challenge conservative cultural values. In France, that would include ageism as one dimension of how hierarchies of capitalist patriarchy condition people to only look *up* to god, to the boss, to the father, to those who make the rules (never to look down, at earth, at our bodies, at our descendants).

A transcendent vision could only have been practically conceptualized in the heat of May by prior existence both of human beings who had taken on responsibility for changing themselves—their needs, aspirations, and ideas—for healing themselves from generations of trauma and isolation from earth and community. The process of reweaving ourselves back into the *whole* would produce human beings who understand our connectedness, not only as human beings but as part of nature. Such beings would also create a variety of revolutionary organizations that refuse to define themselves simply in terms of social divisions brought into existence by capitalism.

The May events came by surprise. Perhaps the privilege of historical hindsight allows mistakes to be made transparent, but it is the future that the legacy of May should serve. It is difficult to assess long-run effects of the taste of freedom in May. People will not simply forget the explosion, nor will the social contradictions that were then manifested disappear of their own accord. Mistakes made and victories won through the courage of those who rose up are a guide for the future. In shoving aside a social order and conditioning aimed to pacify them, the people of France reaffirmed the dignity of human beings, legacy enough for them and people all over the world.

Some Implications of May

Between the direct participation of self-management and a new international reality freed from the fetters of borders lay the power of the French state. The inability of the May insurgents to come to terms with national political power can be defined as their major shortcoming—the primary explanation for collapse of May's impetus to establish a new society and the apparent return in June to the inertia of the established order. Whether or not the French state could have been overthrown in the heat of the May explosion will never be known. That there was no organized force that could have led such an undertaking is also debatable. In the aftermath of 1968, everyone thinks they are a general capable of offering strategic and tactical alternatives that could have led to revolution (or, as some insisted, to disaster). Perhaps it was a blessing in disguise that the May movement did not culminate in a seizure of power. The disorganization of the movement could have produced a monstrosity weighing heavily on future revolutionary movements, once again disillusioning people about the possibilities of socialism.

But such considerations ignore an important legacy of 1968: the *possibility* of revolution in an industrialized country. In the five decades since the demise of the Second International, the prospect of an end to capital's rule did not realistically appear until the May explosion. Revolution in France, practically inconceivable in the decades before 1968, appeared to be back on the historical agenda. If May succeeded in nothing else, it was not a total loss.

Yet there were other results. Less than a year later, on April 27, 1969, the French electorate (by over a million votes) said *non* for the first time to a Gaullist referendum, sending the general into permanent retirement. His power and prestige were shattered in May, making it only a question of time before he would fall. Even before the end of the crisis, three hardline Gaullist ministers had been replaced, and the new minister of justice, although himself a Gaullist, resigned his seat in the National Assembly in May 1968 to protest the government's repressive measures. Fouchet, the hated minister of education, was forced out in favor of Edgar Faure, who in his first appearance before the newly elected Assembly admitted to the government what French common sense had known all along: the grievances of the students rightfully pointed to much needed educational reforms.[53]

Moreover, following 1968, a host of reforms was inaugurated in France which streamlined authority structures and gave a semblance of participation to students and workers. The thrust of most of these reforms was to provide temporary relief to an incurable patient. Increased government planning of the job market and university curricula helped reduce the number of workers and college graduates without jobs. In classrooms and factories, the stuffiness and formalism of pre-1968 France have been replaced by a more casual approach. University problems are now considered by councils that include students. The entire university system has been reorganized into a "co-governing" system, one with a more multidisciplinary focus for each school. An experimental university at Vincennes was created in response to student demands of 1968, and academic disciplines within other universities were redefined and transformed.[54]

While the system's rhetoric may have come to include student power, the reality of genuine student power within universities remains a dream. Student power of the contemporary kind is little more than an attempt to legitimate the administration. Modernization in France has hidden behind the progressive rhetoric of its time, much as the ascendant bourgeoisie temporarily adopted the slogan *liberté, egalité, fraternité* following the struggle of 1848. Accordingly, self-management was made into comanagement, a profitable venture where more initiative from workers may replace some of their supervisors, thereby lowering the company payroll and helping to reduce the "alienation" of workers. While comanagement may help bring the "little people" closer to the decision-making centers, it does not aim, nor will it serve, to abolish the hierarchy of domination.

Comanagement and other reforms institutionalized after 1968 served the authority of the top. Archaic structures inherited from the days of Napoleon were altered according to the modern needs of corporate capitalism, not revolutionized to meet human needs. Such modernization did not call into question fundamental assumptions of the present system—top-down organization of production and consumption for private profit—but merely attempted to make the system more efficient. These reforms were designed to keep protests scattered and ineffective while devising technical solutions for social problems.

A widely propagated conjugation indicated a high degree of consciousness about comanagement and co-optation:

> *je participe* (I participate)
> *tu participes* (you participate)
> *elle/il participe* (she, he, it participates)
> *nous participons* (we participate)
> *vous participez* (you participate)
> *elles/ils profitent* (they *profit*)

May's internationalism also had a use for those who wished to streamline the present system. A top manager of IBM, Jacques Maisonrouge, some of whose children participated in the May events, was heard to mimic them when he said, "Down with borders." After all, transnational corporations are bodies whose wealth and influence transcend any particular country. The global corporation, so he says, increasingly views the world as "one economic unit," a unity that leads to "a need to plan, organize, and manage on a global scale."[55]

But the global vision of transnational corporations is the internationalism of profit making and domination, not of an antiauthoritarian socialism. Here, as elsewhere, the modernization thesis rests on two assumptions. First, that what is needed are new people with better ideas to manage the same structures of society. It fails to conceive of a new type of system, one in which people themselves would govern their lives and institutions. Second, modernists conceive of social problems as technical ones that can be solved through science and technology. The need for fundamental change in the human structures of society is neglected, causing science and technology, originally great forces for the liberation of human beings from material scarcity, to turn into their opposite. Under the modern capitalist system, science and technology increasingly become means for domination and warfare, not liberation and world peace.

In the aftermath of 1968, the political parties also channeled the groundswell of popular aspirations for a better society into parliamentary action. The Communist Party was temporarily swelled with new, younger, and more radical members. More importantly, the Socialist Party (practically nonexistent in 1968) was rejuvenated by hundreds of thousands of new members and millions of supporters, and in 1981, the legacy of May 1968 brought the Socialists to power. Even with the election of François Mitterrand and the formation of his "socialist" government, the aspirations of the popular forces that converged in the May explosion were not satisfied. The contradiction between the *possible* (given modern technology's ability to meet world needs) and the *real* (hierarchical organization for warfare, nuclear power, and the domination of nature) only grew more pregnant. The vision of a self-managed international order remained frustrated.

To be sure, progressive governments can produce significant reforms, but these streamline and strengthen the existing system. They also recruit old radicals to become political operatives. Even Régis Debray, the companion of Che Guevara in Bolivia, accepted a job in Mitterrand's government.[56] Daniel Cohn-Bendit and his *Sponti* sidekick Joschka Fischer became higher-ups in Germany's Green Party. Cohn-Bendit has played an active role in the European superstate in Brussels. Like Fischer, he advocated war on Serbia. As foreign minister in a Green-Social Democrat government, Fischer spearheaded NATO's war on Afghanistan, in which German troops were stationed outside Germany for the first time since Hitler.

The political-cultural contradictions that exploded in 1968 have only deepened. In 1978, for example, it was discovered that only 1 percent of French youth "would give their life for France," compared with 20 percent in 1968.[57] The feminist movement has grown by leaps and bounds since 1968,[58] as has the ecology movement. Another indication of the popular awakening has been the radicalization of the French stage and the emergence of a popular theater movement.[59] All in all, it appears that the French people were transformed more profoundly by the events of 1968 than were French political parties.

Whether frustrations like these will explode in yet another upheaval like that of 1968 remains to be seen. Enthusiasts of the May events will only be satisfied through a genuine revolution that would smash the militarized nation-state, not simply take hold of it. Could a qualitatively new society be built as long as such centralized, authoritarian states exist? In organizing within such formations as "legitimate" opposition, any progressive party is required to conform to existing laws that uphold political, economic, and cultural structures of the global system.[60]

Freedom worthy of the name in the industrialized countries presupposes the destruction of the centralized hierarchical state by an activated population. Such destruction is required of those who would construct a qualitatively new society, a formation that would have little in common with bureaucratic "socialisms" of the twentieth century.

Notes

1.   Ernest Mandel, "Lessons of May," *New Left Review* 52 (November–December 1968): 9–32.
2.   Patrick Seale and Maureen McConville, *Red Flag, Black Flag* (New York: Ballantine Books, 1968), 3.
3.   Andrée Hoyles, "General Strike: France 1968," *Trade Union Register* (London: Merlin Press, 1969), 29; reprinted by the Sojourner Truth Organization.
4.   An anthology of documents from the participants in the May events is contained in Alain Schnapp and Pierre Vidal-Naquet, eds., *The French Student Uprising* (Boston: Beacon Press, 1971).
5.   Seale and McConville, *Red Flag, Black Flag*, 92.
6.   Seale and McConville, 177–78.
7.   Seale and McConville, 48, 183–88, 231.
8.   Chris Harman, "The Crisis of the European Revolutionary Left," *International Socialism* series 2, no. 4 (Spring 1979): 49–54.
9.   André Glucksmann, "Strategy and Revolution in France 1968," *New Left Review* 52 (July–August 2008): 70.
10.   Daniel and Gabriel Cohn-Bendit, *Obsolete Communism: The Left-Wing Alternative* (New York: McGraw-Hill, 1968), 131.
11.   Daniel Singer, *Prelude to Revolution* (New York: Hill and Wang, 1971), 70.
12.   See Daniel Bell, *The Coming of Post-industrialized Society: A Venture in Social Forecasting* (New York: Basic Books, 1973), 165–266.
13.   Seale and McConville, *Red Flag, Black Flag*, 79.
14.   Schnapp and Vidal-Naquet, *The French Student Uprising*, 12.
15.   Hervé Bourge, ed., *The French Student Revolt* (New York: Hill and Wang, 1968), 29.
16.   Bourge, *The French Student Revolt*, 11; also see Raymond Boudon, "Sources of Student Protest in France," *Annals of the American Academy of Political and Social* Science 395 (May 1971): 141–42. Boudon notes that in the wake of May, the findings of a French sociologist bore out Sauvageot's belief: "When the students were asked what were, in their opinion, the causes of the May–June revolt, they quoted much more often the anxiety which they themselves felt in the face of unemployment."

17.   Walter Kreipe, "Studenten in Frankreich: Hintergrund und Potential einer politischen Bewegung," *Kursbuch* 13 (June 1968): 156–58.
18.   Schnapp and Vidal-Naquet, *The French Student Uprising*, 500–509.
19.   See Jürgen Habermas, *Toward a Rational Society* (Boston: Beacon Press, 1972), 50–81.
20.   Schnapp and Vidal-Naquet, *The French Student Uprising*, 437–45.
21.   Schnapp and Vidal-Naquet, 38.
22.   Singer, *Prelude to Revolution*, 85.
23.   See Ralf Dahrendorf, *Class and Class Conflict in Industrial Society* (Stanford: Stanford University Press, 1959); Alvin W. Gouldner, *The Future of Intellectuals and the Rise of a New Class* (New York: Oxford University Press, 1979).
24.   See André Gorz, *Socialism and Revolution* (London: Allen Lane, 1975); Michel Crozier, *The World of the Office Worker* (Chicago: University of Chicago, 1971), 11–12; "White Collar Unions: The Case of France," in *White-Collar Trade Unions*, ed. Adolf Sturmthal (Urbana: University of Illinois Press, 1966); Anthony Giddens, *The Class Structure of Advanced Societies* (New York: Harper & Row, 1975), 179–89.
25.   Singer, *Prelude to Revolution*, 80.
26.   Alain Touraine, *The May Movement: Revolt and Reform* (New York: Random House, 1971), 39–40.
27.   Singer, *Prelude to Revolution*, 211.
28.   See Gorz, *Socialism and Revolution*, 9–29.
29.   We should add from the Earth as well, which capital sees as "dead resources."
30.   This quote and much of the analysis in this section is from Roger Grégoire and Fredy Perlman, *Worker-Student Action Committees* (Detroit: Black and Red, 1969), 49.
31.   See Henri Lefebvre, *The Explosion* (New York: Monthly Review Press, 1969); C. Wright Mills, *The Power Elite* (New York: Oxford University Press, 1956), especially chap. 13.
32.   Lefebvre, *The Explosion*, 93.
33.   Raoul Vaneigem, *The Revolution of Everyday Life* (Oakland: PM Press, 2012), 4.
34.   Schnapp and Vidal-Naquet, *The French Student Uprising*, 172.
35.   Alfred Willener, *The Action-Image of Society: On Cultural Politicization* (New York: Pantheon Books, 1970), 311.
36.   Sylvia Harvey, *May '68 and Film Culture* (London: British Film Institute, 1978), 14.
37.   Willener, *The Action-Image of Society*, 194.
38.   Rene Lourau cited in Willener, *The Action-Image of Society*, 82–83.
39.   Norman Birnbaum, *The Crisis of Industrial Society* (New York: Oxford University Press, 1969), 140.
40.   Herbert Marcuse, *Counterrevolution and Revolt* (Boston: Beacon Press, 1972).
41.   Andrew Feenberg, "Remembering the May Events," *Theory and Society* 6 (1978): 37–38.
42.   Schnapp and Vidal-Naquet, *The French Student Uprising*, 438.
43.   Schnapp and Vidal-Naquet, 439.
44.   See chap. 2, pp. "Europe" on page 84–93.
45.   Cohn-Bendit, *Obsolete Communism*, 166.
46.   Hoyles, "General Strike: France 1968," 29.
47.   Hoyles, 27.
48.   "Universities in Europe Draw Elite," *San Diego Union*, December 25, 1978, A46.

49. Ernest Mandel, "Lessons of May."

50. Schnapp and Vidal-Naquet, *The French Student Uprising*, 427.

51. Rolf Werenskjold, *A Chronology of the Global 1968 Protest, Report No. 13* (Volda: Volda University College and Møreforsking Volda, 2010), 194.

52. Herbert Marcuse, *An Essay on Liberation* (Boston: Beacon Press, 1969), 56.

53. A. Belden Fields, "The French Student Revolt of May–June 1968," in *Students in Revolt*, eds. Seymour M. Lipset and Phillip G. Albach (Boston Beacon Press, 1970), 163–64.

54. Charles C. Lemert, *French Sociology: Rupture and Renewal Since 1968* (New York: Columbia University Press, 1981); Sherry Turkic, *Psychoanalytic Politics: Freud's French Revolution* (Cambridge, MA: MIT Press, 1978).

55. Richard Barnet and Ronald Müller, *Global Reach* (New York: Simon and Schuster, 1974), 18.

56. Debray used the occasion of the tenth anniversary of May 1968 to celebrate the nation-state as eternal. According to Debray, May 1968 marked the Americanization of France: the influx of systems analysis and unfettered technocracy needed to modernize archaic France. In this, the activists accomplished the opposite of what they intended. May 1968 only served to stabilize France since genuine revolution there has been and remains out of the question; the best that can be done is to lend a hand "to the 'barbarians' struggling outside the walls [i.e., in the Third World] against our sophisticated barbarism." Régis Debray, "A Modest Contribution to the Rites and Ceremonies of the Tenth Anniversary," *New Left Review* 115 (May–June 1979): 45–65.

57. *Los Angeles Times*, March 23, 1979, Part VII, 11.

58. Elaine Marks and Isabelle de Courtivron, ed., *New French Feminisms* (New York: Schocken Books, 1981).

59. Judith Miller, *Theater and Revolution in France Since 1968* (Lexington, KY: French Forum Publishers, 1977).

60. Leo Huberman and Paul M. Sweezy, "Reflections on the French Upheaval," *Monthly Review* 20, no. 4 (September 1968): 6–7. For discussion of Mitterrand's administration, see Daniel Singer, "Imagination Has Not Yet Taken Power," *The Nation*, January 29, 1983, and "Mitterrand's Achievement," *Monthly Review* 38, no. 2 (June 1986).

CHAPTER 4
REVOLUTION IN THE UNITED STATES?
MAY TO SEPTEMBER 1970

This is a dangerous situation. It threatens the whole economic and social structure of the nation.
—*Business Week*, May 16, 1970

T
WO YEARS AFTER THE FRENCH MAY EVENTS, THE UNITED STATES came as close to revolution as it had in two centuries. From May to September 1970, the country teetered on the verge of breakdown as revolutionary forces gathered momentum and millions of people went on strike against the Establishment. So great was escalating and increasingly violent domestic repression, many people feared the country was rapidly becoming a dictatorship. Others fought for revolutionary change.

In May, the largest strike in U.S. history broke out. Four million people closed down the system of higher education. In response, thirty-five thousand National Guard were called out in sixteen states to bloodily suppress the movement. The governors of Ohio, Kentucky, Michigan, and South Carolina declared all campuses in a state of emergency. For the first time, the nation's universities were occupied at gunpoint. On many campuses, protesters then opened the universities back up to serve the needs of local communities.

Half a world away, in Vietnam, soldiers wore black armbands in solidarity with the strike, and combat refusal was so widespread on the battlefields, separate companies had to be set up for "search and evade" missions. Mutinies resulted in soldiers killing their officers. The Pentagon reported 209 "fragging" deaths in 1970.[1] According to the *Wall Street Journal*, at least five hundred GIs deserted every day of the week during May 1970. The *London Express* reported that U.S. intelligence estimates were that as many as sixty soldiers a week—the majority of them black—were crossing over to the NLF.[2] The *Express* also uncovered a top-secret campaign to capture or kill these defectors, particularly since some were using their knowledge of U.S. operations to cut in on short-wave transmissions to misdirect artillery fire and lead helicopters into ambush.[3]

Following in rapid succession, a rainbow of constituencies mobilized. On June 28, the first-ever Gay Pride marches dared to take public space in four cities. The march toward New York's Central Park was the largest, filling streets for fifteen blocks.[4] On July 15, led by the Young Lords and the Health Workers Revolutionary Union, about one hundred people took control of Lincoln Hospital in New York. With support from many hospital workers, they provided medical care to their long-neglected community and won their demand for a new building to replace the decrepit existing hospital that had been condemned in 1949. On August 26, a general strike of women brought fifty thousand people into the streets of New York and more than twice that number elsewhere in the entire country. A new and enduring symbol for feminism was created—the clenched fist inside the biological sign for women.[5] Three days later, police viciously attacked the Chicano Antiwar Moratorium in Los Angeles, where more than twenty-five thousand people were peacefully listening to music and speakers. Twice, Chicanos were able to repulse sheriff deputies and to protect themselves from tear gas and batons, but sheriffs used murderous force to disperse the rally, killing three people and injuring and arresting hundreds.

A week later, on Labor Day weekend, about ten thousand people gathered in Philadelphia despite police intimidation to answer the call by the Black Panther Party to write a new U.S. constitution. Delegates from the local black neighborhood and from an array of organizations, including the American Indian Movement, Brown Berets, Young Lords, I Wor Keun (Asian Americans), and the women's liberation movement participated. As an indication of how much existing social antagonisms were transcended, one of the most spirited and well-received groups was the newly emergent Gay Liberation Front. The workshops drafted outlines for an "Internationalist Constitution," not a national one. The Preface began: "We, the people of Babylon, declare an International Bill of Rights: that all people are guaranteed the right to life, liberty, and the pursuit of happiness, that all people of the world be free from dehumanization and intervention in their internal affairs by a foreign power. . . . Reparations should be made to oppressed people throughout the world, and we pledge ourselves to take the wealth of this country and make it available as reparation."

As in France in 1968, the movement climaxed abruptly, posing a threat to power as it reached proportions of historic importance overnight. Like French insurgents, millions of Americans acted according to their beliefs in international solidarity and self-management. Both the scale and intensity of U.S. protests were extraordinary. In the first week of May, thirty ROTC buildings were burned or bombed.[6] At the University of Wisconsin–Madison alone, there were over twenty-seven firebombings, and across the country there were more incidents of arson and bombing (at least 169–95 on campuses alone) than in any single month for which government records have been kept. A $6 million computer, owned by the Atomic Energy Commission and used by New York University, was captured by a racially mixed group of sixty students and held for a $100,000 ransom early in May. The protesters demanded the money be used for bail for a jailed member of the Black Panther Party in New York. After twenty-four hours of futile negotiations, the protesters left gasoline bombs to destroy the computer, but the quick action of faculty successfully defused the explosives.[7] At Fresno State College in California, a firebomb destroyed a million-dollar computer center.

Unlike France, state violence took many people's lives. On May 4, 1970, gunfire from the National Guard in Ohio killed four young college students at Kent State University. Ten days later, two students were shot dead and twelve others wounded at Jackson State University, when the Mississippi Highway Patrol opened fire on a women's dormitory. Altogether in May, more than one hundred protesters were killed or wounded by government violence.[8] Among the casualties were eleven students bayoneted at the University of New Mexico, twenty people wounded by shotgun blasts at Ohio State University, and twelve students shot with birdshot in Buffalo. In Augusta, Georgia, six

Kent State University: May 1970. John Filo.

African Americans were killed and twenty wounded when a riot broke out after a prisoner was beaten to death. Two thousand protesters were arrested during the first two weeks of May.

At the same time, thousands of workers were involved in hundreds of wild-cat strikes. Immediately after the killings at Kent State, union leader Walter Reuther personally addressed a message to Nixon on behalf of the United Auto Workers (UAW) protesting the escalation of the war and the campus killings. The vice chairman of the Union of Teamsters and Warehousemen called on workers to speak out against the war and to take the lead in all actions against Nixon. In Detroit and Chicago, a planned three-minute work stoppage on May 15, called in memory of Reuther (who died in a plane crash on May 10), turned into a day-long antiwar wildcat: two thousand workers walked off the job at one plant alone (Ford Assembly in Chicago's Southside), and in all, thirty thousand workers struck at twenty plants.[9] As a gesture of solidarity, longshoremen in Oregon and Teamsters in Ohio refused to cross student informational picket lines. Ten Chicago union leaders supported local student strikes, and in many counties across the country, central labor councils voiced opposition to the invasion of Cambodia.

In Washington, DC, government workers became restive. *U.S. News* reported that "federal workers, supposedly non-political, are beginning to badger office holders, elected and appointed, on the course of national policy."[10] At least one organization, the Federal Employees for a Democratic Society, modeled itself on Students for a Democratic Society (SDS) and claimed a membership of hundreds within most bureaus of the federal government. Joseph Califano Jr. credited them with the capability to "operate as a shadow government."[11]

Poll after poll found that millions of Americans favored revolution and people were ready to risk life and limb for their beliefs. In 1968, Daniel Yankelovich had reported that at least 368,000 people strongly agreed on the need for a "mass revolutionary party" in the United States, and after the strike of 1970, the same pollster announced that within the universities alone, more than a million people considered themselves "revolutionaries."[12] In early 1971, the *New York Times* discovered that four out of ten students (over three million people) thought that a revolution was needed in the United States,[13] and in 1976, sociologist Seymour Martin Lipset concluded that 75 percent of all college students in 1970, a total of nearly six million people, endorsed the need for "fundamental change" in the nation.[14] On May 17, the *New York Times Magazine* featured six prominent public intellectuals responses to the question, "Are We in the Middle of a 'Second American Revolution'?" The next month's *National Guardsman* magazine warned that the country was "endangered by the rising tide of violence and by the drift toward possible revolution."[15]

In the midst of the upsurge, Nixon and Company launched a vicious counterattack. Already, twenty-five Panthers had been killed, and newly combined police-FBI task forces went into action around the clock. More Panthers were killed, dozens more arrested, and more infiltrators sent into their ranks. White House officials incited tens of thousands of hardhats to attack student antiwar rallies. On one day, more than sixty thousand construction workers rallied in support of Nixon and the war. As police watched, they beat up protesters on national television. Union leaders had been instructed to tell them that if they did not sign the daily roll at their rally, they would lose their pay for the day.[16] Attacks by hardhats in New York and St. Louis were expressions of cultural as much as political conflict. Without the underlying current of resentment against longhaired peaceniks, no amount of manipulation could have made construction workers attack students.

Nixon approved a "top secret" Huston Plan aimed at destabilizing the movement. He feared that the revolt was spilling over to the whole society. The first part of the plan, "Summary of Internal Security Threat," pointed out: "Increasingly the battlefield is the community with the campus serving primarily as a staging area." The Huston Plan was implemented through a campaign of infiltration, mail tampering, burglaries, and wiretapping aimed at a selected list of domestic groups and individuals. Other illegal government counterintelligence operations were intensified: the FBI's COINTELPRO program, the CIA's Operation CHAOS, and similar programs such as the Defense Intelligence Agency, Naval Intelligence, the Secret Service, and a panoply of other federal, state, and local police agencies.[17] As activists refused to be intimidated, Nixon approved even more "dirty tricks"—the Liddy plan, the Segretti plans—aimed at a growing "enemies list" compiled by the White House that came to include Democratic Party candidate for president George McGovern. The path to Watergate was laid in Nixon's attempt to suppress the movement's threat to power. There was so much concern that the campuses would erupt again that the presidential Scranton Commission called for immediate contingency planning to deal with new disorders, including the national expansion of SWAT— Special Weapons and Attack Team—which had first made its appearance on December 9, 1969, when Los Angeles police waged a four-hour gun battle at the local Panther office.[18]

Gunned downed on campuses and beaten in the streets, activists responded with armed attacks during the summer of 1970, a wave of militancy that had been building steadily since 1965, as the map below indicates.[19] On June 9, 1970, the Weather Underground bombed police headquarters in New York City. Two months later, the Army Mathematics Research Center in Madison was gutted (and a graduate student accidentally killed) by a massive explosion detonated in retaliation for that institution's development of an infrared device used by the

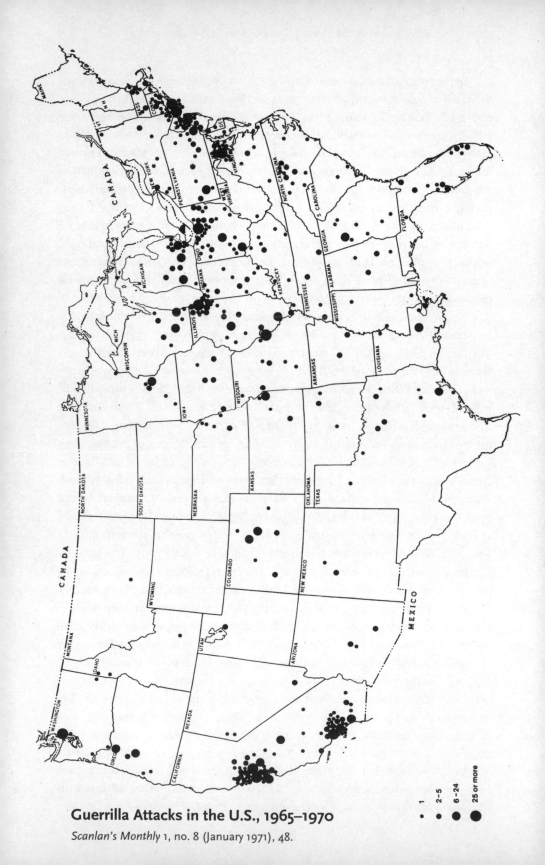

Guerrilla Attacks in the U.S., 1965–1970

Scanlan's Monthly 1, no. 8 (January 1971), 48.

CIA to murder Che Guevara in Bolivia. On August 7, 1970, Jonathan Jackson stood up in a Marin County courtroom with an assault rifle in hand. He freed three prisoners and took a judge and a district attorney hostage, hoping to exchange them for his brother George (a leading member of the Panthers imprisoned for life for his alleged role in a seventy-dollar robbery). A barrage of gunfire directed against their escape van left only Ruchell Magee alive. By September, half of the people on the FBI's most wanted list were radicals, including Angela Davis (indicted for owning the gun used in the Marin Courthouse raid).

The appearance of guerrilla warfare in the United States was one indication of the legitimation crisis of the state, a political dimension of the cultural crisis which spread to young workers like those at Lordstown, Ohio, who refused to work forty hours a week, to soldiers in Vietnam who refused to fight, and to housewives who refused to remain politically marginalized. Returning Vietnam veterans mounted militant protests. Hundreds of them wearing uniforms threw their medals onto the White House lawn. On May Day a year after the campus strike, more than ten thousand protesters were arrested in Washington, DC, when they tried to shut down the city. The Nixon administration resorted to ever more devious schemes involving a secret team of White House plumbers, who were arrested while burglarizing the Democratic Party's national office in the Watergate Hotel.

Only with the removal of the president and a host of reforms was stability restored. Efforts to mollify the movement were made immediately after the national campus strike. Black Panther leader Huey Newton was released from jail in August; voting rights were extended to eighteen-year-olds; the draft was ended; farmworkers won a significantly better contract; women gained abortion rights; new civil rights acts were signed; and, most importantly, the ground war in Vietnam immediately began to wind down. On June 24, the Senate voted overwhelmingly (eighty-one to ten) to rescind the Gulf of Tonkin resolution, which had provided what scant legal grounds there were for U.S. military involvement in Indochina. In the next few months, the Senate's Foreign Relations Committee declared Nixon in violation of the Constitution for his conduct of the war without consent of the Senate. Finally, on December 8, the Senate reaffirmed its ban on committing U.S. troops to Cambodia, an act equivalent to a no-confidence vote, which, in Western Europe, would have forced the resignation of the head of the government.

Prior to Watergate and the removal of Nixon from the White House, no one was sure where the U.S. was headed. In June 1970, the editors of *Monthly Review* warned, "There is no assurance that the U.S. ruling class could find a way out of this tangle. Failure could lead to chaos, attempted military takeover, even civil war with various factions of the Armed Forces pitted against each other."[20]

Historians have neglected these events and even covered them up, but the crisis of 1970 ranks with 1776 and the Civil War as moments when social divisions threatened the established order. Today, with stability long since restored, Watergate is part of everyone's vocabulary. Martin Luther King Jr. is a Great Man of history, but in 1968, however, he was vilified and spied upon, possibly murdered by his own government. After he was killed, Washington, DC, was nearly reduced to ash and cinder, and the crisis continued to intensify. Only a preventative counterrevolution forestalled the impetus for radical transformation.[21]

The middle of 1970 marked the apex of the U.S. movement, but the uprising was not simply a North American phenomenon. In scores of cities around the world, militant protesters demonstrated against the U.S. escalation of the war. Some burned American flags while others went beyond the level of symbolic gesture. In Caracas, Venezuela, National Guard troops fired into the air to repel hundreds of students carrying paint-filled balloons to throw at the U.S. embassy. Near the Central University of Venezuela, two high school students were killed by police gunfire. A few days later, snipers wounded two students during the third day of demonstrations against the invasion.[22] In South Vietnam, antiwar protests became so massive that the government ordered all schools closed. President Thieu publicly vowed to "beat to death" peace demonstrators, and police bloodily cleared antiwar Buddhist nuns and monks from the Vietnam national pagoda, killing five people and wounding fifty-three. In Calcutta, India, the American Center was ransacked and a statue of Abraham Lincoln damaged. In Rome, thousands of demonstrators marched in the driving rain on the U.S. embassy but were kept away by riot police. In Britain, protesters painted swastikas and dumped pigs' heads in American businesses. In Hamburg, Amerika Haus was occupied and renamed "The House of the Four Dead at Kent." In Canada, all major cities experienced angry outpourings of dissent. Hundreds of students at McGill University marched to the American consulate in Montreal and gently laid four flower-laden coffins in front of the building in memory of those killed at Kent State. Several hundred students refused to leave, but police forced them back to campus, and ten people were arrested.[23] In Toronto, ninety-one people were arrested, and in Vancouver, Ottawa, Hamilton, Regina, and Edmonton, major antiwar rallies took place.

The simultaneous eruption of a global movement compelled policymakers to change plans at the same time as it forged international unity among people who recognized in each other the humanity denied them by the existing world system. American college students transcended patriotic loyalty and racial identity. Instead, they identified with Vietnamese freedom fighters and Black Panthers.

The Largest Strike in U.S. History

> The crisis on American campuses has no parallel in the history of this nation. This crisis has roots in divisions of American society as deep as any since the Civil War. The divisions are reflected in violent acts and harsh rhetoric, and in the enmity of those Americans who see themselves as occupying opposing camps. Campus unrest reflects and increases a more profound crisis in the nation as a whole. . . . We fear new violence and growing enmity. . . . If this trend continues, if this crisis of under-standing endures, the very survival of the nation will be threatened.
> —*The President's Commission on Campus Unrest*, September 1970

On April 30, 1970, after President Nixon escalated the war by invading Cambodia, a wave of protests immediately engulfed high schools, colleges, and universities. The National Guard, only just pulled out of ghettos, was unleashed on the nation's campuses. Subsequent killings traumatized the country and spelled the beginning of the end for yet another American president who failed to find a peaceful exit from Vietnam. Outrage was immediate. By May 15, more than five hundred colleges and universities were on strike, and by the end of the month, so were at least one-third of the nation's 2,827 institutions of higher education. More than 80 percent of all universities and colleges experienced protests, and half of the country's eight million students and 350,000 faculty actively participated in the strike.[24] After the murders at Kent State and Jackson State Universities, confrontations and disruptions became commonplace throughout the nation. There had already been many more "disruptive" demonstrations in 1969 and 1970 before the invasion of Cambodia than in the two previous school years, and the proportion more than doubled again for protests after the invasion.[25]

As the eros effect was activated, the world was changed for millions of people. In contrast to prevailing norms and values, they acted according to principles of international solidarity and self-management, not patriotic chauvinism, hierarchy, and conformity. Campus strikers demanded immediate withdrawal from Indochina, an end to the repression of the Black Panther Party, and an end to university complicity with the Pentagon through ROTC and war research. The universal nature of these demands—the fact that they were not for lower tuition, more financial aid, or smaller classes—indicated that students, staff, and faculty were not confined in their goals to their own particular grievances but consciously identified with those at the bottom of the world's social and economic hierarchy.

The essential meaning of the strike was international solidarity of Vietnamese and American and unity of black and white—values that negated the established system's genocidal war and racist violence. Strikers' moved beyond a simple negation of the oppressor/oppressed duality in the universal political content of their demands, and also in the *form* of the strike. Participants not only attempted to stop ROTC and war research but also tried to create dual power based on new ethics and values. Here is one indication of how the movement went beyond rebellion and lived according to revolutionary values. In California, after Governor Ronald Reagan ordered all universities closed, strikers decided to keep the universities open. In a General Assembly in Berkeley's Greek Theater, seventeen thousand people roared their approval to "reconstitute" the university as "a center for organizing against the war in Southeast Asia." Before the meeting ended, Reagan broke his sixteen-month-old vow to keep the schools open "at the point of a bayonet if necessary" and ordered all public universities and state colleges in California to close. Despite his executive order, more than five thousand people gathered on May 8 for an illegal memorial for those killed at Kent State, and on May 10 the school's newspaper appeared under a new title, the *Independent Californian*. As one astonished student at a school that the governor had ordered closed summed up the situation, "My God, everywhere I go on campus, in every building, there are hundreds of people doing things. Organizing, meeting, writing leaflets—it's incredible."[26]

"Reconstitution" (as Californians named their form of self-management) meant secretaries began to talk about significant social issues with their "superiors," not just to take their orders; students sat in on faculty meetings and changed curriculum to include real world issues; law students provided legal help to arrested protesters—in short, the whole authority structure was momentarily transformed. People acted as they thought they should, not as they were told or as accustomed.

Black Panthers Go to Yale

The crisis precipitated by the invasion of Cambodia occurred after both SNCC and SDS had ceased to exist as vibrant organizations. In the summer of 1969, warring factions in SDS had destroyed the organization as they argued about whether it was the working class or the Third World that was the "vanguard of world revolution." SNCC had long since been eclipsed by far more radical currents it had helped to produce. With few exceptions, the old guard of the white New Left's early college days was no longer active, left behind by a movement that had developed far beyond their wildest fantasies. Less than a month before the invasion of Cambodia, the National Mobilization Committee to End the War in Vietnam, sponsor of two massive marches the previous fall, had closed its office a few blocks from the White House, under the impression that President Nixon's promises meant the war was winding down.

The following text appears within the artwork:

1. FREE BREAKFAST FOR CHILDREN
2. FREE FOOD PROGRAM
3. FREE HEALTH CLINICS
4. FREE CLOTHING PROGRAM
5. FREE AMBULANCE SERVICES
6. BLACK PANTHER NEWSPAPER
7. POLICE PATROLS
8. FREE DENTAL PROGRAM
9. FREE BUSING TO PRISONS
10. FREE SHOE PROGRAM
11. FREE PEST CONTROL PROGRAM
   FREE OPTOMETRY PROGRAM
   EE FURNITURE PROGRAM
   RIATRIC HEALTH CENTER
   UNITY HEALTH CENTE
   AL ARTS PROGRAM
   ID AND EDUCATIO
   OR SWITCHBOARD
   TION CLASSES
   MMISSARY FOR PR
   E CELL ANEMIA TES
   L CLINIC WORKSH
   EACH PREVENTI
   ORS AGAINST
   ISABLED PERSONS
   RUG/ALCOHOL AB
   TING NURSES
   NG A

PEOPLE'S FREE FOOD PROGRAM

ALL POWER TO THE PEOPLE

RASHID 7-07-16

rashidmod.com

Art by Kevin "Rashid" Johnson

The Black Panther Party continued its explosive growth, but it was under intense attack from the state. Huey Newton remained in jail, and Eldridge and Kathleen Cleaver were in exile. The only national leader of the Panthers free to walk the streets was David Hilliard, and he was briefly locked up in April for allegedly threatening Nixon's life. Bobby Seale, Ericka Huggins, and other Panthers were on trial in New Haven for the alleged murder of a police informant. With the threat of a death penalty hanging over their chairman, the Panthers organized fervently to save their imprisoned comrades. With the support of a majority of Yale students, the Panthers called for a national mobilization at Yale to free Bobby Seale and his codefendants on the weekend of May 1. On April 15 in Cambridge, the Bobby Seale Brigade rioted at Harvard Square, an action designed as a build-up to May Day, an action described by the *Boston Globe* as the "worst riot in the history of Cambridge."

By Wednesday, April 22, most of Yale College was striking in support of the Panthers. The next day, more than a thousand people gathered on the lawn at the house of the university's president, Kingman Brewster, to listen to speeches by members of the Panthers. Within forty-eight hours, Brewster surprised a faculty meeting with his statement: "I am appalled and ashamed that things should have come to such a pass that I am skeptical of the ability of Black revolutionaries to achieve a fair trial anywhere in the United States."[27] Brewster's last-minute change of heart had the effect of imposing a mandate on the Panthers to control the volatile assortment of radicals they had called upon to come to New Haven.

On April 30, arrival of advance groups of what became fifteen thousand demonstrators coincided with Nixon's announcement of the invasion of Cambodia, making it appear that a confrontation at Yale was unavoidable. But there were only scattered incidents that night, probably due both to insistence by the Panthers not to take to the streets and the presence of four thousand marines and eight thousand National Guardsmen who had overrun the city. The next night, rioting broke out, but not on the scale feared by the Yale administration. Copious amounts of tear gas, police nightsticks, and marching National Guard formations sufficed to quell confrontations.

Brewster's "skepticism" won Panther gratitude and succeeded in avoiding destruction of Yale, and pacification of demonstrators also created a space for the movement to come together. In the "temporary autonomous zone" between two planned rallies, thousands of people discussed the best way to proceed. In a spontaneous assembly in Yale University's Dwight Hall, some two thousand people formulated a call for a national campus strike. The free-flowing meeting was one of those rare moments of optimism and solidarity when imaginations ran wild. Speaker after speaker rose to call for greater resistance and to spread the movement. One activist called for a national student strike. A few minutes later someone called for a general strike. By the end of the meeting, all agreed to organize a nationwide strike beginning Tuesday, May 5. Three strike demands were formulated (and later accepted throughout the country):

1. That the United States government cease its escalation of the Vietnam
    War into Cambodia and Laos; that it unilaterally and immediately withdraw all forces from Southeast Asia;

WE DEMAND:

1 That the United States government end its systematic oppression of political dissidents and release all political prisoners, such as Bobby Seale and other members of the Black Panther Party.

2 That the United States government cease the Vietnam War that it unilaterally and its escalation of into Cambodia and Laos; immediately withdraw all forces from Southeast Asia.

3 That the universities end their complicity with the United States war machine by the immediate end to defense research, ROTC, counterinsurgency research, and all other such programs.

STRIKE!

2. That the United States government end its systematic oppression of political dissidents and release all political prisoners, particularly Bobby Seale and other members of the Black Panther Party;

3. That the universities end their complicity with the United States war machine by the immediate end to defense research, the Reserve Officer Training Corps (ROTC), counterinsurgency research, and all other such programs.

Without the accidental coincidence of the New Haven rally and the invasion of Cambodia, the focus for the strike (particularly the demand relating to political prisoners in the United States) would no doubt have been more diffuse. The movement's universalist vision was the fruit of people's historic choice to stand up for freedom and justice and to move from being spectators to participants. The attacks on the Black Panther Party had the effect of bringing together a spontaneously generated political avant-garde that was able to provide direction to the movement that emerged. The subsequent murders at Kent and Jackson State propagated the strike further than most people thought possible.

The Campuses Erupt

Students exhibited a remarkable capability for self-organization and leaderless actions. Within forty-five minutes of Nixon's televised announcement of the invasion of Cambodia, Princeton students had organized a protest. That night, students at Oberlin College occupied the administration building and demanded that faculty meet to discuss the invasion. During the first six days after the invasion of Cambodia, an average of twenty new campuses went on strike every day, and in the days after the slaughter at Kent State on May 4, one hundred more colleges joined daily.[28] The shootings at Kent State were immediately exposed as having little justification. Students had refused to disperse despite being ordered to do so by the National Guard. As soldiers retreated with no threat against them, Company C suddenly wheeled around and opened fire, hitting thirteen people on campus, including students walking to class two hundred yards away. The four dead in Ohio reverberated across the country—and were immediately immortalized in a Crosby, Stills, Nash & Young song that hit the charts around the world.

A national strike information center sprang to life at Brandeis University and functioned as both coordinator of local protest activities and national information clearinghouse. On May 11, in San Jose, California, over five hundred delegates attended a National Student Strike Conference. On almost every campus, strike coordinating committees spontaneously formed and linked up with each other. At Berkeley, over two thousand activists democratically participated in one meeting of a strike committee after which "action groups" were

After students refuse to disperse, three companies of guardsmen advance with tear gas, fixed bayonets, and loaded weapons at Kent State. Jack Davis.

(CLOCKWISE) William K. Schroeder, Allison B. Krause, Jeffrey G. Miller, and Sandra L. Scheuer, killed at Kent State.

formed. There was the general feeling that "if a person can't find a place to plug in, he can create his own niche."[29]

On less than a week's notice, there was a demonstration of over one hundred thousand people in the nation's capital.[30] From the podium, the American people were called upon to enact a general strike to end the war. Recent strikes by postal workers, truck drivers, and workers at General Electric were all interpreted as responses to inflation caused by the war. Although at least four hundred people were arrested after the rally, the popular surge toward massive civil disobedience was successfully defused from above by the hastily reconstituted New Mobilization Committee, a broad coalition of antiwar forces including pacifists and clergy, as well as Communists and Trotskyites. One key leader of the "New Mobe" wrote later that the committee suffered "an untimely failure of nerve" on May 9.[31] Of course, a confrontation might have made the May 4 massacre at Kent State seem small by comparison, since over twenty-five thousand police and soldiers were standing by (the fourteenth time the District of Columbia's National Guard had been called to riot duty since the 1967 Pentagon march).[32] Two days later, George Winne, a student at the University of California San Diego, died of self-immolation, a desperate act of protest that reflected the national decline of protests after the May 9 demonstration. On May 11, the connections between domestic racism and international genocide became painfully clear in Augusta, Georgia, when six African-Americans were shot in the back and killed after protesting the beating death of a black teenager in the county jail. Three days later came the killings at Jackson State University in Mississippi.

On November 18, 1968, black students protest at Kent State University, winning a black studies program and other reforms. Special Collections and Archives, Kent State University Libraries.

Murder at Jackson State University

Well aware that state violence, only newly directed against white students had long targeted African Americans, Jackson State students nonetheless dared to challenge the forces of order. On May 7, at least five hundred students rallied to protest the Cambodian invasion, and the next day a boycott of classes began. Less than a week later, on May 13, two people threw Molotov cocktails at the ROTC barracks on campus. The following night, after a rumor spread that Charles Evers, brother of murdered civil rights leader Medgar Evers, had been killed, a crowd of students and street people again congregated on campus near Lynch Street. They remained in place after police and highway patrolmen ordered them to leave, so an armored van was brought in. Someone threw a green bottle in its direction. Suddenly shots rang out as police fired at Alexander Hall, a women's dormitory. A journalist described the scene: "The officers in the street crouched, knelt or stood, firing from hip and from shoulder, emptying their guns into the crowd, the dorm windows above, and the darkness about them."[33] It was a miracle that only two people, Philip Lafayette Gibbs and James Earl Green, were killed.

James Earl Green and Phillip Lafayette Gibbs, students killed at Jackson State University.

National reactions to the killings at Augusta on May 12 and Jackson State on May 14 were not nearly as dramatic as after those at Kent State on May 4, and the smaller response to the murders of African Americans served as evidence of racism to many people. While the campus reaction to the murders at Augusta and Jackson State was small in comparison to the outrage after Kent State, it was not inconsiderable. It was, however, mainly black students who mobilized. The National Guard was called in once again to Ohio State University, this time to seal off the campus. Thousands of high school students in New York and Chicago closed their schools in solidarity with those murdered in the South. At Hunter College in New York, a Third World coalition blockaded entrances on May 12 to protest the school not having been shut down in response to the killings in Augusta. New York City memorialized the dead at Jackson State by closing all schools on May 19, 1970.

While racism may have been a reason for people's lack of action after Jackson, systematic cover-up of the violence also shielded the police and state troopers who had done the shooting. The culprits quickly scurried from the scene of their mayhem, leaving National Guardsmen behind. Jackson's elected officials initially denied even that police had fired and said nothing about state highway patrolmen. So lax were officials in investigating the murders that an around-the-clock vigil of students guarded the campus from May 15 to 23 in order to prevent evidence from being taken away by the same Highway Patrol that had done the shooting. The FBI finally came to get the evidence. Jackson State University archivist Juanita Murray explained that while there is an enormous photographic record of the killings at Kent State, at Jackson, "There are no photographs of the bodies lying on the ground . . . there was enough time to cover up what happened before the next newscast."[34] So scant was publicity about Jackson, it took a year before the campus newspaper first covered the tragedy.

Prior to the murders in the South, black and Third World students had not participated in the strike or the antiwar movement to the same extent that they had struggled against racism. In 1968 at Kent State University, for example, 400 of the university's 597 black students quit school to protest that institution's racism, and a solidarity boycott by SDS helped build the impetus that led to the demonstration of May 4, 1970. In February 1970, over one-third of the student body (894 out of 2,300) was arrested at all-black Mississippi Valley State College at a demonstration in support of thirty demands related to improvement of conditions on campus. As late as April 1970, racist university conditions ranked first among the many reasons for campus disruptions. The war in Indochina was close behind in second place,[35] followed by other issues like student power, the quality of student life, and ecology.

When the student strike erupted, black students intensified their struggles around domestic issues. At Southeast Junior College in Chicago, students went on strike on May 13 (the day before Jackson State), not to protest the war or the killings at Kent State (or in Augusta) but to rename the school after slain Panthers Fred Hampton and Mark Clark, for the reinstatement of the black studies director, and for a black college president.[36] Classes there were suspended indefinitely on May 14 after police were called in to quell the second day of demonstrations. On May 8, at Morehead State College in Kentucky, black students interrupted a convocation concerning the war and the deaths at Kent State to present twenty-one demands of their own.[37]

Prior to the strike, the student movement, like the progressive forces in the country, was generally split along racial lines. On March 21, 1970, the day after a shotgun blast had narrowly missed killing a black student, the chairman of the Black League for Action at California State College in Pennsylvania complained about "hippies who cause trouble."[38] At San Jose State College in California, a weeklong ecology "Survival Fair" had culminated on February 20 with the funeral and

On the morning after the shooting, two students peer from a shattered window in the west stairwell of Alexander Hall. Lawmen claimed that a sniper had fired from the stairwell. Associated Press.

burial of a new car to protest smog and environmental pollution. About seventy-five black and Chicano students, supporters of Huey Newton, protested the protest by passing out leaflets saying: "It must be made clear that this is a plot by 'The Man' to mesmerize the people into thinking their environment, meaning the air we breathe, is a basic issue for change."[39]

Antiwar sentiment was most widespread among minorities, and it was disproportionately minorities who fought and died for the Pentagon on the battlefields of Vietnam.[40] Once the strike erupted, ever more minorities joined protests. In Tuscaloosa, Alabama, thirty-seven students at an all-black school were arrested, and in North Carolina, hundreds of black students marched to the state capitol on May 8 to ask the governor to withdraw his support for the Cambodian fiasco. Black students were joined by civil rights activists and college presidents in their protests. The president of Morehouse College issued a call to all 123 black colleges, requesting a meeting to protest the war in Southeast Asia and murder of blacks at home. On May 20, a group of fifteen African American college presidents went to the White House and met with Nixon for over two hours, even though the meeting was originally scheduled to last only forty-five minutes.[41] A March against Repression through Georgia, during which more than 275 people were arrested, culminated in a rally of over ten thousand people in Atlanta, where antiwar and civil rights forces converged on May 22. After the shootings at Jackson State, a coalition of thirty moderate civil rights and antipoverty organizations formed the Mississippi United Front and called for self-defense. Gun shops reported a surge in black customers on the eve of a statewide boycott against white businesses.

Form of the Strike

In 1970, students did not simply strike *against* their universities: they successfully mobilized the members of the universities against national policy and simultaneously transformed the institutions. The movement was not aimed at merely stopping "business as usual"; it sought to redefine international relations, scientific research, and the goals of the whole society. It broke with the assumptions of accepted rules and politics. At Northwestern University, as at many colleges, an alternative university and a new curriculum were established that raised questions about the role of the United States in international events. At Berkeley, experimental curriculum programs sprang up within many departments and were designed to create cooperative relationships based on mutual respect in place of the competitive and hierarchical atmosphere of the university's usual operations.

Challenging authority was an important dimension of the strike. There was also a questioning of everyday roles usually taken for granted. Berkeley's "reconstitution" led some staff members to write, "We are not an integral part of our typewriters; we are human beings with opinions on what is happening on this campus and in this country—and we have the right to express them as fully as the faculty and students are doing. . . . We are all a part of a communal educational process; we should all share equally in all that goes on."[42] Jocks and cheerleaders, fraternity and sorority members, engineers, campus workers, and doctors were all brought into the movement during the strike. Students naturally became a part of department meetings since that was where strike activities were being coordinated. An entire generation of faculty, staff, and students developed new relationships to institutional (and national) authority. As one student put it, "I'll never feel comfortable in a lecture hall again."[43]

The movement transcended a mere defiance of authority and formulated a vision of transformed institutions. One leaflet at Berkeley raised the notion of self-management (or "reconstitution" as it was called there):

> Reconstitution is not a mechanical act, such as electing a senior prom chairman, but a political process—in the special sense, roughly, of a community of individuals publicly engaged in the enterprise of determining

> the management of the events and conditions that affect their lives on
> the basis of some approximation of a common good.... There is no blue-
> print to be followed. There is no specific set of instructions that must be
> obeyed. The form and content of reconstitution will have to be worked
> out by the people who are themselves affected.... Decisions on how to
> implement the process are to be made not by professors, not by adminis-
> trators, not by student leaders alone, but by the very people whose lives
> are involved, acting collectively in their communities.[44]

Participation of people in decisions formerly left to others concretely revealed that consensual decision making produced far better results and higher quality of life than authoritarian management techniques. In the new situation: "Protest becomes an outmoded concept, for this reconstitution movement is not intent on petitioning any leaders to take action on our behalf. We are no longer protesting someone else's politics. Reconstitution is about making our own politics."[45]

Traditionally inactive engineering students joined the protests and began to consider their social responsibility. As one engineering action group's leaf-let said, "We can no longer afford to allow the stereotypes of us as socially irresponsible technicians to be sustained."[46] Staff of the Engineering Library at Berkeley organized an ongoing Social Awareness Collection around the theme of "The Social Responsibility of Engineers in a Peace-Oriented Society," and at City College in New York one thousand engineering students voted to join the strike there until U.S. troops left Cambodia.[47]

Law students commented that when they entered their profession they would "be more likely to change places and to raise political issues in the law firms." Some began to see their roles as "participant reformers" rather than "expert manipulators."

Music and drama students performed in the streets, while other art students built a mobile gallery that traveled around the state. One student wrote:

> The University of California Berkeley has become a piece of art. Though
> its art museum has closed down, its concert halls are empty, its stages
> are dark, this campus for the first time realized the real function and
> meaning of art: to communicate, to change perception, to make us react.
> All sorts of barriers are being broken down: art history students are silk
> screening alongside art practice students, journalism activists are work-
> ing with design majors to make effective leaflets, sculptors are designing
> sets for drama students' street theatre. We've destroyed the artificial
> walls, and our energy and creativity are expanding at a rate unfathomable
> to us just one week ago.[48]

Among students, there was the feeling that the *process* of protest was a significant aspect of the movement and that the bureaucratic mode of work was to be prevented from setting in. At Berkeley, one action group's printed Statement called on all strikers "to enjoy one's tasks and to learn from them. To prevent stagnation, various groups have begun to rotate positions to allow new ideas and faces to flow from one group to another and to prevent bureaucratic entrenchment of ideas and people in single positions."

Besides deepening and consolidating the movement within academia, campus activists also sought to spread the strike to consumers and workers. On May 8, the faculty at the University of Colorado in Boulder voted to accept a strike program that included a plan "to spark a national buyers' strike" and a call for a world economic boycott of the United States to begin June 1.

A popular slogan in the Boston area during the strike was "Shut It Down! Open It Up!" As in many other parts of the country, the striking universities became a base from which the strikers systematically canvassed working-class communities, high schools, and outlying areas. Groups of students and faculty at 40 percent of the nation's universities went off campus to neighborhoods and workplaces during May, some groups traveling up to two hundred miles to talk with people in isolated areas.[49] Around the country, there were a series of widely publicized haircuts that students hoped would make it easier for them to communicate with Middle America.

On May 15, the Cambridge, Massachusetts underground newspaper, the *Old Mole*, called on the striking students to "deepen the strike inside the universities, and to spread it outside. . . . Sure we're a long way from a general strike. But we were a long way from a student strike a few years ago." A wall poster in Cambridge called upon students to "spread the strike" into a general strike against the war on the model of France in May 1968: "Students visited every factory in the Cambridge area Wednesday, May 6 with leaflets calling for a sickout against the war. Liaison committees should be developed in every occupied university to communicate daily with the employees of each major enterprise in the university area. This is just what the French students did in the General Strike of May 1968. We should talk with workers individually, getting to know them, as well as leafleting." A leaflet students brought to factory gates was a direct call to "take power over our lives": "We are not so crazy as to believe that students by themselves have the power to end the evils that oppress us all. This can come about only when all of us act together to take power over our lives from those who wield it today."

Aspirations of student strikers went beyond transformation of the universities or opposition to war. Attempts made to broaden the strike detonated reactions among other sectors of the population, not only bringing new supporters into the movement, but also causing a reaction against the strikers.

Legitimation Crisis

> The present crisis is the most profound one in our entire national history:
> more profound than either World War I or II, more profound than even
> the Civil War, and more profound than the struggle for national indepen-
> dence in the 18th Century. In contrast to the previous crises, the present
> one finds the country not only divided, confused, and embittered, frus-
> trated and enraged, but lacking the one vital element of self-confidence.
> —*Sheldon Wolin* to the American Psychiatric Association, May 1970

The chain reaction of events touched off by the invasion of Cambodia triggered widespread responses throughout the United States. No longer was it possible for Middle Americans to concern themselves with their individual lives while they turned their backs on the international consequences of their tax dollars. With the shots fired at Kent and Jackson, the most important mental health problem in our society became the wars in Indochina and at home. While some chose to act out their aggressions on peaceniks, more focused their anger on the government that perpetuated a genocidal war.

The student movement created a context that affected tens of millions of Americans. Nearly everyone had relatives or friends studying at college, and when the entire university system appeared under attack, fired upon and occu- pied by the National Guard and police and subjected to verbal barrages from the highest levels of government, everyday life became politicized. While some polls showed 79 percent of the American people wanted an end to the war, others revealed that the major problem perceived in the country was campus unrest. Although these seem like contradictory findings, they indicate polar- ization into opposing sides.

Striking students found support for their movement outside universities. One hundred art galleries and several museums closed down to protest the war, and when the Metropolitan Museum of New York refused to close, five hundred artists sat in there. Forty-three Nobel Prize winners (75 percent of all U.S. winners) sent Nixon a joint letter urging an immediate end to the war. On May 8, when the strike was at its height, over 250 officials from the Agency for International Development and the State Department signed a statement opposing expansion of the war. It was rumored that half of Nixon's cabinet was hostile to his decision to invade Cambodia, and in the days following Kent State, more than a dozen advisors and high officials in the White House, including Nixon's advisor for youth, resigned their positions in protest.

During May, more than eleven thousand draft cards were returned to the Selective Service. A Union of National Draft Opposition was set up at Princeton the day before the deaths at Kent State. By the middle of June, chapters had been established at twenty campuses that together hoped to return one hundred thousand draft cards. When organizers tried to give the Selective Service five thousand more cards on June 10, they were turned away without the cards being accepted.[51] The impact of draft resistance was admitted by the Selective Service when, for the first time, they filled less than 80 percent of their national quota.

There was a crisis of legitimacy at the highest levels of power as the ruling circles divided. The chairman of the board of Bank of America, the director of the Bank of Chicago, and the director of IBM all came out against the Cambodian invasion. As Thomas J. Watson Jr., director of IBM, said, "If we continue, I believe we will soon reach a point where much of the damage will be irreparable." On May 25, New York Governor Nelson Rockefeller, never known for dovish views, called for a quick end to the war in order to avoid "greater disasters in the future."[50] The Wall Street Businessmen for Peace and the Corporate Executive Committee for Peace (representing 350 high-level business executives) organized and immediately came out strongly for an end to the war. The Business Executive Move for Vietnam Peace, an organization with a membership of three thousand owners and senior executives of private corporations, launched "Operation Housecleaning," a nationwide effort to help defeat prowar members of the House of Representatives in the November elections.

Twelve hundred Wall Street lawyers converged on the Capitol on May 20 to lobby for an end to the war. Smaller groups of establishment lawyers from fifteen cities staggered their visits to maintain the pressure on Congress. The state legislatures of New York, California, Ohio, Kansas, Illinois, Rhode Island, Alaska, Michigan, Massachusetts, and New Jersey considered, and in some cases passed, legislation allowing draft-age men to refuse to fight in the undeclared war. The Hawaiian State Senate passed a resolution on May 6 urging Nixon to stop the invasion of Cambodia.

The Executive Council of the Episcopal Church proposed to the national Episcopal Convention a multipart resolution that included, "Support the national student strike against oppressive and unjust actions by the government such as harassment of the Black Panther members, the killing of students on campuses by the National Guard and police forces, and the use of American resources for the destruction of human life."[52] Significantly, the May strike also mobilized high school students, workers, soldiers, lesbians and gays, prisoners, activists from the women's movement, and professionals.

Tactical Innovations

During the strike, thousands of students converged in Washington, DC, to lobby Congress, but at the same time, tens of thousands of people in the U.S. chose to battle the police rather than talk with politicians. By their actions, they showed a political understanding that making the system change its policies meant "raising the costs" of continuing the war by disrupting domestic tranquility. Diffusion of militant tactics occurred despite the best efforts of the system (and many within the movement as well).

The state's use of deadly force made militant confrontations dangerous measures. Students spontaneously generated new tactical approaches for confrontations designed to stop "business as usual." Across the country they went in large numbers to block highways, expressways, railroad tracks, and city streets.[53] Blockading traffic might be seen as an adaptation of the sit-in tactic

Photographer unknown.

originally used by striking workers in the 1930s, but students in 1970 contested the operation of the entire society, not only occupying their universities but fighting for control of public space. They insisted that as long as genocidal war and racist violence were "business as usual," normal activities should be stopped. They refused to be "good Germans." On May 1, and again on May 3 and 14, thousands of students at the University of Maryland in College Park closed down Highway 1 and battled police and National Guardsmen who tried to open the road. On May 5, nearly seven thousand protesters from the University of Washington in Seattle blocked both the north and southbound lanes of Interstate 5 for over an hour, during which time they moved along the stopped cars to talk with motorists about the war and the strike. The next day the freeway was blocked again, but this time police moved in and drove protesters away.

At the University of California, Santa Barbara, a noon antiwar rally of five thousand people took over the university center, where nearly two thousand people formed affinity groups and moved onto Highway 101 for over an hour. One hundred feet of the main road leading into campus was treated with lard. At Southern Illinois University in Carbondale, two thousand demonstrators blocked downtown traffic and railroad tracks after buses they had ordered to travel to the May 9 demonstration in the nation's capital were unexpectedly canceled by the school's administration. A running battle with police and National Guard ensued. Scores of students were injured and over two hundred arrested. One thousand people from the University of Cincinnati staged a ninety-minute sit-in in the midst of downtown traffic and were dispersed only after 145 were arrested. A contingent of two thousand people marched from Columbia University onto the northbound lanes of the Henry Hudson Parkway, and at two campuses of the State University of New York (Stony Brook and Albany), at Mankato State College in Minnesota, and at St. John's in Philadelphia, hundreds of students marched off campus to block traffic. At John Carroll University in Ohio, more than three hundred antiwar demonstrators succeeded in bringing traffic to a halt for more than an hour and a half. In Austin, over eight thousand people battled hundreds of Texas Rangers who were called in to move the demonstrators out of the state capitol.

Blocking traffic was not advocated by any central organization but spread spontaneously, with simultaneous decisions made by grassroots groups across the country. Earlier, the burning of the Bank of America in Isla Vista, California, on February 25, 1970, had set an important precedent. Like the Weatherpeople's Days of Rage in October 1969, it defined a new level of struggle across the country. After Chicago's Loop was trashed by Weatherpeople, window breaking and street fighting became commonplace; and after the bank was burned in Isla Vista, firebombings happened across the country. Diffusion of tactical innovations among students was not simply a national phenomenon. When students at Brandeis University took control of the campus telephone system, within ten days, students in England, Italy, France, and West Germany had attempted to do the same thing.[54]

Protests also took on imaginative characteristics. At Cornell University, students laid siege to the ROTC building using a homemade "peace tank" to fire flowers and candy at it. At the University of Connecticut, over one thousand students armed with paint and brushes occupied the ROTC building. They covered the walls with flowers, cartoons, and peace symbols.[55] At Michigan Tech, about two hundred ROTC cadets joined one thousand other students to build a one-acre park in a symbolic protest against the war and the deaths at Kent State.[56]

At the University of Denver, students erected a tent and board city near the student center, which they dubbed "Woodstock West: Peace and Freedom Community." Over one thousand students converged there during the weekend of May 9 to be part of the city that was constructed "as a protest against the war in Southeast Asia, against racism in America, and against the slaying of four students at Kent State University." Although the university chancellor ordered people to disperse, no one paid any attention to him, and he was forced to call in the police. Thirty people were arrested, and the city was destroyed, but almost immediately, six hundred people returned to the site and rebuilt it, this time with heavier nails and bigger beams. While nearly one thousand Colorado National Guard and Denver Police watched, workmen tore down Woodstock West for the second time. That night, students returned, but this time "to love to death" the thirty police guards. They moved from one guard to the next and "discussed, argued, agreed, and laughed together." According to the *Denver Post*: "Several times during the afternoon and evening command officers reminded patrolmen, relaxed in conversation, that their helmets were supposed to be on their heads, not under their arms. The patrolmen responded quickly, but by nightfall the formality had been destroyed, and not one of the night force was wearing his helmet."[57] The next day, 400 of the college's 430 faculty met and voted to support the "spirit of Woodstock West."

In Philadelphia, a National Guard M48 tank bumped a car when the tank's steering broke. A lunchtime throng of Temple University students surged around the tank. Flowers quickly appeared in the barrel and "Free Bobby Seale" was painted on the turret before police could clear a path and get another tank to tow the disabled hulk away.

At McComb County Community College in Michigan, students performed a guerrilla theater. An earmuffed jury connected by strings to judges (who were themselves connected to a villain called "Wixon") condemned a black person, a hippie, and a student as "un-American." The three were then crucified.[58]

Cultural Dimensions of the Crisis

> Tin soldiers and Nixon coming
> We're finally on our own.
> This summer I hear the drumming
> Four dead in Ohio.
> Got to get down to it.
> Soldiers are gunning us down.
> Should have been done long ago!
> —*Crosby, Stills, Nash & Young*

Since 1967, children of the Be-Ins and the Summer of Love created a new territory where careers and compartmentalization of straight society had no validity, where money, prestige, and power were rejected in favor of humanism and naturalism. This new dimension to the culture of industrialized societies may have since become absorbed and acceptable, but in 1970, it was under murderous attack. Hippies and youth communities sprang up across the country (and around the world). The counterculture sought to create human community where it did not exist. Its political expression through the antiwar movement did not express its total rejection of technocratic culture. Young people broke away from deodorized bodies, shiny cars, and plastic. Once the existence of Haight-Ashbury, the East Village, and other havens became widely known, people freely migrated to these Meccas to live their lives according to their own values. At People's Park and elsewhere, they fought (and loved) police and National Guardsmen who were mobilized against them. The Berkeley Liberation Program, written at the height of the struggle for People's Park in 1969, expressed the militancy of a culture under siege:

> The people of Berkeley must increase their combativeness; develop, tighten and toughen their organizations; and transcend their middle-class, ego-centered life styles. . . . We shall create a genuine community and control it to serve our material and spiritual needs. We shall develop new forms of democratic participation and new, more humane styles of work and play. In solidarity with other revolutionary centers and movements, our Berkeley will permanently challenge the present system and act as one of the many training grounds for the liberation of the planet.

Communes and collectives sprang up in major cities, small towns, and rural regions. Experimentation in new ways of living and in raising new generations of children were begun, and free schools, food co-ops, and collective bookstores were created to preserve and spread the new culture. The "underground"

Berkeley: People's Park, 1969. "Welcome to Prague." Alan Copeland.

press quickly spread throughout the country. From five papers which reached an estimated fifty thousand readers in 1966, the Underground Press Syndicate grew to include two hundred papers with six million readers by the summer of 1970,[59] and in high schools, there were an additional five hundred underground papers.[60] Liberation News Service began in 1967, and by 1970, it was supplying over four hundred outlets with a weekly source of up-to-date information on progressive movements throughout the world. As early as March 1969, over 30,000 copies of the *Black Panther* were being distributed across the country. At its peak in 1970, the paper sold over 125,000 per week.[61]

The emergence of this new culture was a time of optimism, and the New Age spirit permeated all areas of society, making its way, for example, onto the stage in shows like *Hair* and performances of the Living Theatre. Electronic music became a significant medium of communication with GIs and young workers. Free concerts in the parks helped create a space where political messages and musical energy flowed together. It appeared that the nihilism of the Beats and their withdrawal from political responsibility had given way to collective action.

On June 28, 1970, the first anniversary of Stonewall, the first gay pride marches took over the streets of Chicago, New York, San Francisco, and Los Angeles. A year earlier, a well planned but unannounced police raid on a mafia-owned gay bar in Greenwich Village took an unexpected turn when patrons refused to be arrested. Led by transvestites and street kids, people fought back against the usual police harassment and violation of gay people's rights. As the brawl escalated, some police were chased out of the neighborhood while a few others were trapped inside the bar. The tactical police force was summoned. As dozens of police formed a phalanx, protesters spontaneously formed a kick line, joyously dancing as if in a theatrical production and singing lyrics proclaiming their liberated sexuality. Even after the police charged and injured many, passersby and bar patrons spontaneously reformed chorus lines and continued to chase the police out of the neighborhood. After that night when Greenwich Village was liberated, gay people would never again return to the closets in which they had been relegated for decades. One participant described how "electricity was in the air." Self-proclaimed street queen Sylvia Rivera felt that evening was "one of the greatest moments of my life." After a second night of rioting, the country took notice. "Gay power" was openly advocated in dozens of cities, and the nickname Gay Liberation Front came to describe and assemblage of groups that sprang up from the grassroots. Puerto Rican people, including gay men, lesbians, and transvestites, were at the epicenter of the Stonewall rebellion in 1969, the seminal event in the birth of the gay liberation movement.[62] Using the moniker of Gay Liberation Front, one group began publishing a newspaper, *Come Out!*, one of more than a dozen gay underground newspapers that appeared in the United States and around the world.

The appearance of gay liberation announced that millions of people were

One of the many affinity groups at the May Day 1970 Panther rally in New Haven. With thousands of National Guard and police in the streets, people came to defend the Panthers.

no longer content to live by the previous rules governing social interaction. From blind patriotism to restitutive justice, previously accepted values lost their magical ability to mold behavior. The work ethic, bureaucratic authority, and compulsive consumption were challenged by the generation born after World War II—a generation raised amid unprecedented prosperity. As the baby

Gay liberation emerged as part of a vast culture of resistance.

boomers began to develop a culture based on cooperation and communalism, it appeared to many Americans that their children had gone crazy, that the comfort they had struggled through the Depression to achieve for their families was being rejected as corrupt. What the Diggers had said in 1966 seemed to express the feelings of millions of people in the early 1970s:

> Don't drop half out. Drop all the way out. Anything that is part of the system is the whole system. It's all hung on the same string. Money is the system; reject it. Give all you have to the poor and do your thing. Wealth, success, security, luxury, comfort, certainty: they are all system-oriented goals. They're what the system uses to reward its subjects and keep them from noticing that they are not free. Throw it all away. The system has addicted you to an artificial need. Kick the habit. Be what you are. Do what you think is right. All the way out is free.[63]

Previous generations of Americans had accepted material advancement as the goal of life, but with the advent of hippies, the baby-boom generation developed a new conceptualization of the good life, a vision not tied as much to material comfort as to ethical and moral concerns. Their aspirations to dignity and love, not wealth and expertise, and the belief that people—not things— are primary were of paramount importance in defining their new culture. The genocidal war in Indochina became the primary focus of the culture that hippies opposed, and the synthesis of culture and politics in 1970 gave rise to political hippies (also known as "freaks"). Resistance and opposition to the war were heightened by the fact that although eighteen-year-olds were not allowed to vote, they were drafted to fight in the jungles of Vietnam.

From its beginnings, youth culture had contained a membership that was motivated by more than a desire to carve out easy lives for themselves. Material deprivation was not part of the experience of millions of younger people at the same time as technological innovations pointed to new possibilities for the reduction of scarcity and toil. It was common sense that Native Americans had been grievously wronged and that the Vietnamese posed no threat to the United States. The legitimacy of material rewards and the Protestant work ethic, so essential to the rise of capitalism in Europe, were being undermined by the system's material success.

Hippies opted to live humanly in an age of specialization. A newspaper from California, *Incarnations*, put it this way:

> Scarcity is an historical condition that necessitates repression, not an unavoidable necessity. . . . This generation is moving into revolutionary action through the discovery that television and new cars do not save. Salvation means wholeness. Wholeness is not found or made in the private consumption of commodities. The needs, limits, and potentials of organisms in their ecological relations must govern our science and our social being, not the needs of a market system or the fantasies of technicians.[64]

On the striking campuses of 1970, many students attempted to integrate questions of everyday life into their opposition to U.S. foreign policy. One action group at Berkeley wrote: "Reconstituting the university means nothing without changing the relationships in our own lives. These relationships extend into our work and into our politics, as well as into our homes."[65] The Scranton Commission's report called "emerging youth culture . . . the deeper cause of the emergence of race and war as objects of intense concern on the American campus."[66]

The summer after May was a time of imaginative and symbolic actions. The flags of the United States, Canada, and the National Liberation Front of Southern Vietnam flew above a summer rock concert attended by 250,000 people on the border between the United States and Canada. On August 6, hundreds of "longhaired undesirables" took over Tom Sawyer's Island at Disneyland and battled with police to stay there, causing a Disneyland ban on hippies for several years. As the politicization of everyday life progressed, repression of cultural events intensified: in Connecticut, thirty thousand people were stranded at a canceled rock festival; in Palo Alto, 260 street people were rounded up on July 12, a week after a July 4 street people's riot in Berkeley. The counterculture's politicization was most consequential on the battlefields.

Revolt within the Military

> In the Army, dissent is a major issue, on a scale unprecedented in the
> history of this nation. Radical newspapers are being published, anti-
> war coffeehouses are being opened, and military discipline is no longer
> accepted at its face value.
> —*Joseph A. Califano Jr.*, 1970

Active-duty soldiers waved the peace sign and often refused to fight.

The eros effect was more successful in touching the hearts of soldiers and sailors than anyone else. After murders on campuses, entire companies refused to
cross over into Cambodia. Their black armbands symbolized solidarity with
antiwar students. Combat refusal became so commonplace that separate companies were set up for men who refused to engage the "enemy."

Although the nationwide participation of GIs in the antiwar movement
reached its highest level in May 1970,[67] it began many years before that. As
early as 1967, the 198th Light Infantry Brigade had rioted at Fort Hood, Texas,
and went to the stockade rather than to Vietnam. In 1969, an entire company
of the 196th Light Brigade had publicly joined the sit-in movement and sat
down on the battlefield. That same year, another rifle company, from the notorious 1st Air Cavalry, had flatly refused (on CBS national news) to advance
down a dangerous trail. The first GI-led march for peace was in February 1968
(during the Tet offensive), when seven thousand people demonstrated in San
Francisco. Across the country, groups of activists formed coffeehouses for GIs,
helped start newspapers, leafleted incoming troop ships and planes, and set up
counseling services for those who wished to leave the armed forces.[68] By 1970,
U.S. soldiers all over the world—England, Germany, Okinawa, South Korea,
and within this country—were marching for peace.

The antiwar movement and the counterculture were forerunners of the GI
movement, and when campuses erupted, many soldiers were quick to join the

spreading movement. For the first time, Vietnam veterans who were patients in VA hospitals got involved in the peace movement in large numbers during May 1970.[69] Members of the Vietnam Veterans Against the War helped to lead student strikes on many campuses. Membership in that organization jumped about 50 percent to 2,000 by the summer of 1970, and two years later there were 2,500 members on active duty in Vietnam alone.

Veterans march from Arlington Cemetery to the Capitol. George Butler.

Never before in the history of the United States had veterans so massively protested while the war in which they had fought was still going on. Not many active-duty GIs in 1970 had spent time on the campuses, but the diffusion of the movement's thoughts and actions into the military, while organized by some, also took the course of music and cultural politics, an opposition to the "military madness" of authoritarianism, enforced short hair, and the overt repression of the base which contrasted so starkly with the comparatively "free" nature of society. *Scanlan's* reported in January 1971 that wigs were one of the biggest selling items at military post exchanges in the United States and abroad.[70] A congressional study in 1971 found that there were at least thirty thousand GIs addicted to heroin.

As morale broke down, officers became legitimate targets for the rifles and grenades of GIs. The Pentagon admitted to 209 "fragging" deaths in 1970, more than twice the toll for the previous year. The *Armed Forces Journal* reported that in one division, the American, fraggings were running at the rate of one a week and that news of fraggings "will bring cheers at troop movies or in bivouacs of certain units." In April 1970, an underground military paper interviewed a former platoon commander, Sergeant Richard Williams, who had served for seven years in Vietnam. "When I was a guard in the Long Binh stockade," he said, "there were 23 guys there for killing their C.O.'s [commanding officers] and 17 others were already on trial for killing C.O.'s."[71] Lieutenant Colonel Weldon Honeycutt, a commander at Hamburger Hill, where his orders to attack had resulted in the deaths of most of his men, was proclaimed "GI Enemy Number One" by an underground publication which issued a wanted poster offering a $10,000 reward for his death. Subsequent reports of grenade and Claymore mine explosions near him indicated that attempts were being made to collect the bounty. According to army records, beginning in 1969, there were at least 551 fraggings that resulted in 86 dead and over 700 wounded.[72] In 1970, the Pentagon counted 209 more killings.[73] In 1973, congressional hearings told that at least 3 percent of all officer and non-com deaths in Vietnam over an eleven-year period were the result of fraggings.

"Resisters inside the army" (RITA) units were established in Vietnam and the United States, a type of resistance which losing armies in World War I (Russia and France in 1917, and Germany and Austria in 1918) and World War II (Italy in 1943) had experienced, but one that had never occurred in U.S. history.

Desertion rates were incredibly high during the period of the student strike. Officially, there were 65,643 deserters from the army alone in 1970— including five hundred every day during all of May. The number of men who left the military in six years (1967–72) reached almost half a million.

Resistance occurred in the navy as well. In March 1970, an ammunition ship was hijacked on the high seas by some of its crewmen and sailed to Cambodia, where the mutineers were granted political asylum. In late May, the destroyer USS *Richard B. Anderson* was set to leave San Diego for Vietnam when someone "threw something into the gears." The destroyer was dry-docked for two months, and the incident was not reported until June 14, three weeks after it happened.

On Armed Forces Day, May 16, at least twenty-two bases inside the U.S. experienced major protests, and normal parades had to be canceled at an even greater number of domestic military installations. Demonstrations at five of these military installations (Fort McClellan, Alabama; Charleston Naval Base, South Carolina; Fort Hood, Texas; Fort Benning, Georgia; and Fort Riley, Kansas) marked the first time that antiwar actions had taken place there. One thousand people, marching through the streets of Killeen near Fort Hood, shouted demands: "U.S. out of Southeast Asia now! Free Bobby Seale and all political prisoners! Avenge the dead of Kent State, Jackson State, and Augusta!"

The military high command was so threatened by the wave of uprisings rolling through the troops that regularly scheduled Armed Forces Day events were canceled at twenty-eight other bases. At Fort Ord, south of San Francisco, most GIs were assigned to their barracks, riot control, or to digging a trench between the edge of the base and Route 1, a barrier against planned demonstrations later reinforced by miles of concertina wire. At Camp Pendleton in Oceanside, California, all marines were restricted to the base, and, for the first time, platoons assigned to riot control received orders to shoot to kill in case of disturbances on the base. At Fort Dix, New Jersey, GIs were restricted to base, and the three thousand demonstrators who attempted to march onto the base were gassed.

On July 4, 1970, one thousand black and white GIs assembled in Heidelberg, West Germany, and were joined by Germans to call for "*Freiheit für Bobby Seale.*" Black Panthers reported they had more members in the armed forces than inside the United States. As black soldiers stepped up their struggle against racism, 250 black GIs at Fort Hood burned down two reenlistment centers as well as one of the base dormitories. Also in July, two hundred black soldiers seized a section of Fort Carson and held it for a time by fighting off military police.[74]

The antiwar movement's political outreach to GIs was intensified after the student strike. By 1972, there were at least twenty-five antiwar coffeehouses and three hundred underground GI newspapers using names like *Star Spangled Bummer* and *Harass the Brass*. Drug abuse became commonplace among American GIs. Dr. Joel H. Kaplan, who helped set up the army's first formal drug abuse program in Vietnam, reported in June 1970 that:

> While I was there, the Pentagon announced that there were only 3500 marijuana users in the entire U.S. Army. My team alone saw that many in our own patient population. My KO (neuro-psychiatric specialist) estimated that 50 to 80 percent of the Army's enlisted men tried marijuana once. . . . I would estimate that between 10 and 20 percent of the GIs in Vietnam were drug abusers. A drug abuser with a daily dependence would smoke a marijuana joint in the morning when he got up, like enjoying a cup of coffee. He would drop some barbiturates during the morning, smoke a couple of more joints at lunch, and in the evening would wind up on opium.[75]

The massive rebellion in the military meant that it was only a matter of time before the United States had to withdraw from Vietnam since its GIs refused to fight. With the return of the veterans, the antiwar movement was provided with a nucleus of leadership in the period after the student strike. The students and soldiers of that time, although segregated into different worlds, came together in the struggle to end the war.

Women's General Strike

By 1970, the autonomous women's movement had experienced phenomenal growth. Women's groups sprouted up on college campuses, in industry, in cities, and in suburbs.

Like the black movement, the women's movement contained a diverse membership, and in 1970, radical feminists became the leading force within the feminist movement. That the "personal is political" had long been discussed by the New Left, but never before had

See Red Women's Workshop, screen print, ca. 1976–78, UK.

the legitimacy of heterosexual relationships and patriarchal domination been challenged as it was in 1970. As radical feminists consolidated their hegemony within the women's movement, women occupied buildings and set up women's centers, and they fought the police for control of their newly won territory. At the Second Congress to Unite Women in New York on the weekend of May 1–3, 1970, more than a dozen lesbians wearing Lavender Menace T-shirts took over the opening ceremony and announced their presence to more than four hundred assembled women from around the country. From that moment on, the entry of lesbians as a public force and the hegemony of radical lesbians within the women's movement became a prominent feature of feminism.[76]

On March 18, 1970, in New York, more than a hundred protesters occupied the offices of the *Ladies Home Journal*, a magazine with circulation in the millions that featured advertisements exploiting women's bodies and had no day-care center for its employees. The activists demanded an entire future issue be devoted to feminism and an end to portrayal of women as mindless commodities. Three months later the magazine complied, including sections on the Equal Rights Amendment and meetings of American socialist-feminists with North Vietnamese counterparts.[77] In the spring of 1970, women's strikes at General Electric, Bendix, and New York Bell Telephone surprised mainstream unions, whose male leadership nonetheless continued to overlook them.

Lesbian and gay pride march, New York City, June 1979. Photographer unknown.

Inside movement organizations, women's voices resonated widely. Among Latinos, the Second National Youth Conference was held in Denver in March 1970. Even more participants arrived than the previous year. The many creative workshops included one on women's rights that issued a report criticizing traditional concepts of females: "We must change the concepts of the alienated family where the woman assumes full responsibility for the care of the home and the raising of the children to the concept of La Raza as the unified family. . . . Everyone, men and women, will work consciously towards the goal of the total liberation of our people."[78] Within the Young Lords as well, their 1969 program as formulated called for equality for women. The revised program of May 1970 went even further: "We want equality for women. Down with machismo and male chauvinism."[79]

In the spring of 1970, the Central Committee of the Young Lords Organization went on a retreat at a Long Island mansion, where they resolved to promote women to the central committee (after a demand, "not a request," from the women's caucus). Their reasoning followed Che's call to "build a new twenty-first-century man (person)." The group organized protests at the Puerto Rico Day march because Miss Universe was the chief marshal.[80]

The women's movement greatly affected the visual arts.[81] In New York, a group called Women Artists in Revolution called on the Whitney Museum to include more female artists. On May 2, 1970, the group opened their first feminist production, *Mod Donna*.[82] At a meeting of some 1,500 people from the art world on May 18, the New York Art Strike was proclaimed in solidarity with Kent State and Jackson State. Some of the resolutions acclaimed an "emergency cultural government" that would sever all ties with the national regime and creation of a fund for resisters against war, repression, and racism through a 5 percent voluntary tax from artists and dealers. Four days later, more than five hundred artists blocked the entrance to the Metropolitan Museum after it refused to honor the strike. A subsequent meeting approved a steering committee of 50 percent African Americans and Puerto Ricans and 50 percent women while adopting the official name "The New York Artists Strike Against Racism, Sexism, Repression and War."[83] To protest the Vietnam War, sculptor Robert Morris called off his own solo exhibition at the Whitney Museum and called for a meeting on May 18, 1970, where over 1,500 members of the art world resolved to create an "emergency cultural government to sever all collaboration with the federal government."[84] Later adopting the formal name "The New York Art Strike Against War, Racism, Fascism, Sexism and Repression," artists organized several demonstrations, most notably on May 23 when over five hundred artists sat in on the steps of the Metropolitan Museum, closing it down in protest of the war. One-day closings of the Museum of Modern Art, the Guggenheim, and Jewish museums also occurred, and an Alternative Venice Biennale helped to raise money for the antiwar movement. In Los Angeles women organized a demonstration against the Los Angeles County Museum, which included no female artists in its exhibitions.

For the first time, rape was made a public issue and previously ignored violations were publicly vilified. Although a 1970 presidential commission found pornography to be harmless, a militant antipornography movement led by radical women quickly changed both consciousness and law. In 2017, the national uprising against sexual harassment provides further indication of the women's movement far-reaching consequences.

In 1970 the National Organization for Women (NOW) embarked on its most ambitious campaign: a general "Women's Strike for Equality" scheduled for August 26, the fiftieth anniversary of women's right to vote. As the date for the strike approached, women staged "tot-ins" to dramatize the need for day-care centers, and Betty Friedan, president of NOW, promised "an instant revolution against sexual oppression." Exceeding organizers' expectations of how many women would turn out, more than one hundred thousand women marched across the country not only in commemoration of the Nineteenth Amendment but to demand an Equal Rights Amendment (ERA). Some fifty thousand women marched on Fifth Avenue in New York, and across the country, there were demonstrations and rallies in more than ninety cities and towns in forty-two states. The next day, a lobbying campaign for an Equal Rights Amendment began on Capitol Hill. Although the ERA never passed, the women's movement continued to gather momentum in the 1970s, changing the common sense of American society while providing women with new possibilities for their lives.

French women organized a solidarity demonstration on the same day, an event which brought together many of the scattered feminists who emerged after 1968 May events and is considered by many to have been the "beginning of the contemporary French feminist movement."[85] In 1970, Simone de Beauvoir took a strong stand against the Soviet countries' treatment of feminism and advocated an autonomous women's movement unconnected to any left-wing parties.[86]

Mass demonstrations to abolish anti-abortion laws, New York City, 1970. Such demonstrations took place all across the country in 1969–70. Photographer unknown.

Latinos Mobilize

New York City was also the center of a burgeoning Puerto Rican movement. New York's medical system all but ignored the needs of Puerto Rican residents, although doctors did find resources for years of unnecessary hysterectomies. Routine care required patients to wait six to seven hours simply to see a doctor in Lincoln Hospital in the South Bronx, and basic services such as X-rays were often not available. The Young Lords "liberated" an X-ray truck and used it to provide medical care to long-neglected patients. Called the "butcher shop" by locals, Lincoln Hospital's building had been condemned in 1949, yet

Young Lords Party, offset lithograph poster, 1971.

no new hospital was being constructed. Disgusted with rats in the emergency room, shortages of personnel, dilapidated equipment and supply shortages, activists moved from protest to the revolutionary action of taking over the hospital and running it as it ought to have been with the willing cooperation of disgruntled hospital workers.

On July 15, 1970, after Carmen Rodríguez, a young Puerto Rican woman, died during an abortion gone wrong, dozens of people wearing purple berets led by the Health Revolutionary Union Movement (HRUM) and the Young Lords took over the hospital. They raised a Puerto Rican flag over the building and educated patients about preventative care and lead poisoning. Altogether, over six hundred people joined the occupation of the Nurses' Residence and pressed demands, including a new building, more Puerto Rican staff, doctors making house calls, and provision of basic services. The occupation was brief but successful.[87] The city agreed the next day to build a new facility (which was completed in 1976). When the hospital still failed to help stem the heroin epidemic plaguing the community, a second occupation began on November 10, 1970. Activists brought more than twenty-five heroin addicts into the hospital for treatment and created a new clinic. Walls were adorned with posters of Malcolm X and Che Guevara. They gave every addict a copy of *The Opium Trail: Heroin and Imperialism*, a pamphlet that instructed readers that revolutionary action could cure heroin addiction better than methadone alone.

Acupuncture treatments were later offered by the clinic, and a convert to them was Mutulu Shakur, husband of Afeni Shakur, stepfather to Tupac.

In Los Angeles, on August 29, three days after the women's general strike, over twenty-five thousand people flocked to Laguna Park in East Los Angeles for the third Chicano Antiwar Moratorium. The event was organized by a broad coalition of Brown Berets, student activists, and the Crusade for Justice.[88] A festive mood prevailed. Marchers were cheered by thousands of people who lined the streets and expressed support for peace. People cheerfully filled Laguna Park and enthusiastically responded to the first speakers. Without provocation, police attacked.[89] The violence began from the rear while music and performances on the stage captured everyone's attention. Out of nowhere, a teargas canister landed on the stage. As people turned to see what was happening, dozens of uniformed sheriffs in riot gear attacked. Twice, people pushed the sheriffs back, but the forces of order attacked in ever-greater numbers and with intensified violence, took control of the park.

By the end of the day, three people lay dead, hundreds had been injured, and over two hundred arrested.[90] Property damage was estimated in the millions of dollars.[91] Respected journalist Ruben Salazar had been murdered as he sat on a stool in the Silver Dollar bar. A sheriff's deputy had fired a ten-inch-long metal teargas projectile through the reporter's head. In retrospect, the assassinations of Ruben Salazar, Lyn Ward, and Angel Gilberto Díaz "were part of a deliberate police terror campaign designed to neutralize and destroy the Chicano Movement."

The state's assault on a peaceful gathering united the entire Chicano community—and many others—in support of the movement. Three days after the attack, an open assembly of more than six hundred people unanimously approved a new protest march for September 16. Refusing to be intimidated despite warnings from police that new violence might be used to silence them, more than one hundred thousand people took to the streets. Amid a diversity of contingents proudly displaying their beliefs with banners and posters, local youth calling themselves La Casa de Carnalismo carried a banner loudly proclaiming "*Tierra y Libertad, Tenemos el Derecho de Armarnos para Defendernos*" (Land and Liberty, We Have the Right to Arm Ourselves for Self-Defense).[92] On January 31, 1971, another Chicano Moratorium was called to protest the war as well as police repression, and the police again attacked, killing Gustav Montag and wounding forty others.[93]

At the same time as the militant wing of the movement was brutalized and dispersed, favorable farmworkers' contracts were signed, effectively dividing the movement. Basking in their victory, Chavez and the United Farm Workers (UFW) continued to advocate tight immigration controls and nonviolence while publicly decrying "illegals" and "green carders" in contradistinction to American citizens.[94]

After the success of a "Free Puerto Rico Now!" conference in September 1970, more than one hundred thousand people marched from Spanish Harlem to the United Nations to support independence for Puerto Rico. Soon thereafter, however, divisions emerged among Young Lords over the question of the role of mainland Puerto Rican émigrés and activists on the island. As the movement split, activists attacked one another, and guerrilla tendencies formed.

Puerto Rican aspirations for independence intensified as part of the global 1960s.

Both the radical Puerto Rican and Chicano movements quickly escalated tactics from street protests to armed struggle. In early 1971, the Chicano Liberation Front staged multiple bombings of banks, schools, and post offices in Los Angeles. To the north, a Chicano revolutionary party promulgated armed revolution on the models of Cuba and Vietnam.[95] Clandestine groups proliferated: the Northern California Frente Chicano de Liberación, the Continental Revolutionary Army in Colorado, the Emiliano Zapata Unit of the People's Forces in California, and FALN (Fuerzas Armadas de Liberación Nacional Puertorriqueña) to name just a few.[96]

As armed groups bombed and robbed banks, it became almost impossible for legal movement groups to continue organizing. In 1972, the Crusade for Justice purchased the apartment complex next to their Denver headquarters, and the entire block became a liberated space. On March 17, 1973, using the pretext of a jaywalking offense, more than two hundred police attacked a party, shooting wildly and drawing defensive fire in which four officers were wounded. Activist Luis Martinez was killed, and over sixty people were arrested.[97] In the aftermath of the confrontation, city officials ordered demolition of the apartment building.

Not as well known as the government's repression of the African American movement, the Latino movement was also heavily attacked. In late May 1974, six activists in Boulder were killed by powerful explosions. In addition to outright murders, multiple false charges were filed against more than a dozen activists. When all was said and done, however, the results were eleven dismissals, two acquittals, and two continuances—and the movement's organizing work had been interrupted.[98] By the end of the 1970s, the Crusade ceased to exist as a viable movement organization.

Like never before, the eros effect of 1970 posed the possibility of unity among all the progressive forces in motion. When thousands of students in Washington, DC, found themselves fighting with police, for example, they were frequently taken in by the black community there, which literally opened its doors to those in need of a safe haven. At the same time, the support for the Panthers provided by the four million striking students bore fruit when Huey Newton was released from jail on May 29 (in the midst of the student strike). With the coming together of blacks, Latinos, and whites in 1970, the movement appeared to be moving toward a genuinely revolutionary position, one that went beyond existing social divisions.

The Chicano Antiwar Moratorium faced severe repression. Raul Ruiz.

The Revolutionary Peoples' Constitutional Convention

On Labor Day weekend, September 5–7, 1970, thousands of people, including sizeable contingents of students, feminists, gay people, Native Americans, Puerto Ricans, Chicanos and Asian Americans, answered the Panthers' call for a Revolutionary Peoples' Constitutional Convention (RPCC) in Philadelphia. Although seldom mentioned in mainstream U.S. history, this self-understood revolutionary event was arguably the most momentous event during the American sixties. Despite the massive police actions designed to scare people away from Philadelphia, as many as fifteen thousand people came.[99] From around the country, spontaneously assembled groups rented buses, drove cars, and took planes. In at least two cities, people reported that buses were suddenly canceled without explanation, compelling people to improvise rides. Twenty-two persons from East St. Louis in a three-car caravan were arrested and charged with firearms violations, and at least one New York Panther was arrested en route to Philadelphia.[100] Organizations and delegates from Florida and North Carolina made a notable impression, as did representatives from African liberation movements, Palestine, Germany, Colombia, and Brazil.[101]

Arriving in the midst of police terror directed against the Panthers, we were determined to defend them as well as to draft a new U.S. constitution. The week before people gathered in Philadelphia, police bloodily assaulted all three Panther offices in the city, arresting every member of the Party they could find. The Panthers had not accepted their fate without a gunfight, and three police were wounded. Afterward, the police forced captured Panther men to walk naked through the streets while being photographed by the press. Police Commissioner Frank Rizzo gloated that he had caught the "big, bad Black Panthers with their pants down."[102]

Publicized widely, the atmosphere of courage amid fear created by police attacks was an important part of the aura of the RPCC. Philadelphia Panther member Russell Shoatz recounts that in the weeks before the RPCC the Panther central office in Oakland made it clear to Philadelphia party members that even Huey Newton was "afraid to come to Philadelphia." Shoatz remembers that they "went on to express their opinion that the racist Philadelphia police would feel comfortable in attempting to assassinate him during the planned Revolutionary Peoples' Constitutional Convention Planning Session."[103]

Rather than facing expected police assaults, we found the homes of African Americans opened to us, their churches, hospitable refuges, and streets alive with an erotic solidarity of a high order. Signs in storefronts read "Welcome Panthers." Five flags flew outside the convention center representing the Panthers, the National Liberation Front of South Vietnam, black nationalism (red, black, and green), Yippies (green marijuana leaf on black flag), and Che Guevara. Evidently the Panthers had done a huge amount of planning for the event, as food was provided for many people. Russell Shoatz recounts how a fifteen-ton refrigerated truck full of frozen meats was commandeered and unloaded on the same day as other Panther squads robbed a bank.

The Philadelphia black community was incredibly supportive. After the police raids, Panther offices had been sealed, but neighborhood people spontaneously opened them back up on their own initiative. The *Black Panther* reported, "In North Philly, two rival gangs had made a truce. . . . They emerged 200–300 strong and when 15 carloads of pigs drove up and asked them who gave them permission to open up the people's office, their reply was 'the people,' and the police had to eat mud rather than face the wrath of an angry armed people."[104]

An extraordinary alliance at the RPCC came together in open assemblies to discuss movement goals and future directions. Most remarkably of all, this diverse convention was able to write down their visions of a free society. History seldom cooperates by providing us with such clarity of participants' thinking in "spontaneously conscious" crowds.[105]

Inside Temple University's McGonigle Hall, a vibrant and festive atmosphere prevailed for plenary sessions. We had won. The police had been unable to stop us. A steady stream of people accumulated, the hall swelled to its capacity, and anticipation grew. Panther security people indicated speakers were about to begin. Suddenly, dozens of gay people entered the upper balcony, chanting and clapping rhythmically: "Gay, gay power to the gay, gay people! Power to the People! Black, black power to the black, black people! Gay, gay power to the gay, gay people! Power to the People!" Everyone rose to their feet and joined in, repeating the refrain and using other appropriate adjectives: red, brown, women, youth, and student.

The first speaker was Michael Tabor, a charismatic young Party member who brilliantly held our attention for over two hours as he enumerated how the original U.S. constitution excluded and oppressed "240,000 indentured servants, 800,000 black slaves, 300,000 Indians, and all women, to say nothing of the sexual minorities." Tabor reminded us that President Richard Nixon, fresh from invading Cambodia and daily bombing Vietnam, "made Adolf Hitler look like a peace candidate." Other speakers included Audrea Jones, leader of the Boston Panthers, and Panther attorney Charles Garry.

During the break in nearby streets, Muhammad Ali, an "ordinary" participant, shook hands, signed autographs, and offered words of encouragement. (The heavyweight champion had been stripped of his title for his antiwar stance and would not win his case before the Supreme Court until the following year.) People talked with old friends or made new ones as they looked for a place to stay. All the while, hundreds discussed their coming task: to draft a new constitution for the United States. Jubilation coexisted alongside criticism but nowhere was fearful resignation to be found.

As evening approached, electric expectations filled the hall as we waited for our first encounter with Huey P. Newton. Thousands more people waited outside hoping for space to become available for them. Only released from prison on August 9, Huey had just published an important essay supporting women's and gay liberation. He also had publicly offered to send troops to fight on the side of the Vietnamese against the U.S. Although many of us had demonstrated for his freedom and read his essays, he was a stranger to practically everyone, even to many Panthers. Huey was everyone's hero but as soon as he took the microphone, we were stunned to discover that he was not at all an eloquent speaker. His high-pitched, almost whiny voice digressed into abstract arguments that had little impact—except to disappoint us, a fact not lost on Newton himself.[106]

The next day, we broke down into topical workshops that could be selected from a menu prepared by a planning group that had met at Howard University a month earlier.[107] As the *Black Panther* reported, "If only for a few hours, representatives of all major constituencies of the revolutionary popular movement huddled together to brainstorm and discuss ideas for achieving our goals of a freer society. The form of the gatherings was quite different than in 1787. Each workshop was led by Panther members, who also coordinated security contingents that insured a trouble-free working environment."

Panthers prevented the media from attending, fearing their presence would only make a circus of the proceedings. While many journalists complained about being barred, the space created by the absence of media was too valuable to sacrifice to publicity. Here was the movement's time to speak among ourselves. Seldom do groups communicate with such a combination of passion and reason. Person after person rose and spoke of heartfelt needs and desires, of pain and oppression. As if the roof had been taken off the ceiling, imaginations soared as we flew off to our new society. The synergistic effect compelled each of us to articulate our thoughts with eloquence and simplicity, and the "right on!" refrain that ended each person's contribution also signaled that the time had arrived for someone else to speak. An unidentified Panther later described how even the children had not been boisterous: "The children were to be for the three days like adults, infected with a kind of mad sobriety." The same author promised: "There is going to be a revolution in America. It is going to begin in earnest in our time. . . . To have believed in a second American revolution before Philadelphia was an act of historical and existential faith: not to believe in a new world after Philadelphia is a dereliction of the human spirit."[108]

In describing the workshops, the Panther went on:

> The pre-literate Black masses and some few saved post-literate students were going to, finally write the new constitution. . . . The aristocratic

> students led by the women, and the street bloods, they were going to
> do the writing. So there were the first tentative meetings, led brilliantly
> by "armed intellectuals" from the Panthers. . . . In the schools and
> churches—the rational structures of the past—the subversive workshops
> of the future met to ventilate the private obsessions of the intellectual
> aristocrats and the mad hopes of the damned.[109]

As the time allotted for the workshops drew to an end, each group chose
spokespersons entrusted to present our ideas to the entire plenary's second
session. As is clear in the documents, differences of viewpoint were sometimes
simply left intact rather than flattened out in an attempt to impose a party
line.[110] Under more "normal" circumstances involving such a diverse collection
of people in working groups as large as five hundred persons, screaming fights
(or worse) might have been expected, yet these workshops generated documents that offer a compelling vision of a more just and free society than has
ever existed. Alongside an International Bill of Rights prohibiting U.S. aggression against other nations, mandates were approved for redistribution of the
world's wealth, a ban on the manufacture and use of genocidal weapons, and
an end to a standing army and its replacement by "a system of people's militia,
trained in guerrilla warfare, on a voluntary basis and consisting of both men
and women." Police were to consist of "a rotating volunteer non-professional
body coordinated by the Police Control Board from a (weekly) list of volunteers
from each community section. The Police Control Board, its policies, as well
as the police leadership, shall be chosen by direct popular majority vote of the
community." The delegates called for an end to the draft; prohibition on spending more than 10 percent of the national budget for military and police—a
provision that could be overridden by a majority vote in a national referendum—and proportional representation for minorities and women (two forms
of more democracy missing from the constitution adopted in 1789).

Universities' resources were to be turned over to people's needs all over the
world, not sold to military and corporate needs; billions of dollars in organized
crime wealth were to be confiscated; there was to be free decentralized medical
care; sharing of housework by men and women; encouragement of alternatives
to the nuclear family; "the right to be gay, anytime, anyplace"; increased rights
and respect for children; community control of schools; and student power,
including freedom of dress, speech, and assembly. Although there is one paragraph in which "man" and "he" are used, the very first report of the workshops
contained a mandate always to replace the word "man" with "people" in order
to "express solidarity with the self-determination of women and to do away
with all remnants of male supremacy, once and for all." As summarized by the
BPP a week later:

Taken as a whole, these reports provided the basis for one of the most progressive Constitutions in the history of humankind. All the people would control the means of production and social institutions. Black and third world people were guaranteed proportional representation in the administration of these institutions as were women. The right of national self-determination was guaranteed to all oppressed minorities. Sexual self-determination for women and homosexuals was affirmed. . . . The present racist legal system would be replaced by a system of people's courts where one would be tried by a jury of one's peers. Jails would be replaced by community rehabilitation programs. . . . Adequate housing, health care, and day care would be considered Constitutional Rights, not privileges. Mind expanding drugs would be legalized. These are just some of the provisions of the new Constitution.[111]

In the society at large: racism, patriarchal chauvinism, and homophobia; at the RPCC: solidarity, liberation, and celebration of difference. From this vantage point, the RPCC provides a glimpse of the break from "normal" business as usual, and of international system to replace the existing one of militarized nation-states and profit-hungry transnational corporations. As a global uprising swept the planet, the Panthers were best positioned as the most oppressed in what Che Guevara called "the belly of the beast" to embody global aspirations to transform the entire world system. These documents convey unambiguous statements of the movement's self-defined outline of a freer society. Although it has been practically forgotten by historians, the RPCC is a key to unlocking the mystery of the aspirations of the 1960s movement.

The Philadelphia constitution's International Bill of Rights was one indication of just how much patriotism was transcended. The popular movement's imagination expounded the contours of a new world—not simply a new nation. The twin aspirations of the global movement of 1968—internationalism and self-management—were embodied throughout the articulated vision. The term "self-management" may not have been used in the documents, but its American version, "community control," was used in reference to schools, police, women's control of their own bodies, and more autonomy for children, students, and youth. In our attempt to create paradise, our immediate task was to mitigate repressive powers of those who wanted to preserve the status quo (police, racism, patriarchal authoritarianism, and the military). We sometimes compromised and agreed to go halfway to paradise, fully conscious that humans will never be absolutely free. If we continually jump halfway to paradise, never reaching it, we nonetheless approach it.

Some of the demands today appear outlandish, particularly those related to drugs. After calling for the eradication of hard drugs "by any means necessary" and help for addicts, the workshop on Self-Determination of Street People stated:

> We recognize that psychedelic drugs (acid, mescaline, grass) are important in developing the revolutionary consciousness of the people. However, after the revolutionary consciousness has been achieved, these drugs may become a burden. No revolutionary action should be attempted while under the influence of any drug. We urge these drugs be made legal. Or rather they should not be illegal, that is, there should be no law made against them.

The RPCC position on drugs displays graphically that more individual freedom was part of the aspirations of the Panther-led bloc, that this impetus, while appearing to some as only concerned with minorities, *actually formulated universal interests*. No one should discount or trivialize the importance of the drug issue. As a symbolic vehicle used for the imposition of class rule and cultural hegemony, it affects hundreds of thousands of people daily. One in three male prisoners in New York was serving a drug sentence in 1997; nationally, that figure was six of ten women; and, in California, one in four male state prisoners (and four out of ten females).[112] The existing system's abysmal failure to wage an effective "war on drugs," its continual enrichment of organized crime syndicates while hundreds of thousands of users languish in jails, and the irrationality of legal drugs daily tranquilizing millions of children and adults, and of alcohol and cigarettes' widespread glorification, are scandalous dimensions of an irrational system. History's judgment may yet prove that RPCC policies are more sane and prudent than those now in place.[113] In the 1970s, Italian youth known as the Metropolitan Indians and Christiania, a countercultural community in Copenhagen, adopted essentially the same position on drugs as the RPCC without being aware of the 1970 convention.[114]

True to the RPCC's call to eradicate hard drug dealers by any means necessary, Panthers went on the attack against heroin dealers, confiscating cash and flushing their stash after giving them plenty of public warnings. In one of the more daring actions undertaken by movement activists, Jamil Al-Amin was captured by police after he robbed an after-hours club frequented by big dealers—a hangout his team and others sought to close. Ron Brazao, underground from a 1970 bust of the Panther Defense Committee in Cambridge, Massachusetts, was killed in a shoot-out with a dealer in Marin, California, in 1972.

More than any other U.S. organization in the latter half of the twentieth century, the BPP accelerated the revolutionary process. The dialectical synchronicity of popular movement and revolutionary party, their dependence on each other and mutual amplification, accelerated and reached its climax at the RPCC. Our gathering accomplished more in a weekend than history usually accomplishes in years or even decades. How much longer must we wait until we again find such space for visionary unity? The Philadelphia convention was the apex of the U.S. popular insurgency. Nikhil Pal Singh eloquently understood the unique human geography that unfolded: "enactment of a Constitutional Convention under the auspices of the Panthers and in celebration of 'radical minorities', excluded in the initial formation of the great document, was an astonishing attempt to is imagine alternative forms of kinship and community to the one organized around a conception of a unitary and universal, national subject."[115]

The CIA held a different view. Their report characterized the RPCC as a "chaotic and nonproductive effort. . . . White radicals in attendance numbered about 40 percent."[116] Not all participants share my optimistic portrayal. Some questioned whether a visible and spirited gay presence existed at the RPCC.[117] Alice Echols mentions a conference of the Lesbian Feminism Movement in Washington, DC, that produced a feminist caucus for the planned second RPCC. She felt that in Philadelphia the BPP was suspicious of feminist activists because autonomous women's workshops (without the leadership of Panther women) were canceled more than once.[118] Ruth Rosen also complained that Huey broke his promise for an autonomous women's caucus to meet.[119] Women did have at least one female-only meeting, but about twenty lesbians left after they were unable to get the group to agree to their demands for women to have "complete control of our social system" and "destruction of the nuclear family." The split broke along the lines of black women wanting to have a "nuclear" family, having suffered centuries of slavery, during which their families were torn asunder. They were fine with lesbians collectively raising children, but they wanted the right to keep their children to their blood family; they were leery of another "state" raising their kids in "day care."

The final report of the Workshop on the Self-Determination of Women sharply contradicted existing society: "We recognize the right of all women to be free. . . . We will fight for a socialist system that guarantees all, creative, non-exploitative life for all human beings. . . . We encourage and support the continued growth of communal households and communal relationships and other alternatives to the patriarchal family. . . . Every woman has the right to decide whether she will be homosexual, heterosexual or bisexual."[120]

Divisions also existed among African Americans. Most severely, the US Organization had murdered Panther leaders Bunchy Carter and John Huggins in Los Angeles in 1969. Antagonisms between the two groups, although exacerbated by the FBI, reflected larger political differences. In Atlanta, on the same weekend that the RPCC convened in Philadelphia, the Congress of

African People gathered in Atlanta, with 3,500 participants from a variety of civil rights, Black Power, and cultural nationalist organizations. The Congress was born out of a series of conferences held in the U.S. and Bermuda from 1966. Atlanta was designed to unite black moderate forces and cultural nationalists—and to differentiate them from the radical multicultural alliance led by the Panthers. Present were Rev. Jesse Jackson, Coretta Scott King, Louis Farrakhan, Queen Mother Moore, Ken Msemaji, and Julian Bond, as well as representatives from many countries. The group restricted its participants to the Third World. In one of the most important speeches, Amiri Baraka (Leroi Jones) warned against "White mythology" written by Marx and Lenin and chided the Panthers for asking us to get "involved with another group of White boys." Ultimately, the group went on to help spur African American politicians to run for office. Baraka would later become a committed Leninist but in 1970, he sought to distance African American activists from white radicals.

At the grassroots level, unity and solidarity prevailed in 1970. The intelligence of popular movements sometimes outpaces even the most visionary organizations, an insight verified by comparing the reformist 1966 Panther program with the revolutionary vision produced at the RPCC in 1970.[121] When held up against the RPCC documents, the program is timid, its vision limited. Nowhere in the program are gay people's rights, the liberation of women, and proportional representation of minorities and women.

Atlanta University students at the final rally of the March against Repression, Georgia, 1970. Roland Freeman.

Comparing the Black Panther Party's 1966 Program and 1970 RPCC Proposals

October 1966 Black Panther Party Platform (black nationalist phase of the BPP)	September 1970 Revolutionary Peoples' Constitutional Convention (revolutionary internationalist phase of the popular movement)
Rights of black people	International Bill of Rights
UN plebiscite to determine the destiny of the black community	USA not a nation; no genocidal weapons; end to NATO, SEATO
Black men exempt from military service	No standing army; no draft; People's militia; return of all U.S. troops from around the world
End to robbery of the black community	Abolish capitalism
Freedom for black prisoners; new trials by peers	Freedom for all prisoners; decentralized revolutionary tribunals
15 mentions of "man" in 10 points	Replace "men" with "people"; encourage alternatives to nuclear family; support for women's and gay liberation
40 acres and 2 mules	International reparations
Education teaching the "true nature of this decadent American society"; student power	Community control of education; proportional representation; national referenda

The original plan was to have two RPCCs, the first to draft the new constitution followed by its subsequent ratification. After Philadelphia, groups worked feverishly to build a second convention scheduled for November 27–28 in Washington, DC. On November 18, Newton gave a speech at Boston College and encouraged people to attend. He announced its theme as "Survival Through Service to the People" and promised to present "our total survival program."[122] In this pathbreaking speech, he reformulated the Panthers' goal as "revolutionary intercommunalism." Rather than seizing national power, he maintained revolutionary forces should instead build up self-governing regional structures that could link together along horizontal lines. In his view, the global village created by the communications revolution as well as the international reach of U.S. imperialism had created the preconditions for revolutionary intercommunalism.[123] According to Newton, capitalism long ago made nations obsolete and treated people everywhere as similar objects for exploitation:

> We see very little difference in what happens to a community here in
> North America and what happens to a community in Vietnam. We
> see very little difference in what happens, even culturally, to a Chinese

> community in San Francisco and a Chinese community in Hong Kong. We see very little difference in what happens to the Black community in Harlem and a Black community in South Africa, a Black community in Angola and one in Mozambique. . . . What has actually happened, is that the non-state has been accomplished, but it is reactionary.[124]

Although the September convention had roared its approval of the program as a whole and thousands of people made their way to Washington, the gathering there never happened. Despite two months of effort, meeting space could not be secured. The FBI and local police agencies had pressured venues such as the University of Maryland and local armories not to allow Panthers to rent their spaces. Howard University insisted upon a $10,000 deposit, a sum the Panthers could not or would not pay. The CIA expected twenty thousand to twenty-five thousand people to attend—double the number in Philadelphia—and predicted even more whites because of sympathy among the "hippie community." When thousands of people arrived, there were simply no facilities available for them. A smattering of events transpired, including an outdoor concert by the Panthers' R&B band, The Lumpen. Newton finally spoke on November 29 to six hundred people inside a packed church, while two thousand more listened through speakers outside, and he promised to reconvene the convention in the near future.[125]

The Panthers Split

In the next eighty-nine days, Newton had an unexpected change of heart and made a snap decision that building a "popular front" to write a new constitution was a mistake.[126] He changed the Party's orientation "back to the black community" and endorsed electoral politics as the defining tactic of the Panthers. He later disclaimed any responsibility for the "crazy Constitutional Convention" and portrayed it as part of Eldridge Cleaver's misdirection of the Party, even though the 1966 Panther program he had written with Bobby Seale pointed precisely toward such a convention. While Newton could not understand it, Cleaver's implementation of the Panther program was part of his desire to follow the leadership of Newton—not, as Huey subsequently maintained, an attempt to overthrow him. Cleaver insisted the RPCC was "actually implementation of Point 10 of the Black Panther Party platform and program."[127] David Hilliard relates that Huey thought his original vision ran completely counter to "Eldridge's plan to create a national popular front with this crazy Constitutional Convention."[128] At the time of both conventions, Cleaver was in Algeria, where he opened the International Section of the Party on September 13, only days after the first RPCC. For a time, the Panthers were afforded official recognition by the Algerian government, and in June 1970 they were given the previous embassy of Vietnam's NLF as their own. They made contact with the governments of Vietnam, North Korea, and China, as well as liberation movements in Africa, Palestine, and around the world.

Huey's erratic behavior precipitated a bitter and bloody internal feud that tore apart the Black Panther Party. Like a mad genius artist who destroys his canvasses, he ripped up the Party in fits of anger. During a televised international phone conversation with Cleaver on February 26, 1971—only eighty-nine days after promising to reconvene the convention—he ridiculed and expelled Eldridge. No one knew it at the time, but with that phone call, the movement's high point passed. In Philadelphia, the popular impetus represented millions of people, but when the split in the BPP turned into internecine war, public revolutionary engagement quickly collapsed.

Eldridge Cleaver and his wife Kathleen in exile in Algiers, 1970. Gordon Parks.

Dynamic tensions among various tendencies contained within the BPP proved unmanageable within their organizational form. Inside one vanguard party were many conflicting directions: formation of armed groups or consolidation of a legal political party; autonomy for African Americans or leadership of an emergent rainbow; plebiscite on a black nation or an International Bill of Rights. As long as the Party was tied to a vibrant popular movement, its various tendencies were able to coexist even though the FBI continually sent false letters to Panthers and employed other "dirty tricks" to exacerbate divisions between Huey and Eldridge. The Los Angeles bureau wrote a memo recommending that "each division which had individuals attend [the RPCC] write numerous letters to Cleaver criticizing Newton for his lack of leadership . . . [in order to] create dissension that later could be more fully exploited."[129]

Rather than continue to build the strident multicultural insurgency, Newton unilaterally undermined and blunted it. Without bothering to convene a central committee meeting, he expelled key activists and forbade members from communicating with them. Insisting the Party go "back to the black community," he confined the Party's public actions to maintenance of Oakland's survival programs and electoral politics. He closed down all chapters of the BPP and concentrated cadre in Oakland where he could personally supervise them. He claimed ownership of the Party, copyrighted the newspaper, and even beat up Bobby Seale to assert his autocratic control. He named himself Supreme Commander and became chief enforcer of party discipline, using a bullwhip to discipline members. In a manner reminiscent of how Stalin had treated Trotsky, every form of political deviation from Huey's new line was blamed on Cleaver. With these revisions underway, Newton secretly tried to control Oakland's drug trade and fell into drug addiction. He pistol-whipped his tailor and brutalized a young woman who called him "baby." With the Party split, the system destroyed the most radical advocates of revolution (George Jackson, the Attica inmates, the Black Liberation Army) while reforming itself in order to prevent further popular mobilization. Attacked by his Party and feeling that exile was a "form of living death," Cleaver saw the revolutionary upsurge receding.[130] After a profound religious experience, he became a Christian and made his way home to the U.S.

As the movement disintegrated, the Philadelphia constitution was apparently tossed into the dustbin of history—or was it? The popular movement's vision continues to animate action. In the decades since the RPCC, millions of people have acted to implement various portions of the Philadelphia constitution. The day after the August 26, 1970, Women's General Strike, a lobbying campaign for an Equal Rights Amendment began on Capitol Hill. For years, advocates work tirelessly for it, garnering support of Congress in 1972 but falling three states short of the thirty-eight needed by 1982. Despite opinion polls showing that more than two-thirds of the country favored it, the ERA never became law. In the 1980s, the disarmament movement sought a ban on the manufacture and use of genocidal weapons. Despite massive popularity, it too never became legally binding.

The most impressive actions in response to Philadelphia's RPCC were undertaken by the prisoners' movement that swept the United States in the months after the Philadelphia convention. From California to New York, imprisoned Americans like no other constituency were activated by the movement's call for justice. As inmates demanded decent, humane treatment, a wave of rebellions swept through the nation's prisons, reaching its high point at Attica State Prison in New York and San Quentin in California. By the end of September 1971, more than fifty persons had been killed in the bloody suppression of the wave of prison rebellions that rocked the nation. The majority of those killed were at Attica, where forty-two people died after Governor Nelson Rockefeller refused to negotiate with the inmate committee coordinating the revolt.

Many years later, RPCC ideas stimulated social movements, and they will undoubtedly do so again in the future. If just two RPCC provisions were enacted—proportional representation and a provision for national referenda— the current political structure would be far more representative of people's needs and desires. How can we call the U.S. a "democracy" after the 2016 elections when the system offered people an abysmal choice between two singularly unpopular, self-serving candidates? Real democracy demands the kinds of decentralized, self-managed forms of governance advocated by the RPCC.

If not for the split in the Party and the disintegration of the movement, where might the hegemonic bloc led by the Panthers have taken us? Barely out of its infancy, the revolutionary movement of 1970 was immature—unprepared to provide long-term responsible leadership capable of leading the whole society forward. Unable to reach the second stage of struggle—consolidation of the revolutionary impetus—it split into thousands of pieces. It would be an enormous mistake simply to blame Huey Newton for the movement's failure to sustain its revolutionary momentum. Indeed, he was a key contributor to the unfolding revolutionary process, but subjective and objective forces of revolution were simply not historically aligned in 1970.

To this day, the RPCC remains unexplored, a unique event that sparkles with insight from the hearts and minds of thousands of participants who represented millions more. At the beginning of the twenty-first century, the phenomenal pace of change accelerates, and shifting group identities, changing affiliations, atomization, and detachment characterize our daily lives. Fragmentation of subjectivity makes it problematic today for any group to provide universal vision. The RPCC was simultaneously the last of the great public gatherings of modernity and the first gathering of our multicultural future. In so being, it was the hinge around which this entire historical period turned.

Workers and the Crisis

If there is any chance of revolution, workers must be key participants. In 1970, however, the working class was far from leading insurgency against the system. No contingents of union members or workers marched as a group into the RPCC. Many workers and union leaders opposed racism and the war, but by and large, the radical movement seemed to be worlds apart from the American working class in 1970. At best, the working class tailed behind others.

Influenced by civil rights, antiwar, and women's liberation movements, rank-and-file rebellions were at an all-time high. Business unions were unable to meet workers' needs, so the number of wildcat strikes rose dramatically. In 1972, more than one thousand miners' strikes were counted, 90 percent wildcats.[131] During a strike in Lordstown, Ohio, a union leader referred to the striking youth as the "Woodstock of the working man." A spokesperson for the Fraternal Association of Steel Haulers suggested his members were the "Black Panthers of the Working Class."[132] After truck drivers surrounded the capital, Studs Terkel referred to them as a "new New Left."[133] These examples portray how much the radical movement helped to change the working class, whose leadership had yet to congeal in the forefront of insurgencies.

Like their college counterparts with whom they shared countercultural values, young people entering the workforce in the 1960s and 1970s spoke up and refused to let grievances be ignored.[134] More often than not, the older generation of established union leaders marched in lockstep with the president. If there was one sector of American society besides the Pentagon that stood behind Nixon throughout the uprisings of May, it was the top leadership of the AFL-CIO.

Clearly, the country was divided on fundamental issues. After the killings at Kent State, a Gallup poll found that 58 percent of the country blamed students for the violence, while only 11 percent faulted the National Guard. While self-conscious revolutionaries may have desired fundamental change, subjective revolutionary conditions did not exist among a majority in 1970.

As inflation picked up speed with the rising costs of the Vietnam War, workers intensified wage struggles. During 1970, some 5,716 walkouts by more than three million workers cost businesses 66 million lost workdays.[135] These strikes involved hundreds of thousands of railroad workers, autoworkers, truckers, postal workers, and electrical workers, as well as tens of thousands of construction workers, rubber workers, airline workers, and taxi drivers. Strike outcomes were not robust. Wage increases barely kept apace with inflation, but as workers drew lessons from these struggles, wildcat strikes outside the control of unions became increasingly common. Strikes were not necessarily progressive. UPS drivers demanded that they be allowed to wear American flag badges on their uniforms.[136]

At the same time as the students went on strike against war and racism, workers' strikes were for higher wages and better working conditions. On May 13, the Federal Mediation and Conciliation Services reported it was mediating 391 strikes, including 166 in the construction industry. In March, the first major walkout of postal workers had occurred over the heads of their union leaders. In defiance of public employee antistrike laws, union orders, and federal injunctions, the wildcat postal strike spread to more than two hundred cities and towns, involving two hundred thousand workers. To deliver the mail, Nixon mobilized thirty thousand National Guard troops to break the strike. Many fraternized with picketing workers, and some deliberately sabotaged mail in solidarity with the strike.[137] In the same month, special legislation from Congress averted a national railroad strike. On April 29, despite a law prohibiting public employees from striking, teachers in Boston went on strike, joining their colleagues in Los Angeles, Newark, Atlanta, Muskogee (Oklahoma), and Baldwin (Pennsylvania) in demanding higher pay and smaller classrooms.[138] In Honolulu, a strike of blue-collar workers was joined by thousands of their white-collar associates and drastically curtailed all public services for almost three days.

In seven states during April and May, dissident Teamsters protesting a tentative national contract negotiated by their leaders set off wildcat walkouts and other disruptions. At one point, the disruptions affected an estimated five hundred thousand workers who were on strike or idled by cutoffs of truck service.[139] Tensions ran highest in Ohio, where over four thousand National Guardsmen were called up under a state of emergency after two-thirds of the state's eighty-eight counties had reported incidents of violence. In Cleveland alone, there was a month-long blockade of city streets and $67 million worth of damages.[140] In St. Louis, trucks and police cars were bombarded with rocks and bricks on May 3 when three hundred strikers tried to prevent a truck convoy from leaving a freight terminal. There were injuries and arrests followed by firebombings and shootings. Gunfire was reported in Illinois, Michigan, California, and Pennsylvania.

The original authorization to call up the National Guard in Ohio had not come because of the disturbances at Kent State but because of the Teamsters' strike. Two regiments, the 107th Armored Cavalry and the 145th Infantry, were on active duty in Akron as early as April 29. It was not until *the day after* the shooting at Kent State on May 4 that the April 29 authorization to call up the National Guard was amended to include the city of Kent.[141]

The epidemic proportion of rank-and-file contract rejections, dramatized best by the April Teamsters revolt against their union leadership, had prompted a panel consisting of the construction industry, the top building trades unionists, and Secretary of Labor George Shultz (before his promotion to the White

House staff) to propose that the right to vote on contracts be taken away from the rank and file in the construction industry.[142] In June 1970, in a decision that astonished many people, the U.S. Supreme Court ruled that employees could be forced back to work if their union agreements contained a no-strike pledge and an arbitration clause.

It was a vicious circle: hardhats were losing work because of the economic problems caused by the war; students who opposed the war might have helped to remedy the situation of these workers but were attacked by them. Furthermore, more than twelve thousand unskilled construction workers (mainly blacks) had shut down all construction in Philadelphia, laying off more than three thousand skilled workers, in a strike for equal pay for skilled and unskilled labor alike. Construction jobs were notoriously reserved almost exclusively for whites, but racism of both the construction industry and unions was under attack in Seattle, Pittsburgh, Buffalo, Boston, and Washington, DC.[143]

Divisions among people made it all the easier for Nixon to maintain order through skillful manipulation. From a prearranged meeting at the White House where he was presented with an honorary hardhat to creation of an all-black police riot squad in Washington, DC, for use against mainly white antiwar protesters, Nixon employed the age-old tactic of divide and conquer in a polarized and racially divided country. The militancy of the Teamsters Union was especially a double-edged sword. In late July, Cesar Chavez and the UFW marched against attempts by the Teamsters to unionize in the Salinas Valley, where the UFW had waged a five-year battle against growers. Teamsters were obviously trying to undercut the UFW base of support. On more than one occasion when disputes broke out, Teamsters beat nonviolent farmworkers. Teachers' strikes also raised racial issues since their demands often collided with perceived needs of the black communities where their schools were located.

Contrary to what was often reported by mass media, students and workers were not at war. As early as November 1969, a strike by workers at General Electric received support at many universities, including Boston University, MIT, the University of Wisconsin at Madison, and the University of Illinois (where the National Guard had to be called out to control students). On May 21, 1970, the day after hardhats in New York City, Buffalo, and St. Louis attacked peaceniks, their coworkers marched through New York City as part of a forty-thousand-strong labor-student antiwar rally, where representatives of twenty-eight unions and seventeen campuses came together in solidarity with those murdered at Kent State, Jackson State, and Augusta. They condemned George Meany and thirty top union leaders who, by a twenty-seven to three vote, had said that Nixon should not be influenced by the antiwar movement. At the end of the rally, nine people were injured when police unexpectedly rode horses into the crowd.[144]

The relationship between striking students and workers on the West Coast was even better. After the invasion of Cambodia, every AFL-CIO county central labor council in the vicinity of San Francisco, representing some four hundred thousand workers, called upon Congress to censure Nixon "for his deception, dishonesty, and violation of our Constitution," to repeal the Gulf of Tonkin resolution, and to cut off funds for combat operations in Indochina by the end of the year.[145] A full-page ad in San Francisco's two daily papers on May 18, signed by 463 trade union leaders (including fifty-three from the building and metal crafts), concluded: "We want a cease-fire NOW! We want out of Cambodia NOW! We want out of Vietnam NOW! We've had it!" One hundred union officers in Ohio signed a similar ad.

In San Jose, California, a standing committee for cooperation between students and the Santa Clara County Central Labor Council already existed. In 1969, a significant alliance between striking workers at Standard Oil in Richmond, California, and striking students and teachers at San Francisco State College emerged. Both struggles had been long and difficult, and police were particularly brutal in their bloody suppression at San Francisco State. At a joint press conference announcing an alliance, Jake Jacobs, secretary-treasurer of Local 1-561 of the Oil, Chemical and Atomic Workers said, "It is not just police brutality that united us. We are all exploited, Black workers more than whites, but we all have the same enemy, the big corporations. And it is corporations like our enemy, Standard Oil, that control the Boards of Trustees of the state colleges the students are fighting."[146]

After the invasion of Cambodia, several union conferences supported the antiwar movement. On May 8, representatives of five thousand faculty from twenty-three California campuses met in San Diego and formed the United Professors of California. After three days of debate on how their union should relate to public stands on political issues, the delegates overwhelmingly voted to "condemn Nixon's escalation" and called for the remainder of the academic year to be devoted to bringing the war to an end.[147] A day earlier, in Denver, a convention of the American Federation of State, County, and Municipal Employees (AFSCME) unanimously passed a resolution calling for immediate withdrawal from Indochina "consistent with the safety of U.S. troops." Union representatives of the Teamsters, United Auto Workers of California, and the AFL-CIO Amalgamated Clothing Workers signed resolutions calling for "Peace Now." On May 11, some eight hundred of four thousand university employees at MIT voted to strike for the three demands of the students, joining workers at Berkeley, Harvard, Columbia, and other universities who followed students' lead.

At a conference in late June, over one thousand trade unionists representing 4.5 million workers called for immediate U.S. withdrawal from Indochina and formed Labor for Peace, an organization dedicated to "inform, educate and arouse the membership to act to end the war now." Will Pary, a district secretary-treasurer of the Western Association of Pulp and Paper Workers said, "Unemployment, inflation, war, racism, repression and worthless labor leaders leave the laboring man in desperate straits. . . . Nixon is the worst anti-labor President we've had."[148]

According to Jeremy Brecher, the student strike of May 1970 helped to create a "sea change in the attitudes of American workers."[149] In the fall of 1970, as college classes resumed, some four hundred thousand auto workers at General Motors walked off their jobs—the first confrontation of the United Auto Workers with General Motors since 1946.[150] Autonomous union formations sprang up and took direct action. New York City telephone operators were predominantly African American or Puerto Rican, and the large majority were women. On December 21, 1970, the first issue of *Strike Back!* contained the program of the Bell Workers Action Committee. Composed of members from around New York City, the group called for "a real union" to represent them. Similar groups emerged in Los Angeles and San Francisco.

During the student strike, truck drivers in Los Angeles met with campus radicals from UCLA to get support for the national teamsters strike.[151] From these initial contacts, Teamsters for a Democratic Union emerged, holding its founding convention at Kent State University on September 18, 1976, with more than one hundred teamsters from forty-four locals in fifteen states in attendance.[152] Miners for Democracy was another major autonomous formation. Joseph Yablonski, leader of an oppositional tendency within the union, was gunned down in 1969, and an uncorrupted miner was elected president in 1972. At the very next national convention, union members rewrote the constitution to increase district autonomy and locals' allocation of dues.

After the student strike, unrest spread to thousands of factories in the United States, as workers developed "informal underground unions" to counter the deterioration in the quality of their daily job lives.[153] A 1973 report of a special task force to the Secretary of Health, Education, and Welfare entitled *Work in America* put it this way: "absenteeism, wildcat strikes, turnover, and industrial sabotage [have] become an increasingly significant part of the costs of doing business." In the words of Peter J. Pestillo, Ford's vice president for labor relations: "We can't run our plants with guerrilla warfare and that's what we've had. We are moving from a law-driven to a personnel-driven situation."[154]

Even though many trade unionists supported the striking students and the idea of a general strike of workers and students repeatedly surfaced in May, polarization of American society made the actualization of a general strike a project for the future.

Restoration of Order

> The people of this nation are eager to get on with the quest for new great-
> ness. . . . It is for us here to open the doors that will set free again the real
> greatness of this nation—the genius of the American people . . . a "New
> American Revolution" . . . a revolution as profound, as far-reaching, as
> exciting as that first revolution almost 200 years ago.
> —*Richard Nixon*, State of the Union Address, January 22, 1971

When the president of the United States echoed the New Left by calling for "Power to the People" and waving the peace sign, it appeared to be nothing more than another example of Orwellian double-talk from a government that claimed to be fighting for "freedom" in Indochina while committing genocide against its people, that "urbanized" Vietnam through saturation bombings of the countryside, and that promised "peace" at the same time as it escalated wars at home and abroad. Few people appreciated Nixon's rhetoric as a signal for the intensification of the war against Vietnam through massive air attacks that would target major population centers. After all, the Senate had voted 81–10 to rescind the Gulf of Tonkin resolution, and Nixon continually promised to end the war.

In the fall of 1970, a host of articles announced "death of the student movement," but tens of thousands of people took to the streets of New York, Washington, DC, and more than a dozen other cities in October to protest Nixon's new escalation of the war. A majority of the country was now opposed to the war, and with each new escalation—the invasion of Laos, the mining of Haiphong Harbor, and the Christmas bombing of Hanoi—the antiwar movement organized massive and militant responses. On May 1, 1971, nearly fifty thousand regionally organized people attempted to disrupt morning traffic in Washington, DC. Their mobilizing call, "If the government doesn't stop the war, we'll stop the government," was direct enough, but illegal arrests conducted by the Department of Justice—more that fifteen thousand in three days—prevented the movement from accomplishing its tactical objective.[155]

Protests following the mining of Haiphong in the spring of 1972 were estimated to have had nearly as many participants as the more than four million strikers in 1970. Students at Kent State were again in the forefront of protests, but this time off-campus at Wright-Patterson Air Force Base, where 152 people were arrested for blocking traffic. There were large demonstrations on a few days' notice in New York (fifty thousand people), San Francisco (thirty-five thousand), and Los Angeles (thirty thousand). At the same time, street fighting broke out at ROTC centers and war-related targets in Berkeley, Madison, Ann Arbor, and Cambridge. Students from the University of Maryland spent three

WANTED BY THE FBI

INTERSTATE FLIGHT - MURDER, KIDNAPING
ANGELA YVONNE DAVIS

FBI No. 867,615 G

Photograph taken 1969   Photograph taken 1970

Alias: "Tamu"

DESCRIPTION

Age:	26, born January 26, 1944, Birmingham, Alabama		
Height:	5'8"	Eyes:	Brown
Weight:	145 pounds	Complexion:	Light brown
Build:	Slender	Race:	Negro
Hair:	Black	Nationality:	American
Occupation:	Teacher		
Scars and Marks:	Small scars on both knees		

Fingerprint Classification: 4 M 5 Ua 6

Angela Davis was arrested in 1970 and acquitted in 1972.

nights blockading Route 1 in running battles with the National Guard. When General William Westmoreland appeared on a base podium in El Paso, Texas, he was pelted with tomatoes by active-duty GIs.[156]

If the 1968 Tet offensive had demonstrated that the United States would never be able to achieve a military victory on the battlefields of Vietnam, the revolutionary upsurge of 1970 blocked U.S. plans to continue the war indefinitely. On May 15, 1970—in the midst of the student strike—McGeorge Bundy, formerly a top military advisor to Lyndon Johnson and president of the Ford Foundation, warned that another escalation of the war "would tear the country and the administration to pieces."[157] In early August 1970, another man near the center of corporate power, Clark Clifford, said that a reescalation of the war "would be traumatic for this country and cause a crisis far worse than the one following the invasion of Cambodia."[158]

In September 1971, the Carnegie Commission published an apprehensive report on campus unrest. In a foreboding section, "It Can Happen Again," there was an acknowledgment that, although a psychic Thermidor (or self-defeating attitude) had set in among activists, a new escalation of the war would have tragic consequences:

> To say that the campuses have been relatively quiet since May 1970 is not to say that they have been pacified . . . Opposition to the war and current national policies run deeper than ever. The signal for any new large-scale confrontation is not likely to come from the campuses or the counter-culture. The student and intellectual communities are now too pessimistic about any movement they would launch having any impact. . . . The spark for the conflagration, if there is to be one, will most likely be a deliberate governmental policy decision—to invade North Vietnam, or to use tactical nuclear weapons.[159]

Addicted to power, Nixon escalated illegal domestic surveillance programs and repressive measures. He sent his team of "plumbers" to steal Democratic Party documents in Watergate, and boldly erased tape recordings of the Oval Office that Congress subpoenaed. As the Nixon administration became increasingly isolated, in a desperate attempt to regain control of the situation, the man who entered office in 1968 promising "never to invade Vietnam or any country in the area" reversed himself yet again and contradicted his lifelong promises to deal resolutely with the "Red Chinese." Given the new mood in the country, Nixon's trip to Beijing boosted his image and carried him through the 1972 elections with one of the largest landslides in American history.

In 1960, it would have been ludicrous to suggest that this politician, whose reputation had been built upon the crudest anticommunism—the heir apparent to Joe McCarthy—would be the one to open relations with the People's Republic of China. Indeed, the attempt to blockade the Chinese Revolution was understood as the principle reason for both the Korean and Vietnam Wars, in which millions of Asians and tens of thousands of Americans perished.[160] Yet this is precisely the stratagem advised by Henry Kissinger to salvage Nixon's presidency.

Despite revelations of secret bombings in Cambodia and Laos from the earliest days of the Nixon administration and the arrest of the Watergate burglars prior to the 1972 election, only when Nixon himself was implicated in the attempted cover-up of White House connections to the Watergate burglary was he forced to abandon the ship of state. Even after he escalated killings with invasions of Cambodia and Laos as well as B-52 saturation bombings of Hanoi, no accusations of impropriety were heard in the halls of Congress. So long as his administration had quietly supervised brutal repression of the black liberation movement and illegal bugging and repression of the antiwar movement, Congress had not considered his leadership of the imperial camp to be improper. Only when he directed the least violent of these same methods against members of the Establishment with the Watergate fiasco had he gone too far. In the skeptical view of Noam Chomsky, the Watergate scandal was "analogous to the discovery that the directors of Murder Inc. were also cheating on their income tax. Reprehensible, to be sure, but hardly the main point."[161]

Although Watergate succeeded in changing the faces of some of the men holding the highest positions of power in the federal government, the American political system remained essentially unchanged. Indeed, it was reinvigorated and strengthened by what did not kill it. Henry Kissinger, one of the great mass murderers of history, was promoted to secretary of state and went on to become a celebrity of the first order. After the Vietnam War ended and the U.S. got its POWs back, not one cent of promised billions of dollars in reparation was paid. An example had to be made of Vietnam for other countries to learn the high costs of opposing the United States.

Using his insights from the historical record, Kissinger helped turn the thrust of the crisis of 1970 into a victory for transnational corporations based in Europe, Japan, and the United States. By 1976, these forces had not only helped to dislodge a president guilty of "ungentlemanly" conduct of office, but they could stage elections where the choice between Gerald Ford and Jimmy Carter was nothing more than a fraternal contest between Nelson and David Rockefeller.[162] The winner turned out to be the one with the least "negative charisma," as the ghost of Watergate lurked on the shoulder of Nixon's hand-picked successor. The loser was American democracy: the federal government had been "saved" by the Rockefellers only to survive as an instrument of their benign rule. In 1970, David Rockefeller called for a new revolutionary change, but few understood that he meant undoing Keynesian reforms. In retrospect, we can see the "New American Revolution" as meaning bloody imposition of neoliberal regimes in Chile in 1973, Thailand and Argentina in 1976, South Korea and Turkey in 1980 and then to the rest of the Empire.[163]

Under neoliberal rules, the United States increasingly resembles countries whose energies and resources are controlled by outside interests. The distribution of wealth and income in the United States today is more in the tradition of the underdeveloped world than in that of an affluent society. Moreover, other characteristics of poor countries have appeared in the United States since 1970: the growing strata of homeless people; transformation of inner cities into playgrounds for the rich and displays of corporate wealth; increasing irrelevance of domestic democracy. As real wages continue to shrink, we are all compelled to work longer hours for more years for less money. The threat of joining the wretched of the earth frightens people into accepting the rewards offered in wealthy countries. We all know that daily thousands perish from starvation and disease.[164]

One of the immediate effects of the Vietnam War was the breakdown of the U.S. Armed Forces among the rank and file. Over the longer term, its command structure was strengthened. Vietnam provided the top command of the Pentagon with a training ground from which they drew lessons and made adjustments in future endeavors to control distant lands and peoples. In 1968, General Westmoreland was removed as chief of combined operations in Vietnam, but he became the U.S. Armed Forces chief of staff and was entrusted with the command of all counterinsurgency operations in Latin America. Ronald Reagan was governor of California during the student strike. The man who advocated "paving over Vietnam" and who reacted to the New Left by declaring, "If they want a bloodbath, let's get it over with," went on to become the commander in chief. A decade before his election, Reagan had already performed in a dress rehearsal for his ascension to power. On February 10, 1969, he played the war-game role of the newly installed chief of state after a military takeover of the United States.[165] After he had rehearsed "saving democracy," all that was left was for him to be "democratically" elected. The Pentagon could not have put anyone more to their liking in the White House.

Legislation was enacted before campuses reopened in the fall of 1970 aimed at repressing campus demonstrators. Over thirty states enacted a total of eighty laws dealing with campus unrest.[166] But of course, the main change in higher education has been its escalating costs—in large part to pay for top-heavy administrations. Students who graduate today do so with an enormous debt burden, a modern form of indentured servitude. The 1% also made sober appraisal of the possibility of less, not more, democracy. As Samuel Huntington put it in his report to the Trilateral Commission: "Some of the problems of governance in the United States today stem from an excess of democracy. . . . We have come to recognize that there are potentially desirable limits to economic growth. There are also potentially desirable limits to the indefinite extension of political democracy."[167] Huntington labeled insurgent social movements as caused by "democratic distemper."[168]

The revolutionary crisis unwittingly strengthened the stranglehold of the rich on American institutions and the system's capacity for domestic violence. Since 1970, local police departments have been armed with tanks, helicopters, and even submarines through federal funding. Specially trained "intelligence" officers and SWAT teams now routinely work within local police forces. Long before the Patriot Act, the FBI reconsolidated itself in the wake of congressional investigations and public concerns caused by its illegal operations, giving itself greater capacity to function in infiltrating and disrupting domestic movements.

Despite its apparent failure, the New Left's decisive break with the Establishment leaves a significant legacy. The U.S. federal government remains unable to regain the kind of popular legitimacy it enjoyed before 1968. The defeat of the United States in Vietnam ushered in an era of successful national liberation movements in Africa and Latin America. The "Vietnam syndrome" temporarily restrained the U.S. military. The draft was ended, two presidents (Johnson and Nixon) were compelled to leave office prematurely, and the vote for eighteen-year-olds was enacted. The movement's political and cultural values quickly became common sense, and millions of people experienced improvements in the daily conditions of their lives. Americans of African descent—and Africans living under apartheid in South Africa—as well as women and gay people all won new life opportunities and enhanced pride in themselves. Changes in norms, laws, and values regarding relationships between men and women came into being (from legalized abortion and widespread birth control to open homosexuality). A new antiracist global culture has permeated even the world of soccer.

Even when it is possible for some people to carve out free spaces, racism and patriarchy continue to shape the overall conditions of our lives. The old Jim Crow system of segregation was largely dismantled by the civil rights movement, but new forms of disenfranchising minorities and more contemporary institutions for racial oppression have been developed. To name just one domain, the number of people in jail or prison has grown from two hundred thousand in the 1960s to more than two million people today, and from majority white to 70 percent people of color.[169] An additional 4.75 million people are on parole or probation. With the Trump presidency, rule by the white 1% is flagrantly obvious. But under Obama as well, the system's prisons were filled to overflowing, financial plunders by a few accompanied continuing starvation for millions, and bloody wars continued unabated. The system, not simply its leaders, is the problem.

For the time being, control mechanisms in the United States are contained in economic disciplining of the poor and working class, vast student debt, a declining standard of living, and continual economic insecurity for millions of people. If such control mechanisms prove insufficient in the years ahead, behind them stands a vast repressive apparatus. The strengthening of the structures of domination—not their weakening—remains an undeniable and unintended effect of the crisis of 1970.

While the revolutionary movement of 1970 may have been dispersed, its legacy lives in a pattern of subsequent global insurgencies.

Notes

1.   Col. Robert D. Heinel, "The Collapse of the Armed Forces," in House of Representatives Committee on Internal Security, *Investigation of Attempts to Subvert the Armed Forces* (Washington, DC: U.S. Government Printing Office, 1972).

2.   "Guerrillas in the Military," *Scanlan's* 1, no. 8 (January 1971): 57.

3.   Monika Jensen-Stevenson, *Spite House: The Last Secret of the War in Vietnam* (New York: Norton, 1997) related that U.S. hunter-killer teams had standing orders to kill certain deserters on sight. Even after the Paris Peace Accord was signed in 1973, at least one Marine claimed the CIA paid $12,000 to $25,000 per kill of renegade Americans. U.S. agencies denied any such program.

4.   Lacey Fosburgh, "Thousands of Homosexuals Hold a Protest Rally in Central Park," *New York Times*, June 29, 1970, 1.

5.   Sharon Howell, "Metaphorical Analysis of the Evolution of the Female Identity, 1961–1982" (PhD diss., Wayne State University, 1983).

6.   Kirkpatrick Sale, *SDS* (New York: Vintage Books, 1974), 637. Reserve Officers' Training Corps, or ROTC, provided military experience for students to go directly into the armed services as officers.

7.   *U.S. News & World Report* 68, no. 21 (May 25, 1970): 20.

8.   The killings began at Kent State in a tragedy caused by Company C of the 145th Infantry National Guard. See Thomas M. Grace, *Kent State: Death and Dissent in the Long 60s* (Amherst: University of Massachusetts Press, 2016).

9.   *Guardian*, May 30, 1970.

10. *U.S. News & World Report* 68, no. 22 (June 1, 1970).

11. Joseph A. Califano, Jr., *The Student Revolution: A Global Confrontation* (New York: W.W. Norton and Company, 1970), 88.

12. Daniel Yankelovich, *The Changing Values on Campus* (New York: Simon and Schuster, 1972). Also see Califano, *The Student Revolution*, 64.

13. *New York Times*, January 2, 1971.

14. Seymour Martin Lipset, *Rebellion in the University* (Chicago: University of Chicago Press, 1976), 58.

15. "The Guard vs. Disorder," *National Guardsman* 24 (June 1970): 2.

16. *New York Post*, May 19, 1970.

17. *Counterspy* 2, no. 4 (Winter 1976); Geoffrey Rips, *Unamerican Activities* (San Francisco: City Lights, 1981).

18. Scranton Commission, *The Report of the President's Commission on Campus Unrest* (Washington, DC: U.S. Government Printing Office, 1970), 169–70; R. Jacob Hedden, "The Rise of SWAT Part 3 of 3: SWAT vs. the Black Panther Party," Law Office of Vijay R. Sharma, December 19, 2012, http://www.vrslegal.com/the-rise-of-swat-part-3-of-3-swat-vs-the-Black-panther-party/.

19. Between January 1969 and April 1970, some 2,800 bombings, arson, and other assaults on institutions took place in the United States. Jeremy Varon, *Bringing the War Home: The Weather Underground, the Red Army Faction, and Revolutionary Violence in the 60s and 70s* (Berkeley: University of California Press, 2004), 3.

20. Paul M. Sweezy and Harry Magdoff, "War and Crisis," *Monthly Review* 22, no. 2 (June 1970): 1–12.

21. See Herbert Marcuse, *Counterrevolution and Revolt* (Boston: Beacon Press, 1972).

22. *Christian Science Monitor*, May 9, 1970, 2.

23.   *New York Times*, May 7, 1970, 20.
24.   *New York Times*, May 7, 1970, 19; Urban Research Corporation, *On Strike... Shut It Down: A Report of the First National Student Strike in U.S. History* (Chicago: Urban Research Corporation, 1970), 1.
25.   Garth Buchanan and Joan Bracken, *Summary Results of the Survey for the President's Commission on Campus Unrest* (Washington, DC: Urban Institute, September 1970), 9–10.
26.   *Daily Californian*, May 8, 1970.
27.   John Taft, *Mayday at Vale: A Case Study in Student Radicalism* (Boulder: Westview Press, 1976), 87.
28.   Scranton Commission, *The Report of the President's Commission on Campus Unrest*, 17.
29.   Richard E. Peterson and John A. Bilorusky, *May 1970: The Campus Aftermath of Cambodia and Kent State* (Berkeley: Carnegie Commission on Higher Education, 1971), 127.
30.   Dave Dellinger, *More Power Than We Know: The People's Movement Toward Democracy* (New York: Anchor Press, 1975), 136; Sale, *SDS*, 637; Varon, *Bringing the War Home*, 131. On October 15, 1969, more than two million people had participated in antiwar demonstrations organized by the Vietnam Moratorium Committee. A month later, the New Mobilization gathered more than half a million protesters in Washington, DC, and several hundred thousand in San Francisco. The hastily convened demonstration on May 9, 1970, drew on these displays of the country's antiwar majority.
31.   A year later, during the first week of May 1971, the frustrated needs for a militant confrontation in Washington were fulfilled in the attempt by thousands of people to close the city of Washington by sitting down in the streets during the early-morning rush hour. Nearly fifteen thousand of the fifty thousand demonstrators were arrested in three days of civil disobedience. Dellinger, *More Power Than We Know*, 137.
32.   "The Guard vs. Disorder," *National Guardsman*, 9.
33.   Tim Spofford, *Lynch Street: The May 1970 Slayings at Jackson State* (Kent, OH: Kent State University Press, 1989), 72.
34.   Cynthia Harrigan, Isabel Irizarry, Elizabeth Yates, and Jessica Kerley, "Jackson State: Ten Days Later," 2000, http://www2.kenyon.edu/Khistory/60s/webpage.htm.
35.   *Urban Crisis Monitor* 3, no. 23 (June 5, 1970): 3–4.
36.   Urban Research Corporation, *On Strike*, 50.
37.   Urban Research Corporation, 58–59.
38.   *Urban Crisis Monitor* 3, no. 13 (March 27, 1970): 44.
39.   *Urban Crisis Monitor* 3, no. 13 (March 27, 1970): 18.
40.   In Puerto Rico, failure to report and refusals to be inducted into the military reached 75 percent of those called in June 1970, as compared with 50 percent failing to report in Los Angeles and Oakland and a California average of almost 40 percent. *Repeal the Draft* 2, no. 7 (July 7, 1970): 3.
41.   *Newsweek*, June 1, 1970, 25; Peterson and Bilorusky, *May 1970*, 3.
42.   Peterson and Bilorusky, 140.
43.   Primary documents for this chapter were also found in the Hoover Institution archive at Stanford University.
44.   Peterson and Bilorusky, *May 1970*, 141–42. Here is an example of the eros effect finding its own form of solidarity, creating previously unexplored types of interaction. Richard Cambridge points out a similarity to Denise Levertov's

understanding of the birth of each poem (in the poet) through a self-organizing internal principal that finds its way to its perfect (organic) form. The spontaneous combustion that happened during the student strike sparked individuals into being whom they could become and not simply whom society/culture molded them to be. For example, shy electrical engineering students at Northeastern found themselves to be orators comfortable addressing crowds of hundreds articulating their transformative process, as well as rewiring Northeastern University's internal electrical grid to serve the needs of the strike.

45. Peterson and Bilorusky, *May 1970*, 141–42.
46. Peterson and Bilorusky, 160.
47. Urban Research Corporation, *On Strike*, 91.
48. *Daily Californian*, May 13, 1970.
49. Peterson and Bilorusky, *May 1970*, 14–16.
50. *Newsweek*, May 25, 1970, 30.
51. *Washington Star*, June 24, 1970.
52. CIA document C00018168, September 10, 1970, at http://archive.org/stream/OperationCHAOS/CHAOS#page/n1/mode/2up.
53. Urban Research Corporation, *On Strike*, 12.
54. Califano, *The Student Revolution*, 53.
55. Urban Research Corporation, *On Strike*, 37.
56. Urban Research Corporation, 75.
57. Urban Research Corporation, 34–35.
58. Urban Research Corporation, 37.
59. *Washington Post*, July 6, 1970.
60. Howard Zinn, *A People's History of the United States* (New York: Harper & Row, 1980), 490.
61. JoNina M. Abron, "'Serving the People': The Survival Programs of the Black Panther Party," in *The Black Panther Party Reconsidered*, ed. Charles Jones (Baltimore: Black Classic Press, 1998), 182.
62. Andrés Torres and José E. Velázquez, *The Puerto Rican Movement: Voices from the Diaspora* (Philadelphia: Temple University Press, 1998), 304.
63. Digger Papers, 1967, box 13, folders 5–6, New Left Collection, 1923–2004, Hoover Institution Archives, Stanford University.
64. Steve Shapiro, "Political Ecology: An Introduction," in *Incarnations* (Irvine, CA), January 15, 1970, Hoover Institution Archives.
65. Peterson and Bilorusky, *May 1970*, 162–63.
66. Scranton Commission, *The Report of the President's Commission on Campus Unrest*, 69.
67. James R. Hayes, "The Dialectics of Resistance: An Analysis of the GI Movement," *Journal of Social Issues*, November 4, 1975, 132.
68. Heinel, "The Collapse of the Armed Forces."
69. Vietnam Veterans Against the War, *History* (Champaign, IL: Vietnam Veterans Against the War National Office, 1972).
70. "Guerrillas in the Military," *Scanlan's* 1, no. 8 (January 1971): 55.
71. "Guerrillas in the Military," 58.
72. David Cortright, *Soldiers in Revolt* (Garden City, NY: Anchor Press/Doubleday, 1975), 44–45.
73. Kevin Keating, "G.I. Resistance to the Vietnam War," *Counterpunch*, October 10, 2014.

74.   Hayes, "The Dialectics of Resistance," 132.
75.   *Look*, June 16, 1970, 72.
76.   Susan Brownmiller, *In Our Time: Memoir of a Revolution* (New York: Dial Press, 1999), 97–98.
77.   Ruth Rosen, *The World Split Open: How the Modern Women's Movement Changed America* (New York: Penguin Books, 2000), 300–301.
78.   Ernesto B. Vigil, *The Crusade for Justice: Chicano Militancy and the Government's War on Dissent* (Madison: University of Wisconsin Press, 1999), 124.
79.   Torres and Velázquez, *The Puerto Rican Movement*, 218; Melendez, *We Took the Streets: Fighting for Latino Rights with the Young Lords* (New Brunswick, NJ: Rutgers University Press, 2005), 236, 238.
80.   Melendez, *We Took the Streets*, 194.
81.   Rozsika Parker and Griselda Pollock, ed., *Framing Feminism: Art and the Women's Movement 1970–1985* (London: Pandora Press, 1987).
82.   Corinne Robins, *The Pluralist Era: American Art, 1968–1981* (New York: Harper and Row, 1984), 49.
83.   Corinne Robins, "The N.Y. Art Strike," *Arts Magazine* 45, no. 1 (September–October 1970): 27–28.
84.   Robins, *The Pluralist Era*, 39.
85.   Simone de Beauvoir, "Feminism—Alive, Well, and in Constant Danger," in Robin Morgan, ed., *Sisterhood Is Global: The International Women's Movement Anthology* (Garden City, NY: Anchor Books, 1984), 230.
86.   Morgan, *Sisterhood Is Global*, 82.
87.   Various dates are given for the occupation. Pablo Guzmán places the date in April 1970, see "La Vida Pura: A Lord of the Barrio," in Andrés Torres and José E. Velázquez, *The Puerto Rican Movement: Voices from the Diaspora* (Philadelphia: Temple University Press, 1998), 165–67. Iris Morales tells us that it occurred in July and again later that year, see "¡Palante Siempre Palante!," in Torres and Velázquez, *The Puerto Rican Movement*, 216. Bryan Burrough says July and again in November, see *Days of Rage: America's Radical Underground, the FBI, and the Forgotten Age of Revolutionary Violence* (New York: Penguin Books, 2015), 449.
88.   Already in December 1969, the Brown Berets had helped to organize the first Chicano Moratorium in East Los Angeles. The effect of bringing so many people onto the streets together was immediate. On February 28, 1970, at least two thousand people marched in pouring rain in East Los Angeles for the second Chicano Antiwar Moratorium. On March 4, 1970, police killed Antonia Martínez, a student at the University of Puerto Rico, during an antiwar demonstration. A year later, another protest there resulted in 31 shooting victims and 169 arrests.
89.   Laura Pulido, *Black, Brown, Yellow, and Left: Radical Activism in Los Angeles* (Berkeley: University of California Press, 2006), 75.
90.   Vigil, *The Crusade for Justice*, 139.
91.   Carlos Muñoz, "Toward a Chicano Perspective of Political Analysis," *Aztlán* 1, no. 2 (Fall 1970): 15.
92.   Antonio Camejo, "Lessons of the Los Angeles Chicano Protest," *Militant* 3, no. 38 (October 16, 1970): 9–16.
93.   See George Mariscal, *Aztlán and Viet Nam: Chicano and Chicana Experiences of the War* (Berkeley: University of California Press, 1999); *San Diego Street Journal*, February 17, 1971.
94.   Luis Valdez and Teatro Campesino departed from the farm worker movement because Chavez distanced himself from Chicano nationalism. Chavez never

supported La Raza Unida Party but maintained direct ties to the Kennedy family and the Democratic Party. Amid a diverse flux of actions and beliefs, many radicals criticized Chavez not only for his organizational style, in which he made nearly all major decisions on his own, but also because of undercutting of militancy and his exclusive focus on the fate of legal farm workers in the U.S.

95. George Mariscal, *Brown-Eyed Children of the Sun: Lessons from the Chicano Movement, 1965–1975* (Albuquerque: University of New Mexico Press, 2005), 35.
96. The FALN alone was responsible for more than 120 bombings between 1974 and 1983.
97. Vigil, *The Crusade for Justice*, 211–13.
98. Vigil, 303.
99. Various estimates of the numbers exist, none of which claims to be definitive. David Hilliard says there were fifteen thousand: David Hilliard and Lewis Cole, *This Side of Glory: The Autobiography of David Hilliard and the Story of the Black Panther Party* (Chicago: Lawrence Hill, 1993), 313. The Panther paper used numbers ranging from twelve to fifteen thousand; *Black Panther* 5, no. 12 (September 19, 1970); *Black Panther* 5, no 18 (October 31, 1970), 7. Social scientist G. Louis Heath states that the plenary sessions on September 5 and 6 attracted five to six thousand people (of whom 25 to 40 percent were white) but doesn't count thousands more who were outside and could not get in; G. Louis Heath, ed., *Off the Pigs! The History and Literature of the Black Panther Party* (Metuchen: Scarecrow Press, 1976), 186–87. The *New York Times* declared there were six thousand people inside with another two thousand outside (about half of whom were white); "Newton, at Panther Parley, Urges Socialist System," *New York Times*, September 6, 1970, 40; Paul Delaney, "Panthers Weigh New Constitution," *New York Times*, September 7, 1970, 13. The *Washington Post*, probably parroting the *Times*, later claimed eight thousand; *Washington Post*, November 27, 1970, C10.
100. *New York Times*, September 6, 1970, 40.
101. Kit Kim Holder, "The History of the Black Panther Party, 1966–1972" (PhD diss., University of Massachusetts, 1990), 131.
102. David Hilliard and Lewis Cole, *This Side of Glory: The Autobiography of David Hilliard and the Story of the Black Panther Party* (Chicago: Lawrence Hill, 1993), 312.
103. Russell Shoatz, unpublished memoir, sent to me by the author.
104. *Black Panther* 5, no 12 (September 19, 1970): 11.
105. I develop this concept further in relation to the autonomous movement (or Autonomen) in Europe to indicate that seemingly spontaneous crowd behavior can have a great underlying intelligence. See *The Subversion of Politics: European Social Movements and the Decolonization of Everyday Life* (Oakland: AK Press, 2006).
106. Hilliard and Cole, *This Side of Glory*, 313.
107. Present at the planning meeting were representatives of welfare mothers, doctors, lawyers, journalists, students, tenant farmers, greasers from Chicago, Latin Americans, high school students, and gays, as well as concerned individuals; *Black Panther* 5, no. 8 (August 22, 1970); *Black Panther* 5, no. 9 (August 29, 1970): 11.
108. "Not to Believe in a New World after Philadelphia Is a Dereliction of the Human Spirit," *Black Panther* 5, no. 13 (September 26, 1970): 19.
109. "Not to Believe in a New World after Philadelphia Is a Dereliction of the Human Spirit," 20.
110. See point 2 of the workshop on the Family and the Rights of Children for one example.

111. "The People and the People Alone Were the Motive Power in the Making of the History of the People's Revolutionary Constitutional Convention Plenary Session!," *Black Panther* 5, no. 11 (September 12, 1970): 3.

112. Laurie Asseo, "Study Ties Drug War, Rise in Jailed Women," *Boston Globe*, November 18, 1999, A18; Chris Bangert, "Marijuana: The Hemp of the Past and the 'Drug' of the Present," unpublished paper, Brewster, MA, 1999.

113. Enforced at a cost of billions of dollars per year and tens of thousands of perpetrators of victimless crimes in jail, the present drug policy includes decades of evidence of the CIA's involvement with both the heroin trade in Afghanistan and Southeast Asia and the cocaine trade in Central America—as well as existence of a Contra-connected crack pipeline to Watts (South Central Los Angeles) first reported in the pages of the *San Jose Mercury-News*. As a result of continual generation of megaprofits based on certain drugs' illegal status (witness the price of oregano or baking soda in any supermarket), control of the drug trade by the "government within the government" is a major source of funds for covert operations hidden from public and congressional oversight. To understand these dynamics, one could begin with Leslie Cockburn, *Out of Control: The Story of the Reagan Administration's Secret War in Nicaragua, the Illegal Arms Pipeline, and the Contra Drug Connection* (New York: Atlantic Monthly Press, 1987). Also see Alfred McCoy, *The Politics of Heroin: CIA Complicity in the Global Drug Trade* (New York: Lawrence Hill, 1991).

114. For more information on these groups, see my book *The Subversion of Politics*.

115. Nikhil Pal Singh, "The Black Panther Party and the 'Undeveloped Country' of the Left," in Charles Jones, *The Black Panther Party Reconsidered*, 87. Richard Cambridge lent me the wonderful phrase preceding Singh's quotation.

116. CIA document C00018170, 5 October 1970, p. 1766/2662 at http://archive.org/stream/OperationCHAOS/CHAOS#page/n1/mode/2up.

117. See Lois Hart, "Black Panthers Call a Revolutionary People's Constitutional Convention: A White Lesbian Responds," http://outhistory.org/oldwiki/images/d/d0/V1_n5_p15-16.pdf.

118. Alice Echols, *Daring to Be Bad: Radical Feminism in America 1967–1975* (Minneapolis: University of Minnesota Press, 1989), 222.

119. Rosen, *The World Split Open*, 133.

120. Echols appears not to have seen the final reports, which are an appendix to this book.

121. For more discussion, see my article, "Organization and Movement: The Case of the Black Panther Party and Revolutionary People's Constitutional Convention," in *Liberation, Imagination, and the Black Panther Party*, eds. Kathleen Cleaver and George Katsiaficas (New York: Routledge, 1997), 141–55.

122. "Speech Delivered at Boston College: November 18, 1970," in *The Huey P. Newton Reader*, David Hilliard and Donald Weise, eds. (New York: Seven Stories Press, 2002), 161.

123. See "Intercommunalism: February 1971," in Hilliard and Weise, *The Huey P. Newton Reader*, 188. Anarchist Murray Bookchin's formulation of "libertarian municipalism" in the mid-1980s has much in common with Newton's conception of revolutionary intercommunalism.

124. Hilliard and Weise, *The Huey P. Newton Reader*, 170–71.

125. "Black Panther Party Revolutionary People's Convention: November 1970," *Washington Area Spark*, https://washingtonspark.wordpress.com/2012/11/25/black-panther-party-revolutionary-peoples-convention-november-1970/.

126. Little is known of exactly what happened to Newton in the eighty-nine days between his November 29 speech in Washington and his televised split with Cleaver on February 26, 1971. Newton expelled Geronimo Pratt in December, followed by members of the New York Panthers who objected to that unilateral action.
127. *Black Panther* 4, no. 28 (June 13, 1970): 14.
128. Hilliard and Cole, *This Side of Glory*, 308.
129. Hilliard and Cole, 317.
130. Kathleen Cleaver, ed., *Target Zero: Eldridge Cleaver, A Life in Writing* (New York: Palgrave Macmillan, 2006), 264.
131. Brenner, Brenner, and Winslow, *Rebel Rank and File*, 128.
132. Brenner, Brenner, and Winslow, 5.
133. Studs Terkel, "The New New Left: Trucker Speaks Out," *New Times*, December 28, 1973, 20.
134. Elly Leary, "Labor Revolts in the 1970s," *Monthly Review* 63, no. 1 (May 2011): 46.
135. Brenner, Brenner, and Winslow, *Rebel Rank and File*, 3, 133.
136. Brenner, Brenner, and Winslow, 25.
137. Jeremy Brecher, *Strike!*, revised, expanded, and updated edition (Oakland: PM Press, 2014), 229–30.
138. *Urban Crisis Monitor* 3, no. 13 (March 27, 1970): 18.
139. *U.S. News & World Report* 68, no. 21 (May 25, 1970): 20.
140. *Cleveland Plain Dealer*, May 11, 1970.
141. Scranton Commission, *The Report of the President's Commission on Campus Unrest*, 286.
142. Al Richmond, "Workers against the War," *Ramparts*, September 1970, 32.
143. *Urban Crisis Monitor* 3, no. 11 (March 13, 1970): 3.
144. *Guardian*, May 30, 1970.
145. Richmond, "Workers against the War," 28–29.
146. Richmond, 31.
147. *Los Angeles Times*, May 11, 1970, Part II, 2.
148. *Vietnam Courier*, no. 305 (January 25, 1971): 6.
149. Jeremy Brecher as quoted in Peter B. Levy, *The New Left and Labor in the 1960s* (Urbana: University of Illinois Press, 1994), 63.
150. Levy, *The New Left and Labor in the 1960s*, 153.
151. Brenner, Brenner, and Winslow, *Rebel Rank and File*, 215.
152. Brenner, Brenner, and Winslow, 215–17.
153. Stanley Weir, *USA—The Labor Revolt* (Somerville, MA: New England Free Press, 1969), 2, as quoted in John Zerzan, *Creation and Its Enemies: The Revolt against Work* (Rochester: Mutualist Books, 1977), 30.
154. As quoted in the *San Diego Union*, February 17, 1982, A-21.
155. Of the fifteen thousand arrests in three days, eight thousand people were swept up on May Day; Varon, *Bringing the War Home*, 131.
156. *Liberated Guardian* (May 1972), 8–9.
157. *New York Times*, May 17, 1970.
158. *New York Times Magazine*, August 8, 1970.
159. Peterson and Bilorusky, *May 1970*, 85.
160. Carl Oglesby and Richard Shaull, *Containment and Change* (New York: Macmillan, 1967).
161. Noam Chomsky, "Watergate: A Skeptical View," *New York Review of Books*, September 20, 1973, 3–8.

162. For further analysis of high levels of power in the United States, see Carl Oglesby, *The Yankee and Cowboy Wars* (Kansas City: Sheed, Andrews and McMeel, Inc., 1976). For background on the Trilateral Commission, see Holly Sklar, *Trilateralism: The Trilateral Commission and Elite Planning for World Management* (Boston: South End Press, 1978).

163. In David Rockefeller, *Memoirs* (New York: Random House, 2002), 405, Rockefeller dealt with the claim that he was part of a secret small group working to destroy the United States and create a new world order: "Some even believe we [Rockefeller family] are part of a secret cabal working against the best interests of the United States, characterizing my family and me as 'internationalists' and of conspiring with others around the world to build a more integrated global political and economic structure—One World, if you will. If that's the charge, I stand guilty, and I am proud of it."

164. In 2003, the World Bank reported that every day some fifty thousand people, including twenty-nine thousand children under the age of five, die from poverty. About 2.5 billion people (40 percent of the worlds population) live in severe poverty—more than half in extreme poverty.

165. See the documents in the appendix of my 1987 book at http://eroseffect.com.

166. Scranton Commission, *The Report of the President's Commission on Campus Unrest* 39; Carnegie Commission, *Dissent and Disruption: Proposals for Consideration by the Campuses* (New York: McGraw-Hill, 1971), 165–66; John and Susan Erlich, *Student Power, Participation and Revolt* (New York: Association Press, 1970), 247–54.

167. Michael Crozier, Samuel Huntington, and Joji Watanuke, *The Crisis of Democracy: Report on the Governability of Democracies to the Trilateral Commission* (New York University Press, 1975), 113–15.

168. Crozier, Huntington, and Watanuke, *The Crisis of Democracy*, 106.

169. See Jordan T. Camp, *Incarcerating the Crisis: Freedom Struggles and the Rise of the Neoliberal State* (Berkeley: University of California Press, 2016).

CHAPTER 5
THE GLOBAL IMAGINATION AFTER 1968

AFTER CREATING CRISES OF REVOLUTIONARY PROPORTIONS IN France in 1968 and the United States in 1970, the insurgencies could not sustain themselves. Whether murderously repressed in the U.S. or assimilated in France, movements imploded and disappeared—or so it seemed. Vast mobilizations momentarily posed threats to the system, challenging police powers, wars, and racism, yet emergent dreams of freedom beyond patriarchy and capitalism remain unfulfilled. The vision of free societies governed through direct democracy, of a world without hunger or an arms race, without militarized nation-states and arbitrary authorities is unabashedly optimistic and possibly unattainable. Yet even discussing such a possibility is a legacy of the global imagination that emerged half a century ago.

Imagination is generally regarded as residing in individual minds, yet I use it in reference to collective actions that embody dreams, aspirations, and desires. Despite enormous cultural differences between France and the U.S., during uprisings in 1968 and 1970 millions of people shared aspirations for international solidarity and local self-management. In their everyday lives during trying times of heartfelt fears and burning desires, people acted according to very similar revolutionary norms and values.

Traditionally, revolutions are understood as changes in elites that control existing economic and political structures, but the global imagination of 1968 envisioned destruction of unjust power and creation of mechanisms for autonomous self-determination. Decentralization and self-government were on everyone's lips—whether "revolutionary intercommunalism" or *autogestion* (self-management). More than a struggle against inherited injustices and irrational structures, people did not want to take over militarized nation-states but to destroy them.

Obsolescence of the nation-state was not an idea invented out of thin air. It was presented by the actual development of history. Neither were nation-states originally "invented" by clever folks, nor inspired by fancy ideas. They emerged as products of humanity's transformation of ancient villages, city-states, kingdoms, and empires. As congealed forms of power that consolidated after centuries of European wars and economic changes, nation-states were then imposed by force upon the rest of the world.

Looking at contemporary forms of political congregation from 1968 to the present, we find the free assembly continually coming into being, not on any-one's orders or any organization's dictate, but from autonomously determined needs of human beings. That kind of governance has little to do with elections and representative "democracy" managed by professional politicians. In an interview in 1968, when asked what form of democracy he wanted, German activist and SDS member Klaus Meschkat responded:

> A form of democracy that is not confined to the heads of states, but is accomplished in all arenas—namely a democracy that is really built from the bottom up. You could say, self-management of producers in all arenas. In the universities, students have seriously demanded democratization of the universities. I believe that such a democratization—including in the factories, the schools, and in all facilities where people work together—is long overdue.[1]

In its internal organization and vision of freedom, the movement strove for popular participation in all aspects of life, including decisions about war and peace, how to run factories and offices, what to teach in universities, as well as what are acceptable patterns of authority in everyday life. The New Left raised the issue of the goal determination of the whole organization of society, a question which—then as now—lies outside established politics, "democratic" or authoritarian, to say nothing about academic theory.[2]

Participatory democracy was central to the global movement's identity from the nonviolent 1955 struggle to desegregate buses in Montgomery, Alabama, to the armed 1980 Gwangju Uprising. Direct democratic norms spontaneously emerged among Polish workers, Copenhagen's communards in Christiania, San Francisco's Diggers, Yugoslav students, Amsterdam's Provos, and Berkeley's People's Park partisans. As in Gwangju, Asian uprisings con-tained parallel forms of deliberative democracy during uprisings in 1973 at Thammasat University in Thailand, and in 1990 at both Chiang Kai-shek Square in Taipei and Kathmandu's liberated Patan. Beginning in the late 1970s, Germany's autonomous movement used consensus in general assemblies to make key decisions and sustained itself over several generations of activism. As they developed through militant actions, the Autonomen transformed them-selves from civil Luddism into a force targeting the whole system of capitalist patriarchy. The 1999 Seattle protests against the WTO were largely prepared by direct action networks based upon strict principles of consensual decision making. In the anti–corporate globalization movement that grew by leaps and bounds after Seattle, social media lubricated the proliferation of participatory ethics. The armed Zapatista uprising involves creating participatory democracy in the everyday life of thousands of people. Rather than trying to seize state power directly, they build counterinstitutions and strive to create a "new person." The Oaxaca Commune of 2006 practiced self-government through open assemblies. Chapters of Black Lives Matter are empowered to take independent initiatives and action not the dictates of a central authority. All of these developments highlight a globally interconnected movement. Given these trajectories, grassroots movements in the twenty-first century will continue to be structured according to a grammar of direct democracy, autonomous self-organization, and international solidarity.

Another dimension of 1968 that remains definitive is an enlarged constituency of revolution—a factor discerned on every continent. Significant participation of the lumpenproletariat among Gwangju's armed resistance fighters, mobilization of the new working class such as Seoul's "necktie brigade" in 1987, and committed protests of Nepalese medical professionals, lawyers, and journalists in 1990 provide empirical instances in Asia. Recent movements rapidly assimilated new technologies like fax machines, cell phones, the internet, and social media. The likes of *Adbusters* and *CrimethInc.* reactivate New Left playfulness, humor, irony, and autonomous artistic expression as opposition tactics.

In the decades since 1968, most noticeable is the growth in size and deepening of vision of globally synchronized insurgencies.

Global Uprisings after 1968

After 1968, the global movement's capacity for synchronous international coordination has grown by leaps and bounds. Not simply a product of social media and technical innovations, internationally coordinated actions emanate from the accumulation of experiences by generations of popular insurgencies. Each wave builds upon victories and defeats of its predecessors. As history becomes increasingly endowed with direct action by self-conscious human beings, our collective intelligence becomes an ever-more-powerful material force. We may regard global insurgencies involving millions of human beings acting in concert with each other as a living organism. Born in 1968 as "the whole world was watching," the infant's development has continued through subsequent uprisings and has yet to reach maturity. Learning from previous episodes, recent global waves have focused on transformation of the world economic system, not simply on opposing its weapons, wars, debt crises, and ecological devastation. Today there are more people consciously opposed to international capitalism than ever before in history, a potential for action that has yet to be fully realized.

In 1968, no one understood the power of global mobilizations better than the leadership of Vietnam. In February 1972, fours years after the Tet offensive, they organized a worldwide peace offensive at an international conference in Versailles, France. Delegates of antiwar movements from more than eighty countries formulated an internationally coordinated action calendar set to begin around Easter in Vietnam, followed by a wave of demonstrations from East to West—from Moscow to Paris to New York and finally to San Diego, where President Nixon was due to be nominated for reelection at the Republican National Convention.[3]

To my amazement, Vietnam's Easter offensive involved, for the first time, tanks among the insurgents' arsenal. Vietnamese forces had disassembled them, carried them south, and then reassembled them without being spotted by the world's most advanced electronic battlefield. Half a world from Versailles, Vietnamese fighters timed deployment of smuggled tanks precisely for the date agreed upon for the start of the international offensive. They liberated the city of Quang Tri and named it capital of their Provisional Revolutionary Government. The U.S. response was to destroy the city. Scarcely a building's wall was left standing after Nixon employed more explosive power than that used on Hiroshima or Nagasaki in 1945. Despite horrific brutality inflicted against its land and people, Vietnam prevailed, reunified itself, and today is increasingly prosperous. In 2001, Vo Nguyen Giáp, military commander of Vietnamese forces that defeated both the French and Americans, summarized the reasons why the Vietnamese were able to win. The antiwar movement inside the United States was a prominent part of his list. For years, Vietnamese leaders cultivated the U.S. movement until it grew into a force with which they were able to coordinate their battlefield tactics.

In 1972, the Vietnamese centrally orchestrated global actions, but no single organization has been responsible for more recent waves of "conscious spontaneity"—for five subsequent episodes of the international eros effect.

1. The disarmament movement of the early 1980s

Beginning in the fall of 1981, Russian and American plans to install medium-range missiles in Europe meant that a nuclear war could have been fought without the Soviet Union or the U.S. being damaged. A key event came on September 13, when U.S. Secretary of State Alexander Haig visited Berlin. Amid a flurry of attacks on American personnel and bases in West Germany, over seven thousand riot police were needed to guard Haig from at least fifty thousand demonstrators in West Berlin. In the ensuing turmoil, hundreds were arrested and over 150 police injured.[4] Less than a month later, on October 10, more than 250,000 people in Bonn marched against the missiles. Within two weeks, similar enormous marches occurred in Paris, London, Brussels, and Rome.

The disarmament movement then spread to the United States. In the spring of 1982, during Ground Zero Week, activists organized events in 150 cities and 500 towns, and the Union of Concerned Scientists sponsored teach-ins at 360 campuses drawing an estimated 350,000 observers.[5] On June 12, at least 800,000 people (some estimates were as high as one million) converged on New York City to express their support for a nuclear-free world. Nuclear freeze initiatives on the ballot in the fall of 1982 won in eight of nine states and in thirty-six of thirty-nine cities and counties. Besides more than 11 million votes (out of a total of 19 million) that the nuclear freeze received in these initiatives, it was approved in 321 city councils, 446 New England town meetings, 63 county councils, and 11 state legislatures.

Besides helping to spark electoral efforts, European street confrontations and mobilizations contributed to the end of the Cold War.

2. The wave of East Asian uprisings, 1986–92

Leading up to the 1980s, East Asian dictatorships had been in power for decades and seemed unshakable, yet a wave of revolts soon transformed the region. In six years, eight dictatorships were overthrown in nine places in Asia, as uprisings exploded in the Philippines in 1986, South Korea in 1987, Myanmar in 1988, Tibet and China in 1989, Taiwan, Nepal, and Bangladesh in 1990, and Thailand in 1992.[6] These insurgencies threw to the wind the common bias that Asians are happier with authoritarian governments than democracy.

After the 1980 Gwangju uprising, the movement suddenly blossomed in 1986, when a massive occupation of public space overthrew dictator Ferdinand Marcos in the Philippines. Overnight, "People Power" became activists' common global identity—cutting across religious, national, and economic divides. East Asia's string of uprisings from 1980 to

Gwangju Uprising. Hong Sung Dam, wood block print.

1998 had a huge political impact, overthrowing eight more entrenched regimes. South Korea's dictator Chun Doo-hwan was disgraced and compelled to grant direct presidential elections before being imprisoned; Taiwan's forty-year martial law regime was overturned; Burma's mobilized citizenry overthrew two dictators only to see their successors massacre thousands; Nepal's monarchy was made constitutional; military ruler Muhammad Ershad in Bangladesh was forced to step down and eventually sent to prison; Army Chief Suchinda Kraprayoon in Thailand was forced to vacate the office of prime minister; and Indonesia's long-time dictator Suharto was ousted after three decades in power.

These uprisings ushered in greater liberties and new opportunities for citizen participation—as well as for international capital. They also inspired Eastern Europeans to act.

3. Revolts against Soviet regimes in Eastern Europe
We can trace a direct line of key activists who kept alive the dream of the 1968 Prague Spring and helped spread it to many other countries, including Hungary, the USSR, Bulgaria, Romania, and Poland. Gorbachev himself was directly changed and inspired by Czech activists, who themselves remained engaged in the process of social transformation. If not for the Western European disarmament movement, Gorbachev and other members of the Soviet establishment would never have been prepared to loosen their grip on Eastern European buffer states—their insurance against a new German invasion. After massive protests opposed to the possibility of nuclear war erupted on both sides of what was then called the Iron Curtain, neither buffer states nor short-range missiles were required to provide Soviet leaders with the assurances they needed. Millions of peace advocates taking to the streets helped convince Gorbachev that Western military intervention in Russia was out of the question.

Grassroots movements against Russian domination have a long history. By the 1980s, they had grown into forces nagging Gorbachev and Soviet leaders, but after Asian uprisings brought People Power onto the stage of history, movements in Eastern Europe gained encouragement and inspiration. Without anyone predicting their downfall, Eastern Europe's communist regimes in Hungary, Poland, East Germany, Czechoslovakia, Bulgaria, Yugoslavia, and Romania were all overthrown beginning in 1989. The Soviet Union could not remain aloof and it soon dissolved. The string of uprisings that swept away East Asian dictatorships and East European Soviet regimes in 1989 was "the continuation of 1968."[7]

Although poverty has increased and life expectancy decreased in these countries since the end of Soviet regimes, and despite massive outside interference leading up to the uprisings, people's self-determined will for freedom was the principal factor spurring the movements. Regime openness to change was also a factor. Sadly, this is not the case in the capitalist "democracies."

4. The alter-globalization wave

As the promised peace dividend at the end of the Cold War failed to materialize and global capitalism was strengthened, millions of people "spontaneously" chose to challenge giant corporations and their international institutions—the World Trade Organization, International Monetary Fund, and World Bank.

Without any central group deciding the focus of mobilizations, people themselves chose the global capitalist system as their target. The 1994 Zapatista Uprising was a huge inspiration. On November 30, 1999, Seattle protesters' victory in halting WTO meetings broke new ground when "Teamsters and turtles,"[8] workers and ecologists, Lesbian Avengers and Zapatista partisans all converged. The worldwide coordination of protests that day involved actions in dozens of other cities around the world.[9] Indymedia organizations were born across the world.

For years thereafter, whenever elite summits took place, tens of thousands of protesters challenged their right to rule. The global movement reached a new level of synchronicity on February 15, 2003, when the U.S. prepared to attack Iraq for the second time. With no central organization, as many as thirty million people around the world took to the streets on February 15, even though the war had yet to start.[10] People in eight hundred cities and sixty countries mobilized. From Damascus to Athens, Seoul to Sydney, and New York to Buenos Aires, millions constituted a global civil society that the *New York Times* named a "Second Superpower." In London 1.4 million took to the streets in the biggest demonstration in that city's two thousand years of history, and three million people appeared on the streets of Rome.[11]

5. The Arab Spring, Spanish Indignados, Greek anarchists, and Occupy Wall Street

In 2011, thousands of Spanish Indignados occupied major city squares and used direct democracy to fight back against the government's austerity programs. In more than a dozen countries, movements simultaneously appeared. Greek anarchists burned much of downtown Athens to protest their government's acceptance of German-imposed sanctions. After the suicide of vegetable vendor Mohamed Bouazizi, a chain reaction of uprisings spread from Tunisia to Egypt, and then to Yemen, Bahrain, Syria, and Libya. In fourteen months, major protests took place in fourteen countries in the region. Millions of people went into the streets. Their increasingly sophisticated use of social media such as Facebook, Twitter, YouTube, and Short Message Service (SMS) and the cross-border speed with which the revolt spread offer a glimpse of People Power's potential in the twenty-first century. Disaster was the outcome in Syria, Libya, and elsewhere as world powers and entrenched regimes obstinately waged war. In Egypt, divisions between Islamists and democrats abetted the military and its U.S. enablers in installing an even worse dictator than Mubarak.

From humble beginnings in New York on September 17, 2011, Occupy Wall Street took control of public space in more than one thousand cities. To illustrate the global interconnection seemingly disparate events, American protesters and Egyptian veterans of Tahrir Square exchanged gifts of pizza deliveries.

These five global uprisings reveal patterns astonishingly similar to the global eruption of the eros effect in 1968. Most recently, social media has facilitated synchronicity, but movements have been accumulating the capacity for international simultaneity since 1968. The global movement's mobilizations have changed from unconsciously synchronized to a form of "conscious spontaneity" as indicated in the chart below.

Global Insurgencies after 1968

Insurgency	Years	Key events	Slogan	Organizations/ Inspiration	Outcome
Disarmament Movement	1981–82	Greenham Common occupation; militant antimilitary protests	Peace	Women for Life on Earth; German Autonomen	Russian and U.S. missiles not deployed; expected peace dividend vanishes
Asian Uprisings	1986–92	Philippines uprising; Tiananmen Square	People Power	1980 Gwangju Uprising; Reform the Armed Forces Movement (RAM)	8 regimes overthrown in 6 years
Eastern European Regime Changes	1989–91	Gorbachev announcement; Chernobyl	Peaceful Revolution	Solidarność; Leipzig Monday demonstrations	Eight Soviet regimes overthrown; increasing poverty
Alter-globalization Movements	1998–2003	1999 Seattle; Genoa 2001; Feb. 15, 2003	Another World Is Possible	1994 Zapatista Uprising; Direct Action Network	WTO meetings halted and subsequent failure; elite summits confronted
Arab Spring, Occupy Wall Street, Indignados	2011–12	Tunisian revolution; 14 countries in 14 months	Out With Them All; We Are the 99%	Egyptian occupation of Tahrir Square; Spanish Indignados, Greek anarchists	Conversation changed to include the 1%; Great Power military intervention and wars in Syria and Libya

Each wave built from its predecessors' victories and defeats. International harmonization from people's intuitive identification with each other in all these cases is noteworthy.

We should expect that future global upsurges will surpass previous waves in cascading global resonance for two reasons: growing grassroots consciousness of the power of street protests and increasing global reach of the world system's impact on millions of people's everyday lives. If the past is any indication, future insurgencies will be increasingly marked by their sudden emergence and proliferation. They will also encounter the problem of sustainability apparent in Occupy Wall Street, which grew overnight to thousands of cities but quickly dissipated.

Some Questions for Revolutionaries

Discontinuities in revolutionary movements and romanticization of past insurgencies have resulted in few critical discussions of lessons and legacies of previous waves of struggle. Many activists today know very little about the May 1968 events in France or even that a crisis of major proportions occurred in the U.S. in 1970. As a result of such dynamics as well as Eurocentric biases, the Gwangju Uprising of 1980 is far less known than the 1871 Paris Commune, a momentous event that took place more than a century earlier. In remarks below, I offer my perspective on issues of central importance to future struggles.

A Centralized Party?

A single centralized party organized along the lines of democratic centralism successfully led the seizure of state power in several countries in the twentieth century, but outcomes of these revolutions are quite distant from the kinds of freedoms now envisioned. Based on the dismal political results of Soviet and Chinese "revolutionary" regimes, we can conclude that the Leninist party does not lead to freedom. In the late twentieth century, Marxism-Leninism hastened the dissolution of the New Left in both Germany and the U.S.

Parties modeled on those of Lenin and Mao Zedong—as was the Black Panther Party—have distinct advantages as well. Historical victories of the Bolsheviks in 1917 and of Mao's Communist Party in 1949 are proof of their power. The Panthers were able to craft unity and discipline among women and men accustomed to behavior far different than serving breakfasts in church basements, writing and selling newspapers, and other daily tasks that made their survival programs so successful. They forged a multicultural uprising in 1970 that momentarily posed the possibility of revolution in the U.S. in the twentieth century. Internationally, Panther emulators sprang up in more than a dozen places, from Polynesia to Bermuda and Palestine.[12]

Yet the Party's democratic centralist structure was also a key reason for its demise. By 1970, the "forces of order" had murdered or locked up the entire central committee. Would a decentralized revolutionary party been better able to withstand assaults of the centralized state? In the words of Herbert Marcuse: "The sweeping concentration of power and control in the nationwide political and military Establishment necessitates the shift to decentralized forms of organization, less susceptible to destruction by the engines of repression."[13]

Too much power was concentrated in the hands of too few people in the Panthers. Factions inside the organization fought for control rather than being able to coexist. Facilitated by "democratic centralism" but without engaging in any meaningful discussion among members, Huey Newton unilaterally expelled dozens of comrades, left others to face decades of prison, and liquidated dissident voices within the Party as he shut it down as a national organization.

The whole point of revolution is to expand freedoms already won through past struggles. If committed activists become order takers of a central committee, how can we expect them to help build a society in which the majority of people decide for themselves, in free and open communal deliberations, the directions we take? The idea that a single party can "unify the broad and fragmented working class into a united movement wherein it is conscious of itself (and its interests) as a class" is often articulated as a key rationale for its existence.[14] Yet I believe that workers—and the vast majority of society—must do this for themselves in order for genuine freedom to flourish.

The difference between heteronomously imposed and autonomously determined unity is vital. The qualitative transformation of the existing society—the break from what has been called "prehistory" and "survival of the fittest"—demands not only breaking the structures of the existing system but also formulation of a new self-consciousness of the human species. Only then could space be created for dignified processes of life and expansion of individual democratic rights. The creation of a society in which patterns of power and authority engendered by capitalist patriarchy are no longer of any consequence depends upon continual liberation of the sensibilities and needs of the vast majority of people, not seizure of power by an armed vanguard. The leap that would be the real "leap into history" would be prepared by the aesthetic and cultural transformation of individuals and groups, whose new needs would prefigure political and economic transformation of society.

Every revolution develops its own theory in accordance with local conditions. In China, Mao insisted upon a break with the Russian Revolution's strategy of seizing power through urban insurrections after mechanical imitations cost the lives of tens of thousands of activists. For his criticisms, he was expelled from the Party. Ultimately, the Party adopted his strategy of building from the countryside into the city and was able to seize power. In Vietnam, Ho and Giáp insisted upon a break with Chinese "human wave" assaults prior to victory at Dien Bien Phu. Instead, they ordered trenches to be dug increasingly closer to enemy positions, saving many lives in the process—and winning a great victory.

As Marx famously said, we do not make history under conditions we select "but under circumstances existing already, given and transmitted from the past." It is no accident, therefore, that a decade after Huey P. Newton articulated his vision of "revolutionary intercommunalism," anarchist thinker Murray Bookchin arrived at a similar conclusion—although he named it "libertarian municipalism." Historical conditions have created the possibility of reduced governmental powers and increased power to the people. We already see emergent forms of direct democracy in the Gwangju Uprising, in Oaxaca's Commune, and seizures of Taksim and Tahrir Squares. The task of revolutionary organizations would be to stabilize the participatory character of communes while lubricating connections from the grassroots internationally. At each level of connection, many formations and types of organizations would be involved. No single vanguard party would lead the way forward, but many vanguards, such as Zapatistas, Lesbian Avengers, Occupy Wall Streeters, Indignados, Greek anarchists, and Tunisian pirates.

In the 1960s, the Provos, the Orange Free State, and Kabouters in Holland, the Situationists in France, Subversive Aktion in Germany, and the Diggers and Yippies in the United States were successful movement organizations modeled more on aesthetic avant-garde groups than on Left parties. Seeking to transform the grammar of people's existence and to change the aesthetic form of life, Yippies threw money onto the floor of the New York Stock Exchange, a Dadaist action that not only succeeded in halting trading. Brokers scurrying for dollar bills also brought wide publicity to young people's rejection of the rat race. By running a pig for U.S. president in 1968, Yippies forever changed politicians' images, not only in the United States. As Stew Albert recalled, the Yippies bathed in the global counterculture of the 1960s: "We turned the streets and its objects into unbounded outdoor props for the creation of TV images."[15] The Yippies and Provos are but two examples of hundreds of playful episodes of autonomously organized resistance to the forces of seriousness and domination.[16]

Direct actions might be more appropriate vehicles than political parties for transformation of contemporary societies. During May 1968, a small group of older activists suddenly occupied the Sorbonne, creating a central meeting place for the movement that became a haven for dissident workers. The liberated Sorbonne became a direct democratic forum where people from different occupations and classes spoke freely. Soon millions of workers were on strike and France was on the brink of revolution. Exemplary actions by avant-garde groups can be powerful catalysts for instigating larger shifts and movements. Without national and international coordination, insurgencies are sometimes not even aware of their proportions, nor can activists comprehend the forces of repression being unleashed against them.

Premature Armed Struggle?

A corollary of centralized parties seeking to take power can be found in small armed groups that attempt to substitute themselves for popular insurgencies. Like babies first learning to speak, revolutionary movements in their infancy mimic elders and create ego ideals in their image. So it was in 1968. In many countries, theory was imported much like any commodity. Revolutionary theory from Russia or China was adopted mechanistically. In the U.S., Che's foco theory was simply applied by the Black Liberation Army and the Weather Underground (also known as Weatherman). Some of Huey Newton's speeches were nothing but restatements of Lenin. "New communists" metaphysically transported the Bolshevik form of organization across time and space.

A very real political difference tore apart movements across the world in 1968: parliamentary vs. armed struggle. Genocide against Vietnam and attacks by police on the BPP made self-defense a necessity, yet many movement activists chose to go underground in the belief that the time for armed revolution had come. By depriving the popular movement of their vision and experiences at the very time the movement erupted, they led in the opposite direction of what was needed. When Weatherman abetted the destruction of SDS (an organization of tens of thousands) and disappeared to carry out symbolic bombings, the movement needed to be reaching out to newly mobilized constituencies by canvassing neighborhoods, workplaces, dormitories, factories, fraternities, and sororities. Interviewed decades afterward, Weatherman Bill Ayers justified his actions by saying, "Militancy was the standard by which we measured our aliveness."[17] A more effective understanding would stress the central importance of movement building, not militancy. Every tactic, every action, should carefully account for long-term movement building and consciousness raising. It should enhance people's confidence in their ability to govern, not build elite groups. Che's foco theory substituted an elite for the popular movement. The same could be said for organizations modeled on the Bolshevik Party.

Hindsight allows us to say that premature armed struggle materially damaged insurgencies in more than a dozen countries, often setting back movements for years, if not decades. While those who undertake armed actions may feel "alive" and justified in their extreme actions (and often feel superior to "less committed" activists), more often than not, such actions undercut popular insurgencies. Rosa Luxemburg understood that "the masses are in reality their own leaders, dialectically creating their own development process."[18] When the time for popular armed uprising comes, as in 1980 Gwangju, and people massively rally to the resistance, it will not be small secretive groups but overwhelming numbers of people who militantly join the struggle. As we look at coming revolutionary moments, our forces will include elements of the police and the military, constituencies readily apparent to nearly every Korean but often outside other activists' comprehension.

A different form of militancy that helps build movements is the Black Bloc, an alternative to both parliamentary and guerrilla tactics.[19] At key demonstrations, activists disguise themselves by wearing all black. Arriving in self-organized affinity groups, they cluster into radical contingents that defend demonstrators from police assaults and attack targets that clarify movement messages. From confronting U.S. President Reagan's visit to Berlin (when the United States escalated the nuclear arms race) to helping defeat the Wackersdorf nuclear reprocessing plant in Southern Germany (which would have provided Germany with weapons grade plutonium), the Black Bloc's resistance to the rottenness of the existing global system resonated internationally. The conscious spontaneity of the Black Bloc relies on popular participation and people taking to the streets, not on armed actions of a handful of people in a centralized party. By opening space for political engagement between ballots and bullets, militant extraparliamentary actions can help to galvanize people's connections to one another and to crystallize an activist milieu for generations.

Militant street confrontations can be a crucible for psychic reworking of needs and desires, a living theater with enormous transformative value. After the 2001 Genoa protests against the G-8 (where two hundred thousand people gathered), one Black Bloc participant told me their experiences "changed me more in a few days than in the preceding years of meetings." Another person called it the "most important experience" of their life. If we accept that consumer culture is a form of cultural colonization, then the Black Bloc's destruction of McDonald's, Nike outlets, and banks are a form of decolonization—a freeing of space from corporate control and creation of autonomous zones not controlled by the police. As Fanon long ago discovered, revolutionary force plays an essential role in decolonization movements.[20] The controlled militancy of the Black Bloc is not only a psychic reworking of individuals in the streets, it is also a moment of opposition to the system as a whole. By making concrete people's desires to be free, decades of deadening consumerism and debilitating comfort can be thrown off overnight.

All models inherited from the past need to be questioned, including the Black Bloc, and even syndicalists' notion of the centrality of the working class. Proletarian dogmatism divides the 99%. The working class has been widely expanded with the enlarged reproduction of capital and the rise of enormous bureaucracies, the expansion of education, and the importance of information to economic development. The universities exist today at the center of production, and as such are critically important to capitalism—as well as to revolutionary movements. The precariat grows by leaps and bounds in the twenty-first century.

No one sector of the population has the capacity to transform society. Building a hegemonic bloc capable of transforming the entire society requires rethinking our past experiences. African Americans played a vanguard role in the 1960s, but they alone were not enough. Latinos' 1960s activism was often unrecognized, and they were left out of subsequent commemorations decades later as well.[21] The 2006 census recorded Latinos as 14.8 percent of population, more than African Americans. As Carlos Muñoz concluded after a lifetime of activism: "We are not islands unto ourselves. Latino/a liberation is not possible without making possible liberation of all people of all colors, including the millions of whites who are not part of the structure of power."[22] Native Americans too are often overlooked, although recent mobilizations at the Standing Rock Sioux reservation indicate their ability to act with unity and to catalyze larger forces. What has only recently been named "the 99%" has long been known as the *minjung* in South Korea. Everyone except the owners of the huge corporations that dominate the economy, the generals in the military and very few at the top united in minjung actions and overthrew an entrenched dictatorship.

Psychic Thermidor

Movements' histories often include internally conditioned, self-defeating behavior, a phenomenon named "psychic Thermidor" by Herbert Marcuse.[23] The cultural roots of the political movement were an important source of the energy of the popular movement, and the New Left's cultural subversion defined one of its most significant dimensions. The spontaneous integration of culture and politics provided vitality to the movement, but it also accounted for the carrying over of oppressive characteristics like sexism, racism, and authoritarianism into the life of the movement. Microcosmic enforcement of enforced structures of domination and oppression divide us from one another. Rather than understanding identity politics formulated along lines of race, gender, and ethnicity as containing a universal dimension in the particular form of oppression being challenged, many activists believe movements based upon identity divide us.[24] Such understanding fails to comprehend that black music appeals universally, and feminism is in all our interests.[25]

The photograph of the advertisement below, taken from the April 1970 edition of movement magazine *Ramparts* (a radical forerunner of *Mother Jones*), is an indication of how sexism and depoliticization go hand in hand. Besides serving to prevent activists from giving and living to their full potential, sexism (like racism) undermines the avowed goals and aspirations of the movement.

In May 1968, no one in the government or the opposition seemed to know what the nine million strikers wanted. The workers themselves were unable to formulate a general consensus for demands and action. As time went on, a psychic Thermidor set in, an impetus to return to "normal" exemplified by workers who punched their timecards when they arrived for strike duty. Within dual

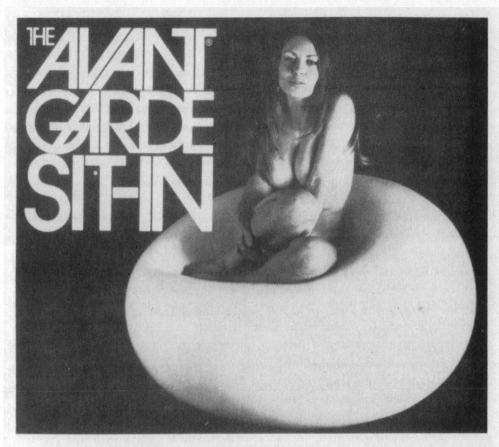

THE AVANT GARDE SIT-IN

Protest against uncomfortable, heavy, square-looking furniture! Take a position in the revolutionary new Avant-Garde Inflatable Sculpture Seat. Use this seat anywhere—in your pad, the office of the university president, even the middle of the Atlantic Ocean. What's more, the Avant-Garde Inflatable Sculpture Seat is completely portable and it can be stored in a drawer. It's made of thick, triple-laminated vinyl and is available in six vibrating colors. Perhaps best of all, the Avant-Garde Inflatable Sculpture Seat easily supports the weight of two—and it bounces!

Chairs similar to the Avant-Garde Inflatable Sculpture Seat sell in department stores for $50. Our deflated price: **only $9.95!!**

To order your Avant-Garde Inflatable Sculpture Seat, simply fill out the adjacent coupon and mail it with $9.95 (plus 85¢ for shipping) to: The Avant-Garde Emporium, 110 West 40th Street, New York, New York 10018. Please be sure to hurry, since the Avant-Garde Inflatable Sculpture Seat is imported and stocks are limited.

You'll really be sitting pretty.

THE AVANT GARDE EMPORIUM
110 W. 40 ST., NEW YORK, N.Y. 10018

Ramparts, April 1970, sexism and depoliticization.

power in factories, universities, and neighborhoods, the forces of order are not simply outside.

Reforms and Revolution

It is sometimes thought that the New Left was merely reformist. That perspective overlooks the movement's impetus from its earliest days to replace national power with cooperative forms of direct democracy. In 1963, at the huge civil rights march on Washington where King gave his famous "I Have a Dream" speech, SNCC leader John Lewis raised the possibility of creating a power outside the established system. In the summer of 1965, a few months after SDS had helped pull together the first national antiwar march, the issue of building an alternative national political structure was raised by Tom Hayden: "Ultimately this movement might lead to a Continental Congress called by all the people who feel excluded from the higher circles of decision making in this country. This Congress might even become a kind of second government, receiving taxes from its supporters, establishing contact with other nations, holding debates on American foreign and domestic policy, dramatizing the plight of all groups that suffer from the American system."[26] In January 1966, SNCC leader Bob Moses asked California activists: "Why can't we set up our own government and declare the other one no good and say the federal government should recognize us?"[27] These early notions of replacing the U.S. government had not yet gone beyond national conceptions of power. Over the next few years, millions of people came to see the U.S. government as an enemy of life, liberty, and the pursuit of happiness. With the widening of the system's crisis of legitimation, there were increasing attempts to put forth alternatives to it, attempts which culminated in the Revolutionary Peoples' Constitutional Convention of 1970. Revolutionary intercommunalism, not seizure of national power, became the movement's goal.

After the vitality of the movement had given way to a return to "normalcy," well-intentioned efforts to reform the existing system have often had the effect of strengthening structures of domination. Take, for example, the campaign for the Equal Rights Amendment in the early 1970s. Whether or not it passed, the campaign's narrow focus on legal equality blunted the questioning of the entire system of capitalist patriarchy, whose structural militarism conditions male domination and vice versa. Feminist questioning of patriarchy was transformed into a question of formal equality within the existing system. In 1970, elements of the women's liberation movement called into question both political structures of power and domination in everyday life. The campaign for the ERA obscured the full extent of patriarchal power.

The relationship between reform and revolution is complicated. The idea of an ERA helped win millions of women greater life opportunities, itself a change of great value. In my lifetime, I have seen feminism turned into its opposite. From a set of beliefs that promised women couldn't rule with the violence and brutality of men, today we are instructed that women should play the same combat roles as men, that women should be just as tough in the corporate boardroom and rule with more efficiency and less sentimentality in a system of worldwide immiseration and alienation. A genuinely feminist revolution would need to free our species from the entire system of capitalist patriarchy: nothing less could redefine the existence of the individual and transform the instinctual needs of men and women in everyday life.[28] The current systematic stratification by gender would have little to do with the lives of free people of all genders. Genuine revolution worthy of the name would be based upon the universal interests of the human species and all life, not just self-interests of a particular nation or sector of the population. It would be a working-class, feminist revolution against white supremacist patriarchy and would necessarily involve transformation of the world's wealthiest countries.

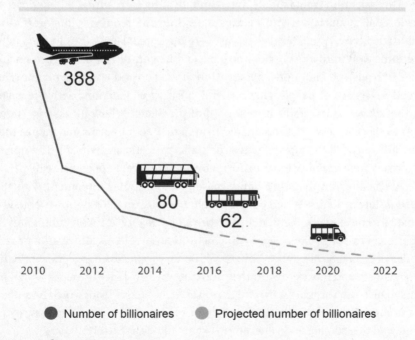

Billionaires who own the same wealth as half the world
And what transport they would fit on

388

80

62

2010   2012   2014   2016   2018   2020   2022

● Number of billionaires   ● Projected number of billionaires

Source: Oxfam, January 18, 2016.

Rebellion or Revolution?

> *The men in power had their universities,*
> *The students took them.*
> *The men in power had their factories,*
> *The workers took them.*
> *The men in power had their radios,*
> *The journalists took them.*
> *The men in power only have their power now.*
> *We shall take it.*
> —poster, Beaux-Arts, May 1968

Even though the first seven lines of this poster were true, the grand finale failed to materialize. Of course, a one- or two-month-long revolution is not possible. But revolution should not be viewed simply as a mechanistic problem of seizing state power or as some other technical transformation of the structures of society. Rather, revolution is a process through which large numbers of people qualitatively transform values, norms, and institutions of society—not simply overthrowing the old rulers and replacing them but creating new kinds of social realities and human beings.

The transition from feudalism to capitalism took centuries, a long process accelerated by uprisings and insurgencies, but one requiring long gestation and birth. Step by step, local customs were uprooted, laws were changed, and freedoms won until a new social order could be consolidated.[29] Forced enclosures of lands and commons, persecution of women and nonmale people, and forced severance of people's natural and spiritual connections with the earth characterized capitalism as it took hold of the planet.[30] Revolutionary visions such as those at the RPCC emanated from a new set of norms and values that contradicted society's racism, patriarchy, and patriotic chauvinism. The uprising posed the possibility for transformation of the totality of social reality.

A rebellion, on the other hand, merely demonstrates discontent with the present state of affairs. When people revolt, they rise up against those perceived to cause a common problem, not to create a new reality. A revolt culminates in negation of existing rulers, values, and institutions, not in the affirmation of new modes of life. As Sartre put it: "The revolutionary wants to change the world; he transcends it and moves toward the future, toward an order of values which he himself invents. The rebel is careful to preserve the abuses from which he suffers so that he can go on rebelling against them. . . . He does not want to destroy or transcend the existing order; he simply wants to rise against it."[31]

The New Left in the United States began in a script dictated by reactions to genocide and injustices perpetrated by the system. In the midst of an escalating spiral of repression and resistance, both the black and antiwar movements reached violent and spectacular culminations. But in 1970, the movement transcended rebellion and went to the next level: Puerto Ricans ran Lincoln Hospital for the good of the community; students and faculty opened campuses for the needs of all; and, in Philadelphia, a multicultural assembly of thousands articulated their vision for a new society.

Karl Marx expected the dull discipline of factory life to help shape the emancipatory proletariat. We can observe today that the material conditions of consumer society, including its spectacles, like the Olympics and World Cup (despite the nationalist wrappings in which they are packaged), help craft an international identity of humanity. Around the world, people identify more closely with each other than ever before. Diffusion of uprisings via the eros effect is one robust indication of such a universal identity, as is diffusion of tactical innovations across borders. People today continue to become increasingly intersectional in their identities, as formerly hard-line divisions of race, gender, and class blur and blend, revealing natural spectrums of identity that bridge formerly imposed and strictly enforced border lines—a signpost that we are awakening to the opportunity for global unity like never before.

While humanity, like nature (and the universe as a whole, according to modern physics), moves indelibly toward intermingling and interdependence, the patriarchal Establishment's impetus to isolate people into easily manageable segments of a societal machine continues to pervade ever-deepening aspects of life. The internalization of the imposed value system (which includes misogyny and body shame, disciplinary "power over" relationships with oneself, believing one is separate from nature, the global epidemic of racism, depression, and suicide) is one of the weapons used against us, so each person self-maintains inner prisons that perpetuate cycles of domination and colonization. Decolonization and healing of each individual's body, psyche, and spirit are more crucial than ever before and are steps toward the creation of liberated spaces, families, communities, and beyond. Another legacy of the global imagination of 1968 is the subsequent reemergence of healing arts and indigenous wisdom traditions that have everywhere been persecuted in attempt to annihilate the natural intelligence and birthright of every human to be connected, healthy, and empowered.

That major new upheavals will occur is certain; their outcomes remain unclear. New explosions could very well precipitate massive right-wing responses. If there is any chance of the aesthetic transformation of the established world system, such a possibility does not rest on any individual or organization. The self-activity of popular movements, the spontaneous emergence of an escalating spiral of actions, strikes, sit-ins, and insurrectionary councils (the eros effect), cannot be brought into existence by conspiracies or acts of will. Neither can these forms of struggle be predicted in advance of their appearance, resting as they do upon the accumulation of political knowledge of the history of our species.

Notes

1. Klaus Meschkat, *Konfrontationen: Streitschriften und Analysen 1958 bis 2010* (Hannover: Offizen, 2010), 210 (my translation).
2. In the original edition of this book, I showed how the movements of 1968 surpassed even the best insights of systems analysis, sociology and academic discourse, and Soviet Marxism. That chapter and other materials from the 1987 edition can be found at http://eroseffect.com.
3. So terrified did Nixon become of approaching protests in San Diego that he sought to deport John Lennon (who had agreed to play there with the Grateful Dead and others) and moved the convention to Miami.
4. I consistently use conservative estimates since I have no intention to appear to be inflating the scope of events in question. At the anti-Haig demonstration, for example, it was estimated by some that at least eighty thousand demonstrators were involved, probably a more accurate number than the police estimate of fifty thousand. German sources include the *Frankfurter Allgemeine* and *Die Tageszeitung*.
5. *Guardian*, April 28, 1982, 5; *Guardian*, November 10, 1982, 7.
6. On South Korea, see George Katsiaficas, *Asia's Unknown Uprisings*, vol. 1 (Oakland: PM Press, 2012); on other countries see *Asia's Unknown Uprisings*, vol. 2 (Oakland: PM Press, 2013). The second volume also contains a critique of capitalism's self-destructive tendencies and calls for its replacement.
7. Giovanni Arrighi, Terence K. Hopkins, and Immanuel Wallerstein, "1989: The Continuation of 1968," in *After the Fall: 1989 and the Future of Freedom*, ed. George Katsiaficas (New York: Routledge, 2001), 35.
8. During the WTO protests, as union workers marched alongside environmental activists, some of whom were costumed as sea turtles, one of the many popular hand-painted signs read "Teamsters and turtles—together at last."
9. See Mark Laskey, "The Globalization of Resistance," in *Confronting Capitalism: Dispatches from a Global Movement*, eds. Eddie Yuen, Daniel Burton-Rose, and George Katsiaficas (New York: Soft Skull Press, 2004).
10. See Barbara Sauermann, ed., *2/15: The Day the World Said NO to War* (Oakland: AK Press, 2003).
11. David Harvey, *Rebel Cities* (London: Verso, 2013), 116. Harvey's valuable contribution does not seem to comprehend the synchronicity of global protest waves, focused as he is on urban dynamics.
12. See Charles Jones, *The Black Panther Party Reconsidered* (Baltimore: Black Classic Press, 1998); Michael Clemons and Charles Jones, "Global Solidarity: The Black Panther Party in the International Arena," in *Liberation, Imagination, and the Black Panther Party*, eds. Kathleen Cleaver and George Katsiaficas (New York: Routledge, 1997).
13. Herbert Marcuse, *Counterrevolution and Revolt* (Boston: Beacon Press, 1972), 42; also see André Gorz, *Socialism and Revolution* (Anchor Books, 1973), 30.
14. For one of Leninism's most articulate advocates, see "On the Vanguard Party, Once Again," in *Panther Vision: Essential Party Writings of Kevin "Rashid" Johnson* (Montreal: Kersplebedeb, 2015), 38–63.
15. Interview, Stew Albert, Portland, OR, December 3, 1999.
16. Benjamin Shepherd, *Play, Creativity, and Social Movements: If I Can't Dance, It's Not My Revolution* (New York: Routledge, 2011).
17. Ayers quoted in Varon, *Bringing the War Home*, 87. At the December 1969 Flint, Michigan "War Council" leader Bernadine Dohrn stood in front of about three

hundred Weatherpeople and extolled the virtues of Charles Manson. "Dig it; first they killed those pigs, then they ate dinner in the room with them, then they even shoved a fork in the pig Tate's stomach. Wild!" Cries of "Fork Power!" and "Free Charles Manson!" could be heard for the rest of the conference.

Two months later, the group accidentally blew up the townhouse in which they were making bombs, an accident in which three Weatherpeople were killed. The group became fugitives, some of whom were never captured by the FBI before they surrendered to authorities. When the Weatherpeople went underground at the end of 1969, the popular movement lost activists with experience accumulated over years of organizing. The type of leadership they exemplified in going underground was a self-destructive force. Because many in the BLA had no choice but to go underground, they were unable to fulfill the promise of a new fusion of politics and culture at the very time when an increasing number of people looked to them for direction. Both groups set out to kill police. Six weeks after Flint, on February 12, 1970, Weatherman's first bombing targeted Berkeley's Hall of Justice complex precisely when police changed shifts "to maximize deaths," according to one participant (Bryan Burrough, *Days of Rage: America's Radical Underground, the FBI, and the Forgotten Age of Revolutionary Violence* [New York: Penguin Books, 2015], 95). The BLA killed a total of seven police, none high-ranking. Reflecting on their actions, Sekou Odinga believes today it was a mistake to "be way out in front of the people" (*Days of Rage*, 538). Tired of being underground, "an increasingly high-cost fantasy" according to Bill Ayers, all members of the Weather Underground surrendered to authorities (*Days of Rage*, 362). On December 3, 1979, Bernadine Dohrn paid a $1,500 fine with a check and walked out of court. Former Weatherpeople who participated in an ill-fated Brinks robbery on October 20, 1981, remain in prison, as do at least six BLA members and many more Panthers, including Mumia Abu-Jamal and Russell "Maroon" Shoatz.

18. "Rosa Luxemburg," *New World Encyclopedia*, July 19, 2015, http://www. newworldencyclopedia.org/entry/Rosa_Luxemburg, see the section on "Dialectic of Spontaneity and Organization." Thanks to Antonia Darder for guiding me to this passage.

19. See Francis Dupuis-Déri, *Who's Afraid of the Black Blocs? Anarchy in Action around the World* (Oakland: PM Press, 2014); A.K. Thompson, *Black Bloc, White Riot: Anti-globalization and the Geneology of Dissent* (Oakland: AK Press, 2010).

20. Following Marcuse, we must always distinguish between the system's violence that kills tens of thousands daily and the movement's militancy. See *Counterrevolution and Revolt* (Boston: Beacon Press, 1972), 53–55.

21. See Carlos Muñoz Jr., *Youth, Identity, Power: The Chicano Movement* (London: Verso Books, 1989; revised and expanded edition, 2007), 14–16.

22. Muñoz, *Youth, Identity, Power*, 233.

23. Marcuse refers to contemporary revolutions' self-defeating behavior, which he linked to conditions of advanced capitalism. See Herbert Marcuse, *Eros and Civilization: A Philosophical Inquiry into Freud* (Boston: Beacon Press, 1966), 91.

24. For an example, see Todd Gitlin, "Fragmentation of the Idea of the Left," in *Social Theory and the Politics of Identity*, ed. Craig Calhoun (London: Blackwell, 1994), 166.

25. See my article, "The Latent Universal in Identity Politics," in *The Promise of Multiculturalism: Education and Autonomy in the 21st Century*, eds. George Katsiaficas and Teodros Kiros (New York: Routledge, 1996), 80.

26. Tom Hayden, "The Politics of 'the Movement,'" *Dissent* 13, no. 1 (January–February 1966): 87.

27. *The Movement* 2, no. 1 (January 1966).

28. Herbert Marcuse, "Marxismus und Feminismus," in Herbert Marcuse, *Zeit-Messungen* (Frankfurt: Suhrkamp Verlag, 1975), 12.

29. See Immanuel Wallerstein, *Utopistics; or, Historical Choices of the 21st Century* (New York: The New Press, 1998).

30. Silvia Federici, *Caliban and the Witch: Women, the Body and Primitive Accumulation* (New York: Autonomedia, 2004).

31. Jean-Paul Sartre, *Baudelaire* (New York: New Directions, 1967), 51–52.

DOCUMENTS

REVOLUTIONARY PEOPLES' CONSTITUTIONAL CONVENTION

September 1970, Philadelphia
Workshop Reports[1]

WORKSHOP ON INTERNATIONALISM AND RELATIONS WITH LIBERATION STRUGGLES AROUND THE WORLD

The Revolutionary Peoples' Constitutional Convention supports the demand of the Chinese people for the liberation of Taiwan. We demand the liberation of Okinawa and the Pacific Territories occupied by U.S. and European imperialist countries. The Revolutionary Peoples' Constitutional Convention supports the struggles and endorses the government of the provisional revolutionary government of South Vietnam, the royal government of National Union of Cambodia, and the Pathet Lao.

Huey P. Newton
Minister of Defense
Black Panther Party

In order to insure our international constitution, we, the people of Babylon, declare an international bill of rights: that all people are guaranteed the right to life, liberty and the pursuit of happiness, that all people of the world be free from dehumanization and intervention in their internal affairs by a foreign power. Therefore, if fascist actions in the world attempt to achieve imperialist goals, they will be in violation of the law and dealt with as criminals.

We are in full support with the struggle of the Palestinian people for liberation of Palestine from Zionist colonialism, and their goals of creating a democratic state where all Palestinians, Jews, Christians and Moslems are equal.

We propose solidarity with the liberation struggle of the Puerto Rican people, who now exist as a colony of the United States and have many groups who are fighting for liberation, such as C.A.L. (Armed Commandos for Liberation), M.I.R.A. and the Young Lords Party.

We propose that, whereas the universities in the United States are used by the imperialist system to provide the knowledge that that system uses to perpetrate the exploitation of the Third World and repression against national liberation struggles, we propose that the universities and their resources be

---

1   Mimeographed originals in the collection of George Katsiaficas.

turned over to use for, by, and of the peoples of the world so that they may implement their vision of a new socialist world.

1. The United States is an international federation of bandits and we denounce its rights to nationhood.
2. We should provoke the destruction of all racists and fascists in capitalistic countries and the world over. We should not rest until all of them are wiped off the face of the earth.
3. We support all liberation struggles throughout the world and we oppose all reactionary struggles throughout the world.
4. Our constitution will guarantee the right of all people to travel and communicate with all peoples throughout the world.
5. We stand resolute in our unrelenting convictions to destroy Pig Amerikka.
6. Wherever the word "men" appears it should be replaced with the word "people" to express solidarity with the self-determination of woman and to do away with all remnants of male supremacy, once and for all.
7. We propose that we declare a just people's war against capitalism and remain in that state until capitalism is abolished from the face of the Earth.
8. We should have an organization or army to defend the kidnapping and terror of pigs as a means of freeing political prisoners of war.
9. We oppose such organizations as NATO and SEATO and all lackeys of U.S. imperialism.
10. We demand immediate withdrawal of all American forces around the world.
11. Reparations should be made to oppressed people throughout the world, and we pledge ourselves to take the wealth of this country and make it available as reparations.
12. We will not allow or accept this country going into other countries and utilizing their wealth.
13. We will administer all foreign aid given by the U.S. by an international body composed of representatives from revolutionary people.
14. We will use our more advanced revolutionary brothers and sisters to better the struggle.
15. We demand an end to the genocide caused by sterilization programs in different forms—nationally and international.

All Power to the People

SELF-DETERMINATION OF STREET PEOPLE

What we want:
We want an immediate end to the crimes of pimping, prostitution, number rackets, gambling, dope pushing, fencing, loan sharking, sexism, rape, theft, pick pockets, bribery, extortion, union corruption, etc., committed on the people by organized crime syndicates which work hand in hand with the pig power structure and those lackeys within our communities who refuse to deal with these problems.

1. Creation of investigative councils run by the people.
2. Encourage informers to turn over information to these councils.
3. Remove by force those elements which have been exposed.
4. Confiscation or destruction of property controlled by organized crime syndicates.
5. The encouragement of all progressive forces and elements to change corruption in government and enforce revolutionary justice.

Education—
All people will be provided with the kind of schooling they desire and need. All levels of schooling will be provided free by the government. Schooling must be noncompulsory. The community will control the schools, education, curriculum, and educators. Education must be part and parcel of the political realities of the time. Education must always serve the people by teaching the true nature of this decadent society.

Dope—
We recognize that hard drugs (smack, speed, etc.) are counterrevolutionary, sapping the strength of the people in their struggle. This problem must be dealt with on two levels. The seller of hard drugs must be eradicated from the community by any means necessary. The user must be helped to rid himself of addiction by the people. We urge setting up of a People's Rehabilitation Center by the people.

We recognize that psychedelic drugs (acid, mescaline, grass) are important in developing the revolutionary consciousness of the people. However, after the revolutionary consciousness has been achieved, these drugs may become a burden. No revolutionary action should be attempted while under the influence of any drug. We urge that these drugs be made legal. Or rather than they should not be illegal, that is, there should be no law made against them.

Land—
We hold that private property is theft.

We demand that the use of parks, streets, rural areas, and unused land to carry on our revolutionary struggle for survival. We will seize the land we need by any means necessary. Streets and urban parks must be liberated to be used for people's needs such as: 1) mass meetings, 2) concerts and recreation, 3) sleeping area, and other everyday activities.

Rural land and large state parks must be liberated to be used for: military training in the techniques of self defense and urban guerilla warfare in order to fight a war of liberation, and land to be used for farming and other productive needs.

Grievance—
All private rural land has been stolen from the people. It originally belonged to the people. It is being used for capitalistic goals and is being destroyed ecologically.

Food, Housing, Clothing, Health—
We demand the right for all people to have free food, housing, free clothing, free medical care and all other rights established by the Revolutionary Peoples' Constitutional Convention.

Recognizing our responsibility as revolutionary street people in this period of transition—

1. We call for free de-centralized medical care and the availability of medical information (curative and preventive) for all the people in the neighborhood to meet the daily situations in a revolutionary manner.
2. We call for the establishment of free inter-relative community food cooperatives to collect, exchange, store, distribute and provide food and cooking facilities for the community needs.
3. We demand community control of the means of production of clothing and adequate sharing and distributing of clothing to meet the needs of the people.
4. We demand the replacement of deteriorated housing with the construction of adequate low-income housing which is available for those people whose housing is replaced and the control of community removal programs by the people in those communities.

Finally, we call for the formation of Revolutionary People's Community Councils to be responsible for the implementation of all collective needs of the community.

WORKSHOP ON THE SELF DETERMINATION OF WOMEN

—We recognize the right of all women to be free.

—As women, we recognize that our struggle is against a racist, capitalist, sexist system that oppresses all minority people.

—This capitalistic country is run by a small ruling class who use the ideas and practices of chauvinism and racism to divide, control and oppress the masses of people for their own greedy gains and profit.

—We want equal status in a society that does not exploit or murder other people.

—We will fight for a socialist system that guarantees full, creative, non-exploitative life for all human beings.

—We will not be free until all oppressed people are free.

Family—

Whereas in a capitalist culture, the institution of the family has been used as an economic tool or instrument, not serving the needs of the people. We declare that we will not relate to the private ownership of people. We encourage and support the continued growth of communal households and communal relationships and other alternatives to the patriarchal family.

We call for socialization of housework and child care with the sharing of work by men and women.

Women must have the right to decide when and if we want to have children. There should be free and safe birth control, including abortion, available upon demand. There should be no forced sterilization or mandatory birth control programs which are now used as genocide against third world sisters and against poor people.

Every woman has the right to decide whether she will be homosexual, heterosexual or bisexual.

Employment—

Whereas women in a class society have been continuously exploited, through their work, both in their home and outside their home, we call for:

1. guaranteed full, equal and non-exploitative employment, controlled collectively by the working people.
2. Guaranteed adequate income for all. This would entail the sharing of necessary, non-creative tasks and the maximum utilization of revolutionary technology to eliminate these tasks.

3. An end to the sexism which forces women into the lowest paying service jobs and the racism that insures that third world women will be the lowest paid of all.
4. Guaranteed paid maternity leave.

Education—

Whereas women historically have been deprived of education, or only partially educated and mis-educated in those areas deemed appropriate for us by those ruling powers who would benefit by our ignorance; we call for:

1. The right to determine our own goals.
2. The end of sex roles regarding training or skills.
3. Self-knowledge: the history of women, our relation to society and the knowledge of our bodies.
4. Guaranteed technological and professional training and in the interim, special programs should be set up in every field in which women have been denied equality, such as child care.
5. Men to be trained in those areas in which they have been denied equality, such as child care.
6. Control of non-authoritarian education by the people it serves in the language and cultural style of the people.

Services—

Whereas the services provided for the people have been inadequate, unavailable or too expensive, administered in a racist and sexist manner, we declare that:

1. All services—health care, housing, food, clothing, transportation and education—should be controlled by the people: and should be free.
2. Services for women should be controlled by the women of the community which they serve.

Media—

The mass media is not permitted to exploit women's bodies in order to sell or promote products. Women must be treated with respect and dignity at all times by the people's media. The people's media will work to eliminate sexist terminology: he, man, mankind; when we mean person, people, humanity.

Self-Defense—

Whereas the struggle of the people must be borne equally by all the people fighting for their liberation, we declare that women have the right to bear arms.

Women should be fully trained and educated in the art of self-defense and the defense of the peoples' nation. We recognize that it is our duty to defend all oppressed people.

Women in Our Own Right—
Whereas we do not believe that any person is the property of any other person, we declare that women have the right to bear their own surnames, not names determined by their husbands or fathers. We demand that all organizations, ranging from health insurance to social security to banks, deal with women in our own right as people, rather than as the property of men.

Equal Participation in Government—
Whereas all revolutionary people must share equally in the decisions which effect them, we are dedicated to the national salvation of all humanity.

All Power to the People!!

STATEMENT OF DEMANDS FROM THE MALE REPRESENTATIVES OF NATIONAL GAY LIBERATION

WE DEMAND:

1. The right to be gay anytime, anyplace.
2. The right to free physiological change and modification of sex upon demand.
3. The right of free dress and adornment.
4. That all modes of human sexual self-expression deserve protection of the law and social sanction.
5. Every child's right to develop in a non-sexist, non-possessive atmosphere, which is the responsibility of all people to create.
6. That a free educational system present the entire range of human sexuality, without advocating any form or style . . . that sex roles and sex determined skills not be fostered by the schools.
7. That language be modified so that no gender takes priority.
8. That the judicial system be run by the people through people's courts and that all people be tried by members of their peer group.
9. That gays be represented in all governmental and community institutions.
10. That organized religions be condemned for aiding in the genocide of gay people, and enjoined from teaching hatred and superstition.
11. That psychiatry and psychology be enjoined from advocating a preference for any form of sexuality, and the enforcement of that preference by shock treatment, brainwashing, imprisonment, etc.
12. The abolition of the nuclear family because it perpetuates the false categories of homosexuality and heterosexuality.
13. The immediate release and reparations for gay political prisoners from prisons and mental institutions; the support of gay political prisoners by all other political prisoners.
14. That gays determine the destiny of their own communities.
15. That all people share equally the labor and products of society, regardless of sex or sexual orientation.
16. That technology be used to liberate all peoples of the world from drudgery.
17. The full participation of gays in the Peoples' Revolutionary Army.
18. Finally, the end of domination of one person by another.

Gay Power to Gay People
All Power to the People
Seize the Time

WORKSHOP: THE FAMILY AND
THE RIGHTS OF CHILDREN

1. The discussion was not truly representative of all oppressed groups, since, for example, there were no children present.

2. Some people felt that the traditional family was so oppressive that it must be abolished and replaced by a different family grouping. Others felt that there were positive things in the traditional family that should be perpetuated in the new world. It was also pointed out that we can't predict what the traditional family might be like under socialism.

3. It was agreed that children are not possessions and are not to be treated as possessions by parents, collectives or the state.

4. General agreement was that children are entitled to the broadest possible education.

5. Children are entitled to be brought up to have the greatest trust, confidence and sense of sharing with the other people in their society.

6. The responsibility for creating those conditions that would enable a child to be a whole human being rests with all of us.

7. We agreed that children's feelings and viewpoints should be respected.

8. It was agreed that children have the right to be breast fed.

9. A child must be reared to be sexually free and have his choices respected.

10. Children are essential to adults as teachers because children naturally resist oppression.

11. Children must be loved in a truly revolutionary manner. Children are people.

ALL POWER TO THE PEOPLE!!!!

CONTROL AND USE OF THE LEGAL SYSTEM
AND POLITICAL PRISONERS OF WAR

The present judicial system in the United States is nothing more than an instrument and tool of class rule, representing the will of the racist ruling class, made into a law for everyone. The laws themselves and the procedural aspects such as bail, cater to the customs and mores of the ruling class.

At this time, in the transitional stage prior to the post revolutionary society, the call for peoples' revolutionary tribunes will be made. The function of these tribunals will be as the peoples' tribunals for revolutionaries who might be at the same time, on trial in the existing legal system of the ruling class. These tribunals will be decentralized and arise out of the area where the incidents or alleged crimes themselves took place.

While the struggle is still being waged, the people must learn to manipulate and utilize the existing court system, through political trials, in order to develop a revolutionary political consciousness and illustrate the true nature of this corrupt legal system before the people.

The courts should serve the people and in this racist society that can only be done by a jury of one's peers. Understanding of the laws is a matter of interpretation which directly reflects one's social, economic and racial background. So if one is to be judged, he must be judged by a jury of his peers instead of by those with the standards and ideas of the racist ruling class.

If we are to talk of creating a legal system that has its foundation in man's human nature, we must talk of transforming the entire society. Therefore it becomes necessary to define for ourselves what is criminal.

Therefore:

Principles are the foundation by which the will of the people is insured. And if we are to talk of legality, criminals and crime, we must first talk of the ultimate crime. That is the crime of exploitation of man by man and the legal system that endorses and upholds it.

Since exploitation deprives people of the necessities of life and the fruits of their labor, it is the supreme crime and the exploiters are the supreme criminals.

We feel that all of the natural resourses of the earth belongs to, and any exploitation, usurpation of man's labors and of the natural resources of the earth is an attack on man's survival and a crime. Any lack of action that denies human beings their right to exist are crimes against the people. Therefore, if the people are to control their destiny and thereby assure their own survival, then we must have a legal system that insures the abolishment of all forms of exploitation.

We recognize the armed body of the state, the fascist police force, is the protector and perpetrator of criminal acts and crimes. Not because the police per se are criminal by nature or criminal men, but because the function of the police and the armed forces in a capitalist society is criminal by nature. So we feel that the police should come from the community in which they live and that there should be no distinction between the people and the police because of their function.

Every man was born and therefore he has a right to live, a right to share in the wealth. If he is denied the right to work then he is denied the right to live. If he can't work, he deserves a high standard of living, regardless of his education or skill. It should be up to the administrators of the economic system to design a program for providing work or a livelihood for the people. To deny him this is to deny him life.

Because the present constitution in words guarantees us the right to live, in practice we are denied this most basic human right, we list the following guidelines as essential to our continued survival and prosperity:

1. All juries must consist of one's peers.
2. All courts should be peoples' courts.
3. All decisions of the people should be implemented in a collective manner by the people.
4. No judge, no policeman, no advocate should serve more than one year in any position of administrative trust without being reviewed by the people.

These guidelines, we, the people feel, are the best pre-requisites needed to insure a just and humane system.

Rights of Oppressed People and Political Prisoners

1. Because of the genocidal acts of the government of the United States, against the people of this country and the world:
   Oppressed people (any class, ethnic group or social group that has its rights restricted by any means by any other group) have an absolute right and responsibility to defend themselves by any means necessary and effective against all forms of aggression, whether this aggression be by a direct act of violence or by the violation of their human rights, among which are the rights to food, clothing, shelter, adequate medical care, education and the inalienable right to self determination.
2. The people have not only the right to self-defense by any means necessary, but also the right to organize against all oppression and exploitation, to alter or abolish all existing legal structures, and to reorganize the society for the benefit of all the people.
3. Because the legal system of the U.S. exists to serve the ruling class and facilitate oppression and exploitation of the people, those people that are

held in jails and prisons have not necessarily been incarcerated for crimes against the people; that therefore all prisoners be returned to their communities for trial by the peoples' court under a revolutionary process.

4. That all charges be dropped against the peoples' leaders so that they can return to leadership of their communities from jail and from exile because they have not committed any crimes against the people . . . Bobby Seale, the Conn. 9, N.Y. 21, L.A. 18, Angela Davis, Soledad Brothers, Ahmed Evans, Martin Sostre. We say that while held, all political prisoners of war must be treated under international agreements regarding humane treatment.

CONTROL AND USE OF THE EDUCATIONAL SYSTEM

1. Liberation schools set up for pre-school age children.
2. Entering school with a political consciousness.
3. Community control of schools:
   a) Parents controlling curriculum
   b) Community elected board officers
   c) Power to hire and fire teachers belongs to community elected board.
4. Intellectual and cultural education shall be available to all persons:
   a) Education will deal with the means of survival of the various portions of society
   b) Education for students will deal with the student as an individual
   c) The working of the system or political education should be taught for constant political consciousness
   d) Schools and institutions will be free and make advanced study available to any person
   e) The schools will encourage all persons to expand and realize their creative aspirations. it will especially encourage study in socialist society, human survival, and the truth and workings of the present society.

STUDENTS' RIGHTS

1. Students in any school will have the right of freedom of speech, dress and assembly
2. Student government should be controlled by the students
   a) No rules set up for who runs for office, ex., grades, conduct, politics, participation in other actives
   b) Student controlled press (paper), student board to decide what goes in paper and what does not go into it
   c) Freedom to assembly whenever problems arise that the students feel should be solved collectively on a face to face basis
   d) Student activities not mandatory
   e) Assemblies left to student decision in accordance with what they feel should be solved relevant to those things that directly relate to them
   f) No guards in schools for any reason. Community and students will deal with all problems, major and minor
   g) Students decide their courses according to what they want and think they need. No set curriculum. Courses will be fit to students, not students to the courses.
   h) New grading system established.

We the people believe that education should serve the people. It should expose the true nature of this society. Education should assist in teaching us our socialist ideas, and stand as a basis for our socialist practice.

The power of education should and will belong in the hands of the people. We believe that education plays a major role in this system of programming. So we the people must generate and seize this tool of the power structure and turn it into a weapon to be used against it.

All Power to the People

WORKSHOP: CONTROL & USE OF
MILITARY AND POLICE

Proposals on the Military—

1. National defense shall be provided by a system of peoples' militia, trained in guerilla warfare, on a voluntary basis and consisting of both men and women.

2. The U.S. shall not maintain a standing army, since historically a standing army has been used for offensive actions against the people of the United States and around the world.

3. No genocidal weapons shall be manufactured or used.

4. All presently existing offensive equipment and installations shall be made inoperable and unserviceable for its original purpose.

5. The people shall be educated and informed on the action of the militia, and all records shall be open to the public.

6. The government shall be prohibited from sending any personnel, funds, or equipment to any nation for military or police purposes. It should also be prohibited from spending more than 10% of the national budget for any military or police purposes. This can be overridden by a majority vote in a national referendum.

7. No person shall serve full-time in the militia; those serving in the militia shall be paid a fair wage.

8. Militia members shall be governed by the laws of the community in which they serve (or governed by the laws of the nation??).

9. National defense shall be provided by a system of peoples' militias.

10. There shall be no conscription for any armed forces.

11. No people's militias shall be stationed outside national boundaries.

12. Government people and military personnel should be defined as one and the same, and not as separate entities in or of the power structure.

13. The people shall have the right to bear arms.
    a) No citizen shall be prohibited the possession, control or purchase of small arms without the due process of law.
    b) Free programs shall be set up in the training and use of small arms.

Organization, Use of, and Control of the Police—

1. The police force shall be a rotating volunteer non-professional body coordinated by the Police Control Board from a (weekly) list of volunteers from each community section. The Police Control Board, its policies, as well as the police leadership, shall be chosen by direct popular majority vote of the community.

2.   There shall not be set up, or permitted to exist, a national body of police, or secret body of police, nor shall un-uniformed police be permitted to exist.

3.   Any citizen can bring charges against any member or officer of the police force before the Control Board, and the Control Board shall have the power to relieve that member or officer of the police force of his or her duty.

4.   Community Police Councils may set up working relations and exchange information with police forces in other communities.

5.   The purpose of the peoples' police force shall be to serve and protect the community.

6.   No person can serve on both the police force and the Control Board at the same time.

7.   Any member of the Control Board can be removed by direct, popular vote of the people.

8.   Funds for community police and for the community's Control Board shall be provided for by national government under direction of the local Control Board.

HEALTH

Health care is a right, not a privilege. We say that comprehensive medical care should not be sold as a commodity by a class of exploiters, interested in profit only. We recognize this profit motive is the outgrowth of a capitalist system which thrives on the exploitation of people and divides them on racist, sexist and class lines. Our solution is to make all aspects of health care meet the demands of all people through prevention, education and community control of health services.

1. Prevention (health checkups)
    a) nutrition (educating people with regard to eating the right diets)
    b) Maternal and child care to put an end to:
        1. genocide
        2. experimentation in the hospitals of oppressed people
        3. experimentation in the public school system as a so-called mental health program
        4. exploitation of children's behavior; children are given tranquilizers and put in a category as threats to the capitalist system.
    c) Senior citizens services (the right to be able to work as long as they can function)
    d) Regular examinations for all people
    e) Better detection facilities (more emphasis should be placed on diseases that are more prevalent in minority group areas, e.g. sickle cell anemia)
    f) Medical teams should be sent out into the communities to seek out diseases and illnesses.
2. Education
    a) health education of the masses (symptoms of diseases in the home, first aid in the home)
    b) training and retraining of present health workers
    c) ending professionalism (titles, etc.)
    d) open admissions to all who want medical training
3. Community Control
    a) right of self determination to have children (not to be told by the capitalist system how many to have)
    b) right to adequate economic means
    c) community boards should run all medical institutions
4. Mental Health
    We consider mental health to include both physical and mental well being. We recognize that much of the mental illness in our society is caused by the

oppression of the capitalist system where psychiatry is used as a tool of fascism. It has also been used against homosexuals.

We are opposed to the medical industrial complex of medicine. We believe in socialized medicine. Inherent in this concept is prevention and free comprehensive, community controlled medicine. The only way to socialize medicine is through revolution.

REVOLUTIONARY ART

The workshop on the Revolutionary Arts and Artists hereby submits the following declaration to the Plenary Session of the Revolutionary Peoples' Constitutional Convention:

We Recognize:
1. That all people are born with a creative potential and that the society must guarantee that every person has the opportunity to develop and express that potential.
2. That art is a creative expression of a people's culture or way of life.
3. We recognize the right of every people's culture to its form of expression and that those forms of expressions should be preserved, encouraged and developed.
4. We recognize that art should be related to the interest, needs and aspirations of the people.

INDEX

Page numbers in *italic* refer to illustrations. "Passim" (literally "scattered") indicates intermittent discussion of a topic over a cluster of pages.

ABOUT THE AUTHOR

GEORGE KATSIAFICAS lives in Gwangju, South Korea, and in Ocean Beach, California. A student of Herbert Marcuse, he is the author of *The Subversion of Politics* (AK Press) and the two-volume *Asia's Unknown Uprisings* (PM Press). Together with Kathleen Cleaver, he coedited *Liberation, Imagination, and the Black Panther Party* (Routledge).

ABOUT THE CONTRIBUTORS

KATHLEEN CLEAVER is former communications secretary and first woman on the central committee of the Black Panther Party. A longtime activist for human rights, she is currently a professor of law at Emory University and is writing her autobiography, *Memories of Love and War*.

CARLOS MUÑOZ has been a central figure in the struggles for civil and human rights, social justice, and peace in the United States and abroad since the 1960s. He played a prominent leadership role in the Chicano civil rights movement. Dr. Muñoz is a Vietnam War veteran, a member of Veterans for Peace, and is active in the immigrant rights movement. He is the author of *Youth, Identity, Power: The Chicano Movement*, which has been published in a revised and expanded edition.

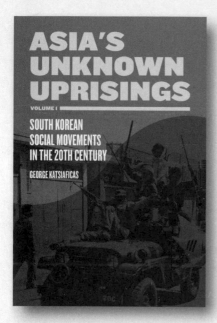

Asia's Unknown Uprisings
Volume 1
South Korean Social Movements in the 20th Century

George Katsiaficas

$28.95
ISBN: 978-1-60486-457-1
6 by 9 • 480 pages

Using social movements as a prism to illuminate the oft-hidden history of 20th-century Korea, this book provides detailed analysis of major uprisings that have patterned that country's politics and society. From the 1894 Tonghak Uprising through the March 1, 1919, independence movement and anti-Japanese resistance, a direct line is traced to the popular opposition to U.S. division of Korea after World War Two. The overthrow of Syngman Rhee in 1960, resistance to Park Chung-hee, the 1980 Gwangju Uprising, as well as student, labor, and feminist movements are all recounted with attention to their economic and political contexts. South Korean opposition to neoliberalism is portrayed in detail, as is an analysis of neoliberalism's rise and effects. With a central focus on the Gwangju Uprising (that ultimately proved decisive in South Korea's democratization), the author uses Korean experiences as a baseboard to extrapolate into the possibilities of global social movements in the 21st century.

Previous English-language sources have emphasized leaders—whether Korean, Japanese, or American. This book emphasizes grassroots crystallization of counter-elite dynamics and notes how the intelligence of ordinary people surpasses that of political and economic leaders holding the reins of power. It is the first volume in a two-part study that concludes by analyzing in rich detail uprisings in nine other places: the Philippines, Burma, Tibet, China, Taiwan, Bangladesh, Nepal, Thailand, and Indonesia. Richly illustrated, with tables, charts, graphs, index, and endnotes.

> "This book makes a unique contribution to Korean Studies because of its social movements' prism. It will resonate well in Korea and will also serve as a good introduction to Korea for outsiders. By providing details on 20th century uprisings, Katsiaficas provides insights into the trajectory of social movements in the future."
> —Na Kahn-chae, Director, May 18 Institute, Gwangju, South Korea

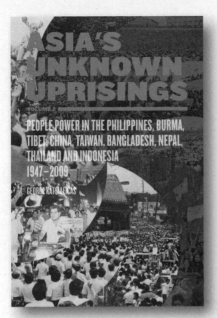

Asia's Unknown Uprisings
Volume 2

People Power in the Philippines, Burma, Tibet, China, Taiwan, Bangladesh, Nepal, Thailand, and Indonesia, 1947—2009

GEORGE KATSIAFICAS

$28.95
ISBN: 978-1-60486-488-5
6 by 9 • 520 pages

Ten years in the making, this magisterial work—the second of a two-volume study—provides a unique perspective on uprisings in nine Asian nations in the past five decades. While the 2011 Arab Spring is well known, the wave of uprisings that swept Asia in the 1980s remain hardly visible. Through a critique of Samuel Huntington's notion of a "Third Wave" of democratization, the author relates Asian uprisings to predecessors in 1968 and shows their subsequent influence on uprisings in Eastern Europe at the end of the 1980s. By empirically reconstructing the specific history of each Asian uprising, significant insight into major constituencies of change and the trajectories of these societies becomes visible.

This book provides detailed histories of uprisings in nine places—the Philippines, Burma, Tibet, China, Taiwan, Bangladesh, Nepal, Thailand, and Indonesia—as well as introductory and concluding chapters that place them in a global context and analyze them in light of major sociological theories. Profusely illustrated with photographs, tables, graphs, and charts, it is the definitive, and defining, work from the eminent participant-observer scholar of social movements.

> "Through Katsiaficas's study of Asia's uprisings and rebellions, readers get a glimpse of the challenge to revolutionaries to move beyond representative democracy and to reimagine and reinvent democracy. This book shows the power of rebellions to change the conversation."
> —Grace Lee Boggs, activist and coauthor of *Revolution and Evolution in the Twentieth Century*

The Revolution of Everyday Life

RAOUL VANEIGEM

Translated by DONALD NICHOLSON-SMITH

$20.00

ISBN: 978-1-60486-678-0

6 by 9 • 288 pages

Originally published just months before the May 1968 upheavals in France, Raoul Vaneigem's *The Revolution of Everyday Life* offered a lyrical and aphoristic critique of the "society of the spectacle" from the point of view of individual experience. Whereas Debord's masterful analysis of the new historical conditions that triggered the uprisings of the 1960s armed the revolutionaries of the time with theory, Vaneigem's book described their feelings of desperation directly, and armed them with "formulations capable of firing point-blank on our enemies."

"I realise," writes Vaneigem in his introduction, "that I have given subjective will an easy time in this book, but let no one reproach me for this without first considering the extent to which the objective conditions of the contemporary world advance the cause of subjectivity day after day."

Vaneigem names and defines the alienating features of everyday life in consumer society: survival rather than life, the call to sacrifice, the cultivation of false needs, the dictatorship of the commodity, subjection to social roles, and above all the replacement of God by the Economy. And in the second part of his book, "Reversal of Perspective," he explores the countervailing impulses that, in true dialectical fashion, persist within the deepest alienation: creativity, spontaneity, poetry, and the path from isolation to communication and participation.

For "To desire a different life is already that life in the making." And "fulfillment is expressed in the singular but conjugated in the plural."

The present English translation was first published by Rebel Press of London in 1983. This new edition of *The Revolution of Everyday Life* has been reviewed and corrected by the translator and contains a new preface addressed to English-language readers by Raoul Vaneigem.

PM Press was founded at the end of 2007 by a small collection of folks with decades of publishing, media, and organizing experience. PM Press co-conspirators have published and distributed hundreds of books, pamphlets, CDs, and DVDs. Members of PM have founded enduring book fairs, spearheaded victorious tenant organizing campaigns, and worked closely with bookstores, academic conferences, and even rock bands to deliver political and challenging ideas to all walks of life. We're old enough to know what we're doing and young enough to know what's at stake.

We create radical and stimulating fiction and non-fiction books, pamphlets, T-shirts, visual and audio materials to educate, entertain, and inspire you. We aim to distribute these through every available channel with every available technology—whether that means you are seeing anarchist classics at our bookfair stalls; reading our latest vegan cookbook at the café; downloading geeky fiction e-books; or digging new music and timely videos from our website.

PM Press is always on the lookout for talented and skilled volunteers, artists, activists, and writers to work with. If you have a great idea for a project or can contribute in some way, please get in touch.

PM Press
PO Box 23912
Oakland CA 94623
510-658-3906
www.pmpress.org

FRIENDS OF PM

These are indisputably momentous times—the financial system is melting down globally and the Empire is stumbling. Now more than ever there is a vital need for radical ideas.

In the many years since its founding—and on a mere shoestring—PM Press has risen to the formidable challenge of publishing and distributing knowledge and entertainment for the struggles ahead. With hundreds of releases to date, we have published an impressive and stimulating array of literature, art, music, politics, and culture. Using every available medium, we've succeeded in connecting those hungry for ideas and information to those putting them into practice.

Friends of PM allows you to directly help impact, amplify, and revitalize the discourse and actions of radical writers, filmmakers, and artists. It provides us with a stable foundation from which we can build upon our early successes and provides a much-needed subsidy for the materials that can't necessarily pay their own way. You can help make that happen—and receive every new title automatically delivered to your door once a month—by joining as a Friend of PM Press. And, we'll throw in a free T-shirt when you sign up.

Here are your options:
- $30 a month: Get all books and pamphlets plus 50% discount on all webstore purchases
- $40 a month: Get all PM Press releases (including CDs and DVDs) plus 50% discount on all webstore purchases
- $100 a month: Superstar—Everything plus PM merchandise, free downloads, and 50% discount on all webstore purchases

For those who can't afford $30 or more a month, we have **Sustainer Rates** at $15, $10, and $5. Sustainers get a free PM Press T-shirt and a 50% discount on all purchases from our website.

Your Visa or Mastercard will be billed once a month, until you tell us to stop. Or until our efforts succeed in bringing the revolution around. Or the financial meltdown of Capital makes plastic redundant. Whichever comes first.